LORD NORTH

By the same Author

CARTERET

The Brilliant Failure of the Eighteenth Century
With 4 Portraits   12s. 6d. *net*

"A penetrating summary of Carteret's career . . .
sympathetic but never biassed"

Times Lit. Supp.

LORD NORTH

From the portrait by Dance in the National Portrait Gallery

LORD NORTH

by

W. BARING PEMBERTON

'Il est plus difficile de s'empêcher d'être gouverné que de gouverner les autres.'—LA ROCHEFOUCAULD.

LONGMANS, GREEN AND CO.
LONDON · NEW YORK · TORONTO

LONGMANS, GREEN AND CO. LTD.
39 PATERNOSTER ROW, LONDON, E.C.4
17 CHITTARANJAN AVENUE, CALCUTTA
NICOL ROAD, BOMBAY
36A MOUNT ROAD, MADRAS

LONGMANS, GREEN AND CO.
114 FIFTH AVENUE, NEW YORK
221 EAST 20TH STREET, CHICAGO
88 TREMONT STREET, BOSTON

LONGMANS, GREEN AND CO.
215 VICTORIA STREET, TORONTO

First Published 1938

Printed in Great Britain by the KEMP HALL PRESS LTD.
in the City of Oxford

To MARY

' Lord North entreats His Majesty to consider him at all times not only as ready, but earnestly desirous of sacrificing every personal consideration to His Majesty's service.   The duty of a subject to his sovereign and the gratitude of a much favoured servant to a most indulgent master requires this of him.'

PREFACE

SOME months ago, when informing a friend I was writing the life of Lord North, I received this singular reply: ' What? Not the fellow who kept a pack of hounds? '

I hope, and I believe, my fox-hunting friend, in confusing the 11th with the 8th Lord North, is an exception. I prefer to think that most people are familiar with the name of Lord North against a less sporting background; that they know he was once Prime Minister and that he was fat; that they believe him to have been equally witty and weak; that they have a pretty strong impression he lost America but rarely his own temper and never his capacity for sleep. If I am right, then what they know of North has been to a large extent gathered from hostile and at least cold neutral sources. And this is not surprising. Lord North had during his lifetime what we should call to-day ' a bad press,' and after his death there was little improvement, except in literary style. To the great Whig and Radical historians of the succeeding century he appeared to be not much more than a puppet dangled by strings in the hands of a sovereign, whose set purpose (so they alleged) was to debauch Parliament and impose autocratic notions upon his American colonies as a prelude to introducing them into Britain herself. As it was just those historians who helped to popularize the eighteenth century, their conclusions have made a durable impression. But not, I submit in North's case, a very convincing one. A Prime Minister, not much better than a confidential clerk, commanding for twelve years and through two General Elections a substantial majority in the House of Commons, is something not quite consistent with a Constitution regarded with universal respect or with the evidence of Parliamentary proceedings and the correspondence of North himself. If it is objected that the example of Lord Liverpool proves length of office to be no indication of a Prime Minister's abilities, I agree; but at the same time I retort that much had happened between the ministries of North and Liverpool to make the Commons and (indeed their constituents) less independent and more docile. Only by adhering to the well-worn assumption that at the time of the American War members were corrupt or indifferent is it possible to deny Lord North the possession of qualities well above the ordinary. If I have not succeeded in removing such an impression from the mind of a reader by the time he has finished my book, then I shall have failed in my purpose which is to shew that, while North was not a great statesman, he is deserving of revaluation. With this slightly limited aim in mind, I have not attempted to write an exhaustive life of Lord North. Little mention has, for example, been made of Ireland, which though it occupied some of his time and

thought, had practically no effect upon his career.
Nor has it been considered necessary to deal with
his financial policy at any great length. If over-
much space seems at first sight to have been devoted
to the causes of the American War of Independence
and the character of George III, it is to be hoped
that, on further consideration, this will appear
warranted.

I have to acknowledge the gracious permission
of His Majesty King George VI to use certain
materials in the Royal Archives at Windsor. I
am deeply indebted to the Viscount Barrington
for generously placing at my disposal papers in
his possession. I have also to thank the Earl of
Minto for allowing me to examine the journal of
Sir Gilbert Elliot. I have likewise to express my
gratitude to the Managers of Brooks' Club for permitting me to study their Betting Book and to Mr.
G. R. Barnes, the joint-editor of the *Sandwich
Papers*, for enabling me to run through the galley-
proofs of the fourth volume. Lastly I am indebted
to my friends Mr. E. Hale of the Treasury for
answering questions dealing with that Department
and Mr. E. H. Goddard, Headmaster of the Haber-
dashers School, New Cross, for reading my manuscript and sparing it as little in criticism as he would
an essay from one of his own sixth-form boys.

August 11th, 1938,
Highgate Village.   W.B.P.

CONTENTS

LIST OF ILLUSTRATIONS

CHAPTER I

LEADING STRINGS

A man in this country is fit for any place he can get.'
GEORGE II (*Selwyn Correspondence*, iv. 103).

THE year 1732 was for Europe one of uncommon
peace. Not a frontier was violated. Not a succession was in dispute. Even the Porte lay undisturbed. It was one of those rare oases of tranquillity which in the eighteenth century can be
counted upon the fingers of a single hand. It was
in fine a fitting moment for two men to be born
who throughout their lives wished to live at peace
and without adventure; who, if a dispute had arisen
between themselves rather than between their
countries, would have preferred to settle it as prosaic
citizens quietly over a bottle of claret rather than as
gentlemen of honour by the sword.

On February 11 (O.S.) in Westmorland County,
Virginia, to Augustine and Mary Washington was
born a son, George. On April 13 in Albemarle
Street, Mayfair, the wife of the seventh Lord North
gave birth to a son and heir, Frederick. Barely
two months separated these infants; one to become
the first President of the United States of America,
the other the last Prime Minister of the First

B   I

British Empire. Both grew up to be men of
ingenuous tastes and of unquestioned integrity,
who would at any moment in their long public
careers have gladly exchanged the burden of
responsible office for the quiet of their own
homes, had not considerations of duty been
involved.

With this, all resemblance ceases. Washington,
the tobacco planter, has become, deservedly, one of
the most respected figures in history. The eighth
Lord North, for fourteen years Chancellor of the
Exchequer, for a dozen consecutive years—a term
only twice exceeded—Prime Minister, has become
an object of derision, if not of contempt: ' The
Minister who lost us America.'[1]

Historical verdicts, if they are to be entitled to
any respect, must be subjected to a constant
revision as fresh evidence is forthcoming and contemporary opinion (frequently the most dangerous
of opinions) can be qualified. Hardly anywhere is
this process more indispensable than in dealing with
the eighteenth century, when pens, while never
more actively employed in recording impressions in
letters, diaries and pamphlets, were never more
directed by passion and prejudice. To contemporaries of the War of Independence, the loss of the
American colonies either presaged the eclipse of
Britain or vindicated the triumph of liberty over
despotism. In either view the man who fought
America and lost had performed a disservice to his
country or his countrymen. Regarded through
the perspective of a century and a half it becomes
increasingly clear that the greatest service any

eighteenth-century statesman could have performed
was to sever the bond that bound Britain to her
American colonies. Had one of the many schemes
of compromise been successful, or, as at more than
one period seemed probable, had the Mother
Country subdued her colonies by force, the rapid
growth of America in wealth, the increasing influx
of non-British immigrants, and the lack, almost
inevitable with the leisurely communications then
obtaining, of any constructive colonial policy from
Whitehall, must have made separation merely a
matter of time. Dependence could scarcely have
withstood the disturbing effects which the Industrial
and French Revolutions must have had upon the
commercial and political relations between Britain
and her colonies. And when America went she
most assuredly would have carried with her Canada,
the West Indies, and more than half Britain's over-
seas trade.* Yet even allowing separation to
have been desirable criticism might (it would seem)
be directed against the ways and means by which
the bond was loosed. Better (it might be argued) a
Round Table conference at which both parties
agreed to separate politically but to remain commercially the best of friends than the bloodstained
heights of Bunker Hill or the bitter tragedy of York
Town. Such a contention, unanswerable in the
twentieth centry, would in the eighteenth have been
preached to incredulous ears. The idea of sitting
down on equal terms with the Adamses, the Rut-
ledges, and the Otises would to its patrician statesmen have appeared as ludicrous as a proposal that

* This argument will be developed below in Chapter VI.

they should marry their mistresses. Moreover, it may well be doubted whether, but for the animosities raised by the war, there would have been found a body of United Empire Loyalists, numbering nearly 100,000, prepared at the sacrifice of all they possessed to pass into Canada, there to create a strong and enduring core of imperial sentiment in a country which till then possessed little and must almost certainly have followed the example of her neighbour. It would indeed have spared poor North many hours of bleak despair could he have glanced into the future and felt that in losing the fight he was indirectly benefiting the country and empire he loved so much. For no man more earnestly desired to quit supreme office than he did during his twelve years as First Lord of the Treasury. Whether Britain would have been the better off had he done so must remain a matter of speculation. Why he did not do so is the tragedy of his life.

.   .   .   .   .

At the moment when Frederick North was born, his family had belonged to the peerage for close on two centuries, and in one direction or another had been active in public service. The lives of the most eminent members from Sir Edward North, in whose person Queen Mary ennobled the family, down to Lord Keeper North in the reign of Charles II, have been celebrated in a work which Jowett considered after Boswell's *Johnson* and Lockhart's *Scott* to be the finest study in British biography.[2] By tradition the Norths were King's men and of the stuff of which Tories were made. Dudley, the third Baron, may have timidly attempted to sit

upon the fence during the Civil War; but his son
and numerous grand-children returned with the
Restoration to unequivocal allegiance. The eldest
of these was created by Charles II Lord Grey during
the lifetime of his father; the second became the
famous Lord Keeper and was raised to the Barony of
Guilford*; the youngest, Roger, later the biographer
of his family, was appointed Solicitor General to the
Duke of York, afterwards James II. Strong Stuart
leanings and associations were not easily deflected
by the Revolution. Roger, who alone of the brothers lived to regret the Stuarts, shrank into voluntary retirement and literary activity. His nephew,
Lord North and Grey, compromised sufficiently
with his conscience to fight and lose a limb at
Blenheim for King James's daughter Anne. But
at the coming of an alien and Parliamentary King,
he, too, drew the line, although not so discreetly as
his uncle. In 1722 he was implicated along with
Bishop Atterbury in the Layer Conspiracy and
spent some months previous to exile in the Tower.
Twelve years later he died on the Continent,
about the same time as his Uncle Roger in England,
and like him childless. The family was now
reduced to the line of the Lord Keeper, represented
by Francis North, third Lord Guilford, the father
of the future Prime Minister.† If Lord Guilford

---

* ' He had not the virtues of his predecessor: But he had parts far beyond
him. They returned to Craft: so that whereas the former Nottingham
seemed to mean well even when he did ill this man was believed to mean ill
even when he did well.' (Burnet, *History of my own time*, i, 297.)

†In 1734, on the death of his cousin, he became Lord North, and this
being a more ancient title than that of Guilford was preferred; but in
order to distinguish him from the subject of this biography, it is proposed
to continue to refer to him as Guilford. Actually in 1752 he was created
Earl of Guilford and thereafter himself used that title.

had inherited any Jacobite sympathies he prudently
mortified them in the interests of the winning side.
In 1730, at the age of 26, he even consented to
serve the alien dynasty in the office of Lord of the
Bedchamber to Frederick, Prince of Wales. This
appointment, which must have clouded the sunset
of his Uncle Roger's life, was to have consequences
of some importance for the future Frederick North.
No man could serve Hanoverian King and Hanoverian Prince. The antipathy between father and
son which characterized the Brunswick Royal
Family, and conveniently provided a safety valve
for political discontent, which might otherwise
have taken an anti-dynastic turn, divided society
into two mutually exclusive camps. Tories who
had shed their Stuart feathers like Guilford, the
ginger-group associated with the name of William
Pitt, jetsam of the Whig party like Pulteney
and Carteret, flotsam like Bubb Dodington,
gathered round the heir apparent at Leicester
House. There they intrigued and there they drank
damnation to Walpole, and a speedy succession
to the Prince who should dispense the loaves and
fishes of office to his faithful and desperately
famished dependents.

Two years after Lord Guilford had joined the
Prince's Court of Great Expectations and four
since he had married the sister of the Earl of Halifax,
his son Frederick was born. The Prince of Wales,
as a matter of course, stood godfather and gave the
child his name. This innocent act of courtesy was
distorted in the most unsavoury fashion, when five
years later his own son and heir, afterwards George

III, was born and exhibited an astonishing likeness
to young Frederick North.* The inference was
too good not to be turned into a scandal. A
common father—and he not the Lord Guilford—
had begotten both sons. Although the similarity in
features, in colouring, and in eyes which protruded
and in the end lost their sight was remarkable, the
pasquinade is unlikely to have had any foundation
in truth. The very fact that the Prince of Wales
constantly alluded to it in jest is its best possible
refutation. A Charles II might have rallied the
husband he had cuckolded; but never a Hanoverian
heir-apparent to whom seduction was more a
matter of routine attached to his position than a
subject for badinage.

. . . . .

The eighteenth century with its Grand Tours, its
Macaronis, its Stowes, its Pump Rooms and its
Gout, saw the burgeoning of the British aristocracy
into its fine flower. Never before and certainly
never since has it displayed itself in such a
riot of colour. Never at home did it enjoy such unchallenged powers and privileges or stand possessed
of such uncontested reversions to the thousand
and one places and sinecures which made the task
of governing congenial and in not a few cases
rendered existence possible. Never abroad did it
post along the highways more arrogantly, more
self-assumingly, more acquisitively. In a manner
which has become legendary, it laid appreciative
fingers on marbles and frescoes; on old masters

* Even fifty years later this resemblance was sufficiently strong for
Wraxall to see in North's countenance a caricature of the King's.
(*Historical Memoirs*, ii. 124.)

and tapestries. It was cultured; it was rich; it was cosmopolitan. It had the *entrée* into the salons of the Esterhazies, the Orlovs, the du Deffands. It conversed with Italians and Frenchmen and Viennese in their own tongues. It was an exclusive club to which there was no qualification but birth, no rules but those instinctive to a gentleman. When even a Pope of Rome confessed he would have been proud to have been born a common Englishman, to have been born heir to a British peerage could have seemed hardly less than heaven.

It was in such a world as this that Frederick North grew up against the lovely background of an unchanging Wroxton Abbey, the Oxfordshire seat of his family. With a father possessed of wealth and consequence, it was merely a question of time —George II could not live for *ever*—before some obliging Minister would be happy to accommodate the son with some pleasant salaried office. Meanwhile all that became the young aristocrat was to proceed to Eton or Westminster, to familiarize himself with Oxford, to learn to dance, perhaps to dice; certainly to make the Grand Tour and to acquire the polish necessary to appear with effect at the Court of St. James's and in the salons of Mayfair.

However, long before the first of these steps could be taken, an event occurred within his own family which was to have an important effect upon North's life. When he was three years old his mother had died in childbirth, and, in the following year, Lord Guilford married the widow of Viscount Lewisham. The second wife brought with her a son nine months older than Frederick North, bearing at the time his father's title though later, on his grandfather's death, destined to succeed to the Earldom of Dartmouth. In a century of aristocrats which began with a Duke of Wharton and ended with an Old Q., the Earl of Dartmouth was the most distinguished exception to a general rule of dissoluteness. Quite early in life he had acquired a reputation for sanctity and never forfeited it. He became closely associated with Selina, Countess of Huntingdon, in the Wesleyan movement, and was believed to have been the original of Richardson's 'most faultless monster' of British fiction, Sir Charles Grandison. To anyone at all susceptible to influence, especially where his affections were concerned, the association with such a paragon in the nursery and in adolescence could hardly fail to have consequences. And North was such a one.

Though an indefatigable husband (he was to marry a third time) Lord Guilford was no prolific father. Besides Frederick, there had been by his first marriage only a daughter, Louisa. By the second came a son, Brownlow, six years junior to Frederick. By the third there were no children. Perhaps it was because the family was small, and of much the same age, that the father was able to exert an unusually powerful and enduring influence over his children.* Unlike his elder son's, Lord Guilford's is not a character which improves on

---

* His wives were (1) Lucy, daughter of the 1st Earl of Halifax, died May 7, 1734. (2) Elizabeth Kaye, widow of Viscount Lewisham, married January 24, 1736, and died April 21, 1745. (3) Katherine Furnese, widow of 2nd Earl of Rockingham. Married June 13, 1751, died December 17, 1766.

acquaintance. Hervey describes him as ' a very good poor creature but a very weak man,' [3] and the picture is perhaps less distorted than many in Lord Fanny's gallery. Moral he certainly was (no Sandwich or Queensberry would have *married* three times), weak he proved himself to be in the precautions he seems to have taken lest his children might develop wills of their own to his personal detriment. Upon a naturally domineering temperament a disagreeable meanness was grafted. The richer he grew by his three prudent marriages, the closer-fisted he became and the allowance made to his heir was meagre out of all proportion to his future expectations.[4] Without an appreciation of the strength and authority of this figure, which to within two years of his son's death stood in the background of his life, much of North must remain an enigma and any account of his life insubstantial.

During Frederick's early years, his father's influence was to some extent beneficial. This much must be conceded to Lord Guilford: his son's integrity in public life and his purity in private life were due in a great measure to the influences which surrounded him in childhood. Homely unaffected virtues were inculcated as much by example as by precept, and there is little doubt that down at Wroxton paternal despotism was of a benevolent kind and the atmosphere devout without being prudish. ' The Christian religion,' Guilford once told his son, ' is strangely misapprehended by those to whom it seems a dull thing. To me it seems to be the only solid foundation of constant cheerfulness.' [5] No lesson was taken more thoroughly to heart. Throughout the vicissitudes of his life, including those last years of physical darkness, North exhibited a cheerful temper, an astonishing lack of rancour, and an amiable disposition which evoked the acknowledgment of his most determined enemies. The influence of Lord Guilford was baneful only in so far—and it went far enough to contribute to his son's ordeal—as it tended to deprive North of an independent will and to accustom him to rely upon judgments other than his own. The spectacle of a Prime Minister of forty-five (and in the eighteenth century this was deep middle age) filially deferring to a septuagenarian father may be unique, may possess even a certain ingenuous charm; but in the practical politics of the day it was scarcely inspiriting. North's notorious irresolution, his habitual deference to the opinions of those whom he loved or esteemed, which characterized and did so much to damage his public career, are directly traceable to habits acquired during his impressionable early years.

At the age of ten North passed to Eton—Lewisham going to Westminster, his grandfather's school. North's transit of Eton had none of the scintillation of Fox's a few years later. Nevertheless, with instruction devoted almost entirely to Greek and Latin authors, a boy who after six years could not produce apposite quotations from the classics or bandy hexameters across the floor of St. Stephen's was emphatically sub-standard. It is significant that Dr. Dampier, the Lower Master, reporting to Guilford on his son's progress, is discreetly silent as to scholarship and confines himself to personality.

'I am pleased to see (he writes) in many instances how both the masters and the boys love him, and that he really, by his behaviour, deserves it from both, which is not often the case. I think he has greatly contributed to the very good order the school is in at present.'⁶ His tutor, on the other hand, was less circumspect. 'You're a blundering blockhead,' he shouted on one occasion, 'and if you are ever Prime Minister it will always be the same—' a remark which, according to North, who loved to tell the story against himself, turned out to be the case.⁷ Although some of his verses appeared in *Musae Etonienses*, it is probable that North learnt only a little more than any boy of superior intelligence. The classical allusions which were occasionally to point his speeches were generally felicitous if not very profound.

From Eton, North went up at the age of seventeen to Trinity College, Oxford, where he was joined by Lewisham. The choice of this college in preference to the fashionable Christ Church was due to the family connexion with Trinity. Wroxton had come to Trinity through the gift of their founder, and for many years had been leased to the North family upon an annual tenancy. At Trinity, therefore, the heir of Wroxton would be received with little less respect than that accorded to the President of the college, and had he wished to indulge in the usual round of wine parties and horse races he might have done so with impunity. That in the freer life of the university there was no falling away from Wroxton standards was probably due to the close

association with Lewisham and the influence of a
most exemplary tutor. The Rev. James Merrick
seems to have had no difficulty in winning the entire
confidence of his pupil, and so engaging his mind
successfully in the contemplation of religion and in
the pursuit of a philosophy of life which laid paramount stress upon conduct and duty. So
thoroughly did the young undergraduate respond
to this treatment that in vacation time it was as
much as he could do to tear himself away from the
companionship of his tutor. At the close of
what proved to be a brief university career, it is
not surprising that he was rewarded with a glowing
testimonial.

' It is an unspeakable satisfaction to me (wrote Merrick) that you have by God's blessing been made sensible
of the importance of religion before your entrance upon
public life. Your improvement in piety, at this season of
your life, will be the best preparation for every scene of it;
and your preserving that cheerfulness of temper and
desire for knowledge which you now have, may be of
excellent use in recommending the example of your piety
to others.' [8]

The President, while acknowledging a parting gift
of plate, added also his tribute to those 'most
amiable young noblemen whose residence with us
was a very great advantage as well as an ornament
to the College.' [9]

Even making every allowance for the partiality
of his masters, it is clear that North by the age of
twenty was already a young man of principles and
promise. Such a paragon (it might be thought)
should surely have taken Holy Orders. Had he
been a younger son he most certainly would have

done so, and the Church would have gained a most conscientious bishop, and the House of Commons have lost one of its most devoted Members. Ecclesiastical preferment however was reserved for young Brownlow, now just entering Eton. For Frederick, there was instead one of the safest boroughs in the country, that of Banbury, waiting dutifully at the door to return him to Parliament as soon as he reached his majority.

To while away the interval between Oxford and Westminster, and acquire what Madame de Staël has called the *esprit européen*, North and Dartmouth, in company with a tutor, set out for a tour of the Continental capitals. They advanced leisurely through Holland, impressed with nothing so much as the absence of good butter, to Hanover where, George II being present on his annual visit, they were hospitably entertained by the Duke of Newcastle,[10] Secretary of State in his brother Henry Pelham's administration. It may have been this visit which healed a quarrel between Guilford and the Pelhams. A year earlier, on the death of the Prince of Wales, the former had been removed summarily from his recent post of Governor to Prince George. Rightly or wrongly Guilford saw in this the hand of the Pelhams and retired in dudgeon to Wroxton. However, very shortly after his son had parted from the duke (who, we may be sure, kissed him effusively on both cheeks), Lord Guilford was created an earl, though no offer of employment was made or probably could be made while the old King lived. The letter of congratulation which he received from his son is worth quoting parenthetically as giving unmistakable evidence of that excessive modesty which, at first perhaps consciously adopted towards a father, became in time natural and demoralizing. Thus, in spite of his twenty years and accomplishments about which Horace Walpole had already heard reports, North could solemnly inform his father:

' You have too good an opinion of me when you imagine me capable of adding a lustre to the dignity you have acquired. I am so far from thinking myself capable of adding a new lustre to it, that I have the greatest apprehension lest I should tarnish and diminish that which it has already.' [11]

Very different, this, from the self-assurance of his future colleague, Charles James Fox, who while still an Eton boy had thought himself fully qualified to step into the Privy Council.

From Hanover, Lewisham, now become by the death of his grandfather Earl of Dartmouth, and Frederick North, shortly to become by courtesy Lord North, passed on to Berlin where at the Court of Frederick the Great they were kept hard at work teaching young Prussian society the intricacies of English country dances. As the nightly balls and masquerades lasted until the early hours, their experience of the city was confined to ' hard exercise and sound sleep'.* Perhaps they were not altogether sorry to move on to Leipzig, where a

*B.M. Add. MSS. 32728, f.163, North to Newcastle. The duke having expressed a wish to hear from him, North tactfully obeyed. This letter, the first of several, contained a lively description of a Prussian military review together with some unflattering observations on Frederick. Newcastle diplomatically shewed it to the King who, heartily detesting his nephew of Prussia, ' was extremely diverted ' and at once began to regard (and to speak of) North and Dartmouth as his two favourites. (Add. MSS. 32728, f.317.)

longish stay was made in order to attend a course of lectures upon the state of Europe by a celebrated professor. But Leipzig proved dull even for such model milords, and during the last fortnight of Carnival they fled to Dresden for diversion and relief. [12] The next objective was Vienna where as in Berlin the difficulty was to find time for work. The problem was resolved by devoting an hour to their Italian master before setting out for the amusements which the Austrian capital offered in abundance; but even this hour cost them an effort.

' Oh, My Lord! ' wrote North to Newcastle, ' how dull a study the first principles of a language! And how very tedious it is to a young man who has been seven years at a public school and almost three at Universities to be obliged to thumb over again his right parts of speech! ' * [13]

From Vienna, the party struck south, penetrated Italy as far as Rome, then returned slowly home by way of Milan and Paris. England was reached early in 1754. The sowing of their wild oats— the harvest must have produced a very stunted crop—was over. Their responsibilities had begun. Dartmouth took a wife and a seat in the House of Lords. North was returned to Westminster by the obedient burgesses of Banbury, who asked nothing more than a good dinner and much ale to perform this ceremony whenever called upon for the next thirty-six years. Though it might have had little choice in its member, Banbury could not have

* So far as German was concerned, notwithstanding his daughter's assertions to the contrary, North seems to have found the task too great. Twenty years later he confessed to the King that he did not understand the language well enough even to read the signature to a letter. (Fortescue, ii. 351.)

chosen one resolved to carry out his duties more
devotedly and more conscientiously.*

One further requirement was necessary before
the elder son of Lord Guilford was properly
launched into public life. He must, following the
example of Dartmouth, marry. Whether the
father supplied the wife with the same facility as he
did the borough is not known. It may be assumed
that the man who had already made two prudent
marriages and was yet to make a third stipulated
for an heiress. Nor was the condition likely to
prove an obstacle. When young Frederick North
descended upon London to attend his first session,
his name must have figured upon the list of every
mother with an eligible daughter. For what
more could be expected of a son-in-law than that he
should possess a title, a wealthy father, a safe seat, a
reputation for wit and an ability to dance the minuet
as well as any beau in town?[14] His present fortune
—a rather niggardly allowance of £300 a year—
was, it is true, not considerable, but then his connexions were full of promise. His uncle, the Earl of
Halifax, presided over the Board of Trade and
watched solicitously over his nephew's interests; the
Chancellor of the Exchequer, Henry Bilson Legge,
a relative of his brother Dartmouth, offered his
services; Newcastle, now by the death of his
brother head of the Ministry, promised never to look
on ' his cousin ' " as Tunbridge or rather Hanover

---

* The correspondence of Lord Guilford contains an interesting insight
into eighteenth-century electioneering. Matthew Lamb, his agent (and
the grandfather of Lord Melbourne), for example, writes on one occasion:
' whatever benefit may have arisen to his constitution from our good wishes,
I am afraid His Lordship's (North) pocket will have suffered more than
usual.'

C

acquaintance which pass off *avec les eaux*."15*

After a year spent in London looking round North married in 1756 Anne Speke of Dillington in Somerset. The bride, who was only sixteen, was variously reported to be ' a lady of great fortune,' ' the Somersetshire heiress of more than four thousand pounds a year.' 16 This fortune, for what it was proved in actuality to be worth, was anywhere but in poor Anne's face. Not even the brush of Reynolds can bring beauty into those pudding-like features and that pert little nose. Yet in this as in so many other respects the couple were admirably matched. Whenever Horace Walpole saw the husband with his bulging eyes, his two pouting lips framed between a pair of inflated cheeks he was irresistibly reminded of some blind trumpeter blowing for all he was worth. This unprepossessing countenance, which recalled to Wraxall the portrait of Leo X, surmounted a body hardly less uncouth. In his Vienna days North might, according to his travelling tutor, have enjoyed ' a comelyness of person,' but it was soon lost in folds of advancing flesh. Once, indeed, during an illness, being asked how he felt, he replied with a smile—what he had not felt for years: his ribs. In fact it is said that North was the original in the story of the man asked by a stranger the identity of the plain-looking woman across the theatre. ' That, sir, is my wife,' came the reply, and when the other in embarrassment pretended to refer to her neighbour, ' That, sir, is my daughter.'

* No evidence of such a cousinship can be discovered. Newcastle probably acknowledged it out of sheer good-nature and North wisely returned the compliment.

LADY NORTH

From the original portrait by Reynolds.   By kind permission of the Rt. Hon. Sir Philip Sassoon, Bart.

What at least lends a touch of verisimilitude to the tale is the very characteristic North conclusion. ' And let me tell you, sir, we are considered to be three of the ugliest people in London.'* Ugliness, in fact, which Mirabeau boasted was for him a source of power, was to North a subject for endless merriment.

Anne North, like her husband, may have been no beauty and gossip may have exaggerated her imme-diate fortune; but when North took her to wife there appeared to be other compensations. A rich and eccentric relative and neighbour, by name Sir William Pynsent, was understood to be leaving her the bulk of his considerable fortune, and for several years after the wedding, North lived under the happy impression that the estate was coming to him as Anne's husband.[17] When eventually the great moment arrived and Sir William breathed his last, it was learned to everyone's surprise, and to the Norths' intense mortification, that the entire fortune had been bequeathed to William Pitt.† A con-scientious vote by North in favour of Grenville's cider tax, naturally abhorred in the West Country, and—according to Walpole—poor Anne's continued lack of beauty, caused the old man to draw up a fresh will.‡[18]

So acute a disappointment might have soured

* Nor did the sons fail to inherit their parents' ugliness. Of his first-born North tells his father ' his beauty is yet to come,' and of another it is said that when on his travels he asked to see the women of the Dey of Algiers the reply came: ' He is so ugly, let him see them all.' (*North MSS.* and Broughton *Recollections*.)

† If Doctor Ruville's theory is correct, there was one man who was not surprised, and that was the fortunate Pitt himself.

‡ He is also reported to have burnt poor North in effigy. Walpole, *Letters*, vi. 172.

many a marriage at a time when wives were valued more for their rent-rolls than for their charms. Upon that of the Norths it had not the slightest effect. In the same degree as her husband, Anne possessed a sweetness of nature and a placidity of disposition which refused to be ruffled by external circumstances. Despite this grave disillusionment, the union of so perfectly matched a couple continued at a time notorious for conjugal laxity, unsullied by the least scandal for thirty-six years and was dissolved only by the death of the husband. Not many daughters of eighteenth-century peers could say with Charlotte North of their mother and father, ' I never saw an unkind look or heard an unkind word passed between them. His affectionate attachment to her was unabated as her love and admiration of him.'[19]

When the Norths set up house on Anne's property down at Dillington and came up to London when the Parliamentary session opened, the miscarrying of their prospects was some way ahead. But for the Somersetshire heiress, her first season in town as a young bride must have seemed unaccountably flat. Lord North, securely wedded to a wife, no longer possessed the same social attraction, and although the wife was well connected and the husband heir to a peerage, the couple spent a strangely quiet and fireside winter in London. ' There are a great many balls this year (he told his father), to none of which Lady North has been invited. She endeavoured to make it up to herself by having a little accidental Hop the other night for some of her particular friends without a

supper.'* [20]   But for the most part they were by
themselves playing chess or quadrille. Not many
years were to pass before such evenings became the
exception, and hostesses who had omitted to
write the name of Lady North on their books were
hastening to do so.

. . . . .

It was not for some time and until the Seven
Years' War was well into its second year and the
coalition of Newcastle and Pitt effected, that the
House of Commons first caught the sound of the
voice of one whom they were to hear with the
utmost frequency during the next thirty years.
While methodically mastering the routine of Parliament, North may have hesitated to make his maiden
speech. Not like Charles Fox or William Pitt did
he leap to his feet early in his first session. He
was, unlike them, no naturally gifted speaker, and,
with his habitual diffidence, he certainly knew it.
His gestures were clumsy, his appearance ungainly,
his tongue was, or appeared to be, too large for
his mouth, causing a certain thickness of speech,
which Horace Walpole likened to ' a rumbling in
a mustard bowl.' For success, he realized that he
must rely upon knowledge of his subject and upon
sheer debating ability. Accordingly, it was only
in his third session and then at the direct request
of the Ministry, that he broke the ice. The
occasion was of some prominence if not of very great
importance. He was asked to second the Address
to the Throne. To his father, waiting anxiously

---

* The last three words were almost certainly added to convince Guilford
that there was no undue extravagance.

for news at Wroxton, he declared with accustomed modesty, that he ' spoke with a loud voice and a tolerable manner and to that more than any matter he owed his reputation.'[21] Old Parliamentary hands, on the contrary, were quick to detect in a happy phraseology and in a commendable lack of hesitation the genesis of a front rank debater. The Earl of Jersey was of the opinion that no maiden effort had given more satisfaction. Uncle Halifax felt he could now conscientiously regard him as having first claim to a vacancy in the Board of Trade.[22] The most interesting comment, however, came from Charles Montagu, Member for Northampton. After reporting that North's performance was ' The subject of discourse in all companies,' he made the following very surprising statement: ' If anybody was sorry, I fancy it was the Secretary of State (Pitt) to have his work taken out of his hands and to see he had so dangerous a rival. I am not singular in this respect.' [23] Whether the suspicions of one who, as Auditor to the Princess Dowager, was in close touch with the political world, were justified or not, it is remarkable that within a month an offer should have come from the Great Commoner which looked strangely like an attempt to remove an unwelcome ally.* Exactly what the offer conveyed is not clear, but in North's letter to his father it is vaguely referred to as ' a foreign appointment', and was therefore presumably of a diplomatic nature.

---

* In justice to Pitt, it was probably not North's promising talents that made him distrustful so much as his connexion with Newcastle and, through his father's supposed association with Bute, a belief that he was a creature of the Scottish Thane. There is no ground for such a suspicion. Indeed there is direct evidence to the contrary in the *North MSS*.

Although the case for refusal seemed so overwhelming that he felt he might have assumed
Lord Guilford's opinion in advance, North dutifully
declined to make any decision until he had com-
municated with Wroxton.

'I am so well acquainted with your Lordship's
tenderness and affection towards me and have
always succeeded so well by following your counsels
that I was unwilling to give an absolute answer to
Mr. Pitt without having first consulted you.'
Quite apart from the difficulty of transporting a
wife and family, he had already noticed that ' most
men who have passed their youth in foreign
employment make no great figure in Parliament on
their return.' Consequently from neither achiev-
ing Parliamentary reputation nor making oneself
indispensable to any Administration, ' one is likely
to be more in the power of those who govern than
any person who can help it would choose to be.' [24]
The sentiments were praiseworthy rather than
wise. A young man who in the last years of
the reign of George II set forth to preserve his
independence was inviting disillusionment—or
penury.

When notifying Pitt of his refusal North hazarded
some hopes for the Board of Trade. For some years
to come a seat on the Board was his immediate
and the Presidency his ultimate ambition: not
assuredly because it was, according to Henry Fox's
prophetic remark, ' the most important place in
England,'[25] but because his attentions were naturally concentrated upon a department of which his
uncle Lord Halifax had been head for no fewer than

ten years. But where Pitt was concerned no man could pick and choose. North was coldly informed there was nothing of the sort to dispose of.

If in his ambition to become a thorough House of Commons man North determined not to be side-tracked, he was to pay for his resolution with many hours of anxious worry. While he was ineffectively sighing for a seat on the Trade Board he began to feel the first twinges of a life-long struggle to make ends meet. The mode of life enforced upon the young husband—a double establishment in Somerset and London—coming on top of the settlements made on marriage so crippled his resources that the future maker of fourteen budgets was unable to balance his own domestic books. Guilford, while enjoying an income of £10,000 a year, had made no offer to increase his son's original allowance as a bachelor[26]; and (though the transactions are obscure) North had been compelled to borrow heavily to make the marriage settlements. Though in return Anne brought in a fair contribution to the common stock, the expenses of having to run two homes (if the husband was to continue his Parliamentary duties conscientiously) were considerable. To add to their liabilities, the North nursery began to fill up. By June of the year following Pitt's offer matters had reached a crisis. Expenses, calculated on a basis of living one half of the year in London and the other in the country, worked out at £2,500. Against it the general income amounted to £2,800; but out of this no less than £840 went in payment of interest on borrowed moneys, leaving a debit balance of £540.

At this rate it was obviously impossible, as North told his father, for him to go on without making some very material alteration in his manner of living. This he was prepared to do 'provided I can ensure myself the satisfaction of making ends meet.' When Guilford from the secure opulence of Wroxton expressed surprise that it was not possible to live on £2,800 less £840, North produced a revised version. It was based upon the cutting down of residence in town by two months 'which by just riding up myself with one servant to London for two or three days at the opening of the Parliament I shall be able to do:' secondly, upon the 'absolute exclusion of every expence that can in the strictest sense be called superfluous': thirdly 'upon the good opinion I have of our new cook who goes upon a much more prudent and economical footing than any of her predecessors.' But even this version failed to balance at £1,960. Still, if Guilford would suggest a plan of life by which the couple could live comfortably and conformably with their rank, North meekly undertook in advance to embrace it. 'All that I desire is to live decently within my income. To everything beyond that I am perfectly indifferent. Whatever you think superfluous in my manner of living, whatever circumstance of magnificence, vanity, pleasure, or even of convenience, you should advise me to forego I do assure you that I am ready to part with without the least regret.'²⁷ Few Chancellors of the Exchequer were to enter office more painfully acquainted with the value of money than poor Lord North.

Relief, though of a somewhat temporary nature, was soon at hand. If Pitt continued shy of the young Member for Banbury, Newcastle had not forgotten his ingenuous correspondent and ' cousin,' and in the matter of office one Newcastle was worth a dozen Pitts. Nine months after the arrival of North's new cook, upon whom so much depended, the opportune resignation of the Earl of Bessborough enabled the ducal jobber to bring Lord North into his own department of the Treasury. ' I hope his appearance in Parliament (he told Pitt in a letter signifying the appointment) will make the choice approved and that he will be in time a very useful and able servant of the Crown.' [28] Newcastle had not been forty years in almost continuous office without possessing some capacity to estimate his fellow beings.

North's promotion to a Junior Lordship of the Treasury was one of the decisive landmarks of his life. It gave him a training and grounding in Treasury affairs to which he owed his ultimate promotion. More immediately important, a salary of £1,400 descended like the dew of Heaven upon the parched economy of Dillington. But for the bad old debt, contracted at the time of his marriage and now hanging ' like a deadweight upon me, keeping me behind hand with everybody and putting it out of my power to make those regulations in my affairs that I desire and that are necessary for me,' life might have been very sweet indeed.

Sixteen months later what everyone had been expecting for a quarter of a century happened with the suddenness that transformed it into a thunder-clap. On the morning of October 25, 1760, George II dropped dead in the act of dressing and places and pensions, their problems and solutions were flung into the melting-pot.

Chapter II

THE ROYAL MASTER

'Men of less principle and honesty than I pretend to may look on public measures and opinions as a game. I always act from conviction.'

Correspondence of George III, iv. 58.

'The history of the reign of George III has too often been written in the style of a political pamphlet.'

Sir William Anson.

THE history of England from 1760 to 1785 is so completely dominated by the person of her King that this quarter century is little more than a volume from the life of George III. So paramount is the royal presence that without some impartial appreciation of the King's character and policy it is hardly possible to reach any satisfactory estimate of his Ministers. Only during the present century has it become possible to sweep away many of the polemical cobwebs attaching to George III. In the cleansing process new colours and unsuspected features have appeared. The portrait of the sovereign handed down from one generation of Radical historians to another emerges much modified. He is seen not necessarily to be a better ruler or a misjudged monarch so much as a victim of circumstances which only an exceptionally strong or hopelessly weak king could have dealt with, the one by confronting and mastering, the other by closing his eyes to and running away from his difficulties.*

* In fairness to earlier writers it should be said that until the publication of the King's correspondence at Windsor, the researches of Professor Namier and the availability of some unpublished material such as the Robinson papers in the British Museum, appearances were certainly in their favour.

28

This reassessment as it were of the sovereign's character must necessarily react upon that of his long-suffering Prime Minister. If in place of the conventional portrait of North, clinging abjectly to office while the British Empire parted in twain, we do not get the outline of a great statesman, we do obtain a picture that should evoke pity and must evoke respect.

George III, born five years after North, was in his twenty-third year when he ascended the throne. For the first time in a hundred years the crown lay upon the head of a young man. Youth, which in a sovereign has generally so popular an appeal, was one feature in his favour. His unaffected piety was another; all the more so since it was in becoming contrast to his two predecessors who had mounted the throne complete with seraglio and its attendant evils. But George III was more than a young king and a pious king. He was a British king in the sense that no sovereign, with the exception of poor bewildered Queen Anne, had been since the Tudors. For foreigners and foreign countries he had a truly British and insular contempt. Like tens of thousands of his ale-swilling subjects he took one red-coat to be a match for any three mounseers, and any British frigate more than a match for the finest ship of war as ever put out from Cadiz harbour. Like any country squire he distrusted at sight all theorists, hair-splitters, and reformers. Like any yeoman farmer, while respecting the honest merchant, he had nothing but contempt for the stock-jobber and denizen of Change Alley. That bold phrase which with his

own pen he slipped into his first utterance as a king,
' I glory in the name of Britain ' would have been
grotesque in the mouth of his predecessors; even
from the lips of a Stuart its sincerity would have been
suspect.   Used by George III those words came
from the depths of his soul.   He gloried in the
country and its empire over which by God's Grace
he saw himself called to rule; he gloried in its free
constitution which he regarded as the pride of the
human race; he gloried in its Church which he believed to be the only sound bulwark against super-
stition and Popery; he gloried in the spirit of his
people whose happiness he considered indistinguishable from his own.   His was a precious heritage, and if
to preserve it intact meant working eighteen hours a
day, he would sacrifice the time willingly, proudly.

And for such a sovereign Britain was ready.
She was wearying of the old gang of politicians who
for two generations had organized, or as it might be
said to-day, had ' rationalized ' the Monarchy in
their own selfish interests.   The country felt that
somehow there had been a betrayal of the ideas of
the Revolution, which since the coming of the House
of Brunswick had become Glorious for a few Whigs
but not hardly for the rest.   The middle classes in
particular were growing impatient with those
governing families who had for so long and to such
indifferent ends monopolized political power.   A
sovereign who set out to put the hands of the clock
back to 1688 would clearly have a large amount of
public support, for there was latent a rich fund of
monarchical sentiment awaiting exploitation.   On
behalf of two middle-aged Germans, one of whom

could not speak the English language and both of whom openly preferred the gardens of Herrenhausen to anything which Britain could give them except a Civil List, enthusiastic loyalty was scarcely possible. But three generations on the throne and a British birth and the collapse of Jacobitism had given to the Brunswick House at least a prescriptive right to the affections of all without distinction.

Had George III proceeded to follow diligently in the footsteps of his forebears he could hardly have enjoyed less popularity than they. There was talk, it is true, of undue petticoat influence by the Princess Dowager as well as of the inculcation of arbitrary notions by the Earl of Bute, his Groom of the Stole. But it was only talk and in any case easily outweighed by the good humour and enthusiasm evoked by the Year of Victories. Coming to the throne on the crest of the most successful war in British history George III possessed, taking all things into account, finer prospects than any king since Charles II had returned from exile exactly a hundred years earlier. Had he done nothing but quietly carry out his duties, agreeing to whatever his Ministers suggested, allowing his hands to be kissed by those they suggested for office, busying himself with petty military detail (for all the Georges were warriors at heart), visiting Hanover every so often, he would have lived and died a model Parliamentary king.* Free to indulge his own

---

* A good and hitherto unpublished illustration of the minute attention paid by the King to military matters is to be found in the Barrington manuscripts. Writing to Barrington at the end of 1775, when the American War was already in progress, he says:

' By the return the Lord Lieutenant has sent of the 68th Regiment of foot on their landing in Ireland I have the pleasure of seeing that it wanted

harmless hobbies his life would have been one of pottering contentment. The shadow of insanity would perhaps never have been thrown across his path—or at least not until extreme old age.* As years passed and younger men came into office his influence for good might even have been considerable.

To do George III justice it should be remembered that such a map of life had little tradition behind it in his own country and none abroad where, on the contrary, Frederick of Prussia was setting his brother monarchs a lesson in the exalted and whole-time duty of service to the State. At a time too when, in the King's private opinion, politicians were 'intent upon their own private interests instead of the public,'[1] it was not the hour to cultivate a garden. Was he who had no axe to grind, no place to gain or lose, whose interests must necessarily be those of his country, not more quali-fied to act the part of Governor than a Temple, a Bedford, or a Newcastle? What peculiar virtues were to be found at Stowe, at Woburn or at Clare-mont which did not luxuriate in more abundance at Buckingham House?

The tragedy of George III's life was that he came to the throne so circumstanced that unless he had been dissolutely idle, middle-aged or an echo of

only fourteen: but in this return, Lieut. Richard Taylor, Ensign Molly (*sic*) Brabazon, Ensign James Bigsby and Surgeon Caleb Barber are returned *absent without leave*. You will therefore write to Lieut. General Lambton to direct them immediately to join the regiment in Ireland and acquaint the Duke of Argyle of it, which will prevent liberties of this kind being taken on future embarkations.'

* The connexion between his attacks of madness and crises in govern-ment was too common to be purely coincidental.

his grandfather, he could hardly have helped adopting a course which led to a generation of chaos, to disaster and finally to insanity. As in some Greek drama, the victim's destiny was cast for him and not all his virtues, not all his good intentions, could deflect its drive.

In the first place there was the influence of his father's little court upon his own impressionable years. At Leicester House in the 'forties, where those out of favour with the King or his Ministers had collected, the governing Whigs had been represented as men determined to make a mere pageant of the throne.[2] It had not been difficult for Pulteney, Chesterfield, Egmont, and others to work up a damaging case against a Venetian Oligarchy which had deliberately filched power and patronage from a Doge of a king. Encouraged in this manner to hate before he could reason it is hardly surprising that the young prince early in life acquired for his grandfather's Ministers an ineradicable contempt. Frederick had died and his shadow cabinets had dissolved, but his ideas of a benevolent ruler working in conjunction with a sort of ministry of all the talents lived on. They were honoured by his son and carefully preserved in the breast of his friend the Earl of Bute. Nor between the two were they allowed to die.

Secondly there were certain indefinable constitutional influences driving the King forward. In its fifty years of life the Hanoverian Settlement designed by Stanhope, completed by Walpole, and veneered by Newcastle had never been subjected to a really critical testing. If two conditions ceased to obtain,

D

that test must be applied and then, unless the country was sufficiently prepared to meet it, a crisis was unavoidable.   The first condition was a willingness on the part of the sovereign to maintain the working agreement, destitute in itself of legal basis, with his Whig bosses.   Except for an occasional guttural outburst George I and his son had been content to run between the rails laid down by those who had made the succession of their House possible and since that time had ' undertaken ' the government on terms mutually satisfactory: the King receiving a handsome Civil List and licence to play the German autocrat in Hanover for six months in every year; the undertakers enjoying political power and, what counted most of all, political patronage.   The second condition was that the King should consider himself exclusively apprenticed to the old Whig families and, as a corollary, exclude Tories and other undesirables from his favour.

Because George I and George II had honoured their bond Walpole's able leadership had been able to develop the constitution at a speed which far outran the political consciousness of the nation. The middle classes could see in those admirable conventions which fostered the growth of responsible government nothing but devices to concentrate power and patronage among a few exclusive aristocratic families.   They knew nothing of the Cabinet except that it was a word that seemed unpleasantly associated with the Cabal of regrettable memory.   As for the fiction of a king reigning but not ruling, it was something puzzling to the country gentleman and quite beyond the comprehension of the artisan.

What then, if before these grafts which the Whig managers had fastened upon the Constitution had taken, there arrived a king who had all the impatience, the enthusiasms and ideals of youth; to whom Hanover so far from being an earthly paradise was ' a horrid Electorate '; who was eager to do his duty by his country; who, like the meanest of his subjects, was jealous of his birth-right; who had ' too much spirit to accept the Crown and be a sypher? ' Here was a contingency for which Walpole in all his wisdom had made no provision. It was as though the Hanoverian dynasty had come of age and the heir was demanding his inheritance. On one side stood the administrators of the estate claiming to preserve their monopoly of power; on the other a young man insisting that he should exercise rights and privileges lawfully his under the Revolutionary Settlement and enjoyed not much more than half a century before by his predecessors, William III and Anne. Between the two parties sat the nation not at all convinced that the trustees had performed their duties satisfactorily and prepared to see the heir given an opportunity at least to show his capacity for management.

Only a ruler with the most pitiful opinion of his own capabilities could fail to ask himself whether he could not do better than men who had bungled the War of the Austrian Succession and, till Pitt had come to the rescue, the Seven Years' War as well. Only the most timid of sovereigns could hesitate to inquire why he must continue to exclude from favour nearly half his subjects because they or their fathers had been Tories. In 1720 the plausible answer might have been given that they were indistinguishable from Jacobites. In 1760 this was no longer possible. Since Culloden Jacobitism had become ' a tale of far off things and battles long ago,' an excuse for a furtive toast knocked back in glasses which to-day have become the prize of collectors. Ideas and ideals which had once fiercely distinguished Whig from Tory had flickered out. A man was Whig or Tory more by heredity and environment than by conviction. He was one or the other much as the present-day schoolboy is Oxford or Cambridge because his father or uncle or favourite master was at one university or the other. In rare cases only would a scholarship or a place prevent respectively an Oxford-minded youth from entering Cambridge or a traditional Tory (like Frederick North) from joining a so-called Whig administration. To ask therefore of any young man in the last decade of George II's reign whether he was Whig or Tory was a profitless question. The only question which really mattered was whether he was in office and, if not, how he could get in.

When at the beginning of the new reign the Have-nots (a term which embraced Whig locked-outs as well as Tory unemployed) turned like sun-flowers to the rising Phoebus; was he to hide his face from them? If he did, then he acted unfairly and for no justifiable reason. If he shone upon them, then at a stroke he destroyed the vested interest in all the good things of public life created by one brand of politicians and betrayed their version of the constitution. Not only that: the moment the sovereign ceased to regard himself as apprenticed to one party, the spring was released and he became what two generations of Ministers had tried to prevent him from becoming, a real personal and independent force in politics.

To-day with competitive examination taking the place of so much patronage, the sovereign entirely divorced from politics, and parties thoroughly organized units, it is not easy to appreciate the effect of such a release upon the minds of the eighteenth century. Even if it had been possible to separate the King from the patronage that was exercised in his name, politicians would have recoiled in horror from the suggestion that he should be above party. Both to the Ins and the Outs such an idea would have had a sinister association with Stuart times when the sovereign for his own ends played off one party against the other. But it was impossible to make any such separation. Only by the assistance of the King and his patronage could any government hope to survive. Hence with groups of politicians competing for office the King became a factor of supreme importance. Hence the attacks on the influence of the Crown by those excluded from government. Hence their silence on that subject once they were within the magic circle of office.

To sum up these constitutional implications as they affected George III: while the forms of government evolved by Walpole and the Pelhams were ready to receive a King above party, and indeed required such a King in order to function properly, neither the country nor its politicians were prepared or able to admit so advanced a conception. For this waste of synchronization Britain was to pay expensively. But the bill should not be sent in to George III. It was his misfortune, not his fault, that he was called upon to reign at a moment of constitutional growing-pains.

The part which poor George was impelled to play by such a variety of accidents was, unhappily for himself and his country, not the one for which he was best equipped. It was not that he was ill-educated—the volumes of essays which have survived at Windsor are enough to dispel such a tradition. It was that, between a mother who strove to keep her first-born uncontaminated from the vices of the age and a grandfather who till his death jealously excluded him from all business, he mounted the throne without practical experience. Lacking this essential qualification, his very virtues became so many handicaps. A clever libertine like Charles II would have played his game admirably; there would have been no Wilkes and liberty—that squinting demagogue would have been won over for life with a bawdy jest and a sinecure; the City would have become more loyal than the King; the displeasure of the colonies would never have been allowed to shift from the Ministers to the throne. But George was no Charles II, whose private life was enough to damn him for ever in his eyes. His conscience was as a millstone about his neck. His piety was acquired at the cost of worldly wisdom, and because of this tended to harden into impracticable obstinacy. Nor had he been given any

Photo : Mansell

KING GEORGE III.

Engraved by Richard Houston after the portrait by Zoffany

opportunity of qualifying impressions acquired at his father's court by being brought into contact with his grandfather's Ministers. Instead, brooding over his real and imaginary wrongs he became a bundle of complexes. The sheltered life, the attitude of George II, a preference shown generally to a younger brother, created in him a sort of persecution mania. He was what in the twentieth century would have been called a difficult child: in the eighteenth he was merely a disappointment to his mother. Starved for affection and yet craving for companionship he threw himself into the arms of the one man who treated him as neither a child nor a blockhead, but a friend. The influence of Bute has almost certainly been exaggerated, but there is little doubt that this most pompous and inept Scotsman did nothing to check the tendency of the Prince to regard all those whose opinions differed from his own as personal enemies, and all opposition as faction.

George III was, in short, a mass of sharp edges which a truly wise ruler is careful to file smooth before he mounts the throne. Compromise, so indispensable to statesmanship, was a word he used with the utmost reluctance. Taking as his beau ideal one of the greatest of English sovereigns he had determined to go straight for his mark.

' When Alfred mounted the throne (ran one of his numerous essays on British history) there was scarcely a man in office that was not totally unfit for it and generally extremely corrupt in the execution of it. . . . He got rid of the incorrigible, reclaimed others and formed new subjects for to raise up his own glory and with it the glory and happiness of his country.'[3]

These words which would have brought tears
of gladness to the eyes of Poor Fred, his father,
faithfully expressed what the Prince felt towards,
his grandfather's Ministers a year or two before he
became King. They might equally be taken as the
motif of the Royal Overture.

The performance, when it came, proved the most
dismal of failures. The King's lofty intentions
miscarried to such a degree that they have since
undergone distortion. Not for a century was any
real attempt made to examine the truth of the
verdict brought in largely by his enemies that
George III, grasping at absolutism, endeavoured to
subvert the constitution, threw the country into
confusion and, in partnership with Lord North,
lost his American colonies.

How far (or how little) the King was responsible
for the American War and for debauching Parliament will be considered at a later stage. At the
moment it is enough to indicate that one half of the
King's troubles came not from any absolutist
tendencies but from a rigid constitutional conscience
which impelled him over-zealously to support the
authority of his Parliament. ' The King would
live on bread and water to preserve the Constitution
of this country. He would sacrifice his life to
maintain it inviolate.'⁴ North, who made this
observation after years of intimate association with
George III, was not exaggerating. A suggestion
that Parliamentary government was threatened by a
Wilkes, a newspaper editor, or a Colony of Massachusetts Bay, found him standing foursquare in its
defence. And how in a country where no *lettres de*

cachet ran and no Bastille stood convenient, could he contribute to this defence in a practical way? Against those men who he sincerely believed were attacking Britain's precious constitution he had no personal means of showing his displeasure save by depriving them of office if they held one in his gift, in the same manner as Temple would have dismissed an audacious gamekeeper who voted for a court candidate.

If it is objected that George III's purpose was to simulate constitutionalism the more easily to use Parliament as his catspaw in the furtherance of absolutist ambitions, the answer is that nowhere in the King's voluminous correspondence is there so much as a whisper of such an idea. For the system of Louis XV he had nothing but outspoken abhorrence. A remark of dubious authenticity, divorced from all context, 'George be a King' has been eagerly swallowed by four generations of Radical historians as proof positive of an autocratic education. The words, if ever uttered, have no more significance than the passing expression of a mother's solicitude. Confounding innocence with wisdom the Princess Dowager may have been foolish enough to have spun a cocoon round her first-born, but at least she did not make the criminal mistake of bringing up a boy who must one day succeed to a great empire without instilling into him the principles, obligations and duties of kingship. Whether his mother was or was not ' imbued with all the aristocratic ideas of a petty German court '5 there is certainly nothing to show that the son aimed at anything more than fulfilling the difficult duties of a constitutionally irresponsible head of a parliamentary form of government. [6]

Equally without foundation is the hackneyed tale of a Prince spoon-fed by Bolingbroke and his *Patriot King*. There is not a shred of evidence that George ever read this vastly overrated pamphlet. The egregious Dodington, whom little about the Prince's court escaped, mentions neither the book nor the author except to record his death.[*] When Horace Walpole observed that following the accession of George III, Prerogative was become the fashionable word, he was merely proving how blind a man in his position could be.[7] George III, who conscientiously sought to tread in the footsteps of William III, never attempted to use and certainly never claimed to possess one prerogative not enjoyed and exercised by this first English King with a purely Parliamentary title.[†]

. . . . .

It was only because Britain was in the thick of a war that George III was unable to put his ideas into instant practice. Such dismissals as he had envisaged in his essay on Alfred were for the moment clearly inadvisable. In consequence the old gang were given an unexpected reprieve, and had they had the sense to make the best of it, all need not have been lost. The one man who, from having

[*] So strong is the legend that it is found surviving as late as 1934. ' Guided by Bolingbroke she [i.e., the Princess Dowager] collected round her at Leicester House in the last years of George II's reign a few men who were to help her son break the Whig party.' (*Fox*, Hobhouse, 14.) On this point it is worthy of note that Bolingbroke died eighteen months after the Prince of Wales and eight years before the death of George II.

[†] And yet the same Walpole can gravely write in 1780, 'the great object of the nation and of the present opposition ought to be to restore the constitution what it was as established at the Revolution.' (*Last Journal*, ii. 382.)

been a member of Prince Frederick's Court, from his intimate family connexions with at least one great Whig house, and from his unparalleled national popularity, might have made a concordat with the King, let this invaluable respite slip away. If ever there was a wicked fairy presiding over the early years of the young monarch, it was the compound of brilliance and blindness, of genius and perversity which went under the glorious name of William Pitt. Like his new master, Pitt took no account of party labels. For years the rafters of St. Stephen's had rung with his pleas for measures not men, and in his own war cabinet this phrase had sprung to life. For a King who sought to merge parties into one national government, here then was a helpmeet indeed ready to hand.* Admittedly, there was one condition. Partnership with Pitt must include Bute, the man who for ten years had possessed, though without the abilities to justify it, the confidence of the Prince. Yet in this there was nothing strange or unconstitutional. The theory that the King must accept and continue in office any Minister or Ministers of his predecessor was held by none, not even by the members of 'the Venetian Oligarchy' themselves. George II had, for example, dismissed the formidable Walpole on his accession and had Sir Spencer Compton proved anything of a financial expert the eclipse might have been permanent. Indeed, 'the minister behind the

---

* Actually, both the King and Pitt were attempting the hopeless task of putting back the hands of the clock. 'Measures not men' had a delectable sound to those starving in Opposition ranks; but as a contribution to contemporary politics it was an anachronism. After having eaten into political life for over fifty years, party could not be exorcised by a few passes from King and Minister.

curtain ' was so much the nightmare of the eighteenth-century politician that it was considered
essential that he should be employed in public so
as to become answerable to Parliament. It had
been an argument used against Pulteney and before
long was to be levelled against Jenkinson. To
criticize George III because he insisted on bringing
forward Bute is to introduce nineteenth-century
canons of criticism to bear upon eighteenth-century
phenomena.

' In England,' Pitt declared six years later when
it was too late, ' there are two possible varieties of
ministry. One consists of those in favour with the
public, the other of men in favour at Court. I
have come to the conclusion that a combination of
the two kinds would produce the best ministry.' [8]
Had he reached this conclusion in the autumn of
1760, and consented to make a working agreement
with Bute, the history of the reign and the career
of Lord North might have been very different.
Instead, his passionate arrogance blinded him to
true wisdom. The man who, three years earlier,
had consented to go into partnership with his old
enemy Newcastle, did not even try to overcome, as
his abilities and prestige would have enabled him
to do, the handicap of Bute's intrusion. Admittedly,
cataloguing the flora and fauna of his Scottish Isle
or, in lighter moments, displaying his shapely legs
at private theatricals, were Bute's true vocations;
still, for all his futility and pomposity, he was
notoriously the royal friend and confidant, and at a
time when the King could not be treated as a
government department this should have been of

supreme significance. A triumvirate of George III, Bute and Pitt with Newcastle fetching and carrying in the background must have been irresistible. Yet when, within two days of the accession, Bute, with his sovereign's approval, approached the haughty Pitt, he was offensively informed that his employment would not be in the King's interests.[9] Even Pitt's stoutest admirers must concede that, except when winning a war, he was imperious, unaccommodating, and temperamental. By denying the King a modest say in the formation of his government, he was being grossly unfair. By preventing the King, of whose character he could not have been ignorant, from exercising his constitutional powers in a reasonable manner he was committing a grave tactical error. So long as the sovereign continued to be the constant, self-contained and decisive factor in politics, so long must he be a magnet to ambitious politicians of all groups. Zeal on behalf of the King must, unless the sovereign were tactfully treated, take the place of zeal on behalf of Newcastle, Pitt or any party chief. And this much could be said for the change: whereas the King's ' undertakers ' had hitherto maintained the principle of ' closed shop,' the King was ready to employ ' non-union ' labour. Moreover, by rejecting the man who above all others possessed the confidence of the King, by declining even to give him rope with which to hang himself, Pitt was inviting his sovereign to set up a double cabinet. For out of the heterogeneous association of persons active on the King's behalf there developed by a natural process a smaller entity of King's Friends, productive of so much misgovernment for the country and unhappiness for North. On Pitt's contrariness and miscalculations rests much of the responsibility for the chaos and disasters that accompanied the first two decades of the reign.

In order to gloss over this unreasonable behaviour of the Great Commoner it has become a tradition to accuse George III of forcing Pitt's hand first by discarding Whigs for Tories and then by prodigal bribery obtaining a subservient Parliament. The one indictment is as weak as the other. Not only had party distinction ceased—and for this Pitt was as much responsible as any man—but a Ministry composed predominantly of hereditary Whigs, such as Grenville, Bedford, Sandwich, and North's uncle Halifax, carried on for nearly four years after Pitt threw up his office in 1761. As for the charge of tampering with Parliament, a comparison between the last of George II and the first of George III yields some surprising results. As the result of the General Election, which Newcastle had been dreading as the end of all things, out of 148 members resigned the old Jobber could count more or less upon two-thirds of their successors. The grand total of those elected upon a definite royal mandate was *three* and these he confessed were ' all very unexceptional.'[10] In other words, the first Parliament of George III, which was to expel Wilkes, pass the Stamp Act, and agree to Townshend's American taxation, was elected, as we should say to-day, upon a Newcastle coupon.

Nor are the references to large-scale bribery,

which will be encountered throughout North's ministerial career, any better substantiated by facts. By the side of the bills which had to be met in half a dozen stately British homes on the morrow of this or subsequent General Elections, the few thousands that the King personally handed over to assist his government were very small beer.* While the Russells, the Cavendishes, and the Temples, might bribe to their hearts' content the sovereign who, to assist the government which possessed his confidence, personally dispensed between ten and twenty thousand pounds at a General Election has been branded an organizer of large-scale corruption.†

Because Pitt obstructed the King and declined to humble himself sufficiently to treat Bute with consideration, the sovereign became more important

---

*In 1768 Lord Spencer spent no fewer than £100,000 on the Northampton election, and as late as 1807 three candidates for two Yorkshire constituencies as much as half a million. (Grego, *History of Parliamentary Elections*, 227, and Halevy, *Hist. of the English People*, i. 165.)

† A good instance of loose generalization is provided by Sir Erskine May in his *Constitutional History*, i. 335. ' The very first election of this reign was signalized by unusual excesses. Never, perhaps, had bribery been resorted to with so much profusion.' For confirmation he gives—Horace Walpole. On such testimony of one who constantly sought for effect in his correspondence, who was a mass of prejudices and whose information was often at second or third hand, so much history has been based.

Again Sir George Trevelyan, writing of the election of 1780, tells us with the air of a man clinching an irrefutable argument that, as soon as its date was decided upon, the King ' sent Mr. John Robinson a packet of bank notes to the amount of £14,000 under cover of a letter, and then he awaited the event with the calmness of an experienced General upon the eve of a campaign, who is conscious that he has neglected nothing which can minimize disappointment and ensure success.' (*George III and Charles James Fox*, iii. 301.) If this proves anything, it proves that George III had, in contrast to his over-mighty subjects, very little to spare for election purposes.

It was never difficult for a hack writer to add on a few noughts. As a typical example, one of these declares in doggerel:

' Sweet are the streams from George's Civil List,
These springs hydropic Pensioners exhaust;
How many *Millions* thus are basely lost! '
(*Taxation the Worst Tyranny* (1778), xi.)

than his government, his cause of greater significance than that of any party group, and the centre of political gravity shifted from Claremont* to Buckingham House. The rising generation of politicians, who no longer thought in terms of Whig and Tory, had little difficulty in adapting themselves to this re-orientation of values. Some did so at once; others, like the young Member for Banbury, after a brief hesitation.

*Claremont was the seat of the Duke of Newcastle.

Chapter III

APPRENTICESHIP

' I was not swaddled and rocked and dawdled into a legislator.'
BURKE, *Letter to a Noble Lord.*

To Lord North the accession of a King, with whose
fortunes he was to become so closely associated for
the best years of his life, passed without immediate
consequences. The Ministerial crises, which disgraced the lustrum dividing Pitt's snubbing of
Bute from the King's declaring he would sooner
have the devil in his Cabinet than George Grenville,
thundered harmlessly over his head. Undisturbed,
though not unconcerned, he minded his business
behind the four walls of the Treasury Office quietly,
conscientiously and, above all, prudently. While
the follies of statesmen were setting the horoscope
which was to determine the course of the reign,
North was building up a reputation for solid financial competence and all-round ability as a debater.
Had he not by his earnest application earned the
respect of his superiors, he could hardly have produced, and in all probability would never have been
given the chance to produce, fourteen budgets, half
of them under wartime conditions. Yet neither at
this time nor in the years immediately to come did

he lift up his eyes higher than the Presidency of the Board of Trade.

When twelve months had passed, and Bute, ' The Favourite', uniting with Newcastle, ' The Minister of Numbers', jockeyed Pitt, ' The Minister of Measures,' into resignation, there was still nothing to interrupt the even tenor of North's existence. The extension and prolongation of the war, which seemed inseparable from Pitt's remaining in office, was hateful to him. Besides, though Pitt was later to make some fulsome observations on North's eligibility for office, it is unlikely that relations between the two had been any closer than coldly official. It was, however, quite another matter when six months later Newcastle, humiliated at every turn, himself decided to resign, and to his mortification was given no chance to change his mind. From the old duke, it will be remembered, North had received nothing but kindness. His first instincts, accordingly, were to follow his chief into retirement; and he could have done so without loss of honour or lapse of duty, always to be two considerations with him of supreme importance. Such self-sacrifice, however, did not altogether suit Newcastle, who through friends and dependents remaining in office, trusted to be still in the Ministry though no longer of it. Such loyalty, it was hinted, was neither desired nor expected. These representations, reinforced (there can be little doubt) by a father who feared to be financially affected by a son's loss of salary and who most certainly saw in North's continuation in office his only hope of drawing some prize from the political bran pie,

bore down any resistance.*   In this, the first, as in
nearly every critical juncture of his career, can be
detected that fatal compliance to the stronger will or
inclinations of those North loved and respected. The
decision now made for him by others shaped the
whole course of his life. Once caught up in the
Bute-Grenville machine there was to be no withdrawing until it was too late.

The peace negotiations which soon followed with
France hastened the estrangement between North
and the Newcastle Whigs. For one thing, the peace
which the duke was hysterically condemning North
considered advantageous: admittedly not so advantageous as it might have been, but certainly not
inadequate enough to warrant the risk and expense
of a further campaign.[1] For another, Grenville
being considered too scrupulous, Henry Fox was
brought forward to ensure the safe passage of the
peace Preliminaries through the Commons; and no
sooner had this been achieved than he proceeded to
deprive of office, pension, or place all who in any way
held of Newcastle. But long before this massacre
of the Newcastle Innocents, in fact within forty-
eight hours of Fox's taking the leadership of the
House of Commons, there came to North from Bute,
now head of the Administration, an entirely unexpected offer of Controllership to the Royal Household at a salary to be specially raised to that which
he was then enjoying as a Junior Lord of the
Treasury. The proposition was, like Pitt's three
years earlier, rejected. To dance attendance at

* See Add. MSS. 33876 ff. 353, 383 for a begging letter by Guilford to
Newcastle and the latter's depressing reply.

Court could have no attraction for one to whom the Commons was every debate becoming more his spiritual home. 'For several reasons,' he told his father, ' many of which will occur to your Lordship, I declined, so I hope to hear no more of it.'[2] Whatever these reasons for rejection they are far less significant than those which led Bute to make the offer in the first place. It is out of the question that anything of this nature could have been proffered in that most realistic of ages without a very definite motive. It could scarcely have been made in order to gain North's support for the Preliminaries —his pacific sentiments could have been no secret. Moreover, there were far too many indigent sons of peers, and even peers themselves, waiting on Bute's doorstep for him to take such pains for one already in an office. As a sop to Guilford, still champing away at Wroxton in indignant unemployment, the proposal was clearly inadequate. Could it then have been an attempt to lure North up a blind alley, at the end of which lay, perhaps, a red ribbon and nothing more? There are several features that make this the most probable explanation. So far from being

> ' the vile domestic of a peer,
>   whose name an Englishman detests to hear,' [3]

North heartily detested the Favourite. He bitterly resented the continued cold-shouldering of his father in the new reign and these sentiments, it may be certain, Guilford used every endeavour to keep alive.[4] On his side Bute had too good an opinion of his own abilities to concern himself about the displeasure of a young and very junior member of his government. Still, it is possible that he may have felt some distaste in having upon his Treasury Board the son of his master's old Governor and the nephew of Halifax (now in charge of the Admiralty), who cordially disliked him. To remove North without advancing him might have led to trouble. To promote him to an office about the Court, where Bute considered himself supreme, would at once eliminate him from the Treasury Board, negative any objections from Halifax, and render North more or less innocuous.

Whatever Bute's intentions—and in the absence of evidence these can only be presumed—they soon ceased to matter for North and his father. Alarmed by the violent hostility he had raised over the Peace terms, he slunk away in retirement, hoping from the pleasanter privacy of his Luton mansion still to direct the footsteps of ' his master and his friend.' In confident anticipation of better and stronger government, the King on his advice handed the Seals to Grenville, a Whig at once by tradition and conviction. In the change-over Halifax stepped up into the office of Secretary of State and North, in consequence, sat all the more securely in the Treasury Office. But not, as it turned out, more happily.

In certain fundamentals Grenville and North confessed the same political creed and might therefore have seemed well-suited to one another. When Grenville reminded a colleague that he had entered office ' from principles of duty, to hinder the law from being unconstitutionally and indecently

given to him (the King),' he was uttering
words which might have dropped from North at
any time during his Premiership.[5] But unfortunately Grenville, who might have been a greater
Speaker than Onslow or as great a Chancellor as
Hardwicke, did not possess the qualifications of a
statesman. Under his administration—according
to Macaulay the worst since the Revolution—
North presently began to repent of his decision not
to have quitted in company with Newcastle. It
was not that he felt drawn towards the Opposition,
with whom the duke was, a little reluctantly,
identifying himself. On the contrary, its oppor-
tunist policy was disgusting him as much as it was
Grenville. Though the country was loaded with
a vast and unprecedented debt, North, from his
knowledge of finance, was as confident as his chief
that recovery lay just round the corner if the public
were prepared to agree to take their medicine like
men. The prescription was, of course, taxation,
so graduated as to spread its burden equitably.
But, instead of agreeing to support so national and
essential an object, Opposition strove to confound
the government's plans by stirring up the passions
of the mob. That men of his own rank could, for
their own narrow ends, indulge the riff-raff of cities
was, for North, complete justification of the King's
condemnation of their conduct as ' faction.' From
these incidents in the spring of 1763 it is evident
North began to regard popular measures so-called
as synonymous with vote-catching devices, and
Vox Populi to mean no more than the cat-calls of a
well-paid canaille. Without going out of his way,

LORD NORTH

Aged about 26.

From a portrait at Kirtling Tower, Newmarket.   *By kind permission of Lord North*

like the young Charles James Fox, to invite unpopularity, he seems thenceforward to have taken
something like a pride in challenging the alleged will
of the people. ' I do not dislike popularity,' he declared some time later, ' but for the last seven years
I have never given my vote for any one of the
popular measures.'[6] Thus, notwithstanding the
squeals of the West Country farmers and its possible
effect upon Sir William Pynsent, he eloquently
supported the Cider Tax of 1763, ' against which
there were never two syllables of commonsense
urged.'[7] Thus was he to fight the proposed
reduction of the land tax, though nothing would
have put the Tory country gentlemen in a better
humour. For the same reason was he to vote
in favour of the Stamp Act and against its
Repeal.

It was not, then, by being called upon to support
Grenville's financial measures that North felt
unhappy and out of sympathy with his colleagues.
It was when the Ministry of Grenville quitted the
paths of peace and retrenchment that North wished
he had gone out with the kindly old duke, who
would never have done what the Administration
proceeded to do before they had been six weeks in
office.

Hardly was the ink dry upon the great Treaty of
Paris than, to North's dismay, the Ministry declared
what proved to be a Seven Years' War of their own
against John Wilkes. In the annals of this in-
glorious campaign there is little that is edifying. On
one side there stood a man whose unabashed purpose was to see how full he could fill his pockets by

trailing his coat, on the other a knot of angry Ministers sticking at nothing to remove a gadfly from their flanks.   Between the two hovered North, uncomfortable and regretful.

On April 23, 1763, there had been published the 45th number of Wilkes' paper *The North Briton*, in which the Royal speech was scathingly criticized. In freedom of expression and scurrility there was little to distinguish this from the thousand and one screeds produced by the violent and venal press of the day, except that rather more care than usual was taken to avoid any personal insult to the sovereign.   The speech was conceded to be the work of the Minister, and references to the King were rather by way of commiseration that ' a Prince of so many great and amiable qualities, whom England truly reveres, can be brought to give the sanction of his sacred name to the most odious measures and to the most unjustifiable public declarations from a throne ever renowned for truth, honour, and unsullied virtue.'   What incensed the Ministry was not scurrilous abuse, characteristic indeed of everything that came from the press of either side, but the charge, particularly galling to patricians like Grenville and Halifax, that they were Bute's lickspittles, ' the foul dregs of his power, the tools of corruption and despotism.' They were not, it seemed, to be given a chance to prove their worth and independence, but were to be condemned unheard and at sight.   Grenville, in effect, was to be assailed with all the virulence which had been levelled against Bute.   If this was to be their portion before they had been a month in the saddle, what might they not expect before the end of a year?

If Wilkes' object was (as he told Madame de Pompadour) to find out just how far the liberty of the Press extended, Grenville was prepared to show him then and there. In this determination every encouragement was given by the King. In the course of his campaign against the Favourite, Wilkes had been spicing his *North Briton* with allusions to immoral relations between Bute and the Princess Dowager.* [8] But it was not these which finally roused the sovereign (who had treated the innuendoes with contempt) but the implication in the 45th number, that he had consciously given his name to a deliberate lie. In this Wilkes had certainly gone too far, and had outraged even many Opposition members. Pitt hastened to dissociate himself from the writer, and Hardwicke thought the paper the most unguarded and audacious thing he had ever read.[9] The Ministry thus had it in their power to deal effectively with Wilkes when in a moment of hasty folly they threw away much of the goodwill they possessed, North's included. Regardless of the Sacheverell affair half a century earlier, they decided to proceed, not by the somewhat dilatory yet normal procedure under which Wilkes would have been arrested, tried and punished like any other editor who had transgressed the bounds of decorum, but by invoking the General Warrant, an instrument of doubtful legality, and

* Of the two most recent biographers of George III, one (Vulliamy) is inclined to credit the scandal. The other (Davies) refuses to believe it. Fortunately, the question of illicit amours of the Queen Mother (as well as those of her son) do not concern the biographer of North.

in this case unnecessary and certainly misguided. To the Opposition this proceeding gave a Heaven-sent rallying cry. To North it caused acute misgivings. To believe that there should be some limit to scurrilous expression of opinion was not the same thing as to approve of methods associated rather with Versailles than with St. James's. It was now that North wished he had gone out with Newcastle, for the warrant on which Wilkes was arrested had been signed by his uncle and friend, the Earl of Halifax.

When Wilkes was released by the order of Chief Justice Pratt, on the grounds that, being a Member of Parliament, he was covered by privilege, he lost no time in carrying the campaign into the enemies' country. Actions were started against the servants of the Crown, principal among whom was very properly the Earl of Halifax. At once the reputation of the Ministry was at stake. But Grenville, a man whose heart and soul were bound up with the rights and duties of the House, was not one to sit idle under such provocation. Parliament, which De Lolme was soon to tell the world could do anything but make a man a woman, or a woman a man, should have no difficulty in overturning the dictum of a Lord Chief Justice. The spearhead of the Government counter attack was offered to Frederick North. The choice was neither surprising, nor was it made at random, yet one of the very reasons which must have suggested his name to the Ministry made him the more reluctant to accept this equivocal piece of nepotism. His choice would be attributed by the outside world not to any merit on his part, but solely to his uncle. Nor was it fair to ask him to bear the burden of attacking a man with whom he shared in common a dislike of Bute.

' As the case stands ' (he wrote, refusing the offer) ' I have personally rather received civilities from Mr. Wilkes and (here breaks in the unmistakable voice of Wroxton) the marks of favour received from His Majesty by my father and myself are not such as to make the world expect that we should be the first in this declaration of duty.' [10]

Brave words these; but, like so many to be uttered in the course of his career, they remained no more than words. The Ministers hastened to meet North's objections. Excuses were made. The blame was thrown upon Bute. The neglect of Lord Guilford, it was pointed out, should not be imputed to the Ministry, who had done, and would continue to do, their best.[11]

Under such pressure North gave way, but with what reluctance only his father knew.

' Nothing,' he told Guilford, ' can go more against me than the business I am now upon, but while things stand in their present ticklish situation, it is impossible to avoid it. You may be sure I shall be very moderate in my expressions, but that will be to no purpose. The part I take will be an unpardonable crime with the other side. I begin heartily to wish I had followed my own opinion in going out with the Duke of N.; I should have spared myself many an uncomfortable moment. From the time one engages one draws closer and closer, until one has so far engaged that one cannot in honour decline taking a part in a thousand affairs wherein one would choose to be quiet.' [12]

The final sentence may be taken as a text

for the next twenty years of North's life.

Another week, and on the first day of the session, North, speaking very effectively, moved that ' The *North Briton* No. 45 is false, scandalous, and a seditious libel containing expressions of the most unexampled insolence and contumely towards His Majesty, the grossest aspersions upon both Houses of Parliament, and the most audacious defiance of the authority of the whole legislature; and most manifestly tending to alienate the affections of the people from His Majesty, to withdraw them from their obedience to the laws of their realm, and to excite them to treacherous insurrections against His Majesty's Government.' [13] When this was carried by a large majority he went on to move that the paper be burned by the common hangman. Ten days later he returned to the attack with a motion, which was carried at two o'clock in the morning, that the privilege of Members did not cover seditious libel.

Meanwhile, to make doubly sure of themselves, the Government were playing out a tragi-comedy within the Lords. A copy of an *Essay on Woman* (a parody of Pope's *Essay on Man*), written by Brother Thomas Potter, son of the late Archbishop, and privately printed by Brother John Wilkes, of the Medmenham Fraternity, had been obtained by means morally, if not actually, criminal.[14] With incredible effrontery and unwisdom, this bawdy effusion was solemnly produced by Brother Sandwich who, in addition to belonging to the Fraternity, had also the recent distinction of being expelled for blasphemy from the Beefsteak Club.[15] While ' the good ' Lord Lyttelton stopped his ears against the flow of obscenities and begged Sandwich to desist, his fellow peers clamoured for more. Their appetites at length satiated, their Lordships proceeded to vote the Essay a breach of privilege for its loose references to the Lord Bishop Warburton, the editor of Pope's Works, as well as ' a most scandalous obscene, and impious libel.' Wilkes, meanwhile wounded in a duel, and disconcerted by this stab in the back, had fled to France. It was probably the wisest thing he could have done. He was no longer the hero he had been. His Essay had estranged numerous friends. His admirers had cooled off. But the mud that he had raised declined to settle at his quitting. North was not to be let off so lightly.

The weakest link in the Government chain had been its use of the General Warrant. These warrants had been used in the past—as recently as the Ministry of Pitt—but conditions had generally been exceptional. They had been directed against Jacobite agents or spies in times of war and crises. In time of peace and tranquillity to arrest half a hundred authors, printers and publishers for a paper, however severely it reflected on the Government, when there were other methods available, revived memories of the Star Chamber. In February, soon after the Christmas recess, the Opposition advanced to the attack with a motion that General Warrants were illegal. The question being primarily one of law, the full brunt was borne by Sir Fletcher Norton, the Attorney-General. But when Charles Yorke, lately Solicitor-General, arose and ripped his arguments to pieces, it was North who

was next put up for the Government, and this fact
is a sure indication of his mounting reputation.
There remains no record of North's or any speech in
this debate, which, for duration, established a
record.   The Government were in a tight corner,
and they knew it.   Well-timed references to Magna
Carta, Star Chamber, and the Stuarts could play
havoc with any majority.   At one stage this had
dropped as low as ten and when, at half-past four
on the morning of February 18, 1746, Members filed
into the lobby for the last division, the life of the
Ministry hung by a thread.   When the figures
were announced, voters for the Government numbered 234, those for the Opposition no fewer
than 220, amongst whom were nearly half the
country members.[16]   It was a victory for the
Opposition in everything but a majority.

Whatever his private sentiments, North neither
at this nor at any time allowed them to interfere
with what he considered to be the carrying out of
his duty.   That he had done as well as any man
could have done in such circumstances was evident
from the regard with which Grenville, never lavish
in his praise, presently spoke of him.   ' North ' (he
said sagaciously) ' is a man of great promise and
high qualifications, and if he does not relax in his
political pursuits he is likely to be Prime Minister.' [17]
In fact, two months later when a report (for which
there proved to be no foundation) was circulating
that Lord Holland was resigning the lucrative Pay
Office, North was one of the two successors suggested.* [18]   This flattering rumour, and the ter-

* Welbore Ellis was the other.

mination (for good and all, it was hoped) of the
Wilkes–General Warrants episode, put North in
the best of humours. ' It is a comfort to see the
Administration conclude their campaign most
reputably and triumphantly, notwithstanding the
most numerous and violent opposition I ever
remember. I do not as yet hear of any mischief
done by Lord B(ute). I own I think that the principal danger is now from that quarter, if his Lordship's power and inclination continue in any degree
what they have formerly been.' [19]

North was unduly sanguine. Bute or no Bute,
the Grenville administration never recovered from
the odium into which the Wilkes affair had cast
them. Though the Opposition was greatly weakened by the deaths of Hardwicke, Legge, and the
Duke of Devonshire, no compensatory strength
accrued to the Government. More ominously,
the Ministers did not even succeed in retaining the
goodwill of the King, who (according to his interpretation of the Constitution) necessarily regarded a
weak and unpopular Administration as a reflexion
on himself and as a danger to the country. Grenville's
prim pedantry and Bedford's arrogant harangues
alike bored and offended the sovereign who, where
his dignity was concerned, was capable of the greatest
resentment. [20] When, early in 1765, following the
first of the King's illnesses, a Regency Bill was, at
George III's own request, being prepared, royal
susceptibilities were roughly handled. In their
ceaseless jealousy of Bute (the legend of whose subterranean activities had many years of life ahead)
the Cabinet attempted to exclude his alleged

paramour, the Princess Dowager. They tricked the King into agreement, but failed to make sure of the Commons, by whom the Princess's name was ostentatiously restored. At the same time the London weavers, aggrieved at the refusal of the Government to adopt Protective measures, were convulsing the capital with riot and uproar. The prestige of the Ministry sank to zero. In despair the King appealed to his uncle; the Duke of Cumberland in turn approached Pitt, and offered him what amounted to *carte blanche*. Once more was a chance given to the Great Commoner; once more did this wayward genius prove intractable.* Disappointed in Pitt, the King was thrown back on Grenville. Never did Prime Minister make more misguided use of victory. As a price of continuing in office, humiliating terms were dictated to the King. Forced by circumstances to accept, lectured and reprimanded at every turn, George III passed through four weeks which probably did more than the previous twenty-seven years of his life to determine the lines of his future policy. They gave him such a horror of ministerial dictation as never left him until insanity descended like a blanket upon his faculties.†

At the end of this memorable month once more the

---

* From the rough drafts made of proposed changes, North was one of the few Ministers to be left undisturbed. (Fortescue, i. 292-293.) On extremely indifferent authority it was stated that the stone of offence (or one of them) was the suggestion, which Pitt naturally rejected, that North should be First Lord of the Treasury. (H.M.C. Various, viii. p. 183.) Inaccurate or not, this is evidence that North was no longer the obscure junior Minister he had so recently been.

† It was at this time that Richard Rigby swore, ' a great Oath that the King should not have power to appoint one of his footmen.'—Walpole, *George III*, ii. 129.

unhappy King turned, although not very hopefully,
to Pitt.   This time, however, he would do his pleading in person.   It was a shrewd move.   Always
dazzled by the light from the throne, Pitt proved
indeed more accommodating.   Ministries were
chalked out, in the first of which North was
deprived of office without compensation, in the
rest was suggested, in company with Welbore
Ellis, as joint Paymaster-General.   Then at the
last moment his brother-in-law, Lord Temple,
refusing to come in, Pitt supinely excused himself,
and advised (of all things) the re-employment
of Grenville.[21]   But a further return to the soured
and offended Premier was impossible.

A second time Cumberland came to the rescue,
and, acting the part of accoucheur-general, brought
forth a Ministry headed by the Marquis of Rockingham.   It was, according to Chesterfield, ' a
jumble of youth and caducity'; to Townshend
(who nevertheless accepted office) ' a lute-string
administration, fit only for summer wear.'   In
addition to the rump of the old Whig party under
Newcastle, it contained Burke and—what particularly concerned North—the Earl of Dartmouth,
who went to the Board of Trade.   Contrary to his
fears, North's recent conduct had not irreparably
alienated old friends and colleagues.   So far from his
removal being insisted upon, his name had appeared
upon every projected list, the last dated twenty-four
hours only before Rockingham took office, as joint
Paymaster.[22]   Within those twenty-four hours
something, or more probably someone, persuaded
North to decline.   That it must have been a

F

weighty or plausible reason which induced him
to separate himself from Dartmouth may well, in
the absence of evidence, be presumed.

Notwithstanding North's aloofness, before six
months had passed a little conspiracy was afoot
between Newcastle and Dartmouth, with Rockingham a consenting party, to lure him back into
office. The negotiations, which naturally fell to
Dartmouth, were accompanied by every blandish-
ment, and when these failed there was flourished a
high court card—the King's expressed wish that
North should return to his service.   High as it was,
it was not high enough to trump North's scruples.
However, some months later, Rockingham, feeling
more than ever the need for reinforcements, again
raised a beckoning finger.   This time the reward
was to be the Treasuryship of Ireland. This time,
as well he might, North went so far as to hesitate.
The temptation of such a lucrative office to an ex-
Minister out of employment, with a clutch of children approaching school age, was so great that it is
no wonder North (according to one account)
' goggled his eyes and groped in his money pocket,
more than half consented, nay, so much more,
that when he got home he wrote an excuse to Lord
Rockingham which made it plain he thought he
had accepted.'[23]   Indeed the Lord Chancellor
went so far as to congratulate the Premier on his
acquisition; and this, coming from the churlish
Northington, was praise indeed. But at the last
moment interest gave place to principle—or was it
to prudence? The sands were fast running out
against the Rockingham Administration and, if

North did not know this, Guilford with his extensive circle of correspondents certainly did. The King, who had almost passionately desired Pitt, had never regarded the Rockingham Administration as much more than a makeshift affair permitting him to mark time until a convenient ' chapter of accidents' should occur.[24] The initial refusal of the Great Commoner to have anything to do with the Ministry, even to give it his confidence, had dealt it a savage blow; the death of Cumberland crippled it beyond hope; the repeal of Grenville's Stamp Act, in a manner distasteful to the King, completed its ruin. North was clearly being invited to 'sign on' a sinking ship.

His refusal, not unexpected by the King, did him no harm. Two months later, early in July, the Chancellor, deciding the hour had come to create the King's ' chapter of accidents,' declined to attend any further Cabinet meetings. On July 7, 1766, the Rockingham Administration was at an end.

This time the Great Commoner, ' penetrated with the deepest sense of your Majesty's boundless goodness to me, and with a heart overflowing with zeal and duty,' consented ' to lay at the Royal feet the poor but sincere offering of the small services of your Majesty's most dutiful subject and most devoted servant.'[25] The basis of the New Deal was to be ' Measures, not Men,' the defence of the Closet against Connexion. The remainder of July was spent by Pitt ministry-making, as actively as a severe attack of gout would allow. By the end of the month most of the blanks were filled in, but there still remained one figure unemployed. On the

28th, Pitt wrote to North. After outlining his Ministry, he declared he had 'the honour and pleasure to open to you by His Majesty's command that the King would see with satisfaction Lord North return to his service.'²⁶ The letter carried an offer of joint Paymaster, which, if North were to accept, Pitt should deem himself happier in having written than in most cases where he had had the King's command to employ his pen. When Pitt wanted his man he left undone nothing that called to be done, and superbly forgot the past. North, in turn, received the letter in the spirit in which it was written, and allowed no resentment over a recent unsuccessful petition against Sir William Pynsent's will to affect his conduct. Unfortunately, this 'very honourable, profitable and agreeable offer, which I see no reason why I should refuse' was alloyed by one unhappy thought. Dartmouth could not be persuaded to continue in the new Ministry. 'Nothing,' lamented North, 'can be more vexatious than to find myself constantly, by the strange political jumbles, opposed to the one of the men in the world that I honour, love and esteem the most. These events damp all the pleasures of preferment.'²⁷

. . . . .

Behind the characteristic torrent of extravagances with which Pitt presently expressed his satisfaction to Guilford that North had consented to honour his administration, one thing had become clear. At the age of thirty-four, qualified by twelve years of conscientious work as a Member of Parliament, eight of them in office, and by the growing regard of the King, North was no longer one whose claims a Prime Minister could afford to overlook or ignore.

. . . . .

The very day on which Pitt strengthened his Ministry by taking in the scrupulous and talented North, he committed, to the consternation of his Cabinet and the amazement of the public, the injudicious, although (in his present state of health) the venial step of accepting a peerage.* This ' fall upstairs,' as Chesterfield called it, by removing from the Commons the most dominant personality it had ever contained, at once forced up North's market value. Left now on the Government benches, of any ability, were only Conway, the Leader of the House, and Townshend, the scintillating Chancellor of the Exchequer.† The first, as unbending as a ramrod in battle, swayed like an osier in every Parliamentary breeze; the second, whose brilliance was soon to become legendary, was notoriously unreliable. Moreover, the Chatham was, like the Rockingham Administration before it, and the North Administration which came after it, a victim of what might be called ministerial

* ' Here dead to fame lies patriot Will,
His monument his seat;
His titles are his epitaph,
His robe his winding sheet.'
(*New Foundling Hospital of Wit*, iv. 84.)

† The Ministry in its chief offices was as follows:

Chatham...	Lord Privy Seal
Grafton	Treasury
Charles Townshend	Chancellor of the Exchequer
Northington	Lord President
Shelburne ⎱ ... ... Conway ⎰	Secretaries of State
Barrington	Secretary at War
Hillsborough	Board of Trade
Camden	Lord Chancellor

hangovers. Clean sweeps, such as became the rule during the nineteenth century, would have appeared almost impious to the mind of the eighteenth-century politician. Where there was no party organization, and therefore no constant integer in politics but the King, holders of office, if in favour at court, or able to satisfy the incoming Minister, might stay on, and did stay on, as a matter of course. Just as Egmont had percolated through from Grenville to Rockingham, so Conway carried on from Rockingham to Chatham. So Townshend, having served under Grenville and Rockingham, was quite prepared to remain in office under their successor; while Barrington, in charge of the War Department for nearly twenty years, passed like a bale of goods as per invoice from one administration to another.* This ministerial continuity (thoroughly agreeable to the King's ideas) did not work in practice, any more than Pitt's ' Measures, not Men,' of which it was a corollary. The one militated against internal strength and a consistent policy; the other, so excellent a rallying cry for the officeless, was when set in motion hard pressed to keep the human element subsidiary. Once the guiding hand of Chatham was removed, disintegration began. When Dowdeswell, who had been Rockingham's Chancellor of the Exchequer, presently likened the Chatham Administration to a collection of discordant atoms, he was not very wide of the mark.[28]

---

* It should be noted that Pitt agreed to Townshend's admission only reluctantly and after Grafton had pressed it strongly. He afterwards bitterly repented of his compliance. (*Autobiography*, 92.)

Such, however, was the magnificent confidence of Chatham, that none of these difficulties, had they even occurred to him, would have acted as a deterrent. He was as convinced that his administration was to be a durable one as he was that the possession of the Royal confidence was his and his alone.[29] Bute had ceased to whisper behind the arras; the tale-bearing Egmont was gone. As a political squib profanely expressed it, Chatham alone ' sat on the right hand of the King, from whence he shall come to judge the good and the bad. And they that have done good shall go into patent places; and they that have done bad shall go into everlasting opposition. This is the Chatham faith, which, except a man believe faithfully, he cannot be promoted.' [30]

Perhaps, as North ascended the steps of the Pay Office, pausing (so it is recorded) to direct that half the fouling of some dog be carried to his co-Paymaster as his equal share of all perquisites, he considered he had arrived at the next best thing in life to the Presidency of the Board of Trade. The work was congenial and not too responsible. Though compelled to pig it on a 'truckle bed ' with a colleague, he nevertheless enjoyed an increased salary. With George Augustus, his heir, on the threshold of Eton, and two sons and two daughters growing up in the happy North nursery, this was no small consideration. Yet within twelve months he was dragged out of this richly appointed snuggery and, though he received a further increase in emoluments, it was at the cost of much peace of mind. At least, looking out in after years through

the windows of Downing Street across to the Pay
Office, he was heard on several occasions to remark
that since he had left it he had never known the
same happiness.[31]

In a well-known passage, Burke has referred to
the Chatham Administration as a piece of diversi-
fied mosaic, a tessellated pavement without cement.
The simile is not altogether accurate. The cement
was there, but it was wholly Chatham's. In
August, and throughout the autumn, it was
holding. When, after a few months of remarkable
activity, Chatham went to Bath for his health,
cracks suddenly and ominously appeared. It was
this debility of its chief which fatally weakened the
government rather than the material with which it
was composed. In his Ministry Chatham became a
passenger, at first querulous, then insensible, leaving
to his underlings the task of riding the storm. And
very indifferently they rode it.

While Chatham had been present, Townshend
quailed before the lash of his eloquence. When
direction was attempted from a sick-bed, Townshend
became once more his gay, irresponsible self.
Having thwarted his leader's intentions by making a
back-door agreement with the East India Company,
he carelessly allowed himself to be defeated on an
Opposition motion to reduce the Land Tax by one
shilling. When Chatham managed at last to
crawl back to London, he did so fulminating
against this ' preposterous union of clashing
Faction ' and wrathfully informed Grafton that he
and Townshend could no longer sit at the same
Cabinet table. But the problem of finding a

successor was not so easy. Dowdeswell, able, though hardly brilliant, was in opposition; Legge was dead; Grenville was naturally out of the question. The only member of the Government who possessed sufficient experience of Treasury matters and enough ability to introduce a Budget was the Joint-Paymaster. For the first but not for the last time in his life North became an inevitable choice. To him, recently (and contemptuously) described as ' a new convert to the Chatham faith ' were Townshend's Seals offered.* 32

The difference between Joint-Paymastership and the Chancellorship of the Exchequer was one of the first magnitude. It lifted its occupant out of the comparative obscurity of the Pay Office into the hard glare that beats upon anyone the nod of whose head must affect the pockets of a nation. But it was not so much the prominence of the office, though this, to one so self-depreciatory as North must have been a deterrent, as the presence across the floor of two such tried ex-Chancellors as Grenville and Dowdeswell (in addition to the prospect of an outraged Townshend eager to confound his supplanter), which caused him, after a period of characteristic hesitation, to decline on the ostensible grounds that his acceptance of the Seals ' would not be of any real service to the King.' 33 Notwithstanding the pledge of secrecy under which the proposal had been made, it has been stated on the authority of Shelburne (who is alleged to have had it from Townshend) that North betrayed the offer, together with this reply, to Townshend himself.

*Grenville Correspondence, iii. 396

The accusation is no light one. Even if the betrayal were made out of pure good nature, it would be quite inexcusable, as indicating a man so irresponsible as to be unworthy of high office. On the other hand, by those most closely affected, no mention has been made of any breach of confidence. Chatham would have been the first to roar, and Grafton, even though he wrote his memoirs forty years later, could hardly have failed to note so heinous a breach of faith. On the contrary, Grafton quotes, in full, a letter from North suggesting that, in order to make quite certain that the negotiations should remain secret, he should be excused from waiting publicly upon the King to notify his refusal.[34] That he should then have gone and told Townshend, of all men, is so unlike any action in North's career that it becomes, not indeed incredible, but extremely improbable. Townshend was no fool. A man of less parts than he possessed (and according to Burke, he was the most brilliant man of his own or any age) could hardly help knowing his conduct was incensing to Chatham, and so envisaging the consequences of his return to London. It could have required little more effort of imagination to realize that North was his only substitute. In fact early in the year when there had been a rumour of Townshend's becoming Secretary for State North had been spoken of as his successor. Therefore, when nothing followed the return of an irate Chatham, it would not have been difficult to assume that application had been made to North and declined.

The knowledge, whether acquired by intuition or revelation, that he was indispensable, gave Townshend added power, which proved disastrous for his country. Only a short time before, he had likened the distinction between internal taxation, to which the American colonies objected, and external taxation (that is for the purposes of regulating trade), to which they did not, as an "ecstasy of madness." In his search for money to compensate for the cutting down of the Land Tax he had rashly declared that he would obtain from the Americans a revenue to which they could offer no objection. Now, revelling in his increased security, he decided to implement his announcement by the introduction of his famous Revenue Acts. A tax on tea, glass, paper and paint thus became the echo by the Chatham Administration to the rousing words of William Pitt not two years earlier: ' Americans are the sons, not the bastards, of England . . . Taxation is no part of the governing or legislative power. . . . America is obstinate; America is in almost open rebellion. I rejoice that America has resisted.'[35]

Having carried his country past a further milestone on the way to Lexington, Townshend made his bow. While in the midst of intriguing to displace Chatham and erect a Ministry of his own, he succumbed to an attack of low fever. ' See that great, heavy, booby-looking, seeming changeling,' he had only recently remarked of North, ' you may believe me when I assure you as a fact that, if anything should happen to me, he will succeed to my place, and very shortly after come to be First

Commissioner of the Treasury." The first part of his jest came true. North reigned in his stead.

But not at once. North might just as well have been expected to cheat at cards as to give an immediate answer to a proposition affecting his career. Inevitably he asked for time; inevitably he refused. The reasons which obtained six months earlier were still valid, with this additional deterrent that there now hung over Wroxton a cloud of depression. The Earl of Guilford lay ill, not dangerously, but sufficiently, no doubt, to be unable to advise. Without the paternal *imprimatur*, the thirty-five-year-old Paymaster could not, or would not, make up his mind. The office accordingly was, in desperation, offered to Barrington, who, like the honest King's friend that he was, took it, as he would have done if commanded the Papal Crown, obediently, though unwillingly. Then, within a week, Guilford recovered, and spoke. At once North unsaid all his excuses, and Barrington gladly handed back the Seals, which he had scarcely warmed. On October 7, 1767, North kissed hands as Chancellor of the Exchequer, and for the next fourteen years directed the finances of his country. A few weeks later, when Conway, who had never been much more than a passenger, yielded up his ticket, North took over the Leadership of the House of Commons. At the same time he was raised to Cabinet rank, although not having ' the vanity to imagine that his advice can be of any consequence in the planning of Government.'*[36]

* So deeply had Bute got under the skin of the Opposition that some of them professed to see his hand even in this appointment. (Almond, *Biographical Anecdotes*, i. 17.)

High promotion had come at last as a well-merited reward for loyal and ungrudging service. Those years in a minor capacity had given an awkwardly made, clumsily moving, altogether diffident Frederick North just those qualifications necessary in a Chancellor of the Exchequer and a Leader of the House. Until swept away fourteen years later in an avalanche loosed by a long, expensive, and unsuccessful war, North carried out his duties ably, faithfully, and conscientiously. Even before he had been six months in his new office he had acquired, according to Selwyn, 'a budget face.' More to the point is the testimony of Richard Rigby, who, with experience that went back a quarter of a century to Pelham, told Bedford, after hearing North's second budget, ' I verily think I have never known any of his predecessors acquit themselves so much to the satisfaction of the House.'[37]

The Ministry was now, in everything but actual name, the Duke of Grafton's. The duke, who preferred Newmarket to Westminster, the plays of Euripides to official despatches, and the arms of Nancy Parsons to both, was not an inspiring leader.* But for the jealousies which weakened and divided the Opposition, and the steady support from the King, who clung to this Ministry as the last outwork against the forces of faction, his administration must have perished with the speed of Rockingham's. Indeed, very soon after North's appointment as Chancellor, it was saved from collapse only by the

* ' Was ever a nation so governed before
By a jockey and gambler, a pimp and a whore? '
(*N.F.H.W.*, iv. 114.)

introduction of the Bedford Party, Gower taking over the Presidency of the Council from the gout-stricken Northington, Weymouth replacing Conway as Secretary of State, and the unspeakable Rigby going to his spiritual home, the Pay Office. The respite was expensively purchased. When problems presently arose requiring tact, restraint and charity, the influence exerted by the Bloomsbury Gang was uncompromising, violent, and malign.

These crises were to throw more and more work upon the shoulders of North. In the Lords, Grafton might shelter behind an assured ministerial majority. In the Commons, despite its success in the general election of 1768, the Government was much inferior in debating strength; when dividing it was always hard pressed and, on occasions, even defeated by the Opposition. Yet it was just these trials which were to bring out the best in North. With his back to the wall and flanked by indifferent allies, he learnt to rely upon himself; to pick out the weak spots at a glance while his enemies were deploying to attack. Under pressure of constant usage his controversial powers developed rapidly. Debate by debate he rose in the estimation of those best qualified to judge of Parliamentary performance.[38] The more he acquired strength and assurance, the more considerately he used his leadership of the Commons, the more firmly he established his claim as the only successor to Grafton.

It would be a mistake to regard North's consistent progress as so many vignettes from the Industrious Apprentice. Sheer industry, of which he had plenty, alone would not have overcome certain conspicuous handicaps: a poor presence, oratory little above the average, a rumbling indistinct delivery. There were many who had as much capacity for solid work as North, but—and it rendered him pre-eminent amongst his fellow-members—scarcely one combined this with three essential qualifications for a mastery of Parliamentary procedure ; leadership, an imperturbable affability and a sense of humour. Unruffled by the hottest debates; taking the severest trouncing with a smile; exchanging pleasantries with his most determined opponents; chuckling with delight at a joke, whether directed against others or himself, yet quick as lightning with a repartee; capable of wriggling out of a corner by neatly turning the laugh against his pursuers; he dominated the House of Commons for the next twelve years as not one of his contemporaries could have done.

Had Guilford died during his late illness it is impossible to estimate the effect upon his son's life. What is clear is that, in the more restrained atmosphere of the Lords to which North would have gone, he could never have acquired such authority nor would it have been thrust upon him. To give his best North needed to be put constantly upon his metal. In a Chamber which rarely contained more than fifty, and of those not half a dozen of any distinctive ability, his qualities would have suffered atrophy. But the rough and tumble of the Commons; the guerilla fire from Burke, Barré, Tommy Townshend, and, for a time, Wedderburn; the tension of Budget night ;

the excitement of a critical division; this was the world in which North was in his true element and the world which, for all its abuse of him, loved North. For how was it possible to hate one who was what every Member with ambition wished to be—a complete House of Commons man? How was it possible to dislike a man who laughed when attacked, who bore no malice, and who, when the debate grew tedious or a Member prolix, lay sprawled across the Treasury bench gloriously asleep?

As a weapon in party warfare this propensity to sleep cannot be ignored as a contributory cause of North's success in Parliament. At first it was no doubt genuine; later, by being carefully cultivated, it came to be used at times with devastating effect. It filled the pompous with impotent rage and reduced the long-winded to negligibility. It disconcerted speakers at moments of intense fervour, as when Burke used a false quantity in a classical quotation and North stirred, murmured a correction, and relapsed into slumber.* The two best-known victims of North's morphetic habit were George Grenville and Alderman Sawbridge, one of the City representatives. When the former once began an involved and academic disquisition North fell asleep, leaving injunctions that he should be woken when, if ever, the speaker reached contemporary times. Later on, being roused, and hearing Grenville referring to the reign of William III, he turned to his neighbour and convulsed the House by exclaiming audibly: ' Zounds, sir, you have woken

*Burke had referred to vectigal with the i short.

me up a century too soon!' As for Sawbridge,
when this turgid 'annual motionmaker' was expos-
tulating against the futility of even attempting to
reach the root of political evils while the Minister
slept profoundly, North merely stirred and mut-
tured: 'No, I was not asleep, but I wish to God I
had been.' [39]

· · · · ·

The first crisis of several which North, in his new
office, was called upon to face occurred even before
he had produced his first budget.   Early in 1768
John Wilkes, who had been outlawed in consequence
of his flight five years previously, returned openly to
England to discover that he was sunk as much in
oblivion as he was in debt.[40]   Had he then and
there applied for a pardon, Grafton would almost
certainly have been willing to forgive and forget.[41]
But such a move was not according to Wilkes' plan.
How could a penniless exile hope to achieve the good
things of life so congenial to an ex-Medmenham
monk by licking the boots of a Grafton?   A timely
General Election provided a more certain and
less humiliating means.   Like some roystering Irish
adventurer out of the pages of Lever, Wilkes
defiantly put himself forward as candidate for the
first City of the world.   The burgesses of London
having, as might be expected, rejected this impudent
outlaw, he turned to the more democratic county of
Middlesex, and, amid scenes of riot and outrage,
swept in at the head of the poll.   His next step in
a well-thought-out campaign was to surrender
himself, as a duly elected Member of Parliament,

G

to the authorities, only to find himself, owing to a
technicality, still a free man.   In order to circumvent this hitch he virtually arrested himself and
betook himself to gaol in a coach drawn by a
halloing mob.   But once more a judicial hair was
prudently split, and the outlawry, which it might
have caused a riot to enforce, was quashed.   On the
original conviction for libel, now four years old,
Wilkes was sent to prison for twenty-two months
and fined a thousand pounds.

The riots which had accompanied Wilkes' election had not only revived in the King's mind that
personal animosity for which, considering how he
had been treated, it is hard to blame him; but, now
that this 'audacious criminal ' had become identified
with the rabble, aroused very genuine fears for the
safety of his crown and the constitution.   In this
alarm his Ministers were thoroughly at one with him.
It was Wilkes' association with the mob, more
violent, brutal, and ignorant than ever before in
living memory, which condemned him in their
eyes.   The forcible intrusion into their midst of a
convicted libeller and a demagogue who appeared
to stick at nothing would, they felt, strike such a
blow at the dignity and prestige of Parliamentary
government as might damage it beyond repair.
If these fears are considered unwarranted, it should
be remembered that Benjamin Franklin, calm and
philosophical, expressed his detestation of the mob-
violence which signalized Wilkes' election and
believed that some punishment must be preparing
for a people who were so ungrateful as to abuse
' the best constitution and the best King any nation

was ever blessed with.'* [42]   Thus when the King
had written to express his opinion that ' the expulsion of Mr. Wilkes appears to be very essential and
must be effected,' [43] he was merely encouraging the
Ministers in a course they had already agreed
to take. Parliament, however, having been prorogued, nothing could be done until the end of the
year. By that time, had Wilkes showed a disposition to serve his sentence quietly, the hand of the
Government, not altogether unanimous on the extreme question of expulsion, would probably have
been stayed.[44]   But would the butts of Yorkshire ale,
the baskets of Newcastle's salmon and the hogsheads
of Maryland tobacco continue to relieve the poverty
of prison fare for twenty-two months should Wilkes
decide to become a model prisoner?   Not only like
the great-hearted Cobbett half a century later
would he use the leisure of his imprisonment to
continue his campaign, but he would do so to
insure the constant inflow of good things.[45]   In
fine, menacing as he might have appeared on the
Brentford hustings, ' that devil ' Wilkes, was going to
be infinitely more threatening behind the walls of
the King's Bench prison.

The first move made by Wilkes was to roll the
apple of discord into the Commons by petitioning as a
Member of Parliament against his past grievances

* No better illustration of the depraved state of the lower classes at the
time can be found than Fielding's description of how, sick unto death, he
ran the gauntlet through rows of sailors and watermen who taunted his
deformity and poured insults upon his misery. (*The Voyage to Lisbon,
Fielding's Works*, x. 209.)

Moritz, too, the German traveller, had his respect for England considerably modified when he encountered at Election time, ' the rampant spirit
of liberty and the wild impatience of a genuine British mob.' (*Travels.*)

and present imprisonment. It was a ruse which, by raising the delicate question of Parliamentary privilege, was in itself calculated to make ample trouble. His next was to publish, complete with his own inimitable libellous comments, a letter, which Weymouth, in anticipation of riots outside Wilkes' prison, had written to the chairman of the Surrey quarter sessions. The riots had duly occurred, and in dispersing the mob some Scottish troops (a most tactless choice of mob-breakers) shot and killed an innocent man. By a liberal use of such tendentious words as 'hellish project' and 'horrid massacre,' Wilkes chose to make capital out of an incident which, however regrettable, would have otherwise passed without very much comment. The use of troops, in the absence of an organized police force, was the usual though unavoidable feature in the dispersal of eighteenth-century mobs.

Accordingly the session of 1768–9 which opened under the shadow cast by Chatham's official resignation, closely to be followed by that of Shelburne, was very largely occupied, to the exclusion of more important matters, with the nuisance Wilkes had been committing. Tempers rapidly became frayed, though North pleaded with the House to proceed in a restrained manner.[46] He himself, as usual, lost neither his composure nor urbanity. He had reluctantly come to the conclusion that Wilkes, by forcing his cause upon them, must be expelled, and for this expulsion had only himself to blame.[47] It was his unrepentant attitude and insolent bearing in the House when Wilkes

appeared to present his petition which seems to have
weighed with North more than his offences. Though
not wishing to be hard on him, and privately preferring to forgive, he considered, as a Minister and
Leader of the House, that expulsion was necessary
at once for the honour of Parliament and for the
tranquillity of the realm.[48]

Before the proceedings on Wilkes' petition had
concluded, matters were complicated by the House
of Lords' requesting a conference on the 'insolent,
scandalous and alleged seditious libel' against
Weymouth. 'No paper,' declared North in the debate which followed, ' ever deserved the appellation
more.   It is not only a libel upon the noble Lord
. . . taxing him with having planned a horrid massacre, but a libel full of much dangerous consequences.'   To represent the calling in of the military
as akin to murder was utterly pernicious. The
letter, in which he saw nothing blameable, but
' great tenderness, great caution,' was not written,
he explained, until the authorities had been
defied, and defied in every way. It was an in-
timation to the magistrates that, if they thought
the civil power ought no longer to be trifled
with, they could count on a remedy. ' Let
Parliament,' he concluded, ' then do its duty; let it
not be said that government and good order, supported by magistrates, ministers and army, are not
supported by Parliament.   Let us, at such a paper
being upon our table, be fired with indignation.'[49]

On February 3, at three o'clock in the morning,
219 duly inflamed Members voted that Wilkes be

expelled as well for the offences he had committed
six years previously as for the present libel against
Lord Weymouth.   The Opposition could muster no
more than 137 votes.   The concatenation of mis-
demeanours had had an irresistible effect upon the
waverers.   Those who might have been unwilling
to expel Wilkes for his libel against the government
were prepared to do so for his observations on the
King; those who considered that neither one nor
the other was sufficient saw excuse enough in his
obscenity.[50]

But upon one body of men North's carefully
worded indictment had no effect whatsoever.   The
Electors of Middlesex promptly re-elected Wilkes
and so thrust the question once more under the
nose of Parliament.   This put up Grenville to make
the finest speech of his career.

' You cannot,' he cried, waving a prophetic finger,
' entertain a doubt but that Mr. Wilkes will be re-elected
after his expulsion.   You will then probably think your-
selves under the necessity of expelling him again, and he
will as certainly be re-elected.   What steps can the House
then take to put an end to a disgraceful contest in which
their justice is arraigned and their authority and dignity
essentially compromised? '[51]

North was ready with his reply:
' The same wise motives that prevailed in 1763
for excluding Mr. Wilkes from Parliament prevail
now . . . Where is the policy of this House breaking
through its own rules in favour of one who is become
the idol of the mob?   By this means we shall make
him the idol of the people.'[52]   North was crush-
ingly logical, but the next dozen years were to prove

the truth of Tagore's observation that logic, like a two-edged knife, can cut the hand that uses it.

Expelled a second time, Wilkes was a third time elected and again the motion was before the House to declare the election null and void. 'If we pursue our present course,' said North, a little more subdued, ' I am aware we may meet with vexation; but I am also convinced it is the only way to preserve our honour and to recover, if we have lost it, the respect of the Country.' But then followed two ominous sentences. ' Constituents should take care to return eligible men to Parliament; and can a man be a true Member who is declared by the only court capable of taking cognizance of it, not to be eligible? If ever this question should again come before us, I shall deem that man the true Member of Middlesex who shall have a majority of *legal* votes.' [53]

The question *did* come before them again within a month. Then was the full implication of North's speech revealed. After his third expulsion, Wilkes had been opposed on the hustings by a Colonel Luttrell, who had resigned a safe seat in order to offer himself as a candidate for Middlesex. Luttrell was defeated by 1,143 to 296 votes; but not the House of Commons. A motion was immediately drafted declaring the election null and void, and the following day another was tabled to the effect that Luttrell *ought* to have been elected.

' In my opinion,' said North, ' the free-holders who polled for Mr. Wilkes threw away their votes. The House of Commons should keep to themselves everything that can relate to their own Members: they have kept it to themselves against the House of Lords, and now truly it is to be delivered up to eleven hundred free-holders!'

If, argued this strong Parliamentarian, the Commons cannot defend their own rights, how is it likely to fare with inferior judicial assemblies? The consequences must be anarchy, confusion, and the end of the constitution. On political grounds, therefore, as well as those of justice, Wilkes should be disqualified, and Luttrell, whose votes alone were valid, elected. 'I am no politician,' he concluded in words which before long were to have a bearing upon the wider field of the American colonies, 'but this principle is engraved in the mind of almost every man. It belongs to no country or province. Tame submission ever produces insult. It is vain to look for respect if you do not dare to assert your rights.'[54]

And so, at two o'clock on a Sunday morning, after an all-night sitting, the House by 197 votes to 143 substituted the name of Luttrell for that of Wilkes as Parliamentary representative for the County of Middlesex. While it is not easy to consider this high-handed action without condemning it, there is no less difficulty in excusing the numerous cases, about which History and Whig historians are strangely reticent, where, on an election petition coming before the House of Commons, the candidate favoured by the administration, although in the possession of a minority of votes, has been elected.* Had it not been for the

* A typical example—they are to be found in all preceding Whig administrations until the practice was rendered more difficult by Grenville's Act—occurred at Bramber only a few days earlier than the Middlesex election. There Lord Winterton with 181 votes was unseated, after the

notoriety of Wilkes, the intention of a desperate
Opposition to exploit his case to the uttermost, and
the fact that the Middlesex was the most prominent
of all constituencies, it may well be questioned
whether his unseating would have acquired much
more publicity than that of Lord Winterton at
Bramber.

North, a House of Commons man to the finger-
tips, viewed the British Constitution in terms of its
Parliament. According to this restricted interpretation, anything that challenged that body challenged
the Constitution and was to be resisted to the last
ditch. His attitude, moreover, was as unrepentant as it was fixed. A year later, when he might
have been wiser after the event, he boldly declared
he would approve the rectitude of those measures
to his dying day.[55] The idea that there could
be something superior to the High Court of Parliament; some body whose rights, when in conflict
with those of the legislature, ought to prevail,
was heresy to one who was sitting in the seat of
Henry Pelham.

Two weeks later, the session was at an end. The
curtain fell on a last act of what a contemporary
termed the tragi-comedy acted by His Majesty's
servants for the benefit of Wilkes and at the expense
of the Constitution. There was to be an epilogue—
but not yet.

.   .   .   .   .

customary perfunctory inquiries in favour of the ministerial choice, with
sixteen votes only. (Manners, *Granby*, 332.) Yet, of the unseating of
Wilkes, a modern biographer of Chatham can write complacently, ' He
(Chatham) quickly gauged how serious a blow had been struck at the
representative system, what a victory gained for the arbitrary power of a
Crown.' (Basil Williams, *Pitt*, ii. 252.)

Compared with the high lights that fell on the Wilkes' affair, there is a certain flatness about the other events of that memorable session: the seizure of Corsica by France and the settling of the King's debt.

The unwillingness of the Government to listen to the appeals of Corsica, early in 1768, to save her from annexation by France and to check French ambitions in the Mediterranean was not neglected by the Opposition. When Parliament assembled in the autumn, this was one of the first topics to be raised. It came in the form of a motion for production of papers, made, as North declared for no useful purpose, but that of ' roasting a minister.' [56] Quite justifiably he protested against this dangerous and profitless device for embarrassing a Ministry —dangerous because of the information it must reveal to the enemies of the country; profitless, because every Member had already made up his mind, which no amount of print was likely to alter. In defending the Ministry's policy he was not quite so happy. To argue (as Bismarck *mutatis mutandis* might have done) that Corsica was not worth the bones of a British grenadier, was hardly consistent with the known importance attached to Minorca.* Nor, had the Government acted from the first with firmness and unanimity, would there have been much likelihood of a single shot being fired in earnest. France would scarcely have risked the consequences of appropriating Corsica in defiance of Britain. Despite all Choiseul had done,

---

* It is worthy of note that, had Britain taken Corsica under her protection, Napoleon, born in 1768, would virtually have been a British subject.

five years were not enough to repair her broken forces, and to mention the name of Pitt was still sufficient to blanch the faces of the most patriotic of Frenchmen. It was all very well for North to declare oracularly: " If we were to attack France wherever she went, we should indeed be the bullies of Europe, and like bullies we should come off with a bloody nose.' [57] The fact remained that, by standing timidly aside, we allowed the enemy we had so recently driven to her knees to score a smart success at our expense. Far more important than the loss to us or the gain to France of a naval base in the Mediterranean was the drop in our prestige. It was an object lesson which the rest of Europe were not likely to forget.

Before the unsatisfactory Corsican business had been as decently interred as North's dexterity could manage, the King informed his ' faithful Commons ' that he was in debt to the extent of half a million sterling. The information was accompanied by a request that this amount be discharged. Only a simple-minded and singularly ingenuous monarch could have chosen such a moment for such a message. The Wilkite storm was at its height; the sentiments of the King in that matter were known; a General Election had just been held; his efforts to see that his Ministry were supported by placemen and courtiers could not have escaped attention. The inference appeared obvious. The debt must have been incurred in corrupting voters and carrying elections.

The motion to relieve the King of his liabilities naturally fell to be introduced by the Chancellor of the Exchequer, and as naturally was meat and drink to the Opposition. Having none of the responsibilities of office, nothing was easier for the latter than to descant upon the twin merits of purity and economy, conveniently ignoring the fact that out of the eight and a half years which had elapsed since the accession, their own Grenville had been at the Treasury for three, and the lately deceased Newcastle for a year and a half, and Rockingham for twelve months. The fault was hardly more the King's than it was his Prime Minister's. If not a penny had gone in bribery the Civil List was almost bound to fall into debt, whatever the administration. Until a beginning was made to overhaul the royal household, wastefulness due to the absence of adequate supervision, the multiplicity of unnecessary posts, and the peculation of their holders, could scarcely be avoided. There is no reason for believing that the debt incurred by George III was due to any intensification of practices which had been going on for the past fifty years.* On the contrary, had the King sought to debauch politics, he would never have surrendered to the nation at the close of the war his rightful share in the various captures made, a sum amounting to three-quarters of a million, with which he could have established a fund for corruption, uncontrolled, and without a rival.[58] That some of the five hundred thousand pounds now required had gone in financing certain ministerial candidates in important or doubtful elections,

---

*Before he had been six years on the throne George I, for example, had incurred a debt amounting to £600,000. *Lady Cowper's Diary,* 128.

or in providing some wavering supporters with minor places or contracts, is indisputable.* There was nothing exceptional in this, and on a smaller scale precisely the same thing was happening with the funds at the disposal of the Bedfords, the Temples, or the Lowthers. As long as the King occupied the position he did in politics it must continue to be so, unless he were prepared to abdicate virtually in favour of a junta. And who shall say that the liberties of the country would have been more secure, the colonies less discontented and politicians less venal, had a Woburn, Stowe or Lowther Castle, and not Buckingham House, been the cynosure of hungry men's eyes?

Apart from sheer bad management, the principal causes of the present deficit were, as North pointed out, the extraordinary expenses to which the Crown was always put during a war, and the frequent changes of administration since the accession. These changes had numbered five, and each First Lord on going out had sought to provide from the Civil List for his faithful servants deprived of employment. North drove this point home very neatly by reminding the House that: ' If gentlemen do not like accommodations, we must have no more changes.'†

More interesting than this cogent defence of the Civil List deficit is the autobiographical apology— the first of a long series—with which North con-

* But not pensions. (See Namier, *Structure of Politics*, i. 232.)

† Even Horace Walpole admits that, considering the expenses of the outset of a new reign, of a Coronation, of a Royal wedding, that the Crown had purchased jewels—the late King's having been bequeathed by him to, and re-purchased from the Duke of Cumberland—the sum expended could not be thought exorbitant. (*Memoirs, George III*, iii. 227.)

cluded his speech. He was Minister *malgré lui*:
' I am not one of those who are anxious to hold
office: perhaps it is a love of ease that induces me
not to wish to continue in office. I never desired
to sacrifice my ease to ambition, but at the same
time I will never sacrifice duty to ease.' As proof
that he was actuated not by ambition but by
principle, he instanced his consistent vote against
so-called popular measures. ' Men may be popular
without being ambitious, but there is rarely an
ambitious man that does not try to be popular.'
Finally, though his inclinations urged him to cut
and run back to the ease and security of the Pay
Office, his political intuition told him that if he
went it would mean the break-up of the administration and the triumph of faction.[59]

And he was right. Far from being a time for
resignation this was one for closing the ranks. Out
of a ragged and stormy sky a new and hardly less
menacing danger than Wilkes had appeared.
A critic of government declared himself, more
scathing than Burke, more vituperative than Barré,
more informed than any Opposition hack. On
January 29 a letter had been published in the
Publick Advertiser. It was signed Junius. No more
brilliant attack ever descended upon a Ministry,
' from which a reasonable man can expect no
remedy but poison, no relief but death.' Grafton,
Weymouth, and Mansfield, Chief Justice of the
King's Bench, came in for the hardest knocks.
North, ' yet to give us proof of his abilities,' was let
off with a very severe caution that he must do better
in the future.

No one has summed up the character of Junius within the compass of a single sentence more ably than Macaulay: ' He must have been a man in the highest degree arrogant and insolent, a man prone to malevolence and prone to the error of mistaking his malevolence for public virtue.' In giving full play to his asperity, Junius invariably hit the nail on the head, when it was obvious; sometimes he hit it guessing its existence; sometimes he struck altogether wide of the mark. Yet so consummate was the skill in directing this rain of invective which has become an English classic, that even to-day it almost compels conviction. The combination of Billingsgate and the Senior Common Room has never been surpassed. Grafton and Bedford were dealt with in a manner that would have pierced the most case-hardened: the one ' sullen and severe without religion, profligate without gaiety,' distinguished from all other Ministers not in doing wrong by design, but never doing right by mistake; the other ' violating the character of age,' and exposing the impotent imbecility, long after he had lost the vigour of his passions. Rejoicing in the immunity of his nom-de-plume and obviously flattered by his reception, Junius deliberately extended the freedom of his invective until at last it reached up to the throne. Eleven months after he had first appeared in print there was published his famous ' letter number thirty-five ' to the King. At the conclusion of much studied insolence His Majesty was bidden ' lay aside the wretched formalities of a King and speak to your subjects with the spirit of a man and in the language of a gentleman.' Otherwise, he was reminded (and George, on this point, needed little reminding), should he plume himself on the security of his title to the crown, that, ' as it was acquired by one Revolution, it may be lost by another.'

While Junius was appealing principally to the London coffee-house *habitué*, the more violent among the Opposition were attempting to enlist the support of the Country. As soon as Parliament had been prorogued in May 1769 endeavours were made, with a success not at all proportionate to the time and labour expended, to induce the counties and boroughs to petition the King to dissolve Parliament on the ostensible grounds that the presence of Luttrell invalidated all its proceedings. The danger of inflaming popular passions, as well as the inconsistency of professed enemies of the prerogative petitioning the Sovereign to exercise that very prerogative, was not lost upon the moderates.[60] Though, in this welter of inspired petitions, it is possible to detect the origin of the public meeting which was to play so notable a part in the succeeding century, the immediate effects were negligible. When it came to the point the government had no difficulty in procuring counter petitions and addresses. Far more critical was the news that down at Burton Pynsent there were strange stirrings. The great Chatham was (almost incredibly) coming to his senses. One July morning, in fact, he walked into the King's levee ' *in propria persona* and not in a straight waistcoat,' and for the last time in his life was closeted alone with his sovereign for the space of some twenty minutes. Having, it is said, expressed to the King his disapproval of recent measures and implored him, very likely in what Burke contemptuously called ' the pompous and true Chathamic style,' to realize that, if he should oppose in Parliament, it would not be from any personal motive, he bowed himself out, though probably not so abjectly as when, in the late reign, Charles Price had seen the tip of his nose visible between his legs.[61] Speculation on his future attitude became less uncertain when he proceeded to treat his late colleagues with freezing ceremony and to make up his old quarrel with Grenville and Temple.   By the autumn he was even hinting at a concordat with Rockingham and his ' knot of *spotless* friends such as this Kingdom ought to have,' and protesting that ' former little differences must be forgotten when the contest is *pro aris et focis.*' [62]

For North to desert his master at such a moment and in circumstances which must hand him over, manacled, to an unfriendly and unpatriotic Opposition, would be contrary to the precepts he had learned on his father's knee and had certainly not forgotten during his apprenticeship to the Duke of Newcastle.   When the once Great Commoner could openly declare, amid the plaudits of faction, that were the enemy to land upon the Sussex coast he would not stir a step until Luttrell had been replaced by Wilkes, it was, North believed, the hour for honest men to rally round the throne.[63]   By the end of the year, so far was North from regretting his determination to carry on, that he ' never felt

H

more perfectly easy, happy and self-satisfied.' To
Guilford he wrote:

' I think I have done what I ought, and what every
reasonable and honest man will approve. I feel myself
totally disencumbered from all connexions, obligations
and engagements, and entirely free to chase the path my
conscience and opinion dictates. A very pleasant feeling
it is! I think I have done by all parties as handsomely as
they could desire, and perhaps more than they could in
justice demand. What is past gives me no regret. My
present situation is comfortable and my future prospects
by no means unpleasing. I may add that my pride,
which was, I confess, a little mortified in the course of the
year, has by the late offer been gratified to the utmost of
its wish.' [64]

What had mortified the pride of North, who, for
all his good nature, was extremely sensitive, is not
known. Perhaps it was some dissension in a
Cabinet which now contained almost as many
divisions as there were Members, perhaps it was
the taunt of Junius. The ' late offer ' can be
deduced with some plausibility. The prospect of
Chatham *redivivus*, ' high in spirits and in fury,' re-
animating the Opposition, had become altogether
too much for Grafton. No longer in the arms of
faded beauty, but in those of a young and handsome
second wife, the distracted Prime Minister had been
searching anxiously for the first favourable moment
to resign, and for someone to whom he could hand
over the seals of office. Such sentiments could
hardly have remained unknown to the King, and a
few days before Christmas, by a message the brief-
ness of which made it significant, North was
summoned to the Palace. Whether the King

sounded him as to his willingness to take over from
Grafton can only be conjectured. If so, and from
North's letter to his father this seems likely, the
overtures came not a moment too soon.

When what was clearly going to be a crucial
session opened on January 9, it was in an atmosphere of bathos. The Royal Speech merely
lamented a distressing outbreak of distemper
amongst horned cattle, and, after a very brief
reference to America, concluded with a prayer to
the House to avoid all heat and animosity.*
Chatham, however, with crutch becomingly laid
and bandage nicely adjusted, had no such pacific
intentions. In a succession of speeches the Government was scorched and seared. Piquant references
to Magna Carta and to the constitution whose
battlements were dismantled and walls tottering,
brought the Chancellor at last into the open. Ever
since Chatham's reappearance it was known to a
small circle that Camden was going to pro-
nounce the Luttrell measure (against which he had
never raised any objection) to be unconstitutional. [65] He now informed their astonished
Lordships that for three years he had hung his head
in shame, and disapproved by looks measures he
had disliked. ' By their violent and tyrannical
conduct, Ministers have alienated the minds of the
people from His Majesty's Government—I had
almost said from His Majesty's person.' A Lord
Chancellor virtually become a member of the

* The session came to be known as the Horned Cattle Session, and in the
Lords it was said that Grafton and Grosvenor, whose wives had been
unfaithful, solemnly bowed to each other during the reading of the speech.

Opposition was something which could not be tolerated. Very properly Camden, whose conduct had been despicable, was dismissed. A spate of resignations followed, the most serious of which was that of Granby from the Ordnance. Nevertheless, a strong successor to Camden, and all might still be well; Grafton might even be persuaded to remain; the Ministry might be lashed somehow together. The King, who had been following every turn in the crisis, had such a man in mind. Charles Yorke, whose father, Lord Hardwicke, had faithfully served the late King as Chancellor for so many years, was known to have set his heart on the Woolsack. He was, it is true, closely identified with the Rockinghams; but then the Rockinghams were less offensive to the King and contained more men of talent, than any other group. To capture Yorke, and through him at least some of the Rockingham party, might give the Government necessary strength and lasting qualities. At the request of his master, Grafton approached Yorke, only to meet with a denial. The King, who never took a first refusal as conclusive, and probably remembered how, five years before, he had succeeded with Pitt, then personally intervened. Under the persistent and eloquent pleadings of his sovereign, Yorke gave way. Three days later, stricken with remorse and the reproaches of his friends and brothers, he died—there is little doubt by his own hand.

The death of Yorke knocked all resolution out of Grafton. The same day he told the King he could remain no longer. To the Opposition it seemed as if the Seals were about to fall into their laps, and in confident anticipation of power they stood four-square.[66] But they counted without their King. It was at such moments as these that George III either went out of his mind, or exhibited that hereditary courage which he so wistfully hoped to find in his Ministers. Rather than yield to the persistent demand for dissolution, he would abdicate, or, in extremities, even resort to the sword, which, in Conway's presence, he half drew from the scabbard. On the twenty-second he sent an urgent message to North; but whatever followed was inconclusive. If North had vaguely agreed to a tentative offer a month earlier, now when it was specifically made he shrank from accepting; but then, so had the unhappy Charles Yorke. The next morning the indomitable King renewed the attack. Weymouth was sent, armed with a royal letter. ' My own mind,' wrote George III, ' is more and more strengthened with the rightness of the measure . . . you must easily see that if you do not accept, I have no Peer at present in my Service that I could consent to place in the Duke of Grafton's employment.'[67] By the twenty-seventh, North's resistance was visibly cracking, and the King had no longer the least doubt ' but that he would step forth on the occasion, though with great reluctance.' Still, there had been no definite promise made which, once given, he knew North would honour. Accordingly, next day, Barrington, whose judgment North was known to value, was commissioned to put before him in the strongest language ' the propriety of making no farther delay least the intention should be divulged previous to the execution; besides, accepting immediately would show a confidence that could not fail in having effect, and would stagger even the warm men in the Opposition; in short, delay may do some harm, spirit must be productive of good.' [68]   This clinched matters.   The next day North was arranging his Treasury.   Grenville's forecast had proved correct and Townshend's prophecy had wholly come to pass.

Chapter IV

PRIME MINISTER

' There is nothing more like a Tory than a Whig in Power.'
(SELWYN CORR., iv., 401.)

In the political history of the reign of George III
the resignation of Grafton is an event of the first
importance. It proved to be the last kick of the
old and widely discredited system of government
which, for fifty odd years, had drawn life and inspiration from one or more of the great Whig
encampments at Houghton, Stowe, Woburn or
Claremont. Thenceforward, until the triumph of
the younger Pitt in 1784, there came into full play
what has been called the New Toryism or the
King's System but which was little more than an
inevitable reaction to the lop-sided growth of the
Constitution under Walpole and the subsequent
failure of the Whig monopolists to adapt themselves
to altered surroundings. While the latter had
progressively broken up into competing groups, the
King, subject to no internal clash of jarring interests, had gained the strength they had lost. The
moment for getting back to what he considered the
salutary system of William III had at last arrived.
Thenceforward nothing should count except devotion to the sovereign and the country, in George

III's view synonymous terms. Willingness to take up duties on such conditions would be the principal qualification for office; refusal to do so would be conduct unpatriotic and therefore factious. Ministers should look to him, the true father of his people, whose happiness was his happiness, and not exclusively to the First Lord of the Treasury. More or less water-tight departments, whose point of contact was the closet rather than Downing Street, was to be the essence of the new system, with which Lord North was, for the next twelve years, to become so closely identified.

When, with all possible reluctance, North took up the Seal of the Treasury retaining, like Walpole, Pelham and Grenville before him, at the same time those of the Exchequer, he embarked upon what Junius believed to be a forlorn hope.[1] This belief, so obviously fathered by a devout wish, might be discounted were it not shared by Horace Walpole, at this moment one of North's well-wishers.* In his opinion the resignation—the King preferred the less euphemistic word desertion—of Grafton had thrown the ministerial party into such a state of alarm that not even the presence of the new Minister, in whom he detected such un-Graftonian qualities as firmness and spirit, could stop the rot.

In whatever terms Junius or Walpole might express themselves, no one admitted his insecurity more thoroughly than North himself.† The pro-

---

* Walpole's friend and correspondent, George Montagu, was North's parliamentary private secretary.

† North's Ministry was as follows:

North	...	...	...	Treasury and Chancellor of Exchequer
Gower	...	...	...	Lord President
Halifax	...	...	...	Privy Seal

cess of counting heads on the morning he took over
the Treasury could not have been encouraging.
" I honour his abilities,' exclaimed Tommy Townshend, said to be the only man whose tongue North
feared, ' I once sat in office with him, and during
that time I learned to admire and revere his ability.
But there he sits without a friend, without an
acquaintance . . . ready to do the midnight
Cabinet work.'* [2] Though there followed a heated
protest against such aspersions, North protested just
a little too vigorously to sound convincing. Townshend's shaft, as was usually the case, struck home.
Beyond 192 placemen who would, as a matter of
course and livelihood, vote with any administration,
there must, on the fateful January 29, have seemed
to North few upon whom unqualified reliance could
be placed. Rigby, the jovial jobber, Jenkinson,
the inscrutable climber, toadies like Jeremiah
Dyson, and ' gentlemen in the wind of the Ministry'† like Ellis and Onslow, would give him their
support just so long as it suited their interests and
no longer. In the Lords, fortunately, a Minister's
majority was automatic, but such Government
talent as did not belong to the cautious Lord Chief
Justice Mansfield was shared by such obscurities
as Gower and Rochford, and by such notorious
rakes as Weymouth and Sandwich—men whose

{ Rochford			
{ Weymouth	...	...	Secretaries of State
Hawke ...	...	...	Admiralty
Barrington	...	...	Secretary at War

The Great Seal was in Commission until, early in 1771, it was given to
Henry Bathurst, created Lord Apsley.

* He had succeeded North for a short time as Joint-Paymaster.

† This happy phrase was used by North at a much later date. (*P.H.*,
xxiii. 317.)

names, sneered Junius, were 'a satire upon all
government.' In the face of such doubtful forces
at his command there was ranged against North
an Opposition more formidable than anything seen
since Walpole had been hounded out of power
thirty years before. Old feuds were being hurriedly patched up in anticipation of an early Opposition victory. Chatham, we have seen, was
already reconciled to Temple, and both of them to
Grenville; Rockingham was basking in the favour
of all three. Here were four names which, between
them, commanded the finest debating talent in
both Houses. In the Commons Barré, Burke,
Wedderburn and the City of London, in the person
of its representative and Lord Mayor, William
Beckford, ' whom no argument can convince, no
defeat make ashamed, nor mistake make diffident,' ³
were capable of keeping up a running fire on every
possible occasion. In the austerer atmosphere of
the Lords, when Chatham's rhodomontade flagged,
capable speeches might be expected from Shelburne,
Camden and Richmond; while in the background,
still urging the Opposition on to the kill, still
pouring ridicule and venom upon their common
foes, forging phrase upon phrase which burnt
themselves into the flesh of his victims and branded
them to all the world as fools and knaves, stood
the bevisored and terrible Junius. If the veteran
Walpole, with a disciplined party and twenty
years' experience behind him as Prime Minister,
had been unable to resist a united front backed by
an unscrupulous press campaign, how much chance
was there for the fledgling North?

These considerations could escape no man's attention, and an immediate fall in majorities was no uncertain sign that those who had been voting with the old administration were showing little disposition to compromise themselves with its apparently puling successor. The Tories in particular, to Sam Johnson's indignation, displayed a 'frigid neutrality.' [4] But not for long. Whether or not, as some thought, North had been selected by the King until an arrangement could be reached with Chatham,[5] it soon became evident that he was developing into the most reliable, as Chatham was becoming the most capricious, man in either House. The reputation he had already gained as Chancellor of the Exchequer, the unwearying and considerable debating powers he had shown as Leader of the Commons; his wit, his courage, and his high sense of duty, combined with the fact that he belonged politically to no one particular party, made North the only possible leader of a Ministry which, in the best and truest meaning of the term, should be His Majesty's Government. No less a confirmed opponent than the great Chatham presently conceded as much: ' I have long held one opinion as to the solidarity of Lord North's situation; he serves the Crown more successfully and more sufficiently, upon the whole, than any other man now to be found could do. This tenure seems a pretty good one. Who, pray, ever had a better? ' [6]

Lord North's negative no less than his positive qualifications—his well-known indolence, his conciliatory disposition, his disinclination to make decisions—were of inestimable value in the first

weeks of his Ministry. An overbold policy, equally
with a cowardly one, would have consolidated more
closely an Opposition which, for all its galaxy of
talent, was united by surface tension only. The
essence of his policy was to be found in his declaration: ' If a man will quarrel with me, I must quarrel
with him. I will never begin, but I will never decline a quarrel.' [7] By pursuing a middle path, by
bending to the storm at critical moments and
resisting its less dangerous buffets, North allowed
his opponents to dissipate at once their strength and
their temper. ' They are a *nihil* administration,'
cried Grenville in scorn.[8] His grievance was well
founded: it was to its negative element that North's
Ministry owed its young life.

North had already given proof of his dexterity
when, during the death rattle of the Grafton
Ministry, an exultant Opposition had moved that
the House was bound to judge according to the law
and the established custom of Parliament. This
laboured reference to the Middlesex election he had
astutely countered by agreement, subject only to the
explicit amendment that Wilkes' disqualification
was conformable both to the law and the custom
of the Constitution. Now, when within forty-eight
hours of his taking office, a fresh variation of the
endless Middlesex theme was pressed upon him,
North was compelled to draw on every resource he
possessed.* It was a case of hit or miss. Defeat
at this juncture meant resignation, and resigna-

* Of this debate, the *Parliamentary History* caustically observes—' That
topic has been so exhausted that the speeches verbatim would neither
contain anything new or exhibit anything in a new light.' (*P.H.* xvi.
604.)

tion meant committing his King into the now
implacable hands of the Opposition. Such
moments will distinguish the pedestrian from the
expert politician, and North stood the test. Speaking
with spirit, much good humour, and disarming
frankness, he began by confessing that the administration had, on Grafton's resignation, been within
an inch of capsizing. Conscious of his own shortcomings, he had, he explained, succeeded very
unwillingly to office, but, having done so, he would
not shrink from any one of the responsibilities
which this entailed. He would defend the King
and the dignity of Parliament against faction and
conspiracy, and, so long as the House gave him a
majority, would never resign while there was
breath in his body. With such sentiments he
eloquently proceeded to encourage the important
body of waverers in the idea that those aboard the
Government lugger were perfectly capable of
bringing her into port, whatever the rage of the
tempest; and then, at one o'clock in the morning,
he called Opposition bluff by moving that the debate
be closed. Amid tense excitement, the Members
filed into the lobbies, and the motion was declared
carried by 226 votes to 186. It was the lowest
Government majority ever recorded in that Session; but it was none the less decisive in establishing North's reputation as a Minister. 'His
conduct,' wrote Hume, 'was reckoned the most
spirited that any man has held since the Revolution,
and he is extolled to the skies.' The Opposition,
who, in anticipation, had been parcelling out
offices, were 'in despair, as there is no doubt that

the Minister will gather force every hour, as he
has upon this critical occasion shown that strength
of mind which is the precise thing hitherto wanting
to give permanence to administration.' [9]   If at the
commencement of his Ministry, with so many
doubtful supporters and such an array of talent
against him, North had been able, however narrowly,
to repel an attack, he might not yet be in sight of
victory, but he could not be far off. The sovereign
thought as much, and with true Brunswick precipi-
tancy advised an immediate counter-attack.[10]   But
North was disinclined to take any risk that might
unnecessarily dissipate his strength, now that every
hour seemed to improve his chances.

When Rockingham, referring to this improvement, sourly complained: ' It is neither men nor
measures, but something else, which operates in
these times,' [11] he was expressing rather more
elegantly what normally occurred to any member of
any minority when he thought of a successful
Minister. Like the Frenchman (according to
Anatole France), the eighteenth-century politician
was never defeated, but always betrayed.   To have
explained away discomfiture by other than corrupt
tactics would have set a Chatsworth dinner-table
rocking with laughter. Rockingham, so lately a
First Lord of the Treasury himself, was not prepared
to go to the extent of telling North:

' At your soft bribe no Senator turns pale,' [12]
but he certainly did imply that he owed his success
to the influence of the Crown fatted to an inordinate size by pensions and titles, sinecures and
contracts.   The facts, however, are against Rock-

ingham.   His pronouncement, for what it is worth,
is applicable to every Ministry in the century.
North had at his command very little more than
any First Lord of the Treasury, Rockingham himself, or Grenville, possessed in virtue of office.   He
could, as a rule (to which there were to be disconcerting exceptions) count upon any of the 192
placemen when they could be whipped-in, a handful of those representing Treasury Boroughs,* and
a small number who out of self-interest would invariably support the powers that be.   When all
these were added up they would not and never
could give anything approaching an absolute
majority in a House of 558 members.

The force which created North's majority in his
first session, and sustained it over a period of a
dozen years, was something which could not be
bought or sold.   The occasional boroughs purchased from venal proprietors like Lord Edgecumbe,
Lord Falmouth, and George Selwyn (invariably
cited as conclusive evidence of the King's corrupt
interference), weighed as no more than a feather in
the balance.   What effectively counted were the
country party and members without any strong
party bias, men for the most part of independent
fortunes and independent traditions, upon whose
elections the influence of the Ministry was negligible.[13]   Had not these been convinced that, taking
everything and everyone into account, North was
the best man available, not all the weapons in the
Treasury armoury could have ensured him a

---

* And as morally bound to vote for the Government as for example the
fourteen Opposition members returned by Lowther Castle were for any
opinion adopted by Sir James Lowther.

majority for a week. It is certainly the case that
North enjoyed what Grenville had possessed only
for a time and Rockingham never, the complete
confidence of the King. But for men who loved
their coverts and hounds more than Westminster
and its politicians, and had as little use for a ribbon
as for a gold-stick, the confidence of the King in
the Minister was no categorical reason why they
should support him. Where North scored with
these stolid fox-hunters was his sincere and artless
political confession. Nothing but a deep conviction
(he was never tired of telling them) that the welfare
of his King and country—for, like George III,
North admitted no distinction between the two—
required the exclusion of those who would put down
the sovereign only to raise a Junta in his place,
could have induced him to sacrifice the ease he
loved so well. This was a point of view homely
squires, anxious to get back to their gun-rooms,
could understand and applaud. Coming, moreover,
from one who had never wholly identified himself
with the old jobbing, place-hunting Corps Connexion, its sincerity was not to be doubted. It
was the faith of a believer who, in the enthusiasm
for his cause, has always one distinctive superiority
over the cynic.

In the second place, North enjoyed an advantage
which no First Lord of the Treasury, with one
exception, had possessed during the past sixteen
years. He presided personally over the Commons,
then very much the senior partner in the body
politic. There, the glance of his bolting eyes kept
watch and ward over his friends and supporters.

His wit entertained them. His dexterity kept them up to the mark. His conciliatory manner humoured them. His comfortable solid form, whether upon its feet, turning a laugh against an opponent, or slumbering away unconcernedly while adversaries prophesied the eclipse of their country, created a feeling of confidence. North, in fact, excellently illustrated the truth of Burke's apophthegm that the House of Commons was more approachable by appeal to its feelings than to its powers of reasoning.[14] Certainly his face, ' so jolly, fat and round,' [15] counted for more than the logic of the great-hearted Irishman. It assuredly counted for far more with the country gentlemen who trooped out to their boiled mutton as Burke rose to deliver one of his masterly orations. Yet not all these advantages would have proved of lasting value had they not been reinforced by considerable political talents, a constant application to his duties, and (as a hostile critic conceded) an ability to detect the weaknesses of his adversaries. With the exception of Fox, he was during his years in office without a doubt the finest debater in the Commons. ' He receives,' continues the same unfriendly writer, ' the attacks of opponents frequently like an electric shock and after haranguing for an hour rather dully, he rises a second time and levels his adversaries in a few words, either in a flow of keen satire or the most sound and pointed argument.' *

Once those uncertain forces, which Richard Rigby wittily termed ' the Opposition to the

* Quoted by Creasy, *Eminent Etonians*, 392.

I

Opposition'[16] and Horace Walpole 'that race of interested stupidity,' were given a lead, once they were convinced that North not only ought to stay but meant to stay, and had the ability to stay, they hesitated no longer. Thenceforward, though Chatham and Junius might revive the bogey of Bute (now a broken man seeking health under an Italian sky) and hail North as his puppet,* though the Burke-Barré-Townshend combination might pour broadside after broadside against the ministerial benches, North's majorities crept steadily up. They reached seventy-five on February 12 in a transparently catch-penny motion by the indefatigable Dowdeswell to disenfranchise Excise and Revenue Officers. Nothing in an eighteenth-century Parliament succeeded like success, and Gibbon, who had had misgivings, now believed that, given another fortnight, North would be secure.[17] That fortnight came and went, leaving North with a comfortable majority of ninety-seven on another specious and concerted motion for an account of the Civil List, and at this time, because of the implication that the increase in amount had gone in corruption, as dangerous a one as could emanate from any Opposition conference.

While every defeat was increasing North's

---

* Even Walpole, who ought to have known better, hints as much, but see *Memoirs*, iv. 61, note. Hume, too, who professed good opinions of North, believed that so late as June 1771 the shadow of Bute in the background kept him on perpetual tenterhooks and made him cautious, over-timid and irresolute. (*Corr.* ii., 245.) As late as 1779 a political cartoon showed North a sloth steering the barque of State on to the rocks, a thistle at the masthead. (Wright, *Caricature Hist. of the Georges*, 342.) Even Prof. Feiling refers to him as one of ' the Leicester House tribe,' *Second Tory Party*, 87.

following, upon the Opposition it was having a contrary effect. This mighty Armada, with all its resplendent names, was fundamentally nothing but a common or garden coalition, and, as with coalitions, failure was likely to be its principal solvent. Unless it could strike quickly and successfully it must presently dissolve into its component parts. The name of Chatham might be tremendous, but the man himself was dictatorial and hardly sane. Rockingham might possess honesty and enjoy the devotion of Burke, but he was proud and reserved. Grenville was already a doomed man, and his followers were pointing ' due West ' towards Downing Street. By the end of February the Opposition could still, indeed, show an outward semblance of unity. But it had ceased to increase, and this was what principally mattered to the harassed Prime Minister. Novelty alone could bring in a supply of recruits and keep together this ' tessellated pavement without cement.'* But instead of novelty, there was only that down-at-heel theme of John Wilkes, and his Middlesex election. It was a rallying cry which put North in mind of a man who had but one story to tell, and dragged it into any topic of conversation.[18]

What was hardly less gratifying to North than the approaching bankruptcy of the Opposition was the recruitment of two talented supporters. Edward Thurlow, whose delivery and assertiveness gave

---

* This, it will be remembered, was Burke's description of Chatham's Ministry. It applies, however, with equal force to the Opposition in which Burke was such an ornament.

conviction to the weakest case, had just made a promising speech and was almost immediately advanced to the office of Solicitor-General. Charles James Fox, the political playboy who had hitherto given few indications of possessing forensic ability, suddenly electrified the House by trouncing the redoubtable Wedderburn. Two days later this ' phenomenon of the age ' was duly rewarded with a Junior Lordship of the Treasury.

Very different, then, was the situation of North from what it had been, when on March 14 the City of London moved up into position. On that day the Livery, preceded by the Lord Mayor, waited upon the King with a Remonstrance. The wording was in true Beckford style; that is, it was arrogant and it was bombastic. After declaring that ' a secret and malign influence ' encompassed the King, it went on to contend that the Commons, because of the election of Luttrell, had ceased to be a truly representative body. It concluded with a prayer that Parliament be dissolved and the evil Ministers removed from His Majesty's councils for ever. As with Junius, so with Beckford, violence of language lost more support than it gained. The words of the Lord Mayor, as well as the interests he purported to represent, were distasteful to the patrician Rockingham. Beckford spoke for the *canaille* and the jobber of Change Alley, with neither of whom had the old Whig aristocracy the least desire to work, but, on the contrary, a wish to shun like the Plague.[19] The Rockinghamites were far more in sympathy with the curt yet dignified reply of the King—the work of Jeremiah Dyson, touched up by North.[20] On the other hand, behind Beckford loomed that incalculable force, the Earl of Chatham, whose only comment on the royal answer had been, ' a more unconstitutional piece never came from the Throne, nor any more dangerous if less unnoticed.' [21] If the once Great Commoner was to become a partner in opposition, it was clear that the noisy and plebeian Beckford must be admitted too. Here was a chink in the Opposition armour which did not escape the eye of North.

When, on the day following the presentation of the Remonstrance, some Government supporters, thinking to take advantage of the revulsion against the City, clamoured for impeachment of Beckford, North prudently held his hand. A hint of persecution, and those uneasy bedfellows across the gangway might become reconciled, and a longer and more dangerous contest than that with Wilkes be begun. But when a Member, who had habitually voted with the Opposition, produced a motion to table the Remonstrance and the royal reply, North saw a way of escape, and his more violent supporters were induced to follow his lead.[22] In the ensuing debate North, speaking, it is said, ' in a very high style,' struck out effectively against the threadbare argument that the exclusion of Wilkes invalidated Parliament. Carried to its logical conclusion it would follow that the forcible exclusion of a Member due to, say, an arrest, would bring the legislature to a standstill. Even in his short Parliamentary career, North continued, he had known several such cases, yet, if the contentions of the Livery were justified, all Acts passed at such a time were null and void.   Besides, he asked mockingly, where was the consistency in those who supported the Remonstrance continuing to attend a Parliament which had ceased to be a Parliament?   If the City were correct, they had better file out of the Chamber without more ado.[23]   This oblique, but nevertheless deliberate, reference to City dictation caused the Rockingham party acute heart-burnings, while the Grenvillites, who had no love for the commercial classes, drifted off into technicalities.   The motion was carried by the surprising majority of 163.

North needed now no spur.   Without giving his enemies time to re-form their ranks, he caused a resolution to be passed stating that ' to deny the legality of the present Parliament or to assert their Acts to be invalid was unwarrantable.'   It was the requiem of the Middlesex election.

These two victories proved crowning and unqualified.   By his own competent generalship, by his indefatigable industry, and by his cool and temperate courage, he had established his Government on what gave every indication of permanency.   That this was not the docile venal affair Whig historians believe, is evident from the number of instances in this and future sessions when North encountered defeats and rebuffs.   Only a fortnight after his fine majority of 163, for instance, there came up the third reading of Grenville's Bill to regulate disputed elections.   This, the last and noblest work of the now stricken statesman, proposed to remove the decision from a Committee of the whole House, where the Ministerial candidate almost invariably succeeded, to a Committee selected by ballot, with power to hear evidence on oath. However admirable in its intentions, the Bill threatened to tamper with custom, and that, in the eighteenth century, was sufficient to ensure opposition. When George III told Lord Chancellor Eldon that he would have no innovations in his time, he was speaking a language which the bulk of his subjects understood and approved.[24] North was neither in the van nor in the wake of his century. Beyond such stock-in-trade arguments as that it was better to bear the ills we have than fly to others we know not of, he had little to offer. He frankly professed his indifference to the Bill, and, to some clauses, his active hostility. When he concluded with a request for more time for consideration he quite openly avowed his hope that it would be shelved indefinitely.

But Grenville's Bill was a case where Parliament ceased to be slavishly representative of popular prejudices. The good sense of Members carried them beyond the limitations of their constituents. The country gentlemen and Tories who had been lately warming towards the administration, marched out shoulder to shoulder with the Grenvillites, and in their train went more than one devoted adherent of North.* Again, three years later, when a motion was before the House to raise the pay of half-pay naval captains, North adopted the

* Four years later when—it having been passed originally for a limited period—Sir Edward Astley moved that Grenville's Act be made permanent, North once more was unsuccessfully in opposition. . . . This time he fought it not so much on the grounds he had previously adopted, but because, it having been admitted to be an experiment, the Act, he maintained, could not be reckoned to have undergone a thorough test until a General Election had been held. (*Egerton MSS.*, cclv.)

thoroughly Treasury attitude. That is to say, he
qualified his sympathy for the lot of the underpaid
officers by a dread of setting a precedent which, if
followed up by other naval (and military) grades,
might imperil finances.[25]   But here again, although
he had given the motion his ' hearty negative,' his
supporters declined to follow his lead, and when the
measure was handsomely carried it was found that
not only the country gentlemen, but most of the
placemen, had voted against the Government.[26]

Meanwhile any elation amid Opposition ranks
at North's abasement over Grenville's Bill was soon
turned to dismay.   Two days after his defeat the
Prime Minister boldly challenged the Committee
on the State of the Nation, which for the last two or
three months had been teasing him by harping
upon the Middlesex election, moved that it be
dissolved, and carried the motion by over 130 votes.

And so, slowly, the nightmare of those first
months of supreme office passed away, and when the
Easter recess came in sight, North piously thanked
his God.[27]   After the holidays the atmosphere grew
palpably lighter, and there succeeded a few uneventful weeks before Members dispersed for six
months' peace and oblivion.   The Opposition had
by then become almost pathetic in its impotence,
and its penury of subject matter a cause of mirth.[28]
At least one member of its shadow cabinet was
already considering throwing in his hand; and
when Chatham remonstrated that by their apathy
they were betraying the people, Rockingham
haughtily declined to be sworn every day to keep
his word.[29]   No wonder then that when North

took the first opportunity after prorogation to visit his eldest son at Eton, he appeared to be bubbling over with health and spirits. 'The blessed effects,' wrote Dr. Dampier, 'of an upright conscience and a prudent heart.' [30] The doctor's deduction in this instance may have been correct; but unless the Opposition had been confounded, neither one nor the other could have raised the spirits of the temperamental Prime Minister, so soon, as it turned out, to be depressed by a fresh crisis.

A few days later, like the cloud no bigger than a man's hand, a sloop reached Portsmouth harbour with the news that Spanish ships of war despatched by Don Francisco Buccarelli, governor of Buenos Aires, had appeared off Port Egmont in the Falkland Islands, and had claimed possession on behalf of Spain. Not for an instant suspecting that, without normal diplomatic representations, the Spanish authorities would proceed to extreme measures, the Ministry felt disinclined to take any steps which might provoke Spanish counter-measures and must certainly cost the taxpayer money. But almost at the same moment as North and his family went blithely down to Dillington, a second force, this time of five frigates and fifteen hundred men, appeared and demanded immediate possession. After a ghost of a resistance, the insignificant British garrison surrendered. A dispute which had hitherto been confined to sea captains and cartographers had become suddenly international and menacing. For, side-by-side with Spain, and linked together by the famous Pact-de-Famille,

stood France, now considerably less in awe of
England since her success over Corsica and the
fall of Chatham. What touched Spain might
touch France, and then everything would be set
for the war of revenge. And this time there would
be no Prussian-British alliance.*

The affair of the Falkland Islands is remarkable
during most of its inflammable phase, not for its
connexion, but for its lack of connexion, with
Lord North, and to this extent may be taken as
illustrative of the weakness inherent in so loosely
constructed a government machine when the
nominal leader failed to possess the welding powers
of a Walpole or the imperious personality of a Pitt.
Except that the news of Buccarelli's coup broke
into his holidays and brought him up to London
as fast as a post-chaise could carry him, he who
was First Lord of the Treasury, principal member
of the Cabinet Council and therefore responsible
for its policy, played a surprisingly small part in
a crisis which, at any moment, might have pre-
cipitated the country into a first-class European
war. To what degree North was responsible for
the demand for immediate satisfaction and the
restoration of the islands, a business which naturally
passed through the hands of the Secretary of State
for the Southern Department, is not known. From
the evidence that exists it would not appear to
have been great. In all papers, official and un-

---

* There seems no doubt that these 'miserable islands' were first sighted
by Davis in the reign of Elizabeth, but no attempt was made to colonize
them for two centuries. Against the British right by discovery, the Spani-
ards set up a claim in virtue of their alleged exclusive dominion of the
Southern Seas.

official, dealing with the matter, it is an affair exclusively of Weymouth acting in conjunction with the King.

But if North had little to do with Weymouth's diplomacy, he knew that upon him must fall, as soon as Parliament reassembled, the task of defending the Government; and the prospect drove his recent high spirits down to zero.[31] It seemed he was back again in the dark days of February. The new crisis had promptly checked decomposition in the Opposition body, and already it was clear that Burke and Barré would make the utmost of this new lease of life. What could not have been so clear was that they would, by their crazy intemperance, let another chance slip through their fingers, and provide the Ministry with additional and badly needed stability. If party government is not to be a sham, it requires that a vigilant Opposition should be prepared to make the utmost capital out of a Ministry's distresses. If Opposition is not to become synonymous with faction it must draw a distinction between distresses which are internal, where full liberty is rightly conceded, and distresses which are external, when ranks should be closed and criticism become sympathetically constructive. This was precisely what the minority failed to do here as later in the early stages of the American War, and showed, if not their unfitness for office, at least how far removed they were from representing the sentiments of their constituents as a whole. Instead of forming a united front to France and Spain, they proceeded to rake up every possible domestic grievance, oblivious of the effect on British prestige abroad. Their attitude was all the more disgraceful inasmuch as, on their own admission, they never hoped to defeat, but merely to discredit, the Ministry.[32] Thus were the Government blamed for not making their preparations early enough, though, had they done so, they would infallibly have been accused of prodigality and provocation.[33] Thus were they blamed for the inefficient state of the navy, although when, subsequently, attempts were made to impress, there came nothing but indignant protests from Opposition benches.*

Finally, as if to prove how entirely factious was their conduct, the Opposition boasted that, unless their grievances over the Middlesex election were rectified, half the country would refuse to fight. ' I declare, Sir,' cried one of their best-known members, ' if I had command of His Majesty's arms and the French or Spanish fleets were upon our coasts, nay, if troops were even landed, I would not budge an inch until peace was made at home and the right of election restored.'† [34] By such unpatriotic language, which at least one of them had the sense to see was far too intemperate, the Opposition played into Lord North's hands.‡[35]

---

* In their criticism of the navy the charge levelled by the Opposition was certainly more justified. But the blame for this state of things should be laid with every administration since that of Pitt. The timber problem, after years of mishandling, was at last come to a head. See *Tomlinson papers*, p. xiii. The hasty building with unseasoned wood during the Seven Years' War and the economies in personnel and upkeep which no Government since then had dared to give up, had brought the navy to what North later admitted to be a ruinous state. (*P.H.*, xvii. 946.)

† The Opposition did not learn by their errors, and expressed almost the same sentiments later during the American War. (See *infra*, Chap. VII.)

‡ William Whitehead, the Poet Laureate, however turgidly, interpreted

But North was skilful enough not to make the mistake of going to the other extreme. Perhaps it would have been impossible for one who habitually shrank from responsibility, who hated the making of decisions, and wanted nothing so much as to live and let live, to work up the Jingo spirit. His speech upon the Address on the first day of the Session thoroughly expressed the views of the average, sober-minded, unemotional Briton. Without attempting to minimize the likelihood of war, he acknowledged his anxiety for peace. But not for a peace at any price.

' Peace without honour is not a peace; it cannot subsist without honour. One tame submission provokes another. . . . I will assert the honour of the country because I am a friend of its peace. Every measure that tends to procure honourable peace is the best measure for this country: every measure that tends to wanton hostilities is a great crime in a minister. You must have the character of moderation ; you must have the character of firmness; you must have the character of strength.'[36]

It was just this essential character of strength which was lacking, owing to the condition of the navy and the conduct of the minority. By noising abroad the external and internal weaknesses of the country the Opposition were bringing Britain into contempt. Moreover—and this made their conduct

far more faithfully the feelings of his countrymen, in his ode for the New Year, 1771:—

> ' O, should Britain's foes presume,
>   Trusting some delusive scene,
> Of transient feuds that rage at home,
>   And seem to shake the nice machine;
> Should they dare to lift the sword,
>   Or bid their hostile thunders roar,
> Soon their pride would mirth afford,
>   And break like billows on their shore.

in North's eyes all the more factious—their allegations that the country was not behind the Ministry were without foundation. ' It would,' he insisted, ' be the raving of a madman, or the dream of an idiot to believe any man would run the risk of becoming subject to France or Spain because he held a particular opinion upon the Middlesex Election.' As to the contention that had the country armed in June, when the first move by Buccarelli had become known, Spain would have proceeded more humbly, it put him in mind of the country parish where the parish officers produced an army of excuses for not ringing their bells on some occasion, one of them being that their church possessed no bells. In the present case the fleet had not the men, and could not have obtained them until the return of the trade fleets in the autumn. Far better, therefore, than to give the appearance of arming ineffectively, was not to arm at all.[37]

Beyond this spirited defence there was little more to say, and a somewhat crestfallen minority allowed the Address to pass without a division. Instead, they fell back on the old-established method of embarrassing Government by demanding production of papers. But North was too practised a parliamentary hand to be disconcerted by such an artifice. Choosing his words with unusual deliberation, he replied that nothing would give him greater satisfaction than to lay every document before the House, the better to be seised of its opinion, before proceeding to the next step. It was, he assured them, no pleasure to have an inevitable enquiry hanging over his head. None the less, if, as a Cabinet Minister, he must welcome immediate investigation, as a Member of Parliament he could never vote for a motion that, by insisting on the production of papers obviously still unfit for publication, must embarrass delicate negotiations affecting the welfare of the country. The House, in which, it was significantly remarked, there were only three Grenvillites present, was of the same mind; and out of 362 members, the Opposition could collect no more than 101.[38]

Provided the dispute could be settled to the honour of his country, North did not greatly concern himself with the question of right of prior ownership on which the Opposition next concentrated their batteries. Quite apart from his normal predisposition to peace, he was too conscientious a Chancellor of the Exchequer to risk sacrificing a policy of retrenchment for the sake of what he contemptuously called 'a barren and useless rock.'[39] On the other hand, there were not wanting experts ready to contend that the possession of the Falklands was closely bound up with the ability to sail the Southern Seas and to such extent was vital to sea power.* Unfortunately, Spain similarly regarded the possession of the islands as a matter of honour and expediency, and where honour was concerned the Spanish Don became as inflexible as British oak. Though Weymouth's note demanding satisfaction had been ostensibly backed by Choiseul, at that moment involved too deeply in a Constitutional struggle to welcome a war, Grimaldi, the

* Lord Anson, for example, had dilated upon their value, and it was largely owing to his advice that they were later colonized.

Spanish minister, professed to read between the lines, and returned a chilly response. He declined to consider Britain as the injured party, and insisted that any concessions Spain might make must be conditional upon others to be conceded by Weymouth. Such terms no Cabinet could lay before Parliament and hope to survive. They were rejected out of hand, and naval dockyards burst into tardy life. Nor was a further reply to a second note much more acceptable. Alarmist reports spoke of a feverish armament race in France and Spain. At home stocks started to fall. The land tax was raised by a shilling to its old wartime level, and North openly referred to the situation as one of ' precarious peace, of too probable war.'[40] In Paris at one time it was actually announced that war had been declared.[41] And to confirm, as usual, the presence of a crisis, the King went sick.[42]

The Cabinet were, with one exception, of the same opinion as North, as the King, and, though in these matters it is hard to generalize, as the country, that everything short of sacrificing honour must be tried before a resort to war.[43] The jarring exception was Weymouth himself. Any watering down of his original demands he opposed with increasing obstinacy. So far indeed from shrinking from the prospect of a war with Spain becoming a war with France, he set out to make this a certainty by advising a lightning attack upon the remaining French possessions in the East Indies where, in justice to Weymouth, Choiseul had, in the event of war, determined to begin hostilities.[44] Whether in such a case Weymouth hoped to displace North just as, thirteen years earlier, Pitt had displaced Newcastle; whether he hoped such a war would once more bring Chatham into power; whether he simply lost his head and clung to a plan with the tenacity of a drowning man to a spar, is one of the minor problems of the reign. If he had any scheme, it certainly miscarried before the united opposition of his King and his colleagues. On December 16, he threw down his Seals. He was succeeded by the harmless Lord Rochford.

From the pride which North took in announcing his participation in the final settlement, it is clear that with the departure of Weymouth he assumed a much more personal share in the nego-tiations. Nothing further was done provocative of a war with France; on the other hand, no attempt was made to whittle down the condition that any settlement must be to the honour of Great Britain. In this one word honour, always so dear to the Premier, was to lie the essence of the problem. Defined by North himself as something which ‘ depends upon every man’s feelings and will guide every man’s vote according to his notion of the extent of the satisfaction we have the right to expect,’ honour did not easily admit of com-promise. As between gentlemen of the eighteenth century there was only one way by which such niceties could be settled—the sword; so between nations it seemed almost hopeless to expect any milder alternative. Rochford had not been three days in office before orders were sent to our repre-sentative in Spain bidding him quit Madrid unless

K

the Escurial consented to give immediate satisfaction. In Thames-side alleyways and stews the press-gangs were busy. The decks were clearing for action.

But a war which might have twisted the course of history and brought Chatham into power was prevented by what Hume sententiously called ' an incident which no Human Prudence could foresee.' [45] The question as to whether Choiseul was or was not sincere in his professions of peace came on Christmas Eve to be of academic interest only. On that day, egged on by an offended du Barry, the doddering French King despatched to his minister a *lettre de cachet* he had been carrying in his waistcoat pocket in fear and trembling for three days.[46] ' My minister,' he thereupon wrote to inform the Spanish King, ' would have war, but I will not.' [47]

Notwithstanding this excellent news, North very properly declined to modify the preparations the country was now making with all possible speed.[48] These measures, combined with the crushing intelligence that it could no longer count on French support, acted like magic on the Court of Spain. On January 22, the Spanish Ambassador signed a declaration disavowing Buccarelli, and restoring the Falkland Islands without condition, but without prejudice ' to the question of prior right of sovereignty.' This harmless and valueless sop to Spanish punctilio the Ministry, in their anxiety to reach a settlement, conceded without demur.

Not so the Opposition. Chagrined at a happy conclusion, which left them still shivering in the wilderness, they fell with fury upon the agreement, and especially its clause shelving the question of prior right, and its omission of any demand for compensation. A weak case they made, as usual, all the weaker by the extravagance of their language. In their mouths the convention became ' scandalous and infamous . . . dishonourable to the Crown and disgraceful to the Nation.' Barré ridiculously threatened North with the loss of his head for having stabbed the honour of the Nation to the heart: ' Four months arming,' he screamed, ' Four months negotiating, and this is all! ' And Junius echoed ' where will the humiliation of this country end? ' Dowdeswell, duller than usual, even raked up the Manilla ransom, which Spain had consistently declined to pay since the conclusion of the Seven Years' War, and demanded: ' If Spanish right is to be saved, why not ours? ' Certainly, to have required compensation, or to have brought up the scandalous evasion of this ransom, might have been a smart stroke of business; but, as North retorted with reason, if, after having stated our terms, we had then risen in our demands, the fear of British ambitions would have alarmed the whole of Europe. ' Just at such an instant to begin a war merely from an imaginary point of honour, when every essential in honour had been satisfied; when the affront offered to us had been disavowed, repeatedly disavowed, would be to inflict upon the country the heaviest of calamities. The whole duty of governors was to keep the country in a sound state of defence, to be prepared to resent insult, but at the same time to act with moderation.'[49] He might have added ' and with circumspection,'

there being little doubt that the state of the navy
had proved an unpleasant shock to the administration, and had compelled them to be the more
ready to snatch the first opportunity of coming to
terms than they might otherwise have been.[50]

With the Spanish Convention approved by a
majority of 118, North's troubles seemed at last at
an end. America, temporarily lulled by the removal of all Townshend's duties save that on tea,
appeared to be returning to normal. The Opposition was not only dispirited by continued want of
success, but a long foreseen and dreaded secession
had taken place from their ranks. On the same day
that Parliament had reassembled, George Grenville
had died. His death provides one of the most biting
commentaries upon contemporary political life.
Hardly was his body cold before Calcraft was
expressing doubts to Chatham upon the loyalty
of his followers.[51]   Hardly was he in his grave before
North was informing the King that ' there is an
opening to acquire not only Mr. Wedderburn, but
all Mr. Grenville's friends.'[52]   No one, least of all
North and the King, imagined that such acquisitions could be obtained for nothing. Wedderburn, about whom Junius had declared ' there was
something that even treachery would not trust,'
was the last man in either House of Parliament to
be off with the old love before being on with the
new.*   It was not until after some weeks of tor-
tuous bargaining, during which the Grenvillites

---

* In their opinion upon Wedderburn Junius and George III made their
single point of contact, George III himself referring to ' that duplicity that
often appears in his political deportment.' (Fortescue, iii. 181.)

became, with the exception of Wedderburn, more and more passengers upon the Opposition craft, that they landed quietly on ministerial soil. Suffolk, regarded as their nominal leader, went to the Privy Seal, Whately to the Board of Trade, and Wedderburn, who was worth more than all the party combined, to the office of Solicitor-General. At the same time, Thurlow became Attorney-General, and the moribund Hawke at the Admiralty was replaced by Sandwich, the most proper person in the world, according to Walpole, to preside over the navy and to restore it to its old form.* North, anxious as ever to embrace Dartmouth as a colleague, made use of this reshuffling to tempt him into the Ministry. Though the offer was accompanied by the King's heartiest endorsement, Dartmouth's principles still forbade acceptance. Nevertheless, such acquisitions as he made constituted a highly creditable victory for North, and in Walpole's view reduced the Opposition to the last stages of consumption.[53] Thenceforward, flanked in the Commons on one side by Wedderburn, on the other by Thurlow, ' *magis pares quam similes*,'[54] with Charles Fox as a guerillero, the Premier might indulge himself in congenial slumbers, confident that the pass would not be sold, yet ready, the instant he awoke, to wind up the debate in a manner which sent Members out into the night tired but contented.

. . . . .

* Sandwich, even more than North, has suffered unreasonably at the hands of historians, who can hardly mention his name without a sneer and a reflexion on his morals. As to these, they were not very exceptional; he was devoted to his mistress and utterly prostrated at her death. In any case they have no bearing upon his abilities, which were considerable.

Most opportunely for North, the Grenville squadron arrived just in time to bolster up an extremely weak case, for which he was not, however, in any sense responsible. One of the most prized privileges of Parliament was, and is, that of excluding strangers. It had not frequently been exercised of recent years, but at the height of the Falkland crisis, when an Opposition peer was about to deal with the insecure state of Gibraltar, the House of Lords had been cleared of visitors. Amongst those excluded had been several Members of the Commons there on business. Stung by this insult, as they regarded it, the Commons, sinking all party divisions, revived their own right of exclusion by way of retaliation. Though in the Commons (but not in the Lords) strangers were soon tacitly readmitted, the incident had frayed tempers, and with Members become privilege-conscious the smallest affront was likely to cause an incident. It was not long in coming.

As a corollary to the privilege of excluding strangers went the still more jealously guarded right to forbid the publishing of debates. ' To print or publish the speeches of Gentlemen,' Pulteney had once airily proclaimed, ' looks very much like making them accountable without doors for what they say within.' [55] Politicians within St. Stephen's might applaud such pronouncements, but the politicians of the coffee houses without clamoured for news, and would not be denied. Biased, garbled, and often scurrilous reports, with blanks, initials, or fictitious names, appeared, chiefly from Opposition presses, and more than one over-bold printer had received the reprimand of the House on his knees. But what if one day a printer were persuaded systematically to use genuine names? What if behind the audacious printer were ranged the embattled Liverymen of London? What if the tempter were none other than John Wilkes himself, now Alderman of Faringdon Without?

Early in February, before the last ripple of the Falkland Islands disturbance had died away, a certain Colonel George Onslow drew the attention of the House to two newspapers which had not only mentioned him by name, but had dared to refer to him as ' little cocking George.' Despite the misgivings of the King, who, while sympathizing with the desire to check this ' strange and lawless method of publishing debates,' preferred that the onus should (as usual in any case likely to jeopardize the Ministry among constituents) fall on the Peers, acting, in this case, as a Court of Record;[56] the printers, Wheble and Thompson, were given a week's notice to attend at the Bar. When they, obviously acting according to plan, failed to do so, a proclamation was issued offering a reward for their arrest. The delay was fatal. If Parliament struck at all (and Burke warned them of the danger of doing so), they should have struck at once, and with effect. As it was, other editors took heart, and upon the head of Onslow, ' that little, paltry, insignificant insect,' descended a rain of abuse. ' Little cocking George ' resolved to be ' a cock that is not easily to be beat,' retaliated by moving that ' three brace of printers more ' be arrested. Then (so far as is known) for the first time in the history of Parliament a minority set out deliberately to obstruct, and it was not until three in the morning, and after twenty-three divisions, that this misguided motion was carried. The matter had become ' the serious affair ' the King had feared.

The Story of the Six Printers is too well known to be detailed. Some of them appeared and were duly admonished; but one, by name Miller, gave the House of Commons messenger in charge for assault. At the same time Thompson and Wheble were collusively arrested and brought respectively before Oliver and Wilkes, only to be discharged on the ground that the Speaker's Writ not countersigned by a magistrate did not run within the City bounds.

Where their dignity or privilege was at issue, the House of Commons became the most intolerant of tyrants. Party distinctions lost their outline in concerted efforts to assert prerogatives on which they imagined their own existence, and the welfare of their country, depended. When even so warm a friend of the City as Chatham could be shocked at the high-handed attitude of its magistrates it is not surprising that North, who is reported to have had no intrinsic objection to the publication of debates,[57] seems to have been infected with the general fever. Although he could hardly fail to be aware that the magistrates were trailing their coats, his zeal as a good House of Commons man to vindicate the privileges of Parliament swept him off his feet. Instead of heeding Barré's reminder that these privileges were meant to be bulwarks against monarchy, and not chains to oppress constituents,[58]

he rhetorically demanded of a sympathetic House:
' If we give up the cause in which our existence is
involved what more shall we have to contend for?
Issue had been joined with the House upon its
essential authority. If we decline the contest, shall
we not be supposed to have given up that
authority?' [59]

Though originally anxious that a moderation
should shape the policy of the House of Commons,
North was soon over-persuaded by his more intemperate colleagues and by his King. Notwithstanding the sovereign's initial mistrust of the business, once issue was joined with Parliament he stood
loyally behind his faithful Commons, declaring that
' Failure to assert the privilege of the House would
put an end to the most excellent form of Government
which had been established in this Kingdom.' [60]
Could his favourite idea of using the Lords as a
cat's-paw have been followed, even at this stage,
the Commons might have saved their face; but
owing to the recent family quarrel, the two Chambers were not on speaking terms, and the lower
House went headlong into one of its most futile and
unedifying contests. First, a wholly unwarrantable
motion was made by Lord North himself that the
messenger's recognizances be ripped out of the
Lord Mayor's Minute Book. Secondly, Brass
Crosby, the Lord Mayor, and Oliver, both Members of the House, were ordered to attend in their
place. Thirdly, John Wilkes, as an ordinary
member of the public, was required to appear at
the Bar. This last move simply invited the re-
joinder which, in due course, it received. Wilkes

agreed to attend, but only if summoned as Member for Middlesex. The riposte was clever, but for once Wilkes' repartee defeated itself. North, having been once singed by such a firebrand, had no desire to renew the experience.* What would be a punishment to others, he argued, would be none, but on the contrary an advantage, to Wilkes;[61] and this advantage he was prepared to deny him. If Wilkes refused to attend as a member of the public, no effective steps should be taken to enforce obedience.† Such circumspect conduct by North side-tracked the villain of the piece East of Temple Bar, what time Brass Crosby and Oliver made their triumphant progress to Westminster. After hurling defiance at the House, Oliver was committed to the Tower; the case of Crosby was postponed for two days owing to his ill-health.

On the morning appointed for examining the Lord Mayor every approach to the House was invested by an ugly-looking mob. As Members arriving filtered their way through, they were hissed or huzzaed as they were foes or friends to the City. In the case of those really objectionable to the mob, such as Charles and Stephen Fox, some violence was used. But these excesses were as nothing compared with those which greeted the arrival of North, doubly offensive on account of his recent motion. In an instant his coach was

---

* A few years later, referring to a remark that one Wilkes was enough for any Government, North replied that he thought it was one too much, ' though to do him justice it was not easy to find many such.' (P.H., xvii. 1013.)

† To save their face the Commons summoned him to appear on a day which turned out to be that immediately following their adjournment.

matchwood. A bully drove a staff into his face. The crowd closed in upon him. Another minute, and Parliament Square might have witnessed its first and only lynching. Fortunately, Sir William Meredith, a well-known member of the Opposition, dashed to his help, and with some difficulty dragged the dishevelled Prime Minister into the safe precincts of the House. Though much cut and shaken, and having been so near a violent death, North quickly recovered his composure, and astonished the assembly by making a firm and unhurried speech.[62] His treatment a few moments earlier gave all the more weight to his words.

' If the City magistrates,' he said, ' could, by virtue of their Charters, prevent the attendance of any citizen summoned to appear before Parliament, then that Parliament was dependent upon and controlled by those magistrates.' ' The Lord Mayor,' he continued, ' must be taught that the authority of the House was not to be trifled with, and the only way of driving the lesson home was to declare him guilty of breach of privilege.'[63]

But the effort of these brave words following on his rough handling exhausted his self-control. The remainder of the speech was merely an apology for his life and work—the second apology within two years but before long to become, due to frequent repetition, almost a formula. The Opposition, grasping at every straw of hope, had been confidently announcing the imminent dismissal of North by a disillusioned master—his elimination was, according to one authority, in everybody's mouth.[64] Tears now gathered in the Premier's eyes as he referred almost wistfully to this rumour which, had it been true, would have meant release from a burden already become too onerous to bear.

' I have heard nothing of it. If it is in consequence of my claiming the right which every free citizen possesses, that of retiring from business, I will tell the honourable gentleman how that matter stands. I certainly did not come into office at my own desire. Had I my own wish I would have quitted it a hundred times. My love of ease and retirement urged me to it; but as to my resigning it now, look at the situation of the country . . . and then say whether it would be possible for a man with a grain of sense, with the least love for his country, to think of withdrawing from the service of his King and country. . . . There are but two ways I can get out now—by the will of my sovereign, which I shall be ready to obey, or the pleasure of the gentlemen now at our doors, when they shall be able to do a little more than they have done this day.' 65

But his sovereign had no idea of dispensing with the only man who could protect him from thraldom, and the gentlemen at the doors were soon too busy calling each other bad names to concern themselves with devoting North to the fate of de Witt.

By 202 votes to 39, Brass Crosby was sent to join Oliver in the Tower, and so actual victory lay with the Commons. But now, as with their official victory three years previously over Wilkes, they learned belated discretion. Henceforward, printers openly reproduced speeches with Members' names in full, and the Commons wisely looked the other way.

But the Lords no less shrewdly maintained their exclusion of strangers, and therefore their freedom from being reported. The original motion, made in a moment of panic, without a thought beyond concealing from the public and the foreigner the nakedness of Gibraltar, had soon shown itself to be a master-stroke of cunning. It deprived the Earl of Chatham of his great and necessary extra-Parliamentary audience which made him so menacing a factor. Henceforward he was left to address impotently what, in his wrath, he described as ' a snug party of unfeeling Lords and the Tapestry hanging. ' [66]

As a second string to their bow, the Opposition had been contesting a point which was of a far less factious nature, and in which, indeed, had they been successful, would have entitled them to gratitude. It had been held by Mansfield and a long line of eminent judges that, in cases of libel, the jury should be limited to the fact of publication only, and the opinion of what constituted libel should be reserved to the court. While the Government took its stand upon opinion and precedent, the Opposition based their objections upon progress and equity. They adopted in effect the more modern and democratic view that juries must be enabled to decide upon the criminality of an alleged libel.

This admirable party-plank, so far from embarrassing the Ministry, actually accentuated the weakness of the Rockingham-Chatham entente, and incidentally provided North's sense of humour with some exquisite titillation. Both Rockingham and Chatham had agreed that under present conditions printers and editors were at the mercy of the courts, and the Press was more or less in shackles. But while Rockingham would be satisfied with an

enacting law which would imply that Mansfield
had been hitherto correct in his interpretation,
Chatham refused to believe that anything so inimi-
cal to freedom could be lawful. Mansfield, he
believed, must have been warping the law to suit
his own sinister Tory purposes. For Chatham,
therefore, not a legislative change, but an incrimin-
ating inquiry, from which the Lord Chief Justice
must emerge loaded with infamy. The result of
this divergence of opinion in the Opposition
enabled North to escape from what might have
proved a damaging defeat. When Dowdeswell,
on behalf of the Rockinghamites, introduced his
Jury Bill, the Chathamites fell upon the measure,
and for five hours the two wings of the Opposition
fought it out between them, with every Minister
save Conway a mute and amused spectator. At a
suitable moment, North, who between naps had
been heaving with quiet merriment, at length gave
the word, and the Government put an end to the
farce by voting with Chatham's followers against
the Bill.[67]   This was the end of the gentleman's
agreement between Rockingham and Chatham;
and for all practical purposes the end of Opposition,
until the advent of the American War.

And so the session of 1770-1, which had opened
so threateningly, closed in an atmosphere of
unexpected placidity. In the Budget speech there
even appeared a few rays of hope. Trade was
flourishing to such a degree that North believed
the following year might see the removal of the
recent shilling on the land-tax. The American
disputes were settled. In fine, there appeared

nothing to interrupt the peace and prosperity of
the nation ' but the discontents which a desperate
faction is fermenting by the basest falsehoods and
with the most iniquitous views.'[68]   Even these
disturbances, he thought, would subside in time;
all that was necessary for the people to distinguish
between their friends and their foes, was a little
firmness on the part of the Ministry.

At the conclusion of the session Crosby and
Oliver were automatically released.   The occasion
was taken for a further outburst of rioting, in which
North's town house was attacked, his windows and
lamps broken.[69]   But already the inspired London
mob was losing its zest.   Beckford's death in the
previous year had, like Grenville's, proved of no
small service to North.   The second had given
him reinforcements, the first divided his enemies.
Once the hand of Beckford was removed the
City had started to split up into factions.   The
cool, unblushing effrontery of Wilkes, his brazen
sponging, his recent failure to obtain martyrdom
alongside of his colleagues, depressed his stock.
In particular his conduct had made an enemy of
his once fervent supporter, the Reverend John
Horne, sometime vicar of Brentford.   This schism
in turn reacted upon the Opposition.   Wilkes and
his party gained the favour of the Rockinghams;
Horne obtained the support of Chatham.   Soon the
latter was referring to the ' narrow genius of the
old corps connexion,' [70] while Burke was writing of
Chatham that ' the least peep into (the) Closet
intoxicates him, and will till the end of his life.[71]
The indispensability of victory as a cementing

agency was evidenced East as well as West of
Temple Bar. While the Opposition toyed with the
whiskered idea of secession, the City continued to
petition for a time, was well snubbed for its pains,
and then for a year or two ceased, like the Opposition, to matter.

North had won all along the line, and deserved,
if ever a politician did, a sinecure. The one with
which a much gratified royal master at this moment
chose to reward his faithful Minister was, of all things
in the royal gift, perhaps the most appreciated. Hearing that the Earl of Halifax was dangerously ill, the
King, on June 6, 1771, made his nephew the offer in
reversion of his uncle's Rangership of Bushey Park.
The next day Halifax died, and North came to be
possessed for the rest of his life of the residence
attached to the Park.* At a time when the week-
end habit for Ministers was creeping into fashion,
the enjoyment of such a retreat within easy reach
of town was highly acceptable to the harassed
Premier. Down to Bushey, for the next ten years,
North and his family would escape from Friday to
Monday. Wandering through the extensive kitchen
gardens, lounging through the peach-house, romp-
ing with his children upon the lawns, North
became for two or three days in every week the
complete family man. To be invited to spend a
Sunday at Bushey *en famille* was a privilege reserved
only to his most intimate friends, and was the more
highly prized for being so.

.   .   .   .   .

The support of a baneful royal influence has for

---

* Actually the grant was made to Lady North.

too long been a convenient explanation of the manner in which North had triumphed over his embattled enemies. To contemporaries of the reign of George III the Closet could account for any feature not to their liking.* Nor since their time has it generally been thought necessary to check their opinion. For confirmation it has been thought sufficient to turn up the pages of Burke, the speeches of Fox, the writings of Horace Walpole, or to refer to the letters of the King himself written to his Prime Minister. Of these sources it is hardly necessary to observe that two are from politicians in opposition, one from a man whose sympathies were mostly anti-ministerial, while the fourth possesses as much value as a one-sided telephone conversation. If, instead, we refer to the man who, as First Lord of the Treasury, must have been in a position to speak with authority; to a man, moreover, who was acknowledged by his enemies, much as they abused him across the House, to be honourable, a different tale is heard. There will be found bitter complaints of sluggish attendance, of spineless support, of votes belonging to placemen withheld, even given to the Opposition; but nothing to indicate the use of artifices other than those hallowed by fifty years of practice. The charge of using royal influence North, in fact, categorically and consistently denied. Speaking, as early as April 1771, he said:

' There never was a time in which offers and threats have been made [less?] use of the last seven

---

* It was even to be made the cause of Cornwallis' surrender at York Town ten years later. (Cf. Fox's speech, *P.H.*, xxii. 705.)

L

years—never a time in which they had less effect.' [72]

Four years later North declared:

' If I have the honour of having an office under the Crown, it follows not that I should prostitute my principles. I never have, I never will use any art, any undue influence, to induce others so to act.'* [73]

Again, four years later, in 1779:

' An honourable gentleman (Fox) had talked much of the influence of the Crown. I do not know if such influence exists, that it has lately increased. For my part I can say with truth that I never endeavoured to exert it or make an improper use of it.' [74]

Finally, in 1783 when no longer Prime Minister:

' I have heard much in my time of secret influence. I never saw anything like it, otherwise I should undoubtedly have relinquished my situation.'' [75]

When North disclaimed such use or knowledge, his language must be judged by contemporary standards. The yard-stick by which the influence of the Crown is to be measured belongs not to the twentieth and hardly to the nineteenth century. A vast accumulation of sinecures and offices which previous generations had heaped upon the Treasury as well as upon other Government departments, in addition to his necessary voice in the distribution of ribbons and titles, gave a Prime Minister, whether he sought them or not, advantages which

---

* A document amongst the Robinson papers (probably written about 1780) gives under the cross-heading ' Payment for Parliamentary Purposes ' the names of nine members to whom contributions towards their annual expenses were made. The sums varied from £50 to £750 and in all did not amount to more than £1,800. (B.M. Add. MSS., 37836, 137.)

a more democratic age would never tolerate.* It
was a venial error on the part of a hungry Opposition to confuse the patronage of the Crown, without which neither Walpole nor Pitt (father as well
as son) could have survived a session, with the
personal influence of the sovereign. That George
III interfered in politics more than once, and with
greater effect than his Hanoverian predecessors, is
as indisputable as the fact that twice only in
North's lifetime did he exceed his limits under the
Constitution. In the first, the Royal Marriage
Bill, North was the unwilling instrument; in the
second, Fox's India Bill, North was to be the unwilling victim. That George III could have done as
much as he did had politicians been more high-
minded may be doubted. But it was not a high-
minded age; and politicians get the Kings, as
peoples get the Governments, they deserve. A
study of the Parliamentary Debates makes it hard
to believe the legend of those ' twelve years of
almost personal rule during which Lord North and
the well-fed phalanx of the King's friends bade fair
to make the House of Commons the mere instrument of the Royal Will.' [76] Without the consent of
the independent Members not a measure could
have been passed.

Until the country was prepared to consent to a

* The ecclesiastical patronage of the Treasury was greatly prized by
North for the opportunity it gave him of preferring men of virtue and
ability. Nor, beyond seeing that Brownlow was well cared for, were his
appointments anything but just and unexceptional. In this connection
there is a story that an ambitious parson, knowing the Premier was to be
among the congregation, chose as his text: ' Promotion cometh neither from
the East, nor from the West, nor from the South.' Promotion (it is gratifying to know) in due course, came from the *North*.

thorough overhauling of its political system it was a
waste of time and labour to inveigh against the
influence of the King or Crown.   Bishop Watson,
stoutly anti-ministerial, was unbiased enough to
admit that : ' You cannot take from the Crown the
means of influencing Parliament, by lodging those
means in any other hands, without destroying the
Constitution, and you cannot (such is the largeness
of your debt, your commerce, your army, your
navy, and the extent of your empire) extinguish
those means.' [77]   And when Burke at a later date
swept away a large number of places, the principal
result was to substitute a coronet for a sinecure.
Pitt the younger, who had been hardly able to find
words strong enough to express his disapproval of
North, created in the first five years of his Ministry
forty-eight peerages to the thirty in all North's
years of office.*

More plausible than the charge of royal influence
is the suggestion that the Opposition, first by
alarming the country and then by falling out
amongst themselves, did North's dirty work for
him.   Even were this a complete explanation, a
Minister who can sit quiet, resist the temptation
to meddle, and allow his opponents to neutralize
themselves, may not be a political genius, but he
has at least progressed some way on the road to
statesmanship.

The principal cause of North's success was
neither the influence of the Crown nor the folly of
Opposition, but the fact that the country gentlemen

---

* In the course of seventeen years Pitt's peers mounted to 140.   (Lecky,
v. 293.)

and independent Members judged him the best
man available and wished him to succeed. They
were weary of the hypocrisy of the old Corps
Connexion, the rantings of Chatham, and the
arrogance of the City. They were prepared to
give a man a chance who, having risen more by
personal merit than by patronage, was indentured
to none save his King and his country. And pocket
boroughs and rotten boroughs, Nabobs and Rigbys
notwithstanding, the House of Commons was at no
time truly unrepresentative of popular feeling.

North succeeded because he deserved to succeed.
A man who, though more fitted to preside at the
head of his dinner table than in a Cabinet Council,
more at home in the Pay Office than in the Treasury,
sacrificed his inclinations to duty, was a man who
possessed principles, and in the long run, with the
average Englishman, principles counted for more
than patronage.[78] Here too was a man who set out
to govern his country without connexion and without violence, whose financial ability (so important
to the taxpayer) was proved, and whose policy was
peace abroad and plenty at home. A country may
ask more of a Minister. It rarely enjoys more.

CHAPTER V

THE INDIA BILL

'If the trading spirit of the English East India Company renders them very bad sovereigns, the spirit of sovereignty seems to have rendered them equally bad traders.'

ADAM SMITH, *Wealth of Nations*, iii. 251.

AFTER the tumults of the previous months there succeeded a period which by contrast was almost moribund. Even the rumbles from across the Atlantic seemed to be subsiding. So placid, in fact, was the political sky that North thought it unnecessary to interrupt the shooting, hunting and Christmas activities of Members until well into January.[1] By then whatever last fleeting clouds remained had vanished over the horizon. With the New Year Junius, realizing the hopelessness of the struggle, determined to quit before a continued want of success tarnished his reputation. On the first day of the session, which promised to be as uneventful as its predecessor had been exciting, he hurled what proved to be his last thunderbolt; and a very indifferent thunderbolt at that. It took the form of a long and laboured letter addressed to Lord Mansfield raising intricate points of legal procedure, far above the head of the general reader. A fortnight later died the Princess Dowager, Chatterton's Carlton Sibyl.* The poor old lady had long ceased to exert any influence good or bad, but her death benefited North's Government to the extent that it deprived the Opposition of one of its principal cock-shies. With Beckford dead, Wilkes very much *vieux jeu*, and Junius retired from business, scarcely any life stirred within the Opposition encampment.

In this sedate Parliament such passions as survived were diverted along theological channels. Two centuries earlier no channels could have been more perilous. By the middle of the eighteenth century religious debates for the most part emptied the House and provoked impatience.

The strong Unitarian feeling which had latterly been growing with some vigour recoiled at the forcible subscription to the Thirty-nine Articles required upon matriculation of every undergraduate, whether destined for Holy Orders or not. Early in February 1772 a petition was presented by Sir William Meredith, signed by 250 persons, some 200 of whom were clergy, praying to be relieved from this imposition. On such an issue so faithful a son of Oxford as North could not hesitate a moment. In this, as in Grenville's Election Bill, was a tampering with a system which had worked, he felt, satisfactorily for generations. But whereas Grenville had merely attempted to introduce a change in Parliamentary procedure,

* ' Oft has the Carlton Sibyl prophesied
    How long each Minister of State should guide.
. . . . .
   Oft from her secret casket would she draw
   A knotty plan to undermine the Law."

                  (*Resignation*.)

Sir William Meredith was, North passionately believed, unwittingly launching an attack against the Church of England, which he loved so well, and in which his brother Brownlow was already starting on his round of episcopal palaces.* It was not that North, and those who voted with him on this occasion, were reactionary; it was that those who petitioned for a change were too far in advance of their times. To the statesman of the eighteenth century the Golden Age lay neither in the past nor in the future, but then and there before their eyes. Only by holding on to the present, and bearing with its accompanying ills, could worse ills be avoided. Once a breach was made in the imposing façade of the Thirty-nine Articles, with what propriety, North reasoned, could they exclude the supremacy of the Pope? ' A thousand doctrines of Popery may rush in at the door the honourable gentleman would open for two or three hundred men.' [2] On this relatively feeble demand North scored a decided point. Only a most widespread movement could justify a change in the fundamentals of an established church, as well as in those of a State; and by no process of reasoning could 200 clergy, out of the twenty thousand in Holy Orders, be said to constitute a demand.

' How can we comply with the desire of a few petitioners,' he asked, ' when the whole body of the clergy oppose them and treat their project not only as mad and frantic, but as irreligious and anti-Christian. The peace of Society ought with us to be the first object; and it is certainly better, in a political sense, that a few prevarica-

---

* He became successively Bishop of Lichfield, Worcester, and Winchester.

tors that make a trade of religion should enter the Church, than that order and good government be subverted, a catastrophe in which the success of this petition would certainly terminate. When our civil dissensions have, thank God, in a great measure subsided, would you introduce religious quarrels? I fear the latter would prove infinitely the more dangerous of the two. Wake but the many-headed hydra, religious controversy, and she will with more difficulty be laid asleep than the Hesperidean dragon. Not all the opium, not all the mandragora and perfumes of the East will lull the monster to rest. Check then such a mad project in the bud, and give not the least countenance to the petition.' [3]

While North's natural conservatism and Anglican training swept him off into such unusually florid periods, he was, notwithstanding the secession of his Solicitor-General, and several habitual supporters, on safe ground. Although the petition was largely supported by the bulk of the Opposition, Edmund Burke, their greatest and most formidable Member, and at heart the stoutest Tory in either House, attacked it with venom and with scorn.[4] ' Suffer men of distempered imaginations, who yet believe in Scripture, to become preachers, and you may absolutely terminate all rational Christianity and bring disgrace upon the very name.' Their only sheet anchor was ' a system of religious laws that would remain fixed and permanent, like our Civil Constitution, and that would preserve the body ecclesiastical from tyranny and despotism, as much at least as our code of common and statute law does the people in general; for I am convinced that the liberty of conscience contended for by the petitioners would be the forerunner of religious slavery.' [5]

After such a display of rhetoric the House of Commons was as convinced as Burke and North. By a majority of three to one* the petitioners were sent about their business.

From not conceding to undergraduates discrimination in their religious beliefs, it was almost an anti-climax to deny to princes of the Royal Family the choice of a wife. Perhaps from having been so carefully diluted in his own case, the hot Brunswick blood ran all the more fiercely in the veins of the King's brothers. After a precocious life of seduction, during which he had been cast in damages for ten thousand pounds, the Duke of Cumberland had, in the previous autumn, openly and at last married the sister of the notorious Colonel Luttrell, a widow the deadly length of whose eyelashes was her most noteworthy qualification. Shamed by this example, the Duke of Gloucester, a few months later, acknowledged publicly a marriage made five years earlier with the Countess Waldegrave, likewise a beautiful widow, and incidentally a natural daughter of Sir Edward Walpole. The Duke of Cumberland and his bride had been forbidden the Court—a widow was bad enough: the introduction of bastard blood seemed to call for sterner measures.

The fact that George III had once had a solitary liaison with the pretty young niece of a London draper, and at another time had come within half a dozen words of marrying Lady Sarah Lennox, a lady of non-Royal blood, made him, no doubt,

* 217 to 71.

all the more sensitive to these matters.* Instead of consoling himself with the thought that his brothers had had the decency to make honest women of their mistresses, as well as a brave effort to settle down into respectable married life, he allowed himself to be carried away by traditional German ideas on the sanctity of Blue Blood. Lord Mansfield was summoned to the Closet, and soon afterwards a measure was introduced into the Lords ' for the better regulating the future marriages of the Royal family.'

The Royal Marriage Act is the swallow that has made a high Tory summer. It is, during the Ministry of North, the one incontestable instance where royal influence and pressure were openly and avowedly employed to bring about a measure to which the majority of the country and most of the Cabinet were indifferent or hostile.[6] It even strained the loyalty of so faithful a servant as North, who prepared to gulp the measure down as a man a dose of physic, but without hope of benefit.[7] Other measures commonly cited of the King's active interference, the Peace of Paris, the affair of Wilkes, the American War, had all a very considerable degree of public support. Here pressure had to be exerted all along the line. On the other hand, George could and did argue that this was a family rather than a national concern. It was not, as he told North, ' a question that immediately relates to

* A recent writer by the liberal use of his imagination claims to put George III back into History ' without a stain on his moral character.' (*George III*, J. D. G. Davies, 33.) But where is the stain? If a crowned head is not allowed one small indiscretion without becoming morally stained, he is surely being subjected to an unjust and unconscionable standard, as compared with his subjects.

administration, but to myself, therefore I have a right to expect a hearty support from everyone in my service, and shall remember defaulters.'[8]

Notwithstanding this warning the passage of the Bill was hotly contested in both Houses in all its stages, and criticism was by no means confined to Opposition speakers. Through the Lords it passed with the administration's customary majority, but in the Commons, where the debates were longer and more violent, North's majority sank on one occasion to eighteen. Here Opposition found no difficulty in making out a case against the cruelty, injustice and tyranny, not to say unwisdom, of the Bill. Men who by law were allowed at twenty-one to be fit enough to govern a realm might very well, Dowdeswell supposed, be thought capable of choosing a wife. The patent weakness of the Government's case was further accentuated by a spectacular defection. Freedom in the choice of a bride was axiomatic at Holland House, and Charles James Fox, with expressions of real regret, begged to differ from his leader. In the circumstances, North's speech in favour of the Bill could hardly have been anything but laboured. After declining to limit its working to the reign of the present King for the very proper reason that ' it is not right to trust any King with power that is not proper to trust all Kings,'[9] he trailed off into a tedious historical survey. Citing a number of examples in support of the Bill, he wound up by declaring ' there is scarce a right of the King and people that has scarce been proved by such a long and uninterrupted series of precedence.'[10] But the House were not

convinced; nor were they sure that any kings *ought*
to possess such an authority. Charles Cornwall, in
fact, went even further and bluntly declared, ' the
present King is not to be trusted with a power over
his children after the age of twenty-one.'[11] The
going was thus uphill and heavy, and half-way
through the debates the Prime Minister, worn out
with the strain of late sittings, ran a high temperature. However, the day after his exiguous majority
of eighteen, he had at last the satisfaction of getting
the objectionable Bill through the Commons with
the moderate majority of fifty-three and earning
his royal taskmaster's thanks for ' the spirit and
zeal you have shown in conducting it through its
different stages.' [12] Nor did the King limit his
gratitude to words. A promise made the summer
before to instal North with the next vacant Garter
was now redeemed. With the exception of Sir
Robert Walpole, North became the only Member
of the Commons to wear the Blue Ribbon since the
reign of Elizabeth.[13]

Encouraged by some phrases dropped in the
course of a debate upon the Clerical Petition, the
Nonconformists concluded the time had come for
them to press for legal relief from certain disabilities
more apparent than real. Here, within two
months, was North's many-headed hydra showing
signs of wakefulness. The King, tenacious of all
that came within the compass of the Constitution,
had no doubt at all how to treat this attempt to by-
pass the Church as by law established. ' I think
you ought to oppose it personally through every
stage, which will gain you the applause of the

established Church and every real friend of the Constitution.' [14]   To North, hardly recovered from the embarrassing shock of that majority of eighteen, these sentiments were magnificent rather than politic. For him the question was not susceptible of such cut and dried treatment. His personal feelings and his traditions were naturally all on the side of the Established Church; on the other hand, the value of the Dissenting Vote could not be ignored. Already, it is clear, the Nonconformist conscience was becoming a thing with which the statesman must reckon. Before many hours were passed even the King came to concede as much. In his next letter he agreed that North ' ought not to press those gentlemen who are brought in on that (i.e., dissenting) interest into Parliament, to oppose this measure, as it would be driving them out of those seats into a new Parliament.' [15] If, in an endeavour to follow the King's heroics, North cracked his whip, the petition would probably be thrown out, but so, at the next election, now within approachable distance, might his Government. If, on the other hand, he did nothing but utter pious exhortations, he must undoubtedly be defeated, for nearly all the Opposition were in favour of the petition, and one half of his own party would either vote in its favour or abstain from voting at all. It was, his supporters naïvely argued, a clear case for rejection by the House of Lords, whose backs were broad enough to bear the indignation of outraged Dissenters. This plan, always a favourite one with the King, being adopted, the sequel became a farce. In the Commons, where abstentions were

BOREAS.

I Promise to pay seventeen Millions in ten Years —if I am Minister.

LORD NORTH making his 1772 Budget Speech

From a contemporary cartoon

many and speakers few (Lord North not being amongst them) the Bill passed by seventy-one votes to nine. In the Lords, obedient to instructions from the Prime Minister, this eight to one majority in favour was converted into a three to one majority against.*

The session closed as sedately as it had begun. In his Budget speech, North, as in the previous year, had even permitted himself the luxury of a pair of rosy spectacles. ' Let it, however, be remembered that I assert nothing as a certainty; I might as well pretend to command the tide and winds as the passions of men. I only assert that at present there is the fairest prospect of peace that I ever knew.' Given ten years of peace, he calculated that the National Debt would be reduced by some seventeen millions, and continued, in words which might have fallen from the lips of some twentieth-century post-war Chancellor: ' We do not stand in need of any conquests. Our dominions are at least as extensive as we could wish; and their improvement, not their extension, should be our chief aim. Thus we see what I believe nobody expected at the conclusion of the last war, some, though no very certain, prospect of gradually reducing the national debt: a step which will necessarily raise our credit and authority in Europe and terrify our enemies into pacific measures. For it is not only an armed force, not only great armies and great naval forces, that will deter our rivals from violence, but the capacity of raising these bulwarks when occasion calls.' [16]

* 102 to 29.

For all these glowing prospects, North was not happy as a less temperamental Chancellor like Pelham or Grenville might have been in similar circumstances. The responsibilities of office (as he never allowed himself or the King to forget) had been undertaken from the first unwillingly, and never ceased to weigh heavily on his mind. Indeed, while preparing his budget, he seriously thought of quitting before he had ' forfeited the little reputation I have gained and done more mischief to the public by my want of knowledge, activity, and talents than I did good to it by preventing the whole frame of administration from falling to pieces in a moment of trouble and danger.' [17] But if North was incapable of remaining an unqualified optimist, it was equally impossible for him to maintain a gloomy aspect for any length of time. In June came the thrill of investiture as Knight of the Garter,* followed, down at Dillington, by a summer so unusually lovely as to calm the most jagged of nerves. The failure of the financial house of Fordyce, and the trail of City bankruptcies which followed failed to disturb his equanimity.†[18] In fact prospects, with North, had a way of looking good or bad according to the mood he was in, and just now he had even more cause for self-satisfaction. The University of Oxford, no doubt in return for his eloquent defence of the Thirty-Nine Articles,

---

* The *Publick Advertiser* announced this event in a couplet:

> ' What a stigma, stars and ribbons, what a blot,
> When North a Garter has, and Chatham not.'

† It is a melancholy reflection, writing in 1937, to note that one of the firms affected by the crash was that of Adams Brothers, whose work on their beautiful Adelphi Terrace was held up for a time.

had offered to nominate him their Chancellor, and
to the surprise of himself, his friends, and his supporters, his election was carried without opposition.[19] And so not even the news that Prussia,
Austria and Russia were digging their claws into
an unhappy Poland led him to revise his favourable
forecast. Instead, he told Sandwich: ' I do not
recollect to have seen a more pacific appearance of
affairs than there is at present: France, neither
from the disposition of her Prince, or her Minister,
or from her own situation, seems likely to engage in
a war for some years.' [20] And to his father he
wrote: ' Public business I do not foresee which is
likely to disturb my repose.' [21]

Exactly a month later the customary reaction had
set in. ' I fear we must be obliged to call the
Parliament together before Christmas.* In short,
there are vexations enough in my office to make me
melancholy amidst all the honours I receive.' [22] A
new problem (or rather an old problem in a slightly
novel form) of the utmost delicacy and importance
had thrust itself into the foreground and demanded
instant solution.

The East India Company had, for some years,
presented a strange paradox. While she was
approaching the verge of bankruptcy, her servants
were waxing fat and prosperous, returning opulent
and arrogant to debauch politics with their money
and Society with their luxury.[23] If Macaulay and
Burke are to be believed, the clerks who were resolved to get rich quickly could have learned little

---

* Despite North's anticipations this did not prove necessary, and Parliament did not reassemble until January 21.

M

from a twentieth-century Chicago gangster: protection sold like so much merchandise; competitors
terrorized out of existence; the necessities of life
cornered; for sanction, a file of Sepoys in lieu of
the Thompson sub-machine gun.   'Animated with
all the avarice of age and all the impetuous ardour
of youth, they roll in, one after another, wave after
wave; while nothing presents itself to the view of
the unhappy Natives except an interminable prospect of new flights of voracious Birds of Passage.'
Though Burke in this and Macaulay in other well-
known passages were by their zeal led to much crude
exaggeration—the bulk of the criminals being
natives themselves, acting under cover of the un-
witting Company—we have Clive's word for it that
Calcutta was 'one of the wickedest places in the
Universe: corruption, licentiousness, and a want of
Principle seemed to have possessed the minds of all
Civil Servants, by frequent bad examples they are
grown Callous and luxurious beyond Conception.' [24]

At home, the Board of Directors had long been
making efforts to set their house in order.   But distance and slowness of communications rendered any
authoritative control from East India House exceedingly difficult.   Moreover, it was just those
servants who had flouted their authority most that
returned home rich and influential enough to
dominate the Court of Proprietors and even to
humble the Board of Directors itself.   In 1765,
Clive had been sent out armed with special powers,
and something was done to purify the springs of
government, every one of which he discovered to
be 'smeared with corruption.'   But half a dozen

Clives succeeding each other at five years' intervals, and not one Clive, were necessary if the work of purification was to be complete; and after eighteen months only, the man who had shown himself to be as consummate an administrator as he had been a general was forced through ill-health to return home.

Meanwhile the Proprietors, more concerned with dividends than morality, and anticipating from Clive's reforms a new Heaven and a new earth, over-ruled their Directors and insisted on raising the dividend from six per cent., at which it had been for many years, to ten. Nothing could have been more unwise and less opportune. The men of North's generation still lived under the tremendous shadow cast by the South Sea Bubble in the days of their fathers, and had an ineradicable suspicion of stockbrokers. No sooner was talk of increased dividends circulating through the windings of Change Alley, than speculation in India Stock began. Memories of the 'twenties were quickly revived, and Government intervention became inevitable. When Parliament had reassembled in the winter of 1766, an inquiry into the Company's affairs was instituted at Chatham's instigation. This, as the Directors, more far-sighted than the Proprietors, had feared, showed no sign of stopping short at dividends. The Seven Years' War, by making the Company paramount in India, had changed her from a trading into a quasi-sovereign organization, enjoying a gross revenue of four million pounds, employing an army of fifteen thousand men, controlling the destinies of twenty million souls, and administering territories nearly the size of France.²⁵ What right could the Company advance to these increased territories, gained with the assistance of British soldiers and sailors, in campaigns which had cost the British tax-payer four millions of money? This was a question which had been lurking in the background ever since the Peace of Paris. Chatham had not the slightest doubt that the claims of the Crown were paramount, and in this he was supported by no less an authority than Clive himself.²⁶ But, his inten-tions were negatived by his illness, and the initiative passed to Charles Townshend, described as the patron of the ' Advocates of the Alley.' Towns-hend's principal motive appears to have been to arrive at an amicable rather than an equitable settlement. And there is this to be said for his temporizing attitude: at no time was respect for Charter rights stronger than in the eighteenth century. Any suggestion, therefore, of taking over territories acquired by the Company appeared to those as politically opposite as the Rockinghams and the Grenvilles, a gross infringement—as it certainly was—of its original Charter. What, accordingly, had emerged from Townshend's nego-tiations was a compromise. The Company bound itself to pay £400,000 annually in respect of its territories and revenues, thus implying, without openly acknowledging, the Crown's sovereign rights. At the same time dividends were to be restricted to ten per cent. It was, as North later confessed, a faulty arrangement, inasmuch as it compelled the Company, regardless of any situation it might find itself in, to pay this tribute.[27]

Two years later, when this agreement expired, Lord North was Chancellor in Townshend's shoes. At first he was filled with a wild hope that matters might shake themselves out without Parliamentary intervention, and that he would be able to sit back and gather in a pleasing revenue from the Company.[28] But the closer he examined the case, the more convinced he became that the Company was once more on the edge of bankruptcy. Yet, when he asked for a proposition, the Company sublimely offered to continue (for a period of five years) the £400,000 which it believed, from its increased sales of tea, it would be easily able to find.[29] In return, it sought leave to raise the dividend to twelve and a half per cent. by more than one per cent. per annum. On the other hand, should the Company be compelled to reduce its dividend, then a proportionate amount should be deducted from its annual tribute; if not more than six per cent. was declared, then the Crown should receive nothing. In other words, the Company promised to become, in North's phrase, ' farmers to the public.' [30]

Like Chatham, North had long held that the Crown had a right to all acquisitions made by the East India Company.[31] According to this opinion, the Company's proposals should have been unacceptable. On the other hand, the Crown's needs were pressing; the £400,000 was a very handsome bird-in-the-hand; to decide on the question of rights and compensation would mean lengthy inquiries, legal arguments, and the possibility of defeat. An amicable settlement was much to be preferred, and North was prepared to accept the terms offered, considering them not only the best obtainable but, through the conditions attached to any declaration of dividend, fortified by the strongest of guarantees.

'All public bargains made with the public should be as simple as possible, and therefore I consider the one proposed, checked by the interests of the petitioners themselves, who are to lose from the dividend as much as they defalcate from the public, the most certain bargain the public can make.' [32]

North was deluding himself. Here, as in the later stages of the American War, he was sinning against light. In his heart he must have known there could be no real solution short of control passing to the Crown. Yet, once he proposed to adopt a scheme which frankly aimed at stamping out vested rights, he knew equally well he could count neither upon a united Cabinet nor a united party. That way lay the delays, the uncertainties, and the turmoil of a Parliamentary battle; the other, a breathing space and two million pounds spread over five years. For any Chancellor of the Exchequer it would have been difficult not to hesitate: for one of North's complaisant temperament it was impossible.

In spite of the opposition of some who, like Burke, declared the terms pressed too heavily upon the Company or of others like Barré, who believed it was being too leniently treated, the new agreement had been adopted by Parliament. Yet Burke was right when he called it a ransom upon the Company, and therefore an uncommercial arrangement, but he was wrong in imputing fraud, violence, and injustice to the Minister. North was mistaken, not criminal, in expecting, and the Company was unwarranted in believing, that such a sum could be paid without the thorough overhauling of an effete organization. The folly of such beliefs was not long in manifesting itself. As the effects of Clive's reforms wore thin, the Company was confronted with diminishing revenues and increasing debts. A failure of the harvest, followed by a famine which, according to official statistics, carried off a third of the population of Bengal, had not the least effect upon the rapacity of the Proprietors, who, at the earliest possible moment, caused the dividend to be raised to its maximum. At such rate, default could not be far ahead.

Luckily for North, the consequences of this short-sighted, makeshift agreement did not at once appear and so synchronize with the critical first year of his Ministry. When in the autumn of 1771 the Indian situation did show signs of embarrassment once more, he was in a position to give it his undivided attention. This time he acted with greater circumspection. Conscious of his own ignorance, he wisely applied to those best qualified to advise.[33] ' The question is in itself a most arduous one,' he told Clive, ' and I confess that I stand in need of much information upon this subject: your Lordship, from your extensive knowledge of it, can be of great service to me, and I have no doubt but your public spirit will incline you to give me every assistance in your power.'[34] The assistance was not denied. Several meetings took place between the two men, and it was probably Clive's account which really opened North's eyes. According to Walpole, the Premier had been saying he did not intend to inquire into petty larceny.[35] Here was something which, as Chatham dramatically expressed it, ' teemed with iniquities so rank as to smell to earth and Heaven.'[36]

When Parliament reassembled, certain pregnant phrases appeared in the King's speech regarding the remedying of abuses which ' from remoteness of place as from other circumstances had crept into the vast and varied concerns of the Country.' [37] Some sort of action was confidently expected to follow. Instead, there succeeded—nothing. Parliament, so Gibbon reported, after a few soft murmurs, fell asleep safely folded in North's arms.[38] For all his assurances to Clive that he was ' seriously bent upon this business and shall certainly prefer no other to it,'[39] North appeared to sink back into his habitual indolence and doze precious hours away while Dissenters petitioned for relief. Actually (as was so often the case) North was very wide awake. No Chancellor, even with the somnolent habits of North, could afford to close his eyes to the very probable loss of four hundred thousand a year out of a Budget of eight millions. Unfortunately, those to whom he had applied for assistance, were by no means unanimous. If experts could not make up their minds, he who held the meanest opinion of his own capabilities, might be excused from making up his own. Having caused veiled threats to be inserted into the Gracious Speech and shown that he was alive to the situation, he trusted that the

Directors of the Company would take the hint and come forward with really constructive proposals.[40] He had, after all, ample precedent in Chatham himself, who, when appealed to on behalf of the Company at the outset of his Ministry, had declared his ' fixed purpose has always been and is, not to be a proposer of plans, but, as a seat in one House enables him, an unbiased judge of them.' [41] And a judge, North repeatedly stated, it was his intention to be.

Not until more than two months had elapsed was the hint taken. Then the Company asked leave to introduce a Bill to restrain the Governor and Council of Bengal from private trading and to improve the judicial system. This may have been a step in the right direction but, following on a recent declaration of a twelve and a half per cent. dividend, it might equally be regarded as an attempt to divert the wrath of the Ministry. Nevertheless, inadequate as he regarded it, North gave the Bill his blessing, while suggesting that the time had come when a Committee of Inquiry might be set up to go into the whole question of India, in preparation for the next session. He was, as he complained, getting rather tired of words.[42] Thereupon Colonel Burgoyne (of whom more will be heard before long), while disclaiming connexion with the administration, took the hint and moved that a select Committee be appointed. This suited North admirably. It relieved him of responsibility; it gave him time. In an excess of gratitude, he promised every assistance in the consideration of such reports as the Committee might make.[43]

Shortly after this benediction, the session closed and North, trailing his Blue Ribbon of the Garter, had gone gaily down to Somerset, leaving Burgoyne and his Committee to swelter in London through one of the hottest summers in the memory of man. As reports from the Committee presently followed him down, a state of things was revealed if not utterly without hope, certainly requiring an over-haul. But the Company had not yet touched rock bottom. In the autumn, while North at Dillington was browsing over Burgoyne's reports, their credit suddenly slumped. Bills had been accepted and could not be met. What was worse, they were now in arrear with half their annual tribute to the Crown, and officials at the Treasury were pressing for payment. In desperation, the Company pleaded for a moratorium, and the loan of £1,500,000. At last their necessities had delivered them, as nothing else could ever have done, into the hands of the Government, and compelled North to decide.* A curtain promptly fell between East India House and the Treasury. The Company was frigidly informed that their request would have to be considered by Parliament. Though Treasury proceedings were stayed on North's instructions, the Board was bombarded with searching questions.[44] This stiffening of attitude, so distressing to Burke, gave the King unexpected satisfaction. ' Till now,' he wrote to North, ' the conduct you have held towards the Directors is much to your honour, but any wavering now would be disgraceful to you and

---

* And in Walpole's opinion there was none at this juncture of affairs more qualified to do so. (*Last Journals*, I. 171.)

destruction to the public, but I know you too well to harbour such a thought.' [45]   North took the hint. A secret Committee was set up, calculated to move with greater speed and effect than Burgoyne's, which, however, was suffered to continue. An eleventh-hour demarché by the Company to escape supervision by sending out supervisors of their own was checked by special Act of Parliament. Finally, on March 9, 1773, North struck.

The loan, more for the benefit of their creditors than for themselves, he granted to the Company, adding that, if this were not enough he would go on piling further loan upon loan until their credit was restored. Accompanying this enforced lending, however, there were to be regulations for the better management of the Company's affairs. They were to be in the nature of experiments which the House must, session after session, correct and amend if need be. ' We must not consider our business at an end when you have gone through what we can do at this session. We must look upon ourselves as engaged in a business likely to hold out long. There must be constant inspection of Parliament over the conduct of the Company.' [46] Appalled by this outlook, the Company, in a slightly Gilbertian manner, petitioned against being lent money. But North was inexorable. They must be forced to borrow. And on North's terms.

The Company's territories and revenues which North calculated were worth two million nine hundred thousand pounds a year, were to be allowed to remain with the Company for six years. What was more, provided they conducted themselves

satisfactorily, they might enjoy them in perpetuity.[47]
Secondly, until their affairs were replaced on a
solid foundation, the public would forego every
penny of its claims against the Company.   To
contribute   towards   their   rehabilitation,   North
thirdly conceded a request that they be allowed to
export their tea, of which they had seventeen million
pounds in bond, free to America.*   In return for
these concessions, crazy declarations of dividends,
which encouraged speculation, were to be checked
by providing a limit of six per cent. until the
Government loan was repaid, and seven per cent.
until the bonded debt was reduced by a million and
a half.   Any dividend over eight per cent. was to be
divided in the proportion of three-quarters to the
Government and one-quarter to the Company.
But most important of all, in order to give the
Company every opportunity of pulling themselves
together, North announced that he would introduce
a series of Regulations.   In the past the Company
had been given liberal chances and had failed to
make use of them.   It was at once the right and the
duty of Parliament now to interpose.[48]

The first step North took was to move a call of
the House.[49]   Quite properly he felt that it would
be wrong to carry his proposals on so important a
subject merely with the votes of placemen, Ministers
and country members.   Thus, when he introduced
his famous Regulating Bill, prefaced by some typical
self-depreciatory remarks, it was to a crowded as

* Great as this amount sounds, it was only two years' supply, and it was
the Company's practice always to have one year's supply in reserve. (*Annual
Register*, 1774, 47.)

well as an excited House. North's reputation for indolence and irresolution had given even his sympathizers the impression that he had neither the mind to conceive nor the courage to carry into operation any extensive scheme.[50] It was, however, his manner rather than his methods which created such an impression. Much as North might prefer the easy road, he never spared himself when, as now, he considered his duty involved. The task was approached in a workmanlike manner, without any attempt at frills or fancies. Abuses were singled out and dealt with one at a time. The glaring weakness of the Board, due to its being elected *en bloc* annually, was to be remedied by providing that members should be elected six at a time for a period of four years. With tenure of office prolonged North trusted that every Director would become less abjectly dependent upon the whims of influential Proprietors and more able to make an independent stand. As a corollary, Proprietors entitled to a vote had to possess a thousand instead of five hundred pounds' worth of stock, and to have held it for at least twelve months. Finally, there was an attempt to deal with the Company at its other, or Indian, end. There, North fairly asserted, ' the sufferings of the people had not proceeded from a want of political freedom so much as a want of government of the Europeans, the servants of the Company, and those who are protected by the servants of the Company.' [51] If power could be confined to fewer hands, and those belonging to persons carefully chosen and thoroughly reliable, such abuses, he believed, would be diminished. He proposed, accordingly, to establish a new Court of Justice in Bengal with superiority over all others, and secondly to subject all British administrations in India to that of Bengal, where supreme authority was to be vested in a Governor-General assisted by four Councillors. These officials were to be specifically named in the Act at a salary calculated to place them above temptation. Future appointments should lie with the Company.

North's diffidence, his feeling that what he proposed was an experiment constantly to be improved upon, and the likelihood of opposition which any tampering with Charter rights must arouse, probably caused him to think that he had done as much as was immediately possible. ' I do not rest my reputation,' he said, ' upon having proposed a law that is to be invariable, that no circumstance, that no case, is to alter. Let the circumstance and the case arise such as ought to convince the world [that there is need of] some alteration, I shall thank the man who proposes and willingly alter, but I must go on in a course I have unwillingly begun, [in] a duty I have unwillingly begun till I find it unwise to continue, or impossible.' [52]

If there had been more truth in the Company's whining protest that the Bill would ' annihilate at once the powers of the East India Company and virtually transfer them to the Crown,'[53] North's regulations might have worked with greater success. Instead, the supremacy of the Crown was suggested rather than specified. Warren Hastings, the first and only Governor-General under the Regulating Act, was left without power to over-ride his Council, and the Council without the necessary powers of rewards and punishments.[54] In practice, North's Act proved a failure: as an experiment along the right lines it was a commendable effort in statecraft.

Never did North emerge with greater credit than he did with the long and tedious debates through which his Regulating Act dragged.* Throughout all discussions he tried to ensure that so important and national a question should be a non-Party one. He desired to be considered in this affair not a Minister, not an Advocate, but a Judge, and he hoped all Members would feel as he did.[55] It proved a vain hope. Almost every sentence in the Bill provoked censure and criticism. The City of London petitioned against it. Dowdeswell called it ' a medley of inconsistencies dictated by tyranny, yet bearing throughout each line the mark of ignorance.'[56] Burke likened it to ' a football kept up between Heaven and earth by the buffets it received.'[57] But North, patient, accommodating, sweet-tempered, always ready with a humorous thrust, by his moderation and modesty triumphed over the most unscrupulous attempts to depict him as a destroyer of corporate rights. The Opposition had not even the satisfaction, as in their annual flagellation over the Middlesex Election, of flogging a dead donkey. They were

* For the most part these are unpublished, the *Parliamentary History* giving only a few; but in Sir Henry Cavendish's reports amongst the *Egerton MSS.* they fill several volumes, although, owing to gaps, they are difficult in place to follow.

simply beating the air. To argue with Governor Johnstone that the Act was ' fatal to liberty,' or with Burke that there was all the difference in the world between entering a house to regulate its management and entering it to rob and steal, was sheer nonsense.[58] Even Chatham, hostile and aloof, deigned to think that ' an attempt towards Reformation in a case so urgent does some honour to a Minister.' [59]

While the destinies of a great Company were being discussed, dissected and debated, those of an individual hardly less renowned were at stake. Quite early in the inquiry, a suggestion, said to have come from Thurlow, was made that all monies acquired by public servants in India should be confiscated by the Crown.[60] Whether Thurlow had Clive in mind, or not, certain members of the Select Committee, including Burgoyne its Chairman, were very quickly convinced that they had to look no further for the villain of the piece. The great cleansing services which Clive had performed during his memorable eighteen months, had filled returning East Indiamen with irate Europeans who, on arrival, made Leadenhall Street echo with tales of their woe. To such men, the appointment of Burgoyne's Committee provided an unlooked for opportunity of getting their own back on Clive. Whatever the latter might have said or done, his immense wealth branded him as easily the chief of the Nabobs, and prejudiced his position unfavourably. Due to some skilful lobbying, this Committee soon became little more than an inquisitorial court for breaking Clive, actually one of their own Members.[61]   By extending the scope of their inquiry some fifteen years back, they brought the Baron of Plassey within the terms of reference, and, as he bitterly complained, examined him ' more like a sheep-stealer than a Member of the House of Commons.'[62]

While North's Regulating Bill was still in Committee stages, Burgoyne had presented a further report followed by three Resolutions, all of which were carried without a division. These asserted that territorial acquisitions of the Company belonged to the State, that grants made to its servants were illegal (a thrust at Clive's Jaghire), and that large sums had been acquired and appropriated to their private use by persons vested with civil and military authority.

These resolutions, so obviously pointed at Clive, were not altogether relished by North. He and Clive were on friendly terms, and there is no doubt that he wished these relations to continue, in order to have the benefit of the other's advice. Drawn one way by his conscience and the other by his inclinations, he spoke in a half-hearted manner, justifying his attitude with the flimsiest of excuses. While he agreed with the sense of the resolutions, he disliked the wording; while he thought Burgoyne actuated by the best of motives, he declined to take part in the debate, save as a private Member, owing no allegiance and being owed none. ' I would not,' he said, ' have it considered that a question of justice was to be carried like a question of policy, and that the opinion of a man in office, as a man in office, should have weight or influence, in the House. Therefore, I do not think it peculiarly

N

[proper] for the First Lord of the Treasury to make [a case?].' [63]

This Pilatesque attitude pleased neither Burgoyne, who felt the pass was being sold, nor Clive, who must, after their conversations, have considered North ought to know him better.   When some days later Burgoyne took the next obvious step and moved that Clive, in consequence of powers vested in him as Commander-in-Chief, had illegally acquired monies to the detriment and dishonour of the State, North was driven into a corner.   ' It is one of the most difficult duties,' he complained, ' for a man of Society to enter into an inquiry of this nature, when you must at every step give offence.'   On the other hand, it was impossible for him to shirk his duty at a time when ' the temper of the Age leads to conniv-ance, to excusive mercy rather than to agitation of mind and violence of temper that has often marked the proceedings of Parliament in other cases.' [64]

Here was North's difficulty, in which, incident-ally, he had the fullest sympathy of his sovereign. While both acknowledged Clive's services to be unparalleled—in fact it was on North's express recommendation that Clive had been recently decorated with a K.B. and made Lord Lieutenant of Shropshire—both felt he had set an insidious standard for others who lacked his own matchless qualities.   Though a glorious example in one field, he was an iniquitous one in another.   ' How, Sir,' asked North, ' shall you pay a just tribute due to the services of Lord Clive, without permitting guilty men who had done no service to the State [to go unpunished?].'[65]   Clive's virtues might more than balance his faults, but his bad example remained, nevertheless, if something were not done. ' To receive a present by virtue of any public authority is wrong, always wrong—it is a clear wrong. The moment it is allowed the State is ruined.' What North would have preferred was for the House of Commons to find for Burgoyne's censure; then, having established a principle, to take no further action on the ground of Clive's eminent record.

' If his services have been great, state his services.   If in the result the noble Lord fares better than other persons in India, let it be known, not that you approve of these presents, but because the noble Lord has done services to this Country and others have not.   If you will refuse to find this fact as it stands, postpone the censure, but if you start and then refuse to find that fact as it stands, it will be in vain to suppose that the House will support any inquiries against any other men.' [66]

The House thought otherwise. ' Upon the whole,' wrote Thomas Bradshaw, Secretary to the Treasury, who sat through the debate and voted consistently with North, ' I felt a pleasure in the good humour of John Bull. He will speak and write daggers, and hang and cut off heads without mercy in the newspapers; but when the culprit has submitted, and John has him absolutely in his power, he will not hurt a hair of his head.' [67]   First of all, the House with North's consent, split Burgoyne's original motion into two and unanimously agreed Clive had accepted £234,000. Next, in the teeth of North's objections, by 155 votes to 15, they struck out words conveying that Clive had received this sum through the influence of powers with which he was entrusted. This, as North had warned them, made the whole thing illogical. ' To say a man does an illegal act does not convey censure; what makes his action censurable is his intentions.' [68] Thus, when Burgoyne went on to move the second part to the effect that Clive had abused his powers and set an evil example, it was, after the previous motion, considered useless and was rejected without a division. Finally, at twenty minutes to five, what was left of the original motion was moved and carried, likewise without a division. Then, Wedderburn putting the question, it was unanimously resolved that ' Lord Clive did at the same time render great and meritorious services to this country.'

The numerous vexations encountered, as well from within his own ranks as from without, during the passage of his Regulating Act, North had found exceedingly galling. Although ' not unused to contradictions nor unacquainted with storms,' on this occasion his feelings seem to have been genuinely hurt. Having throughout the proceedings approached the subject from the most detached and disinterested angle, to be accused of personal or vindictive motives was unjust and humiliating. So keenly did he resent the attacks on his good faith that at one moment he had definitely decided to throw in his hand.[69] Had he done so—and there were Members even of his own Cabinet who would have shed few tears—North could have retired to the back benches conscious of having kept his country out of a useless war, preserved its constitution from novelties, and done his utmost to save his King from faction and India from chaos.

North did not go. And the reason is clear. Like Samson, he was tied to a pillar, and if he went he could only do so by bringing down the edifice. It would have been easy enough to have found a peer to take over the Treasury, but an analysis of the Government personnel is enough to show that there was not one man with the reputation, the ability, or the experience, to lead the Government in the Commons or to introduce a Budget. If even Chatham could acknowledge North to be indispensable to the Government, how much more so did the King? With George III it was not merely that North was his only line of defence against men whom he feared and distrusted; he believed that those moods of dejection which swept over his Prime Minister were pathological in their nature, and would respond to treatment. To lose North in one of these temporary attacks of malaise would, from his point of view, be deplorable mismanagement. The King accordingly acted as any constitutional irresponsible head was entitled to act. The tocsin was sounded from the Closet. A mass attack headed by Dartmouth was launched, with instructions to overcome North's resolution, so ' destructive to his country, his King who loves him, and his honour.' [70] While it could be shewn that the Commons still supported him with a majority, North had really no defence to offer. The white flag was hoisted and then, as if these periodic resolutions to resign were necessary to the building up of tissue, North was immediately his

old self again.   Indeed, so that others might have
no cause to question his new-born resolution, he
took advantage of the Budget speech a few days later
to frame it in unequivocal language.

' Others might succeed to the Temple of Fame by parts,
by eloquence, or a great genius; but he, having none of
these qualities, thought himself happy in doing in this
instance what was right and his duty to do; that he
entered upon his great office at a moment when things
were not in the most pacific situation; that he had hitherto continued in it with resolution to do his duty, and that
he should persist in what he thought right, in defiance of
all noise and clamour; that he was determined to abide in
the post in which he had laboured, and should not willingly relinquish the trouble of it; that those who looked
into his conduct might perhaps see indolence and a love of
ease, yet they should not find a want of an honest per-
severance in a great and public cause.' [71]

For six months North had no reason to put this
bold declaration to a test.   The second half of the
year 1773 was the quietest period in the whole of his
ministerial life.   A little trouble with a proposal
from Dublin to impose an Absentee Tax, some work
in preparation for a Bill to regulate the gold coinage
of the Realm, scarcely rippled the placidity of the
stream.   The calm in America promised to last;
Clive had departed for Italy, proving that he bore
North no manner of grudge, by leaving his ten
boroughs in his charge; Guilford was made happy
by being promoted Receiver-General to the Queen.
Yet, if ever there was a lull before a storm it was in
the six months ending December 31.   On the 18th
of that month the inhabitants of Boston had committed the entire contents of an East India Company's tea ship to the sea.   For the next eight

years North's public life was to be one of anxiety and perplexity.

It was just at the moment when these trials were about to descend upon him that North was compelled to dismiss one who had hitherto been his most mettlesome supporter. Charles James Fox, whose original connexion with North had so pleased his mother, had for some time been ceasing to please his Chief. He had airily resigned from his post as Junior Lord of the Treasury in order to oppose the Royal Marriage Bill. In view of his own private opinion upon the Bill North had taken such a defection with the utmost good nature; but when Fox next defeated the Government by one vote on a Bill to repeal the Marriage Act of 1753, such irresponsible conduct became a little trying. The wisdom of having such a fellow inoculated with office was evident even to the King who, in other cases, was not prepared to forget the defaulters on his own Marriage Act. Before the end of the year a special reseating of Government posts was actually effected in order to bring in the twenty-four year old Fox as a Commissioner of the Treasury. But nine months of liberty had, besides acquainting him with Burke, brought about some disturbing changes in the quondam rising hope of the stern unbending Tories. He who had, over the Royal Marriage Act, begged humbly to differ from his leader, now did so whenever the fancy moved him, and without so much as a by-your-leave. Whether in such conduct the young man was actuated by pure puckishness, whether by the love of notoriety, or whether he felt he had made a mistake in re-entering the Ministry, and sought to provoke North into dismissing him, are questions which no biographer of Fox has satisfactorily answered. Perhaps it was something of all three motives which urged him to see exactly how far North's well-known placidity could be challenged.

In February 1774, shortly after the meeting of Parliament, an attack on the Speaker's alleged impartiality having appeared in the *Publick Advertiser*, its printer, Henry Woodfall, was summoned to the Bar. There he revealed the identity of the writer, one John Horne, the Brentford parson, who had once assisted Wilkes in his election. Such accommodating attitude, together with an hitherto blameless record, clearly inclined the House to deal leniently. Woodfall was about to be committed to the gentle custody of the Sergeant-at-Arms, when Fox sprang up and demanded that he should be sent to Newgate. A more disturbing, as well as a more unauthorized proposal, could hardly have fallen on North's ears. Newgate being within the City of London, and the memory of the Six Printers still vivid, a proposal to compel the Sheriffs to receive one of their citizens in their own jail for having infringed the privileges of Parliament would certainly re-open the quarrel. With America threatening once more, the last thing North or the King desired was another squabble with the City. On the other hand, when it had been a question whether Woodfall should in the first place have been summoned before the House or prosecuted in the courts for criminal libel, North had come out strongly for applying, whatever might be the consequences, the ancient constitutional method of asserting their own rights without seeking the aid of the Crown.[72] To hand the Printer over to the Sergeant at-Arms after such grandiloquent declarations might well be considered an anti-climax. North was compelled to wriggle out of the dilemma into which Fox had drawn him by proposing an amendment, committing Woodfall instead to the Gate House of Westminster, and then urging his own supporters to join with the Opposition in defeating the motion.

Such conduct in a subordinate Minister no self-respecting Prime Minister could afford to ignore, however amiable he might be. Even while North hesitated as to the best means of showing his displeasure, Fox, not in the least contrite, took advantage of Horne's appearance further to upbraid him for his pusillanimity. This left North no option. He sat down and addressed to Fox the neatest letter of dismissal ever penned: ' Sir: His Majesty has thought proper to order a new Commission of the Treasury to be made out, in which I do not see your name.'

North did not pay for this piece of laconic humour by adding one more enemy to the Opposition. Events were already happening which would have offered to Fox an irresistible temptation to cross the floor of the House. Even while the Commons were debating just where their privileges began and ended, Government clerks were drafting Bills which were to bring Parliament into conflict with a body of men infinitely greater and more resourceful than the Aldermen and Sheriffs of the City of London.

Chapter VI

AMERICAN COMMENTARY

' It is a widely different thing, Sir, the quelling of a paltry riot in Moor-fields or Bloomsbury Square to that of making two millions of people distributed from one corner of the American Continent to the other all unanimous in the opinion of right being on their side, submit to your deci-sions. It matters little to the question whether they are in the right or not, they think themselves so.'

NICHOLSON CALVERT, *P.H.*, xvi. 109.

NORTH's long and devoted services to his country; his laborious husbanding of her resources; his patient efforts to purify the springs of the East India Company; his sacrifice to duty of that freedom from responsibility for which he sighed, lie buried beneath the tombstone which pitifully recalls the passing of Britain's first Empire. His epitaph is brutally brief—the Minister who lost America.

That this loss may have turned out an advantage is a consideration which cannot be allowed to intrude into Lord North's balance sheet. If a Minister sets out to achieve an object and fails, he is not entitled to be credited with the possibility that, in the long run, his failure accomplished more than success could ever have done. On the other hand, if it can be maintained that the secession of the American colonies was as inevitable as the Swedish traveller Kalm had, thirty years before, predicted it to be, [1] then one considerable item should in fairness be expunged from the debit column.

If Lord Balfour is right and Englishmen do, in
fact, possess a passion for self-disparagement, we
need look no further for the basis of the popular
and persistent theory that American independence
was born of the arbitrary ambitions of King George
III, and the criminal shortsightedness of his
Ministers. It was an explanation which agreeably
titillated the smug complacence of Victorian England by underlining the foibles and follies of the
previous and less enlightened century. It is,
therefore, perhaps, not surprising that theories attri-
buting the struggle rather to the selfish, wanton
and unaccommodating attitude of the Americans
should have been more effectively developed from
across the Atlantic. As is frequently the case in
questions of magnitude and diversity, the truth
would seem to lie suspended between the two stand-
points. American contrariness contributed to the
separation equally with British short-sightedness.
But considered neither singly nor together can they
be regarded as conclusive causes. Except the centre
of Imperial gravity had shifted (as some indeed
imagined at the time it must be shifted) from
London to New York, it is hard to see how separation could have been avoided. Hard, that is to
say, unless eighteenth-century statesmen, Whig as
well as Tory, had been endowed with modern
conceptions of Imperial relations and had enjoyed
modern facilities of transport and communication.
There can be little doubt that the British Empire
would not be functioning to-day in its frictionless
state had it not become as easy to keep in touch
with Capetown and Canberra as with the Board

of Trade across Whitehall, or were Delhi and
Ottawa no more distant in time than Edinburgh
or Dublin a century and a half ago. A Statute of
Westminster passed in the early years of the reign
of George III would certainly have postponed,
perhaps for a considerable time, separation. The
colonists who, until the eve of the war, professed
a more or less genuine attachment to ' the best of
Kings,' would cheerfully have agreed to a settlement which gave them everything they claimed and
cost them nothing in return. But to imagine an
eighteenth-century Parliament passing a Statute of
Westminster is to imagine that august assembly
suddenly taking leave of its senses. It could no
more have contemplated such a measure than it
could a Parliament Act to deprive Peers of their
veto.

  . . . . .

 ' The fundamental principle of the Revolution
was that the Colonies were co-ordinate members
with each other and with Great Britain, united by a
common executive sovereign but not united by any
common legislative sovereign.' [2] These words of
Madison, which, if uttered to-day by a Dominion
Premier at some City banquet, would evoke hearty
applause, would have been received by North
and his contemporaries in frigid silence if not with
expressions of alarm. A suggestion that the inhabitants of His Majesty's Plantations were to be
considered in any sense the equals of the governing
classes at home would have been taken as a
joke in very poor taste. Moreover, to the
logical mind of the eighteenth century there

was something darkly sinister in ' a claim which supposes dominion without authority and subjects without subordination.' [3] Settlement purchased at the price of admitting Parliament had no jurisdiction over its colonies, but must stand aside in favour of a King holding a Parliamentary title, was no settlement at all.* It was insidious: it must set all Ireland in a flame and act like a solvent upon the West Indies. It was heterodox: a King exercising authority for which the Cabinet was not responsible, and able, by direct application to individual colonies, to obtain monies behind the back of Parliament, revived the worst memories of the Stuarts.† To colonial writers brought up largely on seventeenth-century text-books and in a very different social environment none of these considerations counted for much. To them the problem of Empire was infinitely simpler. They had no difficulty in visualizing a more democratic framework than was possible for the patrician statesmen of Whitehall, steeped in high Parliamentary traditions and lisping the complacent catch-phrases of the *Our* Colonies School. Although a long way from unanimity on the exact measures to be adopted they showed far more ingenuity and willingness to co-operate in settling the Empire upon some Commonwealth basis than any who on this side of the Atlantic paused to reflect upon imperial relationships. They

---

* There was thus every justification for the remark of the King on the outbreak of war, ' I am fighting the battle of the legislature.' (Fort., iii. 256.)

† Cf. the ludicrous remark of Wilkes, which nevertheless was characteristic of the Opposition mentality. ' Every friend of the Constitution saw early in the support of the American cause a vindication of the rights of Englishmen against an old exploded usurpation of the Stuarts, revived under the third Prince of the House of Brunswick.' (*P.H.*, xxi. 892.)

realized, as probably not one Englishman in a hundred thousand did, that the old machinery would no longer serve for an Empire expanding rapidly in size, wealth, and population. All they asked for, at this period of transition, was a reasonable redefinition of their status. The request was not a fantastic one. The imperial government had merely to give legal effect to what was in practice already existing. But no such answer was forthcoming because no British statesman, not even Pitt, was prepared to admit the full implications of such a reply: namely that King and Parliament were not in fact supreme over every square yard of Empire. Yet this much can be said in extenuation of the attitude adopted by North and his contemporaries from the days of the Stamp Act to the first shot at Lexington: if they gave the stone of Parliamentary Supremacy when the colonists asked for the bread of partnership, they did so without any intention to affront. They acted consistently with the traditions of their fathers and the men who had made the Glorious Revolution. And in after years those who survived could have consoled themselves with the reflexion that, had Parliament under the spell of some chimerical dream consented to adopt one of the many American schemes for federation, the thread which would have held the colonies must have been so fine that it could never have withstood the industrial and political strains to which it must have been subjected at the close of the century. For the separation of the colonies began neither with the Stamp Act nor with Lexington, but when the first

Pilgrim Father stepped ashore from the *Mayflower*.

Starting from the very infancy of the American settlement, a variety of forces had tended steadily to weaken connexion between the settlers and the Mother Country. Their habits of life and their tenets of theology favoured a republican rather than a monarchical regime. They had quitted England at a time when prerogative was being fiercely contested and ideas current of fundamental rights which no man or body of men could override. Because subsequently the absolutist sovereign had been put down from his seat, for them it did not follow that Parliament had stepped into his shoes. The privilege of a subject not to be taxed without his consent lay not only, it was believed, embedded in the immutable laws of God and nature, but had been constitutionally confirmed by Magna Carta, and the statute *de Tallagio non Concedendo* of Edward III. To America, they argued, they had carried this and every right and privilege belonging to British birth without reservation or equivocation; and the knowledge that three thousand miles of water separated them from their nominal rulers allayed any fears they might have had of giving expression to their opinions. Conscious of their birthrights, self-reliant and uncompromising, these pioneers, the flower of England's middle-class, made magnificent colonizers, but only indifferent imperialists.

The coming of the eighteenth century witnessed the gradual dilution of this stiff-necked Puritan stock by emigrants who, in increasing numbers, now flocked across from Scotland and Ireland, some of them of poor quality and many of them (especially the Presbyterians from Ulster) hostile to or careless of the British connexion. These were in turn followed by settlers from the Continent, especially the Germans, who brought their trades and industries and highly resented all commercial restrictions.[4] On the eve of war, indeed, so considerable had been the influx, that settlers of purely British blood numbered no more than two-fifths of the white population.[5]

On their side the Home Government made no pretence that the plantations existed for any purpose beyond exclusively benefiting the Mother Country. Theirs was a conception implicit in the still unchallenged Mercantile System. ' Such is the end of colonies,' declared a member of the Board of Trade fifty years before the outbreak of war, ' and if this use cannot be made of them, it will be much better for the State to be without them.'[6] Forty years later no less a person than Chatham was to threaten America with the whole weight of Britain's displeasure if she should so much as manufacture a stocking or forge a hob-nail. Even Burke, with all his American predilections, is found complacently admitting that ' the great object for which the Colonies were founded (was) navigation and commerce.'[7] Yet, so far from weakening the imperial connexion, the much abused Mercantile System with its Navigation Acts and intricate network of Protection did, to a great extent, knit together the farmers of New England, the manufacturers of Birmingham, the shippers of Bristol, and the sugar growers of Jamaica by bonds stronger than those of mere sentiment.[8] Definite markets, protected from rivals, were assured; bounties were given; and if there were any harshness in the regulations, evasions were more or less connived.* Even the restrictions placed, in accordance with current theories, upon American manufacturers —Adam Smith's 'impertinent badges of slavery imposed upon them without any sufficient reason '— were minor hardships in a country where land was cheap and labour was dear.[9] Nor, considered dispassionately, was it unreasonable of the British taxpayer, called upon to defend frontier posts from France and her Redskin allies, and seaport towns from pirates, to expect some practical return. Regarded by contemporary standards, the British Government did not require very much. And here, perhaps, lay one of their cardinal errors: they asked too little, or they asked too much. So many attributes of liberty did the colonists enjoy that the few restrictions effectively enforced acquired an irksomeness out of all proportion to their incidence.†

Had the Home Government rigidly adhered to the mercantile system and kept their colonies in a state of rigid political and commercial subjection similar to those of Spain; had they appointed and paid colonial governors, judges, and officials; restricted immigration and denied settlers all effective local

---

* Wholesale smuggling, in which even certain Colonial Governors were involved, made, for example, the unpopular Molasses Act, 1733—passed, be it noted, by Walpole, who is given so much credit for declining to impose a Stamp Act—a dead letter. Grenville's Revenue Act passed to ensure its enforcement became, by offending the American merchants, an important cause of the war. (Cf. Schlesinger, *The Colonial Merchants*, Chapter II, and Van Tyne, *Causes of the American War of Independence*, 126.)

† The Constitution of Rhode Island, for example, was considered so liberal that it survived the war by nearly sixty years, and remained unchanged till 1842. (Acton, *Lectures on Modern History*, 311.)

government; a revolution might have long been averted. The very fact that the British colonies, and not the Spanish or Portuguese, first rebelled against their Mother Country is a testimony to the lightness of their yoke. Men do not rebel when they are fast bound in misery and iron, but when they hold many of the ingredients of freedom and desire to be possessed of all.

The almost idyllic calm in American affairs which George Grenville, by his Stamp Act, is supposed to have rudely brushed away, is a necessary premise to the theory of British folly as a cause of the War, but, unlike that theory, it is not only misleading, but basically false.* For one set of factors making for harmony there were half a dozen exerting a contrary effect. For close upon a century one disputed point after another had been cropping up. Governors' salaries and powers, Charter privileges, Admiralty Courts, Writs of Assistance, royal Quit Rents, the colonization of Indian territories, a threat to establish episcopacy, had all provided grounds for complaint or quarrel. The widespread, prolonged and generally successful evasions of the law, especially the Revenue Laws, tended to encourage a spirit of defiance, which, unchecked, became more pronounced and more militant. In the words of a recent American writer:

' The thirty years or so before the American Revolution were years in which the balance of power in all loyal

* (Cf. Stanhope, vii. 124.) ' Provinces, which at the peace of 1763, had been as contented and loyal as the shires along the Severn or the Thames.' Even Mr. Basil Williams, fifty years later, in his excellently documented *Life of Pitt*, falls into this error and speaks of that ' hazy state, quite free from bitterness,' which is supposed to have preceded the Stamp Act. (*Life of Pitt*, ii. 181.)

provinces* was clearly shifting from the Crown to the assemblies. The Constitutional history of the provinces in the eighteenth century is fundamentally the history of a series of controversies between assemblies and the prerogative in which the former won victory after victory.' [10]

Under the strain of the Seven Years' War the weakness of the royal prerogative had become increasingly pronounced, and old controversies acquired a new lease of life. The assistance asked for by Pitt was granted, but often at a price which left the Governor little beyond his patent and his pomp.[11] Nor after the war did the obloquy of the Bute Ministry or the dispute with Wilkes do anything towards restoring lost prestige. As Hume asked, pertinently enough, 'How could we expect a form of government to maintain its authority at a distance of three thousand miles when it could not make itself respected or even treated with common decency at home?' [12] The more these impressions sank into the minds of the colonists, the more they became constitutionalists, the more they demanded their full rights (as they conceived them) of British citizenship, the less they were prepared to undertake any of its duties.

'The Revolution,' declared John Adams, 'was effected before the war commenced. The Revolution was in the minds and hearts of the people.' [13] This is admittedly a rhetorical flourish; but it is nearer the truth than Thomas Cushing's sugary pronouncement that (in the summer of 1773) the people of Boston were 'as faithfull and as

---

* i.e., New York, Massachusetts, Virginia, North and South Carolina, New Jersey, Georgia—the first three being, in agitation-value, worth all the rest combined.

loyall subjects as any ye King has in any part of
the British Empire; ' [14] and much nearer than his
own words three months after the battle of Bunker
Hill: ' If such an idea (of independence) really
obtains amongst those at the helm of affairs, one
hour's residence in America would eradicate it.
I never met one individual so inclined, but it is
universally disavowed.' [15] Pronouncements upon
the avoidability of the American War made by
colonial leaders must be read with the utmost
caution. Having a very considerable body of
their own countrymen averse from independence,
and knowing that the friendship of the English
Opposition might easily be forfeited by too outspoken language, politicians were guarded in whatever they elected to write or say. The King or
Parliament was blamed according to whether
they were dealing with their English supporters or
Americans with loyalist sympathies. Written when
there was no longer need for restraint, John Adams's
declaration, if applied to a determined and considerable minority, is incontestable. Like the English that preceded and the French that followed, the
American Revolution was largely the work of an
organized body of resolute men imposing itself
upon an unwilling or indifferent majority. On the
outbreak of war it was computed that as much as
three-fifths of the population was well disposed
towards the Mother Country. The remainder,
principally to be found in New England, where
Puritan ideals had suffered little modification in
150 years, would not require much incentive to
become Separatists. ' There are,' wrote General

Gage, the British Commander-in-Chief at New York, who, having married an American, might be supposed to know something of colonial sentiment, ' three fundamentals on which the people of this country endeavour to establish the political doctrines they have promulgated, and as they fail in producing proof from the one have recourse to the other. These are Charter Rights, British Constitution, and the Laws of God and Nature.' [16] With these premises at their finger-tips, New Englanders were never in want of an argument whatever the grievance.

It should have been obvious that a population growing in numbers but weakening in sentiment required discriminate and careful handling. A merely commercial nexus was not enough. Gage, far from being the choleric imbecile of history, had been driving this point home.

' Surely,' he wrote, ' the people of England can never be such dupes to believe the Americans have traded with them so long out of pure love and brotherly affection? That they will manufacture when they are able is easy to conceive, in spite of your laws to prevent them, but this is looking into futurity. That they will struggle for independency, if the good folks at home are not already convinced of it, they will soon be convinced. From denying the right of internal taxation, they next deny the right of dutys upon imports, and thus they mean to go on step by step till they throw off all subjection to your laws.' [17]

Wise direction from home, inflexible in essentials, indulgent in accidentals, acting rarely, but never without effect, might have helped to erase unhappy memories, ironed out real or imaginary difficulties, and ultimately have made the colonists, for the

time, at least, loyal if not contented. But not only
was there no attempt in Whitehall to understand
colonial problems, but the royal executive in
America was poorly qualified either as administrators or as advisers. From Governor to humblest
tide-waiter, applicants were selected less by merit
than by favour. To the ruined gentleman, America
was manna from on high. 'Most of the places
in the gift of the Crown,' runs a well-known complaint, 'have been filled with broken Members
of Parliament, Valets de Chambre, electioneering
scoundrels, and even livery servants.'[18] This state
of things might not have been so bad if, while
feathering their own nests, these Nabobs of the
Western World had honestly kept their masters in
touch with real American opinion, and so enabled
them to propound some remedial policy. But,
despising the 'Colonials,' and finding nothing to
attract in the social life of their province, they lived
principally amongst themselves, or in the society of
American office-holders. They never came to know
the real American—the farmer of Connecticut, the
merchant of Boston, or the backwoodsman of Virginia. As a consequence the authorities at home
remained ignorant or misled, and as late as 1763 a
Virginian was writing: 'The ministers see nothing
with their own eyes that is passing amongst us, and
know nothing with their own knowledge, and are
therefore very improper legislators to give laws to
the colonies.'[19] This lack of knowledge was, as much
as any one factor can be so regarded, the cause of
the Revolution; and this handicap was not confined
to Frederick North. Chatham during his last years

and the Opposition throughout the dispute and the war showed by their language how thoroughly they were out of touch with effective American sentiment.*

Apart from their ignorance of America, the King, the Ministers, and the Legislature of an essentially unicellular state like Britain were utterly at sea when called upon to deal with a conglomeration of restless provinces differing from each other in climate, creed, and outlook. The only relationship they could visualize was one of parent and child— eighteenth-century parent and eighteenth-century child—possession and authority on one side, duty and deference on the other. George III perhaps might be excused from descanting upon ' the obedience which a colony owes to its Mother Country,' [20] but Rockingham, for all his association with Burke, was no better. ' I shall always consider,' he wrote, ' that this Country, as a parent, ought to be tender and just; and that the colonies, as children, ought to be dutiful.' [21] Had it only been possible for George III, Rockingham, North, or any Cabinet Minister to have visited America during a summer recess, the future might have been much modified Instead, knowing nothing of conditions so completely different from those at home, ignorant of the colonial attitude towards constitutional problems, all they could do when relations deteriorated was to evoke the supremest authority they knew—the High Court of Parliament. ' By what means,' asked North, and his rhetorical question may be said to epitomize the misguided but

* Cf. Hertz, *Old Colonial Policy*, 28.

intelligible British standpoint, 'By what means is authority to be maintained but by establishing that authority from Parliament.' [22] Even so, had Parliament agreed to delegate plenary powers to a council capable of action, something might have been done; but until within seven years of the Revolution there was no department which could deal authoritatively with America. The Board of Trade and Plantations, nominally in charge, could advise, but could not act. The Secretary of State for the Southern Department could act when he had time, but then not necessarily in accordance with advice.* A system of government that jogged along well enough for a line of scattered and under-populated colonies had become hopelessly inadequate as a means of guiding the destinies of thirteen thriving communities containing in all nearly three million souls.

It was by a sort of malign fate which seemed relentlessly to pursue the British Government for the next dozen years or more that, just when they turned to America for contribution towards imperial defence, there should have been less spirit of accommodation in the colonies and more weakness in the executive than ever before. The French menace from Canada, which had made the presence of British forces so necessary, had been removed by the Peace of Paris, and the colonists might pertly question the necessity of keeping up any military establishment whatever. To most of

---

* In 1766, two years before the office of American Secretary was set up, Chesterfield made one of his habitually astute epigrams: 'If we have no Secretary of State with full and undisputed powers for America, in a few years we will have no America.' (H.M.C., *Dartmouth*, iii. 182.)

them a standing army, with its Caroline associations, was hateful. Secure as they now felt themselves to be in their townships, they could not see the slightest reason for tolerating anything so abhorrent to their traditions. To tell them that France was certainly planning a war of revenge and would be likely to strike at Canada was unimpressive. To tell them that there remained still one real danger in their midst, the threat of a Red Indian war, certainly carried more conviction; but only in those districts most likely to suffer. While to the frontiersmen of the middle States the menace of the Redskin was no imaginary one, to others it was something remote. Shoulders were shrugged, excuses were made, and, as usual, the burden was shifted to the broad back of the British Exchequer, which received very little in return. Nor was the burden an inconsiderable one. The line of forts was long and costly, and (what made it the more irksome) it need have been neither one nor the other. Had the colonists, especially the fur traders and land speculators, treated the Indian in an honest and decent fashion, nearly every outpost, with a very few exceptions, might have been evacuated. But Gage, who would have liked nothing better than to have withdrawn his men from the backwoods to the seaport towns, where they would have been more amenable to discipline, felt that the moment the troops were no longer policing the frontier, practices would revive which had in the past caused Indian wars and had incidentally induced the majority of Redskins in the late war to favour the French. Even under the shadow of

British bayonets it was as much as he could do to prevent the peace from being violated.

' The abandoned fellows,' he wrote, ' who trade, and the lawless banditti upon the Frontiers, particularly Pennsylvania, Maryland and Virginia, are ever guilty of some injustice and violence, and the Indians get no satisfaction though some of their tribe should be murdered.' [23] That, over and above bearing the expense of a war which had freed the colonists from the French incubus, at a cost to the Mother Country of something like £100,000,000, and had given them extended markets, the British taxpayer should be called upon to pay for protecting Indians against the colonists, as much as for protecting colonists against Indians, was unreasonable. It might not even be considered politic. Gage seriously considered that: ' If we took less trouble about the savages we should be full as friendly with them (the colonists) as we are now. In short, if the Americans will not pay to save their own scalps, they deserve to lose them.' [24] In other words, to leave the Western frontier defenceless would effectively keep the colonists weak and dependent. However, it having been decided to do otherwise, the problem before the Government was to find a method of passing on a share of this expenditure to the colonists. The number of troops required was estimated at 10,000, and their cost at £300,000.* A scheme for an all-American Parliament responsible for defence had been turned down,

---

* It should be remembered that this sum was no less than a twenty-fifth of the national expenditure. The same proportion in a present day Budget would have been rather more than forty millions.

owing to inter-State jealousies. Application to individual colonies would have raised a cloud of objections. A system of voluntary quotas had already been tried without success.

In reviving an old idea to raise money by the sale of stamped paper George Grenville prided himself on having found an agreeable solution. To him (as to North and to all save a handful of Opposition members) the proposed tax seemed, he told the London agents of the Colonies, equitable and easy to collect. Its entire proceeds moreover were to be earmarked for, and spent within, America which, even then, would by these measures contribute not more than one-third the cost of its protection. Nevertheless Grenville was so anxious to deal fairly by the colonies that, instead of introducing his proposals forthwith he gave them a year in which to put forward for his ' due consideration ' any alternative suggestions. When twelve months had elapsed and nothing feasible had been recommended, the Stamp Act was proposed. It slipped easily and expeditiously through a House, too lethargic to perceive that it was not quite the simple equitable measure Grenville had hinted. The Act ran to fifty-five resolutions by which a tax was raised varying according to the nature of the transaction from one half-penny to ten pounds. Nor were these transactions remote from the life of the ordinary colonist. Tax was to be paid for example on all appointments to office worth more than £20 a year, for marriage licences, retail-liquor licences, for all pamphlets, newspapers, advertisement, deeds of apprenticeship, paper wrappings to playing-cards and dice (the last bearing a stamp of ten shillings), not to mention all contracts, leases, and bills of sale.[25] Introduced piecemeal over a term of years the Act might have succeeded with little more than the grumblings which proceed from the most loyal of subjects when taxed.* But the Stamp Act was not only a formidable measure in itself; it was a novel one. The prospect of being taxed right and left was for the Americans alarming enough without the introduction of a new factor. It was not only that it was the first, and they feared that if successful it would not be the last, attempt at direct or internal taxation. Hitherto they had seen their liberties threatened principally by royal Prerogative in the person of the Governor. With the Stamp Act they came face to face with a power which, though it had played little part in the internal life of the country, was infinitely more formidable than the King's representative. The Governor they knew pretty well how to circumvent; with Parliament it was different. If the rights of this body to impose taxation internally from a distance of three thousand miles were admitted it seemed to them they must lie defenceless for all time. Previous Parliamentary legislation such as the Mutiny, Molasses and Navigation Acts had principally affected New York and the sea-port towns; but the Stamp Act involved the whole country while particularly in-

---

* Notwithstanding its widespread incidence there are grounds for believing that the Stamp Act would have provoked no very great resistance had it not been for the recent unpopular measures taken to put down smuggling and their effect upon American commercial classes along the sea-board. Cf. Schlesinger, 66.

censing its three most influential bodies, the lawyers, the merchants and the journalists. So widespread indeed and unanimous was the feeling aroused that it infected many who, like Dulany, eventually became loyalists and suffered for their faith.

As mail after mail brought home advices of fierce and unprecedented opposition, the King and his Parliament might excusably profess astonishment. If prominent and patriotic Americans like Jared Ingersoll of Connecticut, John Hughes of Pennsylvania and Richard Lee of Virginia had been willing to accept office as agent for the sale of the stamps,[26] it seemed not unreasonable to conclude the agitation to be purely factious and capricious. But in their ignorance of America statesmen at home reasoned incorrectly. Opposition to the Stamp Act was neither fortuitous nor was it transient; rather it was symptomatic of that undercurrent which was every year bearing the colonies farther away from the Mother Country. In the clash of conflicting ideas, sentiments, and aspirations a stone of offence was bound to be unearthed sooner or later. What Grenville's Stamp Act did was, in the opinion of a political opponent, merely to anticipate by twenty years or more the inevitable struggle.[27]

Faced by these unexpected developments inherited from Grenville, the Rockingham administration, after much hesitation and many a heart-burn, repealed the Stamp Act. Except amongst the merchants threatened by an American boycott of British goods, there was so much prejudice against and so little feeling favourable to the colonial attitude[28] that it was possible to pass the repeal only by yoking it to an Act declaratory of Britain's right to bind the colonies ' in all cases whatsoever.'

The immediate sentiments of North towards the Stamp Act and its repeal are unrecorded in any speech or letter. But from later pronouncements it is not difficult to deduce his opinion at the time. He viewed America in the same half-light as his King, who in turn may fairly be said, in this as in so many other questions, to have represented the vast majority of his subjects. In his defence of the unpopular cider tax two years previously, he had shown that he believed in ' a steady, manly resistance to the impatience of those who want to ease themselves of the burthens left by the war.' [29] Not knowing that Americans—especially the inhabitants of Massachusetts—were heavily taxed by their own local legislatures, he had no difficulty in persuading himself that arguments which applied to a country where the burden of Imperial taxation was 25s. a head, applied with crushing weight to one where it appeared to be but 6d.[30] He did not wish to draw, nor did he think it possible to draw, a considerable revenue from the colonies; but he did feel, as a sorely taxed land-owner and citizen, that they should co-operate in a fair proportion to the expenses of the Empire.[31] He felt that the Stamp Act judiciously achieved this purpose, as it ' interested every man who had any legal dealings or any property to defend or recover.' [32] The vote he gave on its behalf was one of principle which a year later he saw no reason for revising—no reason, that is, except force, and force to North was never an argument. To give way to threats by the colonies was to introduce ' anarchy and dissolution into American policy.' He therefore opposed the repeal (although apparently he did not himself speak against it) and never repented of having done so. To it he afterwards attributed, and with some reason, the source of so much calamity. Its lesson, he believed, was never lost upon the colonists. They took to heart the efficacy of their non-importation agreements and the strength which comes from united effort. They learned that they might, with impunity, make a long nose at the majesty of Parliament, and the luxury of such a sensation was not readily abandoned. The rejoicings and bunting which followed the news of the repeal and were continued every anniversary until the war, might well be regarded as due to a desire to keep alive the memory of so successful a triumph rather than as an indication of heartfelt gratitude. Moreover, to prove the truth of North's anticipations, in Boston, the storm centre, the repeal failed to have any sedative effects, and even in New York continued outrages and bloodshed shocked and oppressed the friends of America.

' The moderation and forbearance hitherto shown by Great Britain has been,' Gage reported a year or so later, ' construed to timidity, and serves only to raise sedition and mutiny to a higher pitch.' [33] North could not have expressed the thoughts which troubled his mind more succinctly. With his long Treasury training, he had all the civil servant's horror of creating a precedent. If the colonists set up a claim that the Stamp Act was the thin end of a wedge of systematic internal taxation, he had a ready reply that repeal was equally a wedge splitting asunder the framework of Empire. If, in the face of agitation, one Act was repealed, why not all? Why not the Mutiny Act, why not every Revenue Act applying to America, and even that Palladium of British Liberty, the Navigation Laws? To have modified the Stamp Act and then, when America had quietly submitted, to have repealed it out of consideration for the colonists would have been to achieve the same result as Rockingham had done, but in a very different manner, and (he believed) with very different results.

Sincere or otherwise, the rejoicings over the repeal of Grenville's Stamp Act were soon damped down by the news of Townshend's tax upon lead, glass, paint, paper and tea. These new taxes were supposed to pander to the susceptibilities of the Americans, who, Franklin had assured the Ministry, would not question the power of Parliament to impose external duties for the purposes of regulating imperial trade. Commissioners were appointed for carrying out the Act and, at the same time, for sealing up loopholes through which the colonists had hitherto escaped the provisions of the Mutiny and Navigation Acts, to the detriment of the British taxpayer. From the estimated yield of £40,000 from his taxes, Townshend proposed to pay the salaries of governors and judges, thus removing one fruitful cause of friction, and at the same time usefully strengthening the executive. Any balance was to go to the defence of the colonies. The absurdity of taxing British exports—for this is what it amounted to—seemed to have escaped everyone in the Government but North, and he, not yet being in the Cabinet, probably did not think it of any use to object.

Thus, once more, the British Government played into the hands of the extremists, who in press, pulpit and market-place, had not been idle since the Stamp Act. As usual, Massachusetts took the lead. Non-importation, so successful in the past, was immediately revived; but because they did this in a more sober manner, to Camden, at least, the attitude of the colonists seemed more menacing than in 1765.[34] Even more sinister, though at the time less spectacular than the boycott, was the circular letter which the same indomitable Massachusetts sent round to other provinces, ostensibly asking for advice, but by implication suggesting concerted measures. Unanimity in action was still some years ahead, but from New Hampshire to Georgia there appeared unanimity in determination, actively or passively expressed, not to submit to the Townshend Revenue Acts. While the struggle was a fiscal one with Parliament, few colonists, however strongly Tory, supported the authority of the British legislature. According to one traveller, scarcely one in a hundred was not firm on this point, and ready to argue that they had as much right to fight for what they considered liberty as the people of Great Britain had done a century or more earlier.[35] Nor did anything contribute more to keep this spirit at a steady level than the appearance of the famous Farmers' Letters of John Dickinson of Pennsylvania. Written in a simple, homely idiom, abounding in

P

question-begging epithets, they brought the issues from the counting-house and the committee room to the hearth and the backwoodsman's shack.

While Dickinson's readers were being told that any tax levied upon the colonies was bad, and were being urged not to become as ' abject slaves as France or Poland can show in wooden shoes and with uncombed hair,' the direction of their affairs passed from the hands of the Earl of Shelburne, whose American sentiments had harmonized with those of his friend and patron, the Earl of Chatham. In 1768, probably too late to be effective, an American Department was at last carved out of the Southern Secretaryship, and the Earl of Hillsborough appointed to the office. Nevertheless, it was a step in the right direction, and for all Shelburne's eclipse, not an unpromising one. Hillsborough had voted against the Stamp Act [36] and Franklin believed that his present inclinations were still favourable towards America. There was even a rumour that he would engage the American savant himself as his private secretary.[37] Hillsborough, moreover, was what Shelburne was emphatically not, a personal friend of North, who lost no time in persuading him of the uncommercial nature of Townshend's taxes. Between them, they had actually decided on a general repeal, when advices from America suddenly took a grave turn.[38] Townshend's measures to render effective the Revenue Laws had touched Boston more vitally than any other American town. The efficient manner in which the Commissioners were carrying out their duty threatened its smuggling merchants with ruin. The seizure of a sloop belonging to one of the prominent townsmen, by name Hancock, brought matters to a head. An inspired mob grew out of hand. Officers were tarred and feathered; others were manhandled; the civic authorities could not or would not raise a finger. In fear of their lives, the Commissioners fled the city.

Here was an entirely new situation, calling for entirely different treatment. The very suggestion of physical compulsion by those whom he honestly believed to be in the wrong, or at least misguided, was enough to make the amiable peace-loving North don the mail shirt of a crusader. To admit that there was something stronger than law was to admit the existence of something more authoritative than Parliament. To acknowledge that Parliament was not omnipotent was to rip the Constitution, the pride of the human race, from top to bottom. ' I hope,' he cried, ' we shall abide by the Declaratory Law and neither to-day nor at any future period repeal an Act of Parliament in consequence of any resistance the Americans may give to it.' [39] All thought of concession was now drowned in a spate of resolutions condemning the proceedings of the Colony of Massachusetts as of ' a most unwarrantable and dangerous nature, calculated to inflame the minds of His Majesty's subjects in other colonies.' [40] Troops were ordered to Boston, since the authorities there were powerless, and a police force there was none. The venom of the Bloomsbury Gang even caused an old statute of Henry VIII to be revived whereby American sedition-mongers might be brought to England for trial.

Whatever North's prejudices against repeal, and his refusal to be driven to it by downright force,[41] they could not override economic considerations. Nothing the Americans could do or say would render intrinsically unsound taxes commercially sound. Townshend's duties North had always considered to have been ' preposterous,' and he even confessed it was beyond his comprehension how they ever came to pass an English House of Commons.[42] A tax on British manufacturers must damage what was only less sacred than the British Constitution—British Trade. Moreover, much as Members of Parliament might resent favours granted to ungrateful and insubordinate colonies, yet if the invariable response to a tax for raising revenue was a ruinous trade boycott, such a tax must go. The Cabinet agreed and in a circular letter to the American governors Hillsborough not only stated that all duties (with one exception) would be repealed, but that it was not the Government's intention to lay any further taxes on America for the purposes of raising a revenue.[43] Yet it was very far from being their intention to give up all thoughts of raising contributions for imperial purposes from America.[44] To preserve their rights while the colonies were being approached with this object, the Tea Tax, which North considered perfectly sound commercially, was, by a majority vote of one in the Cabinet, retained agreeable to the maxim that favours once granted can never be recalled. Though North had some ' personal reasons,' probably connected with Dartmouth, for wishing to repeal the tea as well as the other taxes, he regarded its retention as vital if Britain was not, for all time, to lose all rights over her colonies. Had he felt that these would have been truly grateful for such a capitulation, and not have taken it as a precedent, he would certainly have voted with Grafton, Camden and Conway, and so carried the complete repeal of the Townshend duties. But, as he had already complained, every concession from home had been taken for weakness, and followed by further demands all tending to impair the imperial tie. At this moment, to remove an altogether irreproachable tax in response to popular outcry, would be to capitulate to extremists who were patently aiming at an independence which even so fervent a friend to the colonies as Shelburne believed would mean the ruin of Britain.[45]

This was North's difficulty. Where was one to put a term to American pretensions? Already there were demands that every Revenue Act from the accession of Charles II should be repealed. What would then remain?* It is as easy to deride a paltry threepence a pound imposed on tea and reckoned to bring in only three hundred pounds in a year, as it is to sneer with Rockingham at this ' uncommercial, unproductive peppercorn rent.'† [46] But it is not so easy to believe that a man of North's financial capabilities could consent to retain a tax

---

* The Duke of Richmond, too, the most extreme of American partisans, had declared to Burke that if Britain gave up her sovereignty she gave up her trade and her wealth. (Burke, *Corr.*, ii. 30.)

† Or with Burke at ' so paltry a sum in the eyes of a financier, so insignificant an article as tea in the eyes of a philosopher,' which ' has shaken the pillars of a commercial Empire that circled the whole globe.' (*P.H.*, xvii. 1222.)

so trivial and risk consequences so grave unless
some principle was at stake on which he believed
the prosperity, if not the very life, of his country
depended. As long as the tax was on the statute
book and enforced, so long would there be a symbol
of colonial dependence upon the Mother Country.
But if, as Grenville declared, ' Great Britain gives up
her right of taxation, she gives up her right of sovereignty, which is inseparable from it in all ages and
in all countries.' [47] Sovereignty, it was considered,
must either be absolute or else it did not exist. As
Johnson put it: ' In sovereignty there are no grada-
tions.' Authority divorced from the power to tax
was to the statesmen of George III clearly a contradiction in terms. When a member of the Commons
declared that ' A peppercorn in acknowledgment of
right is of more value than millions without ' it
was felt that here was a complete answer to the
Marquis of Rockingham, and not a piece of impolitic bombast.[48] An association of ' autonomous
communities within the British Empire, equal in
status, in no way subordinate to one another in any
respect of their domestic or external affairs, though
united by common allegiance to the Crown,'*
would have been entirely meaningless to North
and his generation. Nor, in the composition of the
House of Commons and the state of communications
then existing, would such a formula have proved
workable. Unless there was commercial advantage
to the Mother Country or due acknowledgment of
her sovereign rights (and that all these implied), an
empire upon such a basis would have been accept-

* *Resolution of the Imperial Conference*, 1926.

able neither to the old Mercantile nor to the new Chatham Imperialist School. George III spoke for every Member of Parliament with hardly an exception when he declared: ' Distant possession standing upon an equality with the superior state is more ruinous than being deprived of such connexions.' [49] But, while it was easy enough to state the alternative coldly on paper, where was the statesman who could come forward and solemnly propose the amputation of a limb which was, as North and all parties readily agreed, ' the basis of the wealth and power of the Kingdom.'

If there could be no compromise from the British standpoint, there could be equally none from the American. When the Speaker from the Massachusetts House of Assembly told Hutchinson that: ' If Parliament could bind the colonies they were all slaves,' he was making an assertion which was just as positive and just as representative as the King's.[50]

It was in this inability of either side to admit of compromise that lies the essence of the tragedy to which Britain and her American colonies were now hastening.

.   .   .   .   .

By a strange coincidence, on the very day, almost at the very hour, when North was deploring his inability, owing to American behaviour, to remove, for the present, the duty on tea, there occurred on the Rope Walk an incident which by gross distortion of fact became known throughout the whole American continent as the Boston Massacre. A small body of soldiers, taunted and

assailed beyond endurance, opened fire upon a mob
of roughs, five of whom fell dead.   At the trial and
acquittal of the soldiers it became abundantly clear
that the shooting was done in self-defence. Already,
before this climax, the commercial classes and those
with a stake in the country had begun to falter; they
had now ample excuse for doing so. The wave of
indignation which had at first passed across the
colonies was, outside New England, quickly subdued
by the feeling that Samuel Adams and his fellow
extremists had overreached themselves in their
exciting of mob passions. When subsequently the
news arrived that all duties but that on tea had been
repealed, it was willingly embraced as an occasion
to forgive and forget. There was even some
reaction in favour of the Mother Country. Gage,
to his surprise, could hear of no ill-humour anywhere,
and even in Boston a tendency to let bygones be
bygones showed itself in subscription balls where
British officers and American merchants danced to
the same measures.[51] But the resistless logic of
American life was already at work, sweeping aside
the merchant and property owner, once in the van
of colonial radicalism, but now rapidly hardening
into Toryism. The struggle, when it revived, was
to be between the Government and the common
people.

.   .   .   .   .

For three years there followed a lull upon the
American continent. It was a period of marking
time rather than of peace. There were occasional
incidents, showing in which direction the wind
was continuing to blow. Gage, on the spot, was

unimpressed, as well he might be. Scrapping
went on as before between the various governors
and their Assemblies, and in 1772 the preventive
schooner *Gaspee* was burnt at Providence.   Nor did
the hearty encouragement which a thoughtless
Opposition were ceaselessly sending across the
Atlantic tend to heal old wounds.   To tell the
colonies that ' Demands which are made without
authority should be heard without obedience ' was
gratuitous if true, and wanton if incorrect.* [52]
Gage might prophesy that, unless Britain exerted
' her near annihilated authority,' the end of her
Empire was in sight, but North, engaged first in
securing his position at home, and then in the affairs
of India, was content to let sleeping dogs lie.
Dartmouth, whom at last he had in 1772 persuaded
to take office as American Secretary in place of
Hillsborough, was certainly not likely, from his own
conciliatory disposition, to give any fresh grounds
for friction.

Nevertheless, that the *status quo* could have continued indefinitely, however circumspect the behaviour of the British Government, can hardly be
believed.   Only the edge of the hatchet was buried:
the haft stood invitingly above ground.   In every
province there remained a hard-working radical

---

* The harm that men like Burke, Wilkes, Pownall and others were doing
by their utterances and correspondence was the subject of frequent complaint from Gage in New York.   In this, however, he was not alone.   In a
memorandum written in 1774, but misdated by Fortescue 1773, George III
wrote:

' Perhaps no one period in our history can produce so strange a circumstance as the gentlemen who pretend to be Patriots instead of acting agreeable to such sentiments, avowing the unnatural doctrine of encouraging the
American colonies in their dispute with their Mother Country.'   (Fort.,
iii. 48.)

ginger-group committed in their hearts to independence. They were canny enough not to rush their slower-witted brethren, but clever enough never to miss an occasion for keeping alive discontent or taking every advantage to further their aims. Thus, for example, a congratulatory address to Dartmouth on his appointment from the Massachusetts Assembly contained a typical sting: this happy omen, they trusted, would be productive of American tranquillity ' consistent with their rights as British subjects.' [53]   This ceaseless stressing of rights to the exclusion of duties was one of the most ominous features in American politics.

That it should have been Lord North himself who provided grounds for an incident which led directly to the war is, when considered in perspective, one of the grimmest jests in history. How could the Prime Minister, how, for that matter, could anyone, have foreseen that ability to drink their cup of Bohea at half the cost to their English brethren would call up a resistance that should prove decisive.[54]   It will be remembered that one of the concessions made to the East India Company at the time of the Regulating Act was liberty to export tea free of duty from their immense stock warehoused in London to America, subject only to the tax of threepence per pound on entering the colonies. The net effect of this was substantially to reduce the price there while at the same time retaining the symbolic right of taxation. As, by this time, the duty, either quietly paid or more or less successfully evaded, had ceased to worry all but the most inexorable, and tea itself was being freely drunk even in dour New England, there could be no ground for believing this concession to American housewives would be received as anything but a favour. It was, as North correctly insisted, ' relief, not oppression.' [55] And so, no doubt, it would have been considered, but for an error of judgment on the part of the East India Company. Instead of consigning their tea to established American merchants accustomed to handle the commodity, they picked out men known to favour the government. This action wiped out all beneficial effects of the Boston Massacre and once more threw the merchants back into alliance with the irreconcilables. Samuel Adams, with his finger ever on the American pulse, leapt at this favourable conjunction of circumstances to commit his colony and his country to revolution, if not to independence.

If ever there was a deliberately planned and designedly provocative act, it was the Boston Tea Party. Elsewhere, the tea had been prevented from being landed, but no violence had been used. Wanton destruction of property in a century when property was venerated as never before or since met, to the mortification of the Bostonians, with as little approval in America as in Britain. Their brethren elsewhere were a long way from endorsing what John Adams exultingly called an ' epocha ' in history. Their reaction was more akin to Franklin's severe comment upon the proceedings as ' an act of violent injustice.' The merchant class, especially timid in the face of mob action, were already repenting of any renewed encouragement they had given.[56]   The only thing that the British Government therefore had to avoid was the turning of Bostonians into martyrs.   Though they took more than a month to act, and cannot, therefore, be accused of proceeding without deliberation, this is exactly what the Cabinet of Lord North did.   Yet in the circumstances, it should be admitted, any other course would have been so difficult as to have been almost out of the question.   Modern statesmen, assisted by rapid transport, telephonic communications and prompt Royal Commissions, might have dealt with the situation successfully.*   The Ministry of North, hampered by unavoidable delays, the impossibility of getting swift and reliable information, was reasonably certain of doing the wrong thing.   It was perhaps on this that Adams and the Massachusetts extremists were counting.

A highway robbery on Hounslow Heath, it was said, signified more to the country than all the disturbances in America.[57]   Generally speaking, this was so ; but the deliberate jettisoning of fifteen thousand pounds' worth of merchandise could not be overlooked, much less pardoned.   The news of the Tea Party reached London shortly after Parliament had reassembled on January 13, 1774, and shocked the shop-keeping conscience of the nation. Unfortunately, the man who at this critical moment might have successfully advised the Government had just been transmuted into an implacable enemy. As agent for Massachusetts, Pennsylvania, Georgia and New Jersey, where his son was Royal Governor, Benjamin Franklin had naturally been consulted

* Cf., West Indian Riots, 1937.

upon American affairs, and, it will be remembered, had even been spoken of as Under-Secretary to Hillsborough. As a man of science, who had invented the lightning conductor, and the most eminent of living Americans, he had the entrée to every great house. On one occasion, the rumour that he contemplated returning to America had even distressed North, who, ' very obligingly ' expressed in person his hopes that ' we shall make it worth your while (to stay).' [58] Just when Franklin might have made some return for the hospitality and regard of British society, no such return was any longer wanted or indeed possible. Some months previously there had come from America a printed collection of letters from Thomas Hutchinson, Governor of Massachusetts, to the late Thomas Whately, the friend and sometime private secretary of George Grenville. The letters were private and personal, written, with one exception, before Hutchinson became Governor. Generally their theme had been the factiousness of local agitators (accompanied by some pert pen portraits), the weakness of the executive and the necessity for sterner measures. It is tempting to believe that the fury aroused in Massachusetts by these letters was due largely to Hutchinson's having hit the nail repeatedly on the head. Suspicion of having stolen the letters falling upon a certain John Temple, Whately's brother challenged him to a duel. Luckily no fatality occurred, because at this point no less a person than Benjamin Franklin himself stepped forward to acknowledge that he had despatched these letters to America. They were,

he explained, transmitted under a pledge of secrecy
with the specious intention of proving to the
Massachusetts Assembly that their worst enemies
were not British politicians, but men of their own
flesh and blood.

How far Benjamin Franklin wrote with his
tongue in his cheek is a matter of controversy.   If
he secretly looked forward with confidence to an
independent America, he certainly meant it to be
a friendly and associated America.[59] However
thin Franklin's excuses, his confessed purpose was
achieved. By the most bare-faced of pretexts,
the pledge of secrecy was broken, the letters were
published, and the wrath of the Assembly was
instantly diverted from England to Hutchinson
and his brother-in-law, Peter Oliver. A petition
was thereupon forwarded to the King, praying
that the offenders be instantly removed from
their offices. Precisely at the moment when the
consideration of this petition came before the
Privy Council there arrived the astonishing news
of the Tea Party. The atmosphere was thus
unfavourable enough without one member deter-
mining, out of loyalty to Grenville's friends, to give
the Massachusetts agent the dressing-down of his
life. Although Franklin was not directly involved,
and attended the consideration of the petition rather
as a spectator, Alexander Wedderburn, the Solicitor-
General, directed the full blast of his withering
invective against the ' wily New Englander ' whose
arts surpassed those ascribed by the dramatist to
' the bloody African.' Placing his finger dexter-
ously upon Franklin's really vulnerable spot—the

unexplained means by which he had come into possession of the letters—he continued, in words which for sheer malevolence matched anything which ever came from the lips of Pulteney or Pitt.

' Into what company will the fabricator of this iniquity hereafter go with an unembarrassed face, or with any semblance of the honest intrepidity of virtue? Men will watch him with a jealous eye. They will hide their papers from him and lock up their escritoires. . . . I can compare him only to Zanga in Dr. Young's Revenge. . . .

> ' No, then, 'twas I,
> I forged the letter—
> I disposed the picture.
> I hated, I despised,—and I destroy.'

Such language could not have been heard within the decorous precincts of the Council in the memory of man, and, with one exception, all the Members, the President included, gave themselves up to laughter and applause. Alone of the Privy Councillors, North behaved with decent gravity. Not because there was, according to Sir George Trevelyan, ' something like death in his heart,' but because in his character there is to be found no trace of personal hatred or vindictiveness.

Calm deliberations and suspended judgments were hardly possible following the heats aroused by the Massachusetts Petition and the advices from Boston. When, early in March, North rose to announce the Government's policy, none could have expected and few could have desired moderation. Making the unassailable premise that had the Boston outrage occurred in any foreign port, no question would have been raised against a stern demand for satisfaction, North went on to argue that, in the present instance, satisfaction was not enough: there must be security for the future.[60] Assuming that there could be no other course open to government than ' to punish, control, or yield,' he moved that Parliament should take such measures as might be best calculated to put an immediate stop to the disorders and ensure ' the just dependence of the colonies upon the Crown and Parliament of Great Britain.' [61] The motion, expressed in rather stilted language, was what nine Englishmen out of ten were saying more coarsely in the coffee-houses of the City and ale-houses by the roadside. They, no more than their King or Parliament, could visualize any relationship between themselves and *their* colonies but one of dependence. ' America,' as Mrs. Montagu put it, ' is our child, and a very perverse one.' [62] A province which flouted their King's authority, boycotted their trade, and finally ' canted ' fifteen thousand pounds worth of good British merchandise into the sea, for no apparent reason than that of wantonness, must be taught a lesson.

Parliament correctly interpreted the sentiments of the country in a series of coercive Acts directed against the Colony of Massachusetts Bay. In all of them North did the piloting through the Commons, unwilling only to the extent that ' no method of punishment ever came from him but with great regret.' [63] At the same time he pleaded for unanimity at home, without which he had no hope that any measures would bear success. The occasion was a critical one. Now was the hour

to make a stand, or never: to defy the colonies
with firmness and without fear, or to yield for all
time.[64] Yet, though the proceedings he had in mind
were designedly severe, North was careful to insist
that there was nothing in them inconsistent with
existing law. Parliament's reactions to the Boston
outrage, he urged, should be inspired not by political convenience but solely by policy and by policy
he sincerely endeavoured to proceed.

The first measure was the celebrated Boston
Port Bill. Its outline came from Dartmouth, a
fact which showed how gravely the violence of the
colonists had shocked this genuine friend of America;
its phrasing from the pens of two law officers,
Thurlow and Wedderburn, who had at length
found some subject on which they could agree.[65]   In
introducing it, North made the very obvious comparison with Edinburgh, punished forty years
previously for its Porteous Riots. But whereas
Edinburgh had gone berserk for one night only,
' Boston had been upwards of seven years in riot and
confusion.' As a punishment he therefore proposed
that the port should be closed and the Customs
transferred to Salem, until the town gave evidence
of repentance by making compensation to the East
India Company and giving guarantees for her
future behaviour. At the same time, he expressed
the hope that the lesson it was proposed to mete out
to Boston would not be lost upon America. Though
he admitted disarmingly he was not altogether
happy in these measures, yet, after an unhurried
deliberation, he felt they were the best so far suggested. The Bill at least had one great advantage

in the eyes of a careful Chancellor of the Exchequer; it was cheap. Its provisions could be carried out by three or four frigates only. To have proposed measures that required co-operation with the army would have entailed vast expense; yet, he uttered ominously, he would not have anyone think that to enforce due obedience to the laws of this country he would boggle at the price.[66]

It is not difficult to criticize this, which, more than any single measure, cleared the decks for rebellion; but it is not so easy to offer an alternative which would have been acceptable. The Tea Party with its repercussions strikingly illustrates the difficulties of Empire management before the acceleration of transport and communications. The outrage was six weeks old when the news reached London. Admitting (what even the pro-American party conceded) some punishment to be necessary, if evidence was to be taken, explanation required, and opportunity given for repentance, many months must have passed before a final decision could have been reached. By that time the incident would, so far as America was concerned, have become blurred, and any action taken by way of punishment, however mild, must necessarily have appeared vindictive. The immediate objection too that, however provocative its conduct, North had denied the town a chance of repentance was more apparent than real. Any belief that Boston would be prepared to see the error of its ways received a crushing set-back when the news presently came that there had occurred, towards the end of February, a *second* Tea Party, although on a smaller scale.* Any suggestion that the first outrage had been committed on the spur of an angry moment and was already being regretted was no longer possible. North might well ask ' Is this seeing their error? Is this reforming? Is this making restitution to the East India Company? Surely no gentleman will, after this, urge anything in their defence.' [67]

The second item on the Ministry's coercive agenda was a Bill for regulating the Government of Massachusetts. This was a proposal designed, North explained, to purge its Constitution of its ' crudities,' and to give ' strength and spirit to the civil magistracy and to the executive power.' *Quis custodiet ipsos custodes?* When those in whose hands lay the civil power were the ones most actively engaged in rioting or inciting to riot, there must patently be ' a total defect in the constitutional power throughout.' Were they then to sit still and deny the Governor their support, while His Majesty's subjects were being tarred and feathered, or remain unconcerned while all authority was being flouted and all advice spurned? But, until the executive authority was vindicated and control removed from the democratic parts of the Government, it was idle for Parliament to attempt any regulations for the colony. Under the Government of Massachusetts Bill the Governor would have power to appoint all officers exercising civil authority, to nominate all members of the Council, and to curb the freedom of local assemblies.[68]

* This damaging event is very properly mentioned by Stanhope, vi. 6, but is completely ignored by Lecky, Trevelyan, and by even the impartial Van Tyne.

Massachusetts, in fine, having declined to be ruled
by kindness, must be ruled by management.[69]

The third measure—a Bill for the impartial
administration of justice—was a corollary of the
second. It was equally futile to reform the magis-
trature while juries were empanelled upon a system
which made too probable the acquittal of any
homespun agitator and the conviction of any
servant of the authorities. Juries elected upon a
popular vote—grand-jurors for life, petty jurors for
a twelvemonth—could hardly fail to suffer from
local bias. As some violence, perhaps resulting
in bloodshed, might result from the enforcement of
the coercive Acts, or the suppression of riots, it
would not be fair to ask men to undertake duties
without the assurance that, should they be accused
of assault, or even of murder, they should have a
fair trial.*[70] Under this Bill the Governor was to be
empowered to send an accused for trial either to a
neighbouring colony, or, in extreme cases, to
England. If precedent were required for so exceptional a measure, it could be found, North explained,
in the arrangements made for trying the Scottish
rebels of the Forty-Five in England.[71]

The Governor chosen to function under these
Acts and to supervise their enforcement was General
Gage, now at home on leave, who in a careless
moment had rejoiced the King's heart by promising
to bring Boston to heel with four battalions of
infantry.

---

* It is the case that Captain Preston was acquitted on such a charge at the
time of the Boston Massacre so-called. But much had happened since
1770 further to inflame passions ; nor could everyone rely upon being able
to persuade John Adams to be counsel for the defence.

North's plea for unanimity had not been made in vain. All three Bills were passed by formidable majorities, the Opposition being hopelessly divided by Boston's misbehaviour. Cheered by this gratifying endorsement North hoped, though not over-confidently, that his measures would achieve their purposes. The sooner they did so, the sooner could he allow his merciful instincts full play. ' We are now (he said) to establish our authority or give it up entirely: when they are quiet and return to their duty, we shall be kind, whether by repealing this tax or what-not, I cannot tell: but this I will answer, that when they are quiet and have respect for the Mother Country, the Mother Country will be good-natured to them.' [72]

Because this was a mistaken attitude to adopt towards a people who, having reached their majority, were demanding a latch-key, it is no reason why it should have been misrepresented. No sinister, concealed purpose lay behind North's penal code, which from first to last was drawn up to apply to what it was hoped were purely temporary circumstances. The King, North, and Parliament would have rejected with contempt any measure which cut down the liberty of a British subject, whether he lived in Massachusetts or in Berkshire. To see America free and happy was the supreme end of their colonial policy, whether regarded through the eyes of the merchant or of the imperialist. But it was freedom construed in a qualified, not an absolute sense: it was freedom under the law and under the Constitution. Outside the British family, America might assuredly be free, but it was felt—and the feeling was shared by a large body of Americans who later suffered for their loyalty—she could be neither prosperous nor happy; while Great Britain, with her Constitution and Empire the envy of the world, and her ships on the seven seas, must, deprived of her American colonies, sink into a power of the second class.*

Nothing more tyrannous underlay the attitude of North towards the colonies than ninety years later determined that of Abraham Lincoln towards the Southern Confederacy. To preserve their respective heritages, no cost, sacrifice or effort was considered to be too great.† For Great Britain, in the interests of their common weal, to expect her colonists to take some trivial share in the cost of their government and defence, to require them to acknowledge the authority of a parent, to punish them if they wilfully misbehaved, could hardly justify the charge, set out in the Declaration of Independence, of seeking ' to reduce them under absolute government.' There is this excuse for Congress, that their declaration was indited at a time of war, but there is little justification for Fox's ceaseless refrain that the successes of the Ministry meant the death of Britain's liberties, or for such claptrap as Horace Walpole was transmitting to Mann, as when half-way through the war he wrote, ' easy am I that so far the ill success of the American

---

* The learned Mrs. Carter was more than half a century ahead of her times when she believed that when colonies wished for independence, the truest policy is at once to give up the struggle. (*Letters*, iii. 31.)

† The analogy cannot, the circumstances being so different, be pursued further but it is worth while considering what Lincoln's reputation would have been to-day had Gettysburg and the Appomattox been for him what Saratoga and York Town had been for North.

War has saved us from slavery.'* If there were any
' badges of slavery ' they were not worn by the free
citizens of New England, but rather by the wretched
denizens crowding those dark satanic mills in the
great unenfranchised towns of industrial England.
If Ministers had been the pliant instruments of
a sovereign determined to aggrandise the power of
the Crown and so threaten the Constitution, they
would have hastened to agree with the colonies
who, in the ten years following the Peace of Paris,
would cheerfully have come to terms with ' the best
of Kings ' behind the back of Parliament.[73] In
attempting, on the contrary, to assert the supremacy
of Parliament, the Ministry was (as North, in fact,
made the extremely neat point), carrying into
practice traditional Whig principles. It was the
colonies who, in their claim to belong solely to the
Crown, were talking the language of the Tories.[74]
But tyranny was a good word with a wealth of
classical antecedents. Once resolute separatists
like Samuel Adams, Patrick Henry and Christopher
Gadsden, were able to persuade their countrymen
that neither their pockets nor their consciences were
safe, the conviction that Parliamentary legislation
affecting the colonies was unconstitutional, illegal,
and therefore tyrannical, followed as a matter of
course.

If, despite his hopes to the contrary, North by
his string of Acts contributed to the ultimate loss of
America, he must be allowed to have saved Canada.

*There is even less excuse a hundred years or more later for Trevelyan's
dilating upon ' a tyranny which was trampling out English liberty in the
colonies.' (C. J. Fox, 555.)

While his coercive Bills were passing through
Parliament, he fearlessly introduced and carried the
Quebec Act.   Although this great and statesmanlike measure was principally the work of Sir Guy
Carleton, the Governor of Quebec, it had lain with
North either to carry it into effect or, as Newcastle
in the circumstances would certainly have done,
to pigeon-hole it until too late.   The Quebec Act,
the culmination of so much thought and labour,
was the implementing of the fourth article of the
Treaty of Paris which had handed Canada over
to Great Britain.   The Roman Catholic inhabitants
of the ceded province, who, as late as 1774, out-
numbered British settlers by something like four
hundred to one, were to be allowed to profess their
faith freely and their clergy to enjoy tithe, subject
only to the supremacy of the King.   Religion was
to be no disqualification for the holding of property
or for membership of the executive Council, on
which it was North's intention that the minority
should be French-Canadian Roman Catholics.
The establishment of an Assembly was for the
moment held in abeyance.   On this, Roman
Catholics would naturally have an overwhelming
majority, and there was, North feared, ' something
in that religion which made it not prudent in a
Protestant Government to establish an Assembly
consisting entirely of Roman Catholics.' [75] English Law, with trial by jury, was to be introduced
in criminal cases.   In all other causes, French law
and custom, in which there was no jury, were to
hold.   Finally the boundaries of Canada were to be
extended southward to the Ohio and westward to

the Mississippi in order to embrace eighty thousand French settlers in those parts.

So incensed had the irreconcilable element of the Opposition become at North's coercive Acts, that they refused to believe anything good could come out of his portfolio. In deference to the colonies, where objection to the Act was hardly less violent than to the penal laws, they were prepared to tolerate an injustice to Canada, as well as a breach of faith on the part of their own country. Chatham, who had done so much towards the acquiring of Canada, now, in his tenderness to the New England conscience, raved against this ' child of inordinate power,' [76] and strove to make their Lordships' flesh creep by picturing an arbitrary Governor packing his Council with none but Roman Catholics. If North had listened to such unstatesmanlike rant-ings, the American Revolution would have been delayed by not so much as a day; but Canada would have been lost to the Crown for ever. To his lasting credit, the Prime Minister, who had declined to tamper with the Thirty-nine Articles, and was shortly to reject as untoward a proposal to grant commissions to Roman Catholic citizens, remained inflexible.

.   .   .   .   .

North believed, on information which he later acknowledged to be false, that the colonies would not ' take fire ' at the punishment meted out to Boston. On the contrary, once it was proved that Britain was not afraid to control, he was convinced obedience would follow. The bluff of the agitator had only to be called for the American ferment to

subside. ' Let us,' he said, ' conduct ourselves
with firmness and resolution throughout the whole
of these measures, and there is not the least doubt
that peace and quietude will soon be restored.' [77]

It was a most unfortunate prophecy. If Members
recollected these words in the black years that lay
ahead, they remembered too that ominous sentence
which had closed the speech of an independent
Member who had rarely voted against the Government. ' If ever there was a nation running headlong to its ruin, it is this.' [78]

When the news of the coercive Acts reached
America (by a strange mockery in the ship *Harmony*) there arose from New Hampshire to Florida
a howl of indignation. The cause of Boston became
the cause of America. Resentment, for some
strange reason, was more outspoken in other
colonies than in Massachusetts. The scrapping of
her Charter and the elimination of local juries
was, by skilful propaganda, despite North's express
pronouncement that the Acts were directed against
Massachusetts, ' the ringleading province,' made to
appear so many precedents which an arbitrary
government would, at the first favourable opportunity, seek to apply to other provinces. When a
few weeks later, the news came that the Quebec Act
has been passed, it was received as additional proof
of the Ministry's infamous conduct. Although
North had been careful to stress the fact that the
Act affected no part of America regularly planted by
British settlers,[79] its preamble establishing the boundaries of Canada on the Mississippi and the Ohio
incensed the Middle Colonies. Its toleration of

Roman Catholicism infuriated New England. Popery now became bracketed with slavery as the badges which an unscrupulous British Government were seeking to impose upon the colonies. Under the successive blasts of land-greed and religious bigotry, the American furnace burnt to a white heat.

Throughout the summer of 1774, events moved towards their inevitable end with gathering momentum. Gage, as Governor of Massachusetts, soon proved, as George III was the first to admit, unequal to the task.[80] The Committees of Correspondence between the colonies, that had functioned at the time of the Stamp Act, were revived, and by September the first Continental Congress had assembled in Philadelphia. This illegal body resolved to suspend all trading with Britain until grievances were redressed: in other words until every Act affecting America passed since 1763 should be repealed. To ensure that these Resolutions were to be more than pious homilies, an Association was set up to see that they were carried out. Finally, it despatched addresses to the King and the peoples of Great Britain. The conservative element was just strong enough to ensure that the wording was tactful. There were reference to ' Your Majesty's faithful subjects ' and to ' affection to our parent state,' but it was a mere playing with words before a back-cloth of unreality. In New England, in much of Virginia, and in New York, they were under no illusions. Drilling was openly taking place on village greens; patriots were cleaning their muskets. In the streets Tories were insulted and assaulted—if John Adams had had his way they would have been hanged from the nearest tree [81]—and at the very moment Congress was lisping its loyalty, cannon and munitions were secretly on their way from Europe.[82] The King was still spared because he was regarded as ' a deluded monarch.'* The villain was Parliament and the arch-villain Lord North, ' cursed from morn till noon and from noon till morn by every denomination of people.' [83]

In the face of such open preparations there were two courses only open to the Imperial Government —to resist or to give way. As between the two it was impossible for any British statesman to hesitate. To give way would, as North admitted, have ended the dispute there and then, for the very good reason that America would become virtually independent and an Empire acquired at so much labour and cost lost for ever.[84] From such a prospect even the great Chatham shrank in horror. Moreover, soaked as they were in the sacrosanctity of the Revolutionary settlement, and firmly believing that ' the whole of our political system depends upon the preservation of its great and essential parts distinctly, and no part is so great and essential as the supremacy of the legis- lation,'† the Cabinet were bound to resist what they considered a challenge to Parliamentary govern- ment as well as to the Constitution and unity of

---

* His health was even drunk in a Connecticut Volunteers' Mess several weeks after Bunker Hill, and for some time to come Washington spoke of the *Ministerial*, not the British, army.

† The words are not from the pen of any reactionary Tory but from that of General Burgoyne, a stout Whig, and, after Saratoga, an inveterate opponent of the Ministry. (Quoted by Fonblanque, 171.)

the Empire. When the King in the face of New England's open arming declared that ' Blows must decide,'[85] he was merely putting in his pithy and logical manner what his Ministers were taking several hours of Parliament's time to propound. When he went on to declare that he was fighting the battle of his legislature he was saying what in their hearts all but the extreme members of the Opposition must believe.[86]

While New England was becoming one vast camp and Gage was virtually a prisoner in Boston, North, availing himself of the privilege of his office, advised a dissolution.*[87] The fact that the General Election was premature by six months and caught the Nabobs and the Opposition unawares, cut both ways.† Preparations which every Government habitually made for such an event were impossible, and North in consequence feared a much reduced majority.[88] But a rising tide of patriotism (although still far too sluggish for the Premier's liking) was too strong for the Opposition. The election—one of the least corrupt for many years—thoroughly endorsed the Government's policy towards America. Taking a most conservative figure, North was able, in a House containing 170 new faces, including those of Gibbon, Wilkes, and forty young Etonians, to count on three hundred and twenty-one as certain out of five hundred and fifty-eight in all.[89]

The result of the General Election was to North

* Gage's earlier tune of four battalions was quickly altered to twenty thousand soldiers, ' regulars, German huntsmen, picked Canadians and three or four regiments of light horse.' (*Barrington MSS.*)

† And incidentally cost Charles Fox, who had betted George Macartney Parliament would not be dissolved before Christmas, a hundred guineas. (*Brooks' Betting Book.*)

like the draught of physic no self-indulgent eighteenth-century statesman failed to take at frequent intervals. It cleared away the humours that had been settling on his spirit. He became now as confident as the King that the Mother Country having spoken in no equivocal manner, the colonies would see the wisdom of submitting.[90] This confidence, confirmed by reports from colonial governors contemning any possibility of armed resistance, together with his own confessed difficulty of reaching any arrangement to stave off war without overdoing concession,[91] caused him to face the new Parliament—to the wrath of his die-hard friends—without any plan whatsoever.[92] The Government having declared their intentions, the next step, he declared, must now come from the colonies. But at the same time, to show how entirely averse he was from wielding the big stick, or in any way making a provocative and irrevocable step, he insisted on reducing the armed forces. The navy, already weak, was cut down from 20,000 to 16,000 men.[93]

But nothing came from America save the tramp of armed men and—now that it was too late— alarming reports from the colonial governors. It was no longer possible to remain passive. On the second day of February, in a speech of unusual length, in which he reviewed the whole American situation, North concluded by proposing that His Majesty be requested to enforce obedience to the laws of Britain and the supremacy of her Parliament. Yet, still unwilling to seal up the last loophole, he declared that he would listen to any reasonable proposition and, provided America would allow Britain her constitutional right of taxation (which she had no longer any intention of enforcing), the quarrel might forthwith be concluded.[94] Four days later, under pressure it may be presumed from his more violent colleagues, he moved, it is true, that the recalcitrant New England provinces be restrained from trading with the British Isles and their fishermen from the Newfoundland Banks. But here, too, he showed his dislike of such provocative measures by insisting on limiting the period of their operation, and doubting whether it would be possible to limit their scope to New England. Should this restriction have to be applied, as he feared, to Virginia and the other colonies, war must be immediate and certain.[95] While there remained one chance of avoiding this deplorable conclusion without loss of prestige, North would take it. On February 20, he introduced his Conciliation Bill.

This was merely a development of his early contention that nothing but an acknowledgment of Britain's bare rights stood in the way of peace. While the authority of this country was in dispute, Parliament could enter into no negotiations, agree to no compromise. As soon as any province consented to contribute a quota to the common defence of the Empire, the administration of its justice and the support of its government, then the supreme rights of the Imperial Parliament would be implicitly recognized and North would undertake to levy no duty or tax save those necessary for the regulation of commerce. These terms would preserve

the unity of the Empire, meet certain reasonable prejudices in the colonies, and enable the
more lukewarm provinces to break away from the
thraldom of Massachusetts.   Still North offered no
opinion as to the likelihood of his ' auction plan '
proving acceptable, confining himself to a declaration that in the event of its being rejected blood
must lie on the head of the colonists. [96]   Chatham
might scoff at the Conciliation Bill as ' a mere ver-
biage and a most puerile mockery ' and at the same
time he was not far wrong. On the other hand it
was an infinitely more statesmanlike measure than
his own Bill a few weeks later, which was based on
a misconception of the colonial situation greater
even than North's.   Introduced ten years earlier
the latter's proposals might (for a time) have
provided a solution.   In the early spring of 1775
they satisfied neither the friends of America nor
her critics.

   To the Opposition, the most sinister feature in
North's Conciliation Bill was the inducement held
out to the milder colonies to yield.   Based on ' that
low, shameful, abominable maxim *divide et impera*,'
it threatened, in their opinion, to split up America
and break down that ' generous union in which the
Americans stand as one man in defence of their
rights and liberties.' [97]   To the men of North's own
party the Bill was a shameful capitulation to the
twin forces of violence and faction.   North, who
had expected opposition from every side, laboured
hard to justify himself.

   ' If there be any persons (he said) who think we ought
to make no advances towards accommodation because

they understand such to be a concession which we ought not to make—if there be any who think the terms which this Resolution holds out are disadvantageous, I would not wish them to agree to it. But they will give me leave (who think that even were we to impose terms in the hour of victory itself, this proposition would be a just one) to propose it now, before any blood is shed.' [98]

Between the mortification of the bellicose Bedford group on one side and the rage of Barré, Burke, Fox and others on the other, North fought desperately. Six times he rose to appease the storm and for two hours it seemed he must be overwhelmed. Then Sir Gilbert Elliot, hitherto uncompromising in his attitude towards colonial aspirations, declared definitely for the Prime Minister, and the Bill was carried.

Critics on both sides of the Atlantic, as well as North himself, might have spared their breath. Had proposals been lenient or stern, simple or involved, the course of future events would scarcely have been modified in a single detail. Before the Act could be digested in America, blood which North had hoped so fervently to avoid had been shed plentifully and in earnest. On April 19, a British force sent by Gage to destroy a cache of arms at Concord was waylaid and attacked at Lexington on its return to Boston. Two hundred and seventy-three officers and men were killed, wounded or missing.* The war had begun.

* An illustration of the degree to which faction could go, thereby justifying the King's loathing and North's contempt of the Opposition, is shown by the collecting under the auspices of John Horne of £100 for the relief of the widows, orphans and aged parents—not of the poor ambushed Red-Coats—but ' of our beloved American subjects inhumanly murdered at or near Lexington.' (Quoted Hertz, *Old Colonial Systems*, 152.)

R

Chapter VII

THE AMERICAN WAR

' The American War is held up to our view as if it had been the war of the Crown, in contradiction to the wishes of the people. I deny the fact. It was a war of Parliament, sanctioned throughout its whole progress by both Houses. It was more. It was the war of the People, undertaken for the purpose of maintaining their rights over the dependencies of the Empire.'

WRAXALL, iii. 407.

' The American War was a constitutional war: it was a popular war.'

NORTH, *P.H.*, xix. 607.

No sooner had the dispute with the American colonies become an affair of muskets and generals than it tended to recede into the background of Lord North's life. It became a disturbing, unhappy, and at times exceedingly sombre background; but it bore little direct relationship to the pathetic, often bewildered, figure in the foreground. Once the gloves were off, the initiative necessarily passed from North. His principal concern was to meet unprecedented demands upon the Exchequer and to repel the ceaseless assaults of the Opposition. In the Cabinet where, on his own confession, he was at the best of times unable to choose between the clashing opinions of his colleagues, he made fewer decisions than ever.[1] Possessing neither the driving force nor the imperious personality necessary to control a Ministry under war conditions, he co-operated rather than

directed, he advised rather than resolved. Decked
out with all the trappings of authority, he enjoyed
increasingly less of its realities. The war became
George Germain's war, Lord Sandwich's war, King
George's war, before it could be considered, if,
indeed, at all, Lord North's war. Anything like
a consecutive account of the struggle forms, therefore, no part of his life, as it must that of Germain
or Sandwich. Events in America are of importance
only in so far as they affected North personally and
ministerially.

If the American War brought to North nothing
but distress of mind; if he suffered privately for
what, publicly, he had little power to prevent; if in
the closing stages he even saw its futility and hopelessness, it may very properly be asked why he
consented to remain in such uncongenial surroundings when Bushey with its lawns and glass-houses
beckoned unceasingly? To the complete eighteenth-
century mind there was only one explanation possible: the emoluments of office outweighed its
vexations.* This point of view, expressed independently by Walpole and Fox,² both in their way
highly representative of their age, is, in North's
case, an increasingly unconvincing explanation the
closer his career is studied. Admittedly his total
emoluments were considerable, but when the
expenses of Bushey, Downing Street, and Dillington had been taken into account, in addition

---

* In *The Duenna* by Israel Pottinger (1776) Boreas (North) chants:
    ' 'Tis true I'd dispense with the post that I hold
    If with it I should not dispense with my gold,
    But avarice seconds ambition so well,
    That I'd follow my old Master *Walpole* to hell.'
The whole play is a laboured, but not unamusing, attack on the Ministry.

to the immense prodigality which in those days it was almost impossible for a public man to avoid, little was left over for luxuries.*[3] Once North had retired—and it would have been clean contrary to practice to have done so without the offer of some substantial pension—once Downing Street and perhaps even Bushey had been given up, his financial straits must cease, and there would be sufficient to live upon in comfort. Moreover, the cynics who so glibly attributed his retention of place to the basest of motives did not know, what is known to-day, that on at least one occasion North offered, in order to keep the Ministry alive, to give up ' the profits, the honours and the future expectations of his situation, and to reserve only the responsibilities and the fatigues of it '; [4] and on another, in order to make things easier for his successor, to retire without honour or even pension.[5] They did not know that when the King, to encourage him, hinted that the longer he stayed in office, the more opportunities he would have of benefiting his family, North replied without art that his duty and attachment to his sovereign required no stimulus.†[6] Nor could they have been aware of the

---

* Shelburne, it is true, believed that a man of rank could live on £5,000— about half what North was getting—and keep up all appearances, but it is doubtful whether this could apply to a man of rank who was also a First Lord of the Treasury. (Boswell, *Johnson*, ii. 200.) Newcastle actually lost money during his years in office, and William Pitt died hopelessly insolvent.

† Nor indeed could they know, who had seen the Newcastle system in its high summer, the limited scope of reward which North, at least for the first six years of his Ministry, had enjoyed. Soon after he became Prime Minister, a regiment was given at his recommendation. It proved unique as late as 1776, when he wrote to Barrington: ' . . . Having seen several military favours granted to the application of my immediate predecessor, I had falsely conceived the notion that I might sometime expect to see the same attention paid to mine, not sufficiently considering that I have no

repeated occasions on which North had pitifully, abjectly, pleaded to be released from the burden of his office. These appeals, at first made at infrequent intervals but, after the disaster of Saratoga, of almost monthly, even weekly, occurrence, were based on three or four themes, played over and over again, separately or in unison.

There was first that of unworthiness. North was not equal to the trust.[7] ' In his conscience he thinks himself incapable so far as having any hopes of seeing them [his King and Country] honourably and happily relieved from their present difficulties.' [8] He therefore cannot ' conceive what can induce His Majesty, after so many proofs of Lord North's unfitness for his situation, to determine at all events to keep him at the head of the administration, though the almost certain consequences of His Majesty's resolution will be the ruin of his affairs.' [9]

These depreciatory reflexions are in the second place varied with purely physical considerations as to why he should be allowed to resign. His memory is gone; his strength exhausted; his capacity worn to a shred.[10] His mind, always weak, has become ten times weaker as the difficulties themselves have increased tenfold.[11] He is thus daily becoming more mentally and physically infirm and ' totally unfit in every respect to cope with the ardours and difficulties of his situation.' [12] Abject as was this confession, a year later North finds ' his

pretensions to be put upon the same footing with him. Six years experience have thoroughly convinced me of my error, and your Lordship shall have no longer any reason to complain of molestation on the part of your very faithful, humble servant—North.' (*Barrington MSS.*)

spirits and his frailties both of mind and body
much less equal to his situation than they were
this time twelve month.' [13]

Thirdly, there is the National theme. How can
public business be carried on as it ought, when
those at the head of affairs actively dislike their
situation? [14] ' Every hour convinces me more and
more of the necessity Your Majesty is under of
putting some other person than myself at the head
of affairs.' [15] No arrangement can be so effectual
to the public services as one that shall alter the
person at the head of the Treasury.[16]

The final variation is a resultant of the three
preceding. It is that of remorse. North alone is
guilty of the ruin of his country's affairs. ' For I
must look upon it as a degree of guilt to continue in
office while the Publick suffers and nobody approves
my conduct.' [17] His remaining in office (he is
convinced) ' is to be reckoned among the principal
causes of the present dangerous position of the
Country.' [18] ' What ever he does must be attended
by some disgrace and, what is worse, perhaps,
with some detriment to the Public.' [19] Than
this anguish of mind, better impeachment, better
even capital punishment.[20] As for this, he was
willing to die disgraced for what he could not
prevent, but he pleaded ' let me not go to the grave
with the guilt of having been the ruin of my King
and Country.' [21]

Were these protestations genuine? Charles
Jenkinson, once Bute's private secretary, while
allowing for the immensities of North's labours, was
of the opinion they sprang from an intermittently

LORD NORTH

From a caricature by Boyne

diseased mind.[22] He believed North would carry on as long as he possibly could provided it could be made to appear that he was acting under pressure and was not directly chargeable with failure.[23] John Robinson, North's Secretary at the Treasury, whose views, based on greater intimacy, are entitled to more respect than Jenkinson's, preferred to trace his Chief's despondent moods to private financial worries, but agreed in thinking North had no intention of parting with power.[24] The King, more charitable than his servants, attributed North's fits of gloom exclusively to ill-health, especially about budget time, which, according to North himself, was always one of ' anxiety and labour.' [25] The weakness of the Jenkinson-Robinson is the same as that of the Fox-Walpole theory. North out of office, and pensioned, would not be very much worse off, if at all, than in office. Of the King's more kindly view it may be said that one who invariably knew his own mind could scarcely be a fair judge of another whose mind was a confusion of complexities, and whose spirits rose and fell with the regularity of the tide. To his father and to Dartmouth North unburdened himself in a manner which discounts all artifice, pretence or mere ill-health. To the first he wrote:

' I am almost worn out with continual fretting. It may very possibly be that my uneasiness proceeds from my own faults, but the fact is that so long a continuance in a situation that I dislike, and for which I am neither adapted by temper or capacity, had sunk my spirits, weakened my understanding, impaired my memory, and filled my heart with a kind of uneasiness from which nothing can deliver me but an honourable retreat.' [26]

To Dartmouth, his friend and companion from nursery days, there went out, in one of the blackest hours of the war, a cry straight from the heart: ' I am in a fever with my situation. I have been kept in it by force. If the House falls about my ears I cannot help it. All I can do is not to quit a falling house, and to use every means in my power to sustain it as long as possible.' [27]

If these two letters can be said to prove the sincerity of North's sentiments, the next question that must be faced is why, as a free agent in a free country, did he not insist on ' an honourable retreat '? The answer supplies at once the clue to and the tragedy of North's life.

Since the publication of the King's letters to North the explanation that had seemed most satisfactory—had the facts been known to North's contemporaries it would have seemed completely so—was what might be called the theory of the Gilded Cage. North, in other words, if not actually bribed, was put under such obligations as to make resignation in defiance of the King's wish out of the question.

The story starts on a certain day in September, 1777, when Robinson, in reply to a letter from the King expressing concern at the harassed state of North's mind, wrote: ' Mr. Robinson thinks he perceives what oftentimes adds to Lord North's distress of mind when the weight of public business oppresses him, but that Mr. Robinson durst not on any account presume to mention it to His Majesty without His Majesty's special command.' The King having commanded Robinson to be more explicit, there came four days later a further letter of considerable length, going into details. Ever since he became First Lord of the Treasury (Robinson writes) North's expenditure had considerably exceeded his income.* A variety of causes were blamed: a falling away in his own and Lady North's private income; the largeness and growing expenses of his family; his preoccupation in public affairs making it impossible for him to devote time to private economy; the heavy expenditure incidental to his position. What with this persistent deficit, monies borrowed, debts to tradesmen, and an outstanding mortgage of six thousand pounds, North had told Robinson it would require close on eighteen thousand pounds to clear him and put him at ease; for 'the thought of this situation frequently distresses his mind and makes him very unhappy.' [28]

It was clear to the King that a Minister teased by such anxieties could not be expected to give his best attention to business. Therefore, without any more delay, George III took up his pen and wrote to North.

'*Lord North.* From delicacy I take this method of opening to you an affair that dwells much on my mind, but that I can more easily express on paper to you than in conversation. I have now signed the last Warrant for paying up the Arrears due on my Civil List, and therefore now, and not till now, find myself perfectly at ease, and therefore seize with pleasure this instant to insist on doing the same for you my Dear Lord; you have at times

* In the Robinson Papers there is a rough draft of his first letter to the King containing a sentence subsequently erased giving this annual debit balance as varying between twelve hundred and fifteen hundred a year. (Add. MSS. 33823, f. 208.)

dropped to me that you had been in debt ever since your first settling in life and that you had never been able to get out of that difficulty. I therefore must insist you will now state to me whether 12, or £15,000 will not set your affairs in order, if it will, nay if £20,000 is necessary I am resolved you shall have no other person concerned in freeing them but myself; knowing now my determination it is easy for you to make a proper arrangement and at proper times to take by degrees that Sum. You know me very ill if you do not think that of all the letters I have ever wrote to you this one gives me the most pleasure, and I want no other return but your being convinced that I love you as well as a Man of Worth as I esteem you as a Minister; your conduct at a critical minute I never can forget, and am glad that by your ability and the kindness of Parliament I am enabled to give you this mark of my affection, which is the only one I have ever yet been able to perform; but trust some of the Employments for life will in time become vacant that I may reward your family.

GEORGE R.

Kew. Sept. 19th, 1777.

$\dfrac{M}{46}$ pt. 11 a.m.[29]

If those twenty thousand pounds were really what Sir George Trevelyan calls them, ' his richly gilded chain,' North earned every penny by five years of rarely alleviated anxiety. But from all that is known of his life and character it is impossible to believe that gratitude for a gift specifically given for services rendered could by itself have induced North to continue in harness, when every fibre of his being recoiled at the prospect. A Minister who declined to accept the usual Treasury perquisites of free coals and candles (a very considerable annual item) and paid for these out of his own purse, was

not the type amenable to bribery.[30] Moreover, as no
condition was attached to the King's bounty, clearly
North could have resigned at any time without
feeling he had ignobly repaid his master. That
gratitude did place him under a certain obligation
and supplied an additional reason for acceding to
the King's wishes cannot be doubted. A letter to
Thurlow shortly afterwards makes this abundantly
clear. After referring to his anxiety to retire, and
his determination to do so at the earliest moment,
North went on: ' I am under such obligations to the
King that I can never leave his service while he
desires me to remain in it and thinks I can be of any
use to him, which he possibly may as long as I
continue in the House of Commons.' [31] But to see
in such obligations only gratitude for a gift of money
is to leave out of account two supremely important
factors in North's life—his own character and the
personality of the King.

The incident of Charles Yorke and of North
himself in that memorable month of January, 1770,
had proved the remarkable powers of persuasion
possessed by the sovereign. As then, so in the years
of the American War, he pleaded with all the
passionate and extravagant emotion of which he
was master. To North's timid appeals for release
came counter-appeals, bristling with unequivocal
allusions to ' real duty,' ' affection for my person,'
' the sense of honour which must reside in the breast
of every man born of a noble family.' North was
entreated in a wealth of superlative to stand firmly
at this hour ' to the aid of him who thinks he
deserves the assistance of every honest man': [32]

to deliver him from a set of men who would not only reduce him to a government department and betray the cause of the country, but cruelly proscribe all who had hitherto served their royal master.[33] The King's dexterity as a reader of character enabled him to pierce North's armour as he had pierced Yorke's, by penetrating references to what lay nearest the heart and was perhaps dearer than life: honour and duty. North had only to mention resignation to be reminded that ' he who so very handsomely stepped forth on the desertion of the Duke of Grafton would lose all merit by following so undignified an example ';[34] or to be told with less circumlocution that such a step ' though thought necessary to him, is very unpleasant to me,'[35] or was ' highly unbecoming at this hour '[36] or even ' productive of evil,'[37] or to be asked (the most torturing of all questions to one so sensitive as North) ' Are you resolved, agreeable to the example of the Duke of Grafton, at the hour of danger to desert me? '[38]

Though George III has been severely criticized for insisting on North's remaining in power, the strictures are not altogether justified. It was not that he absolutely declined to release North—to such a course he soon became reconciled on conditions—it was that he refused to give up a policy which he firmly and rightly believed had the general approval of the country. The King was far too astute to be blind to the obvious faults of his Minister, his irresolution and preference for lines of least resistance; but he declined to see any truth in North's pitiable contention that 'there is not a

single member of the present cabinet, or a single
member of either Houses of Parliament, of any
clique of eminence, that is not more fit than I am.' [39]
He believed, with every excuse, that North was the
linch-pin of the Cabinet, as the Cabinet was in
turn that of the American policy.   Withdraw that
pin, and, unless there were guarantees (which were
not forthcoming) a change of Premiers must mean
a complete change of programme.   Such an event
in the midst of a critical war would do irreparable
harm to the country, and encourage her enemies
in a manner no victory in the field could ever
do.*   North may have lacked the strength, personality and vision of a wartime Premier [40] but
who else could be said at that time to possess
those qualities save Chatham, and he three-parts
insane?   Certainly it was not to be found in an
Opposition one half of which deplored every
rebel defeat without producing a single scheme
(other than abject surrender) which Congress
would have considered for five minutes;   the
other half of which adhered desperately to the
Declaratory Act, yet opposed its physical enforcement.[41]   It was North's misfortune to be, during the
American War as he was in 1768 and in 1770, the
only real choice.

* On the subject of George III's estimate of Lord North, a conversation
with George Germain reported in *H.M.C. Various*, vi. 267, is illuminating.
Germain having stated that the King would be hard put to fill North's
place in event of his resignation, George replied:
   ' So I should, for although he is not entirely to my mind and there are
many things about him I wish were changed, I don't know any who would
do so well, and I have a great regard for him and a very good opinion of
him.'

Directed upon one inured from childhood to defer to the influence of others and to rely upon the decisions of those he loved or esteemed, such royal reproaches and pleadings, reinforced by emotional appeals within the Closet, crushed any resolution out of North. Duty to his sovereign, a sincere belief that he stood between an attempt, on the one hand, to carry on a just war in which honourable settlement seemed for so long almost round the corner, and on the other a surrender, humiliating alike to King, Country and Empire, prevailed over personal inclination and, as the war became more expensive and more hopeless, over private reservation. Bouts of determination thus alternated with moments of abnegation; and so it went on. In answer to piteous prayers he assured his master he had ' no idea of deserting His Majesty while his faculties of mind and body will enable him to continue in his service.' [42] He will ' sacrifice every personal consideration to His Majesty's service, in which he will die rather than abandon His Majesty in distress.' [43] He will endeavour to go on in his ' most arduous, most irksome and most embarrassing situation,' because it is ' Your Majesty's pleasure and because I understand from Your Majesty that you cannot without distressing yourself form another Ministry at this moment.' [44] Having embarked on the Ministry by His Majesty's command, ' by the same gracious command . . . whilst he remains under the same much-revered imposition, he will serve.' [45] What Selwyn rather contemptuously called his ' scholastic puritanical education ' [46] gave North perhaps an exaggerated sense of honour and duty. He could not—his tradition and training made it impossible—forsake his master in the hour of need.

Yet this faith, which bound North so effectively to his master, was not by any means an absolute one. If he personally could not unloose the bonds, there was for this thorough Parliament-man a body to whose inclinations every consideration must give way. This reservation, which runs throughout his correspondence with the King, is best expressed in North's own words. ' There are two grounds (he told the Commons) upon which a Minister ought to stand, the King's undoubted right of naming his own servants, and the approval of the people's representatives in Parliament, without whose assistance neither King nor Minister himself could carry on.' [47] Only when Parliament withdrew its support would North go, in despite of royal entreaties to stay. But in the autumn of 1775, and for many a year to come, it had no mind to withdraw that support in favour of Fox or Barré or Shelburne.

North paid dearly for his political faith, however much it might be qualified. As it was under his Ministry that the war was lost, so upon his head appeared to rest the chief odium of defeat. And it was this knowledge which harrowed his soul to the day of his death. But it was not North who lost the war; it was not Sandwich or Germain (though the latter may be said to have contributed as much as any one man); it was not even King George III. Britain lost the War of American Independence because she failed to produce either a strong man at home or a military genius abroad; for without one or the other a system of government, which had lost the advantages of an autocracy without yet gaining those of a democracy, was certain to bungle any war. Hostilities, especially those at a great distance and requiring closest co-operation between land and sea forces, subjected it to an almost impossible strain. The so-called King's System only partially aggravated the trouble by rendering the various departments more self-contained and therefore making it more difficult to achieve unity of direction.[48]

' There must be consultation, union and a friendly and hearty concurrence in all the several parts which set the springs at work, and give efficacy and energy to the movement, without which the machine must fail.'[49] Such essential centralization of authority, as Robinson, who may be presumed to speak for his chief, here envisaged, was not to be found within North's Cabinet, which its members considered rather as an association of equals than the file of obedient colleagues it had been under Walpole; in which, moreover, the man in whose control lay the military operations in America actually considered himself to be an independent unit.*[50] The Prime Minister, on his own admission, was ' not capable of forming wise plans of combining and connecting the whole force of Government.'[51] Nor, if he had been capable, had North the vibrant personality that should have riveted the Cabinet into one united whole. The only man (besides Chatham)

---

* Rigby, the Paymaster-General, though not of the Cabinet, adopted much the same attitude as Germain, and in his case showed it by declining to sit on Government benches. (Wraxall, ii. 212)

who might have done this was the King; yet had he possessed the qualities of a Frederick, or even of a William III, the conventions of the Constitution would have rendered them sterile. Seven years later, when no longer First Lord of the Treasury, North was to tell Fox:

' If you mean there should not be a Government by departments, I agree with you; I think it is a very bad system. There should be one man or a Cabinet to govern the whole and direct every measure. Government by departments was not brought in by me. I found it, and had not the vigour and resolution to put an end to it.' [52]

In the last two sentences lies the immediate cause of North's weakness. He had not the resolution to terminate those subterranean activities which went on between the various departments and the Closet without passing through 10 Downing Street. He had not the vigour to enforce his authority over colleagues who ignored, betrayed or plotted against him. Instead he suffered to go on under his very nose intrigues and disloyalties which not only helped to lose the war but at moments dragged such harrowing cries from him as when he wailed to Robinson, ' I see every day more and more the disgraceful footing on which I am likely to continue while I remain in office, which God knows I have other causes enough to quit.' [53] But when it came to resigning we have seen what confronted the despairing Premier.

·   ·   ·   ·   ·

Rarely has a country begun a war with more indifference or with less preparation than Britain did the War of American Independence. Though

s

the prospects of fighting their own flesh and blood, however reprehensible their conduct, could not be contemplated with any enthusiasm, it is not to be inferred that the country as a whole was hostile to the Government's determination to crush the American rebels.   The country gentlemen, the Church, the Universities, the Dissenters, a high percentage of the commercial classes—not excluding those of Bristol with its extensive American trade—were solidly behind North, when they thought of America or listened to the atrocities retailed by a now steady stream of refugees fleeing from the fury of their compatriots.[54]   But in the summer and autumn of 1775 not everyone was thinking of America.   The upper classes were diverted with the affairs of the bigamist Duchess of Kingston. The commercial classes were enjoying a trade boom due to Continental peace and demand.   The masses, owing to one of the finest harvests within living memory, were employed and contented. Nor, if thoughts were turned across the Atlantic, were they followed with feelings of over-confidence in the authorities at home.   In a Prime Minister they looked for something more at such a time than amiability, somnolence and *laisser faire*; and they doubted whether they should find it.   Gibbon, while acknowledging North to be one of the finest companions in the world, was far from impressed with his ability to conduct a war.   ' As to your old dog Bosun,' wrote another and stronger supporter of the Government, ' he is as fat and lazy as ever; he does very well to keep the hall and has a good tongue there, but he is not fit for the field.' [55]

Preparations were on a scale with the reputation of the Minister. Since the disconcerting revelations at the time of the dispute with Spain, Sandwich at the Admiralty had been doing his best within the limits of economy budgets, but the navy was still a long way from what it had been. In the army, recruiting, always sluggish, showed no disposition to improve.* It was this difficulty in raising recruits that presently led to the Gilbertian spectacle of Barrington the Secretary at War, pleading for all he was worth for an exclusively naval war; an idea which, at the Admiralty, must have filled Sandwich with dismay.

Disaster, which, taking everything into account, must have been a tolerably safe bet at Brooks' before the first shot was fired at Lexington, appeared almost a certainty when Bunker Hill showed that the despised Colonials were able to stand up to regular troops. To think of trying to conquer such people at a distance of three thousand miles was by many considered to be sheer imbecility. ' Ridiculous idea!' cries Caen Wood† (in a political skit), ' ten thousand times more ridiculous it is than the attempt made some years since to place our old friend on the throne.'[56] Yet in no war did the British soldier exhibit finer qualities or more reckless bravery than in this contest, which began in gloom and ended in humiliation. Time and again those ' croakers of faction,' who, like Fox and Selwyn, were confidently predicting defeat,[57] were on the point of having to eat

* In the summer of 1775 there were, exclusive of Guards, only nine marching regiments of effective strength, 3,226 rank and file in the country —a number without parallel for many years. (*Barrington MSS.*)

† i.e., Mansfield still supposed to be trailing Jacobite sympathies.

their words. However inevitable the secession of
the American colonies, a Colonial military victory
over the Mother Country was far from being
certain. Despite their natural and moral advantages, the Americans found the game more than
once, in Washington's own words, ' very nearly
played out.' Had Britain possessed a War Minister
with a tithe of Pitt's ability to organize and to
inspire, or a Commander-in-Chief strong enough
to conduct his campaign from his own tent, and not
under instructions from Whitehall, Washington's
fears must have been realized. What could not
Clive, who, had he not perished by his own hand,
must have been the Nation's choice, have made of
those men who returned to the famous third charge
up the slopes of Bunker Hill? Can it be doubted
in those circumstances a complete (and magnani-
mous) British victory must quickly have ended the
war? But in its vital early stages there was no Clive;
only a Gage, bewildered by events; a Howe whose
heart was never in the struggle; a Burgoyne, brave
but pedestrian.* Well might North exclaim, ' I do
not know whether our generals will frighten the
enemy, but I know they frighten me.'†

Though North might find time and occasion for
jesting in company, there was no jesting on the
subject of recruiting in his correspondence with his
Secretary at War as the summer months dragged

* At least Burgoyne should be given credit for suggesting that a Viceroy
armed with supreme powers be sent out. The idea, of course, was quite
unacceptable to Germain. (See Fort. iii., 244.)

† *The Political Life of Barrington*, p. 185. The saying has also been attributed to Wellington. But the Bishop of Durham writing during the Napo-
leonic Wars would hardly have attributed to North so contemporary a *bon
mot*.

by. If, as he hoped, the war might be brought
to a successful conclusion in one campaign during
the coming year, it was imperative to throw at
least twenty thousand troops into America before
the spring. Had twenty thousand elephants been
required, the prospect could have appeared hardly
more difficult.

It would be a mistake to read in the poorness of
recruiting a moral disapprobation of the war.
What was harassing the British War Office was a
matter of equal concern to Washington. In
America, where, the Opposition pamphleteers
were never tired of repeating, the fight was for
liberty and freedom, out of three million inhabitants
it was with extreme difficulty that an army of
fifteen thousand could be raised, and then only on
very precarious terms. When it is remembered
that the American soldier was fighting for hearth
and home, and the British recruit realized that he
was to cross three thousand miles of unfriendly sea,
too much stress will not be laid upon the latter's
reluctance to step forward.

Still, whatever the causes of this hanging back,
something had to be done in Britain, as in America,
and the ordinary methods of recruiting discarded.
In common with Barrington and the King, North
was against the raising of new corps, commanded
by those who recruited them and officered by their
friends. There was only one thing to be said for
this system: ' it would engage gentlemen of property
in different parts of the Country in the cause of
Government, and give a credit to our side of the
question, of which it is rather in want.' But whereas

the King objected to it as unfair on serving officers, the Chancellor of the University of Oxford believed there was no objection so deadly as the opportunity it might give of ' putting papists into command.' [58]

If the British Protestant would not fight, and the British Papist could not fight, there remained one unfailing source of man-power—the foreign mercenary. Taking everything into account, North considered there was no way at once so cheap and so effective as the time-honoured hiring of soldiers, whose expenses would cease with repatriation at the close of war. ' I wish much for an assistance of foreigners,' he wrote to Barrington, ' and shall think your Lordship does an effective service to the Country if you can make such agreements as will bring us a considerable supply, either by private recruits or by corps.'* [59] In the end, however, every method was tried. Prisons gave up their able-bodied felons; townships offered bounties; new regiments were raised; the East India Company was induced not to compete beyond a ten-mile radius of London; mercenaries were hired from Germany; even Russia was approached, though without success, for twenty thousand men. By such laborious, expensive, and humiliating expedients, within six years the army was increased in numbers from 17,500 to 110,000 men. [60]

The control of this very considerable force was vested virtually in the American Secretary, its operations falling within his jealously guarded province. No wonder then the pious, peace-loving

---

* As it would no doubt have been damaging to recruiting at home, North publicly was forced to dissemble his sentiments on the question of hired troops. See *P.H.*, xviii. 858.

Dartmouth shrank from such a responsibility.* North regretfully agreed that the waters had become too deep for his half-brother, and before hostilities had begun in earnest steered him into the Privy Seal lately vacated by Grafton. The seals of the American office were given to George Germain, who, as Lord George Sackville, had been court-martialled fifteen years before for cowardice at the Battle of Minden, and had never been allowed to forget it. At the same time Weymouth returned like a prodigal and the ' good ' Lord Lyttelton, another holder of strong anti-American views, took office. The choice of Germain was entirely North's, and, in his opinion, a most propitious one.[61] A tall, commanding presence combined with a Parliamentary reputation as a forceful speaker, gave the impression of a man of action. To a lazy, affable Premier, a man of action has little difficulty in passing as a man of parts. To some extent, in this case, there was no imposture. Germain was certainly no imbecile.† Had he been more of a nonentity he might, to the advantage of his country, have been a harmless figure in the hands of those better qualified to direct operations.‡ What probably counted with North was a feeling that a large share of his burden would be taken from his shoulders. But Brownlow North, now Bishop of Worcester, who knew his brother better

* Though he later repented of his timidity, see Fort., iii. 284.

† Some indication of his considerable talents was evidenced by his being regarded as Junius. (Cf. Haydn, *Book of Dignities* (1851 edn.), 173.)

‡ In a century rich with epigrams, there are few better than John Wilkes' on Germain shortly after his appointment. Alluding to Pitt's famous, ' I will conquer America in Germany,' he said: ' George Germain may conquer America, but it will not be in Germany.' (Walpole's *Letters*, ix. 330.)

than most men, feared, and, as it turned out, with reason, that North had taken on an unfortunate colleague, whose unpopularity, impracticability and ambitions were likely to give trouble.[62]   In fact, within three months Germain was disloyally calling North a ' trifling and supine Minister,'[63] and within six was badgering the King behind North's back for a sinecure office strictly belonging to the First Lord of the Treasury. He was neatly snubbed; but when, some months later, Lady Germain gave a grand ball, the Prime Minister and his wife were about the only people of note in London not invited. ' Which,' Lady North might pertinently remark, ' is something odd.'[64]

But it was not Germain's incivility so much as his gullibility which was to confound the Prime Minister. An extreme contempt for the rebels caused him to swallow over-readily tales of loyalists waiting only the lead and opportunity to declare for King George.   Than this fiction, lovingly embraced by the American Secretary, nothing proved more damaging to British strategy. Between a King anxious to reassert dominion over as many provinces as possible in the shortest time, Sandwich pessimistic about the navy, Barrington all for a naval war, Weymouth eager to make New England smart for its sedition, North wielding a sword in one hand while still clutching an olive branch in the other, the Ministers were sufficiently distracted without being haunted by the chimera of loyalist co-operation. The simple-minded Dartmouth had, quite naturally, been impressed by the bleats of refugee governors, like Martin of North Carolina

and Lord Dunmore of Virginia; but better things
should have been expected from his professionally-
trained successor than isolated expeditions to the
South, while New England remained unsubdued.
To these North, unfortunately, gave his cheerful
and confident approval, failing, like Germain, to see
that when the Northern colonies had been isolated
and reduced, the Southern would return to allegiance fast enough of their own accord.

Nor was the prospect of bringing the belligerent
and embattled New Englander to his knees so
fantastic as to justify diversions elsewhere.   By gaining control of the line of the Hudson and Richelieu
Rivers, the Canadian end of which already lay in
British hands, the other or New York end (as events
were to prove) easily attainable, Britain could have
isolated New England from the more half-hearted
provinces.   If at the same time, consistent with
North's belief that the navy should play the
principal part in the reduction of America,[65] a
rigid blockade of the Northern coastline had been
enforced, it is not unlikely that within six months
New England would have been ready to capitulate
and the rebellion virtually at an end.   Instead,
owing to a deplorable lack of direction which
Chatham alone could have supplied, the Hudson
Valley plan was shelved in favour of Germain's
schemes further South, and no attempt was made to
impose an effective blockade of the Northern coastline, notwithstanding the Cabinet's knowledge that
essential assistance was pouring into America from
Europe.

Nevertheless, the year which was to see the

publication of the *Decline and Fall*, as well as the Declaration of Independence, opened with the glad news that an American attack on Canada had been successfully repulsed by Sir Guy Carleton. With the Canadian end of the Hudson Valley more than ever secure the plan to isolate New England should have been a step nearer realization. But at this point, instead of pressing on to capture New York, and advancing up the Hudson Valley while the season permitted, valuable months were thrown away preparing for the campaigns in Virginia and the Carolinas which North had allowed himself to be persuaded were of supreme importance. There was no time to spare a thought for the wretched Howe who, after taking over from Gage, spent a winter of great privation in the Massachusetts capital, although at his back lay the sea on which Britain held command. When eventually, in the spring, he evacuated ' that damned Boston ' he was kept hanging about Halifax without instructions and, what was worse, without reinforcements. It was not until late in the summer, when joined by the unsuccessful expeditions to the South, that he was able to seize Long Island and capture New York. This was some consolation to North, who had set high hopes upon the expeditions to Cape Fear and Charleston, and was bitterly chagrined at their miscarriage, though he had tried to laugh it off. ' Faith, my lord,' he told the Duke of Newcastle, ' if fretting would make me thin, I should be as sorry as your Grace, but since it won't have that effect, I bear it as well as I can.' [66]

If by the time New York was occupied it was
too late in the year to think of joining up with
Carleton, it was not too late to crush the dispirited
and retreating army of General Washington.
Indeed, for a moment, it looked as if the mantle of
Clive had descended upon the shoulders of Sir
William Howe.   After the capture of Long Island
he had pushed on to rout the rebels decisively at
the battle of Brooklyn.   He had only to follow this
up to annihilate, if not to capture, the only colonial
army worthy of the name.   At this point began
Howe's apparent aversion from a complete military
victory which henceforward characterized his operations in America.[67]   So perilous was the plight
of the Continental army that it seems impossible
Howe's restraint after Brooklyn could be due to
military and not to political reasons.   It is here that
North makes one of his few definite points of contact
with America, and with such unfortunate results.

As chief of a wartime Cabinet it must be admitted
Frederick North, with his hesitations and irresolu-
tions, was not inspiring, and this lack of inspiration
reflected itself in the earlier stages of the war.   It
was not that, as with certain of the Opposition, he
was a defeatist at heart, still less that he had no
stomach for a fight.   Within the House of Commons
he would contest every inch of ground.   There
North was in his correct milieu; there he knew
his own mind; there, whether in defence of his
Budget, the Civil List or a colleague, he continued
to demonstrate the sparkle of his wit and the quick-
ness of his brain.   The bleaker the prospect, the
more menacing the tone of his opponents, the more

did old *Boreas* divert members with his conceits.
Outside the House, on the other hand, all virtue
forsook him. In the Closet he was a mountain of
doubt and indecision; in the Cabinet he havered,
slept, or for peace of mind chose a course not always
best calculated to win the war. Moreover, in
spite of the brave front he promised his rather
sceptical supporters that he would adopt, he was
unable to shake off the persistent and venial hope
that, even at this twelfth hour, war with its train of
unbalanced budgets, ceaseless anxiety and inevitable harsh measures so repugnant to his nature,
might be avoided. If his conciliatory plan early in
1775 had been received with contempt, even in the
Quaker city, he might argue that America was then
exulting over Lexington and in no mood for recon-
ciliation. But now that Britain had shown that she
was in earnest, and had given a foretaste of her
displeasure, might not the colonies prove more
amenable? The Minister, who had always set his
face against giving way to force, had never been
against making concessions in return for submission.
Unlike Germain and Weymouth, he had no
desire to rub salt into American wounds. In his
opinion, the best use to which any victory could be
put was to bring about peace, and not to punish.[68]
Thus, while declaring Britain would throw such an
army into the field as would *look* America into
submission,[69] and taking steps to prohibit all
commercial intercourse with the colonies, North at
the same time proposed to send out commissioners
with power to receive into the King's peace those
colonies which agreed to make some contribution

to the Exchequer for defence purposes. Conceived
from the security of a Downing Street armchair,
the plan had much to commend it. It was cheap,
it was reasonable, it was an advance upon anything which had emanated from Whitehall. It
would have saved the face of the Mother Country
without entirely humiliating the colonies. The
King approved, as well as fire-eaters like Rigby and
Elliot, though Wedderburn caustically observed it
was like proposing to finish the War without
finishing the dispute.[70]   Late as this olive branch
was in budding, at least one friend to the colonies
believed in its possibilities had the matter been
canvassed with some American closely in touch
with the sentiments of his countrymen.[71]   North
would then have been warned that to send out
Commissioners having no authority to recognize
Congress, even to concede Washington his military
title, was a mere waste of time.

It was not the failure of North's conciliatory
plan—that, in the circumstances, was assured—but
its unfortunate effects upon the Commissioners
themselves which makes it of importance. Considered either as olive-branch bearers or as com-
manders-in-chief, Lord Howe and his brother Sir
William would have been unexceptional choices.
Enjoying a wide American acquaintance, which
included Franklin, brothers to the gallant Howe
whose statue the citizens of Boston had recently
raised, the Howes had definite qualifications as
peace-makers. Possessed of a creditable record in
the navy and army respectively, Lord Howe and his
brother were equally qualified for command of

naval and military operations. It was only the combination of their two commissions which proved disastrous. ' No mistake,' writes the historian of the British Army, ' is more common or fatal in British statesmen than the attempt to wage war under the principles of peace.' This is precisely what the British government did endeavour to do during the first year of the American War. Sir William Howe's dual commission hampered instead of facilitating his work, as general as well as negotiator. His restraint after the battle of Brooklyn, which every text-book and the flimsiest knowledge of strategy must have told him to be inexcusable, can scarcely have been due to anything but a conviction that his overtures might be more favourably received if the Americans were not rendered desperate by the loss of their army. For this confusion of purposes North must bear a large share of responsibility. The Howes were his choice. The Peace Commission was his pet idea. It was one of his few definite contributions to the war, and it was based upon a misunderstanding of the colonial situation as great as that under which the Opposition laboured, and no less harmful. Although he had been warned that no concessions would be entertained short of complete capitulation,[72] he placed upon the Commander-in-Chief (who, having taken up his duties reluctantly needed little encouragement to go slow) a restraining influence precisely at a moment when a smashing victory might have ended the war.[73]

Notwithstanding the failure of the Commission, by the end of the year things all round were cer-

tainly looking more favourable.* At home, the
Opposition was in eclipse; Rockingham had retired
to the country; Fox was in Paris forgetting ' the
terrible news ' of Brooklyn. In America, Washington was finding the tale of his daily diminishing
troops poor compensation for the recent Declaration
of Independence which had given his country a
status in the eyes of a watchful Europe.†

With the Americans at such a disadvantage,
Britain had still time to repair all her errors and
miscalculations in a campaign that seemed to her
enemies not only unavoidable but, notwithstanding
their own snap victory at Trenton on Christmas
day, likely to be overwhelming. To Washington,
bravely struggling, in spite of the interference of
Congress, to create something like an army, the
prospect seemed without hope. To him it was
inconceivable that anyone could fritter away such
an opportunity as Britain possessed in the early
months of 1777. But Washington was counting
without George Germain. The campaign which
ended one autumn morning at Saratoga, an event
which, after York Town, proved the most decisive of
the war, is perhaps the unkindest illustration of a
Whitehall-waged war. Germain adopted one-half
of the Hudson Valley plan. Burgoyne was ordered
to advance down from Canada under minute and
positive instructions, preposterous as coming from

---

* In an intercepted letter Robert Morris writes on December 20 to Silas
Deane, one of the American delegates at Paris: ' The unfortunate case of
American affairs at this period leaves no room for joy in the mind of a
true friend to this country.' B.M. Add. MSS. 34413, f. 121.

† The desertions were on such a scale that by December the main American army numbered no more than three thousand ragged troops. (Fort.,
British Army, iii. 194.)

one who had no personal acquaintance with the conditions or nature of the country through which the army was to advance. Had Howe at the same time been ordered *up* the valley, there might have been some hope of success. But Howe had never liked the idea of invasion from Canada, and since Trenton he liked it still less. Instead, believing that Pennsylvania was full of anxious loyalists and waiting like a peach to fall into British hands, he proposed instead an attack upon Philadelphia, by which means he hoped to take Washington from the south and rear. One plan or the other by itself might have worked. To attempt them simultaneously and according to instructions from which in either case no power to deviate was given, must risk almost certain disaster Yet this was the risk undertaken by the American Secretary who had already shown his dangerous ignorance by likening their victory at Trenton to ' the last effort of the Americans.'* Howe was instructed, likewise minutely, to pursue his plan, Germain airily expressing a hope that ' whatever you meditate, it will be executed in time for you to co-operate with the army ordered to proceed from Canada.' [74] A letter to North from John Wesley warning him that the colonists were ' terribly united ' and would dispute every inch of ground was probably pigeon-holed or, if passed on to Germain, certainly ignored. [75]

In the face of such gross mismanagement and stupid miscalculation, the bravery of troops and the competency of generalship were alike useless. Though Howe covered himself with glory at the

* B.M. Add. MSS., 34413, f. 267.

Battle of Brandywine and marched in triumph into Philadelphia, exactly four weeks later the remnant of Burgoyne's fine army was piling arms just out of sight of the victorious New Englanders.

The news of Saratoga reached London on the second day of December. For the Ministry the shock had been partially absorbed by a secret intelligence four weeks earlier to the effect that Burgoyne had been checked and was in retreat.[76] Even so, they reeled beneath the force of impact. George Germain was as a man stunned; William Eden, his Under-Secretary, felt like the victim of some hideous dream. As for North, who, only a few weeks previously, had been flattering himself on the favourable turn of events,[77] he burst into tears, and, making straight for the Closet, begged His Majesty to allow no considerations or predilections to keep him in office or exclude others therefrom.[78]

How far was North responsible for a disaster which led to foreign intervention and ultimately to the victory of the colonists? He certainly approved Germain's strategy, however guardedly. ' I am neither soldier enough nor well enough acquainted with the Country,' he wrote, ' to reason upon the situation of the army, but it seems to me that if Sir Henry Clinton and General Burgoyne make themselves masters of the North River and Sir William Howe cuts off Washington from the Southern provinces, Washington must, after a little time, be reduced to fight, or disband his army.'[79] Though this is evidence that he endorsed Germain's instructions, North did so because he believed the possession of Philadelphia would lead to a speedy

T

peace. He can hardly be charged with the criminal carelessness of allowing the two generals to
fall out of step; nor, indeed, did the Opposition
(nor even Burgoyne himself) accuse him personally
of this, although in other respects, they abused
him freely.[80] Appreciating, perhaps, that the
Prime Minister had sufficient to answer for without
being saddled with the sins of the American Secretary, they directed their rage and their Billingsgate
exclusively against Germain. And such was North's
depression that for this neglect he was pathetically
grateful. At the close of one of Fox's most flagel-
lating speeches, threatening Germain with a *second*
trial, he turned, and whispered audibly, ' Charles, I
am glad you did not fall on me to-day, for you was
in full feather.' A few days later he even expressed
his satisfaction that Fox had abandoned attacking him, an old hulk, in order to assault ' a man of
war.'[81]

Though North might console himself with the
thought that he was little to blame for Saratoga,
the defeat was, he realized, not merely a staggering
blow at the prestige of the Government. Seventy
years before Stanhope had surrendered with twice
the number of men at Almanza, yet Britain had
gone on to win the war. The full significance of
this defeat was to be sought not on the field of
battle, not even in America, but in France. For
two years the French Court had been doing everything short of declaring in their favour to assist the
rebels. Until they felt that the Americans were
likely to give a good account of themselves, they
hesitated to commit themselves further. Upon an

always clamorous French war party (baulked in 1770), the effect of Saratoga could be predicted with certainty. Even Lord Stormont, the British Ambassador, who hitherto had been sending reassuring despatches from Paris, was now convinced France meant war.*[82]

If North before had felt lacking in qualifications to deal with the revolted colonies, here was a situation which filled him with consternation. From a contest with France, waged on land and sea, in America, India, the West Indies, perhaps even Ireland, Britain might emerge successful, but (he was convinced) bankrupt.[83] And it would be he who would have the thankless task of finding the money and receiving in return only the execration of an over-taxed and ruined country. On national and personal grounds these changed circumstances clearly indicated and justified a modification in attitude towards the colonies.[84] By a timely surrender to America it was always possible to cut the ground from under the feet of France. Nor need that surrender necessarily be abject. All was far from well with the Americans. Having put out George III they were finding their own Assemblies as tyrannical and unconscionable as ever he was alleged to have been; and Congress more incompetent than ever had been the Imperial Parliament. A flood of paper money was causing high prices and much distress. Attempts to invoke the aid of

---

* For months the British Ambassador's messages had been completely contradicted by those of the Government's secret agents, but, because North had an ineradicable dislike of brokers and all they stood for, and he believed his spies to be ' bears in the Funds,' he (and the King) suspected their reports. (Cf., Add. MSS., 34414, f. 196.)

a Bourbon and Papistical power was a hard and distasteful thing for many a colonist to stomach. Though the King accurately prophesied that, even at such a time, America, or rather the Congress, would laugh at any British proposition, he too agreed that the American War as now secondary to that with France. Fortified with the King's consent, North, though without over much confidence, resolved to go forward.

Within ten days of the news of Saratoga the Prime Minister caused Parliament to be adjourned, letting it be known at the time that he was seeking to open negotiations with America, without, however, parting with the fundamental rights of Great Britain. Though Horace Walpole might observe that North's only honesty was his impudence, the sarcasm was purely churlish.[85] As against Saratoga, Britain had much to set off: Canada was secure, New York was firmly held, Philadelphia was hers, Washington, wintering in Valley Forge, had been reduced to a desperate plight. And so, all through the Christmas holidays, while military and naval preparations were being surreptitiously hurried on, in order not to alarm France into precipitate action, North's pen was busily throwing off draft after draft. The mass of material buried in the Auckland Papers is proof of the genuineness of North's intentions and, incidentally, of the obstacles encountered. Over and above the difficulty of proposing anything likely to be accepted by Congress, which would not mean utter humiliation for England and for him the obloquy of the nation and the curses of his hitherto loyal supporters, pervaded always his sense of unfitness for the task. He could hope for no qualification in the eyes of his enemies but his love of peace, and even that might well be suspect.

At last, by the middle of February, his task was done, and on the 17th he rose in the Commons to deliver his Conciliation Bill. Briefly, everything asked for by the colonies as late as the summer of 1775 was granted, if not specifically, at least implicitly. The Government of Massachusetts Act was expressly annulled. The Tea Duty was repealed, and with it went all intention to tax America for the purposes of obtaining a revenue. (This, as he told the King meant precisely nothing, because, whatever might happen, it was quite certain England could never levy any further taxes in America.)[86] Even the modest contribution towards Imperial defence was no longer insisted upon, though colonies declining to assist in this should be given to understand they could not look to Britain for support in an emergency. In the second place, Peace Commissioners were to be sent out, but on this occasion with very much enlarged powers. Unlike the Howes, they were to be restrained by no punctilio. They could recognize and address Congress. They could give Washington his full military titles. They might promise the repeal of obnoxious Acts. Indeed, they were to be limited by two restrictions only: independence they could not concede; American hands must not be allowed to touch Canada.

' They certainly consider it,' wrote North of American designs in that direction, ' as a step favourable to the uniting Canada to themselves as a fourteenth State and till that is accomplished they will be always obliged to pay attention to Great Britain. If we have recovered and preserved that Province by arms, we must take care not to lose it by treaties.'* [87]

In selecting the Commissioners, North was exceedingly anxious that they should, both in appearance and in fact, carry the Government's mandate.[88] He desired them to be ' men of ability, shrewd negotiators, men of character, inviting confidence from both sides.' He therefore magnanimously ignored party labels. But though the invitations were widely distributed, there followed no rush of acceptances. It is, therefore, perhaps unfair to North to criticize the appointment as Chief Commissioner of the youthful and inexperienced Earl of Carlisle, whose name had not even figured on the provisional lists in any capacity.[89] It is also unnecessary, because, whatever its personnel, a Commission which was precluded from granting the one thing upon which the Americans would insist, their independence, was doomed before it set sail.

North's speech introducing these proposals lasted for two hours, and was reported to have been eloquent and able. As usual, there was much autobiographical detail and penitence. He main-

---

* According to Granville Sharpe, North was even prepared, in view of the imminent war with France, to grant independence on such terms as would establish intimate commercial relationship between the two countries, thereby trusting to draw as much benefit from America as if she had remained under the British flag. In this purpose, laments Sharpe, North was prevented by the violent declarations of Chatham and Shelburne against independence. (*H.M.C.*, *Dart.*, iii. 255.)

tained that any charge of inconsistency was more apparent than real. He had never believed it to be possible to extract a beneficial revenue from America. He had inherited such a policy, and would readily have given it up in return for some gesture of goodwill. He had always been for conciliation, witness his two earlier attempts. If, since then, he had not repeated his offers it was because he felt the moment of victory was the moment to make concessions.[90] If not a groan interrupted this speech, not a cheer greeted its conclusion. Instead, there succeeded for some moments a ' dull melancholy silence.' Propositions that, after an expenditure of some thirty millions, gave up practically everything for which the country had been fighting, could evoke little enthusiasm from the Opposition, whose thunder was being stolen, and none at all from the Government benches, where mortification was evident. For all Lord North's care, or perhaps because of all Lord North's care, his Bill was a half-measure, which pleased nobody, least of all America. ' Though it might be but the shadow of power for which Lord North contended, it was a shadow which would have darkened for ever the brightness of the American constellation.' The young Walter Stanhope, Member for Hull, could hardly have anticipated the reactions of Congress more prettily.[91]

The Commons might have spared itself its melancholy, North his labours, and Stanhope his simile. Eleven days earlier France, fearing the effects such an offer might have on war-weary Americans, had hurriedly signed a treaty recognizing

their independence. Two days after the Royal
Assent to North's Conciliation Bill this recognition was intimated to Great Britain in terms
so insulting that Stormont was recalled, and war
ceased any longer to be a matter for speculation.

Hoping rather than believing that ratification
might be denied to the French treaty in America,
North, in now more anxiety than ever to ensure
success for his Commissioners, resolved to sacrifice
himself.   It was quite unnecessary for the Opposition to remind him that his presence at the head of
the Treasury was an impediment to any understanding with America.   The man who had
imposed the Boston Port Act, the Prohibitory Acts,
and had declined to remove the Tea Duty, had not,
and never could have, a good Press in America.
None knew this better than North himself, whose
wish it had long been to go as soon as he could hand
over to another without feeling that he had betrayed
his King and Country.   Never was the identity of
that successor more positive than in the spring of
1778.   If the Americans learnt that at the head of
the Government sending forth the Peace Commissioners sat their honoured and revered Earl of
Chatham, would they not feel a sense of security,
and hasten to avoid a hateful accommodation with
France?   Might not even France, in such circumstances, hesitate to implement her treaty?   On the
day preceding his proposals North had begun to
prepare the way with the King.   Chatham, then
described as ' of all the Opposition the person who
would be of most service, and probably the least
extravagant in his demands ' [92] was now formally

proposed as his successor. The royal reply was only partially encouraging. Although he expressed general indifference to the project, the King had no objection to Chatham's being approached. But it must be on the clear understanding that North remained at the head of the Treasury, and that that 'perfidious man' should act as supporter, and not as dictator. Though he declined to have any such personal dealings with Chatham as he had had ten years earlier, George made no objection to receiving his followers, amongst whom, though not a Chathamite, he named Fox, and granting them minor offices. It was as far as he would go. To no purpose North insisted 'the condition of the country is most critical, and it becomes next to impossible to carry on government except upon a broad comprehensive plan.' [93] The King was adamant. He would accept what the Opposition had to offer towards strengthening the Government on a more or less national basis, but they must understand they entered, not as conquerors, hardly as partners, but as auxiliaries. How was it possible to accept on more generous terms men like the 'patriotic Duke' (almost certainly Richmond), who, told Gilbert Elliot, with joy sparkling in his eyes, that a British ship of war had been lost in a storm, and not one of its crew of a thousand had escaped? [94] With his vivid memory of such things said and done by Minority men and their paid hacks, even to go as far as he did gave him pain, but the King did it (he let it be known) solely to ease North's anxieties. Seventeen years on the throne—and especially the first ten—had given him such an opinion of

Opposition (which he preferred to call Faction) that he would run any risk rather than submit to a body of men who, he was honestly convinced, would, if given the chance, reduce him to bondage and plunge the country to destruction. Rather than wear his crown as a puppet in disgrace, he would lose it for ever.[95] However pardonable in an individual, such sentiments become less excusable in a ruler. Much as George III had suffered both before and since he had ascended the throne, he should have known that the moment had come to forgive and forget. Moreover, it was a time of violent and exaggerated language and, once entrusted with office, there can be little doubt that every member of the Opposition, not excepting Richmond, would have hastened to obliterate former extravagances. Fortunately the King's error on this occasion had no effect other than to preserve the reputation of Chatham. By that time the American situation had become altogether too complex for the once great Commoner. Even had the King capitulated all along the line and Chatham had assumed office, his ministry could scarcely have been anything except one of humiliating failure. In any case, North's hopes and fear, the King's heroics and prejudices, the journeyings backwards and forwards to Hayes, ceased to matter when, on April 7, Chatham collapsed in the House of Lords, and passed out of practical politics.

'May not the political exit of Lord Chatham encline you to continue at the head of my affairs?' So wrote the King, too little of the hypocrite to feign sorrow over the death rattle of one by whom he considered he had been abominably used.[96] But nothing so objective could ever have inclined North to remain beyond the end of the session: this was the limit of his undertaking. Such a promise was obviously not good enough for the King. Fortunately, at this critical moment the royal task-master was able to supplement his passionate entreaties by appealing to North's sentiments in a manner which broke down resistance. The Earl of Holderness had most opportunely died, and the Wardenship of the Cinque Ports, promised twelve months before to North, at this moment fell vacant. Although the King declined to make the appointment for life (as he had done in the case of Holderness), despite North's contention that any shorter tenure would be construed as a want of confidence in his Minister, he made it clear that this office, together with the reversion of another, would be given him *whether North consented to carry on or not*.[97] It was one of the cleverest gestures ever made by a man whose knowledge of human character was truly royal. The fact that no condition was attached touched the sensitive North so deeply as to make it impossible for him to desert so kind a master—for desertion he knew it would be considered. Yet how little the place in itself acted as a bait is evidenced by North's readiness to take it without a salary, and ultimately accepting £1,500 a year, instead of the usual £4,000, in order to relieve the expenses of the Civil List.* [98] And so, from having consented to

* One can hardly help suspecting that Pitt's refusal of this place on the death of North was little more than cheap ostentation. To refuse such an office and then to die leaving tradesmen and others in his debt for many thousands which the country ultimately settled was a queer form of probity.

see the session out, North was committed to stay on until the King could make other arrangements, a time which, so far as the latter was concerned, might be conveniently relegated to the Greek Kalends. Besides how was it possible for him to make other arrangements? The Chatham squad, without its leader, had ceased to possess much *raison d'être*. The Rockinghams, now thorough-going defeatists, were impossible.*

As in January, 1770, it was once more a case of North or nothing; of carrying on the government which still had the support of the nation, or of handing the King over body and soul to a knot of politicians whose future conduct might excusably be gauged from their past endeavours to throw every obstacle in the way of raising men and supplies. It was Britain's misfortune that in this critical stage of her history there existed no alternative party prepared to put an end to the existing system yet determined to carry on the war with patriotic resolution. Much as their management of the war was open to criticism, the Government was, in the eyes of the nation, the only body of men who were prepared to attempt the recovery of America.† [99]

Though it had seemed to North that, with a new enemy in the field, the Ministry must be overthrown, actually the outbreak of war with the traditional enemy rallied the bulk of the nation behind the Government. [100] The trickle of recruits

---

* It was in opposing one of their motions to withdraw all forces from America that Chatham made his swan song.

† A good illustration of Opposition mentality is to be found in a letter of Walpole to Mann at this time. ' France has a right to humble us.' March 17, 1778.

swelled into a torrent. Offers of regiments poured in from peers and commoners, as well as from the cities of Manchester, Liverpool, Glasgow, and Edinburgh. Within six months of Saratoga 15,000 men were in training. At Almack's club young men about town were discarding opera wenches and racehorses as topics of conversation in favour of drill-sergeants and firing control.* [101] Thus a session which had opened in the shadow of Saratoga, closed on a note of mingled confidence and defiance.

On the same day that Parliament dispersed, Thurlow, the Attorney-General, received the Great Seal, and ministerial debating powers in the Lords promised to be materially reinforced. But previous indications of this promotion, for which the King was largely responsible, had roused the wakeful jealousy of Wedderburn, the Solicitor-General, whose services North had been the first to acknowledge. His anxiety to keep these two essential auxiliaries sweet had for months been giving the Prime Minister the utmost concern. Not daring to disappoint Wedderburn he plagued the reluctant King for consent to a peerage, and then at once repented. The prospect of losing one pillar of support was grave enough, but what if both went to the Upper House? Moreover, Wedderburn's promotion would raise a cloud of similar requests from others equally entitled to peerages, but not equally necessary to the Minister. Teased to such an extent by these problems, North actually fled into the country for twenty-four hours to collect

* Yet Trevelyan continues unctuously to refer to the war as 'Lord North's war.'

his thoughts and, as he told the King, to recover his understanding.[102]   George III treated his Prime Minister of forty-six as a mother might a feverish child, and prevailed upon Wedderburn to waive his pretensions for the time and to content himself with stepping into Thurlow's shoes as Attorney General. For this arrangement North expressed himself truly grateful, and showed his thankfulness in a sudden access of energy.   He let Robinson know he was proposing to turn over a new leaf, and of his own accord conceived and set in motion an expedition which captured Goree later in the year.[103]   But the King was not impressed.   He realized that North was on the verge of a nervous breakdown.   The repose that the coming recess offered he trusted would restore to him something of his old vigour, and enable him to take a decisive lead in the Commons.[104]

Had the war prospered during the summer it is possible that North would have fulfilled the King's expectation.   But the profit and loss account, by the time Parliament had reassembled, was not flattering to the Ministry.   The entry of France, with an efficient fleet, and the probability of Spain following her example, had necessitated a re-adjustment of operations.   For the moment the colonial struggle passed into the background.   To defeat France would almost certainly bring America to her knees, whereas the converse would not necessarily hold.   The better to concentrate against the Bourbons, Philadelphia, Howe's great achievement of the previous year, was accordingly abandoned without a shot being fired.   North's Peace Com-

missioners, who arrived at this unpropitious moment, were cursorily told by an exultant Congress
either to acknowledge American independence, or
withdraw their army as a preliminary to discussions. At sea, which the British had ridden victori-
ously for so many years, there was fought only the
indecisive battle of Ushant, which in turn was soon
to lead to as indecisive a battle in the Commons,
between Keppel, the admiral in command, and
Palliser, his subordinate. Finally, when Burgoyne
returned on parole, and started to air his grievances
against Howe, likewise a Member of Parliament, the
House became convulsed by personal quarrels, instead of getting on with the war. The introduction
of political feeling into the higher command of both
services was, in fact, one of the most regrettable
features of the war, and one for which the Opposition was the more blameworthy.*   When Tommy
Townshend declared that Admirals like Keppel
and Howe, and others who had resigned largely for
political reasons, would be fit for Bedlam if they
ever trusted the Ministry again, he was truly representative of an Opposition who made the Palliser-
Keppel professional quarrel a party affair, and were
soon to revile Cornwallis because, like a good soldier,
he was carrying out his duties notwithstanding his
vote some years before against the imposition of the
Stamp Act.† [105]   Not till the days of Nelson

* It even spread to those of lower rank. ' I am sorry to say that the
poison infects even some of the officers employed in the troops sent to us
last year, but (General) Vaughan treats them as they deserve.' (Rodney to
Sandwich, 27.4.1781, *Sand.*, iv.)

† On this occasion North scored smartly off Townshend by retorting
the Ministry would themselves be fit for Bedlam if they ever employed
such Admirals again. *P.H.*, xxi. 920.

was the political canker excised from the Navy.

As the session approached there arose too a question which North had not had to face since the early days of his Ministry—the maintenance of a majority. Habitual Government supporters, even amongst the faithful Lords, felt keenly the humiliation of Saratoga, and dreaded its European repercussions. They distrusted Germain with, and Sandwich without, reason; they feared that North, for all his amiable qualities and darting wit, was not the man for the critical situation which appeared to be developing—a conclusion, incidentally, to which none subscribed more heartily than North himself. Even in the previous session they had ceased to attend in their usual numbers, leaving the Prime Minister, as he complained bitterly, standing alone and unsupported. No less a confirmed ministerialist than Barrington felt the draught and, had he not been Secretary at War, he too would certainly have followed the ' rats.' [106]

It was clear that something must be done if the Administration were to survive the session of 1778-9. Business-like, as ever in such matters, the King urged that prevention was better than cure. He requested North to produce a plan, in support of which the usual sanction of royal displeasure against all shirkers was promised. Characteristically this most careless of correspondents, who had been known to leave important documents lying about the privy, allowed a fortnight to slip by, and then had to be sharply reminded, before producing a scheme. This, manifestly the work of Robinson, proposed the circulation of members with an

additional or second whip, the stressing the need
for attendance, and the holding of a preliminary
meeting of placemen for instruction in their duties.
The rest of the communication was undiluted North,
and went with surprising frankness to the root of
his difficulties. There were two points, it was
explained, which were of supreme importance to the
Government of the country:

' The first is, That the public business can never go on
as it ought whilst the Principal and most efficient offices
are in the hands of persons who are either indifferent to,
or actually dislike, their situation.

' The second is, That in critical times, it is necessary that
there should be one directing Minister, who should plan
the whole of the operations of government, and control
all the other departments of administration so far as to
make them co-operate zealously and actively with his
designs, even though contrary to their own.

' Lord North conceives these two rules to be wise
and true, and therefore thinks it his duty to submit the
expediency of His Majesty's removing him as soon as he
can, because he is certainly not capable of being such a
minister as he has described, and he can never like a
situation which he has most perfectly disliked even in
much better and easier times.' [107]

Having more specifically unburdened his conscience than ever before, but still without hope of
release, North was prepared to acquiesce in the
royal pleasure and carry on till the King could see
his way to replacing him. The King on his part
believed that, provided North's proposals for bolster-
ing up attendance were followed up with spirit,
there would be no need to search for a successor,
though, as he warned Robinson, North must ' cast
off his indecision and bear up, or no plan can

U

succeed; he must be more exacting in answering
letters or let others do it for him, and he must
let measures be thoroughly canvassed before undertaken, and when adopted must not quit them.'
What, he asked pertinently, was the use of whipping
up supporters if, when they attended, their leader
could not make up his own mind? [108]

At first it seemed the King's optimism was justified. North's pre-sessional harangue proved so
promising that Sandwich confessed he had never
seen the Prime Minister more disposed to carry on.[109]
But the mood soon passed. The Opposition came
crowding to Westminster, jubilant at seeing their
prophecies of woe coming true, and with the
avowed object of clogging the wheels of government.[110] Under such conditions the stimulant
administered by North soon lost its virtue. Majorities which not long before Burke had been calling
' blind, biased and manacled '[111] once more became so
perilously sluggish that at last even the sovereign
agreed that in the circumstances, without a coalition,
' the present system must be overturned.' [112] Here
was a definite concession by the Closet, and early
in the New Year negotiations were opened with
those parts of the Opposition who still declared
against the independence of the colonies. Howe
was offered the Admiralty. Germain was to be
kicked out of office and up into the Lords. North
was to be considered as no longer at the Treasury.
But this attempt to divide the Opposition failed,
owing to the surprising firmness of Grafton and
Shelburne, who refused to come in as auxiliaries,
and insisted upon the admission of the pro-American

Rockinghams. Such an attitude the King naturally regarded as sheer dictation in his constitutional choice of Ministers, and, rather than suffer as
he had done under Grenville, professed his intention
of retiring to Hanover.

Driven back North found no comfort amongst
his own Party. Wedderburn was again up to his
game of exploiting his market value. The Bloomsbury Gang, with one eye, as usual, upon their
emoluments and the other upon the Opposition, were
known to be ready to sell the pass if a sufficiently
high price could be obtained.[113] North's homilies
to his own rank and file had worn thin. Finally,
after a night rendered sleepless by the attacks on
his house during the riots following the acquittal
of Keppel, he was defeated on an Opposition Bill
to exclude members from taking Government
contracts.* As a result of this motion ' so personal
to the First Lord of the Treasury ' he told the King,
' it becomes clear they no longer wish to see Lord
North in that situation.' [114] If he was not prepared
to go quietly now while he could still count on some
sort of majority, he would soon be compelled to go
violently and be treading—who knows?—the path
to Tower Hill. When the King replied that,
unless his Minister did not mind occasionally being
in the minority as they were in the days of King
William, the country could never regain its proper
tone, he was speaking a language that North was
rapidly unlearning. But when he went on to
insist that ' the day of trial is not the honourable
one to desert me,' he was appealing to something

* The Bill was subsequently thrown out by the obedient Lords.

that was still dearer to North than life. To this there was no reply so long as Parliament showed its readiness to support him on the essential issues. North must go forward, with Jenkinson and Robinson, both under royal inspiration, urging him, the one to adopt 'the doctrine of rewards and punishments,' and the other impressing him with the advantages of possessing so gracious a master.[115]

Surely no Minister needed more encouragement. After their triumphant return from Portsmouth, where their darling Keppel had been acquitted on the charges preferred against him by Palliser, the Opposition became more clamorous than ever. With cool audacity, the men who had been doing everything to put spokes in the wheels of the fighting services and deploring every manifestation of public zeal, now set out to accuse the Admiralty departments of criminal lack of preparation. Charles Fox, now in his thirty-first year, bestrode the House, and with one motion after another assailed the Earl of Sandwich. North was never lacking in courage to defend a colleague. Though he had again and again maintained that there was no such person as the Prime Minister, and that his responsibility extended only to his own departments, the Treasury and the Exchequer, yet when Ministers were attacked he did not hesitate to fling his mantle around them and insist that the Cabinet stood all for one and one for all. A censure on the Admiralty was, he contended, a censure upon himself and the Cabinet.[116] This argument, thoroughly sound according to the Walpolean conception of the constitution, but hardly deducible from existing practice, succeeded in so far as it deterred waverers from voting, as they probably would have done, with the Opposition if it had been simply a case of the unpopular Sandwich.

As in 1770 so in 1779 North obtained more assistance from the conduct of a misguided Opposition than from his own supporters, whose attendance continued to be uncertain and capricious. A little more discretion, a little less irresponsible and destructive criticism on the part of Fox and others, and North's departure might have been ante-dated by some three years.* They should have learnt by this time that though shock tactics might drive North's spirits to a vanishing point, forensically he could always give as good as he got. Though the Empire might be sinking by the stern, the crew mutinous, the captain could be depended upon to stand four-square, his flabby form conspicuous behind his Blue Ribbon of the Garter, lolling upon the Front Bench five days a week, his witty responses infecting with laughter both his friends and his foes. Just now he tickled the House with a lively picture of the Opposition fastening like barnacles upon the gallant Keppel, whose bottom would become so foul and whose course so slow as to require an overhaul. He convulsed Members by likening a discursive speech of Fox's to an ancient chart which the geographer was, for lack of know-ledge, compelled to fill up with representations of beasts.[117] And when an opponent contemptuously

---

* Horace Walpole, whose sympathies were anti-ministerial, cursorily dismisses the Opposition at this period as ' not able.'

referred to him as ' that thing called a Minister,'
North adroitly turned the laugh against him by
patting, almost lovingly, his own considerable
anatomy and replying, ' To be sure I am a thing;
the member, when he called me a thing said what
was true, and I could not be angry with him.   But
when he added " that thing called a Minister " he
called me that thing which of all things he himself
wished most to be, and therefore I take it as a
compliment.'[118]

But such efforts were visibly telling upon North's
nervous system.   Sometimes the effects showed
themselves in unreasonable petulance and even
in unusual shortness of temper; sometimes too in
needless incivility to his friends and colleagues.
It is clear that North, with his nerves becoming
ragged, did not know where he stood, and he saw
no further ahead than the next Parliamentary
division list.   Throughout the session his spirits
rose and fell, often within the space of a few days, as
varying news came from the fronts.   The repulse of
the French from Jersey, the capture of St. Lucia
and the restoration of Georgia to allegiance hardly
compensated for the long-expected declaration of
war by Spain.   The saluting of Union Jacks by
Georgian colonists, however flattering to royal
esteem, was no solution to a problem become
infinitely more involved by the possibilities of what
a combined Franco-Spanish fleet might do.   In
Scotland anti-Popish riots—the shape of things
shortly to come in England—were raging; Wales
was in a ferment; Ireland, where sympathy with
America ran high among the Protestants, was

threatening, North feared, to run ' the same course
with America.' [119]   Nearer home, Wedderburn
was once more pressing his claims and teasing North
to distraction.   In the Commons tempers became
looser as the summer advanced, and Paul Jones
was insulting the British coasts.   Personalities
descended like hailstones upon the head of the
Prime Minister, who implored his master to
release him from the anxieties and miseries of his
situation.   In return he offered to provide His
Majesty with something lamentably wanting at
that hour—' a member of Parliament out of place
who would be ready on every proper occasion to
support the measures of government to the utmost
of his abilities.' [120]   The recent declaration of war
by Spain enabled the King to reply with irresistible
force that any wish to retire ' would be highly
unbecoming at this hour.' [121]   What could North
do with any honour to himself and in duty to King
and Parliament, who still both trusted him, but
continue in office ' till His Majesty can replace
him without inconvenience.' [122]

A few days later the session closed, but not
before the House had been treated to the spectacle
of their imperturbable Premier dissolved in tears,
and on the following day delivering the least prolix
and most convincing defence of his personal
conduct.   During a motion to double the militia
the blustering Sawbridge shot straight off at a
tangent and accused the Noble Lord in the Blue
Ribbon of never being awake save when some particularly lucrative reversion was being disposed of.
The attack was particularly ungenerous as it must

have been commonly known that his infant son Dudley, on whom he doted, lay dead at Bushey. To rebut this entirely groundless accusation, North started to make one of the most pathetic of his apologies for ever having been born. In twelve years of office, he declared, he had asked for nothing. Everything he had received had come to him unsolicited. Nor was this list a long one: a reversion valued at £1,000 for the lives of two sons, a small place worth £500, and the Cinque Ports during pleasure at a very much reduced salary by his special request. Being ready to resign the last on demand, all he stood to possess when going out of office would be £1,500 a year on which to support a large family, and this after twenty-five years in the House. At this point the memory of his dead son came before him, and he broke down. The House, respecting his grief, brought the debate to a close.[123]

The occasion of his defence of his policy occurred on the day following in reply to a threat from Fox to bring the Minister to punishment unless he instantly resigned.

' The Hon. gentleman says, why not resign at this, why not resign at that, why not resign at another period? I will tell the hon. gentleman why I neither did, nor could resign. I was always determined never to resign as long as his Majesty thought fit to accept of my poor services, and till I could do it with honour. Could I have resigned with honour when America first resisted? I answer no. Could I have resigned with honour in the prosecution of the American War, while the event of that war was yet depending? No. Could I have resigned with honour when France interfered and acknowledged American independency? Most certainly not. And ought I to resign at this period, or could I do it with honour to myself, or discharge my duty to my country, now that we have the united force of the House of Bourbon to contend with? I am persuaded I could not. My language has always been uniformly the same, never to resign, till a fit person was found out to succeed me. I have not heard that person yet pointed out, nor do I know him. I am well convinced that many persons of abilities, infinitely superior to mine could be found. I know no man more fit in some respects than the hon. gentleman himself; but his abilities, so far as they respect me, are out of the present question. He and his friends think differently from me on matters of very essential importance. I hope I have as great a reverence for the constitution as that hon. gentleman; but his ideas are not perhaps exactly consonant to mine on that subject. I am for supporting the just and constitutional prerogatives of the crown, and the rights of parliament, according to the best of my own judgment; and upon those opinions I must continue to act, and can never consequently consent to call any set of men, be they whom they may, as far as my feeble voice can reach, of whose political doctrines I do not approve. The good of my country and my own honour, therefore, will not permit me to follow the hon. gentleman's advice and subscribe to his opinion, that this is the proper time for me to resign.'* [124]

This year prorogation brought less respite than ever to the harassed North. A combined Franco-Spanish Fleet, outnumbering the British by two to one, paraded the Channel. Invasion was expected hourly, in England probably, in Ireland for a certainty. The press gangs worked overtime. Plymouth Harbour was hastily boomed. The country was roused as it had not been these twenty years. A martial spirit penetrated even the City of

* This was the speech which Hazlitt regarded as the most characteristic of North.

London. Amid such scares and activities Dillington became impossible that summer. But though North remained within posting distance of the capital, a torpor settled on him. His heart (he said) was oppressed with a thousand griefs which totally unfitted him for work. He trembled as he opened every despatch from America.[125] The routine of office, the filling up of vacancies, was neglected. Soon he had sunk into a dull indolent apathy from which Robinson despaired of moving him.[126] Sandwich tried to make him use his leadership with spirit and decision.[127] Weymouth coldly intimated his intention to resign.[128] Wedderburn renounced all personal intercourse. Gower told him to his face that nothing could save the country from ruin but a coalition, and in reporting this conversation to the King North added ingenuously that, having been of the same opinion for some years, he could not argue the point.[129] At one time during this black summer it was even rumoured the Minister had at last resigned.[130] But what would have been a merciful release was not possible so long as the King held him to his promise not to desert him while other arrangements were pending, and then, unable to forget the past, placed such conditions in the foreground of any negotiations as made their success extremely unlikely.

' My wish, and what I really believe would be the best measure in the present moment,' North wrote to the Chancellor, ' is that His Majesty would call to his assistance a part of the Opposition, or indeed the whole, and that he would make use of my resolution of not deserting him only for the purpose of forming a new administration, and then let me depart; but the King cannot, I believe, make up any proper system in the present moment; at least, he seems much bent on trying to go on with those of his servants who remain with him.[131]

In his renewed determination to keep North tied to his stake, the King at first tried to encourage him to trust in Providence (as he himself was always ready to do) and in the fortitude of the British Tar.[132] But when this evoked nothing but pitiful pleas for coalition and self-effacement, he drew off his gloves. In a letter to Robinson he declared that, unless North pulled himself together and treated his colleagues with civility and confidence, there was likely to be no end to the present mischief. This letter, which Robinson, very likely on purpose, left lying on his desk, was seen and read by an appalled and stricken North. Though the King later expressed regret at having hurt his Premier's feelings, he retracted not a syllable.

' I am ever ready (he told Robinson) to take any burthen on my shoulders to assist him in the prosecution of public affairs, but he must not expect that I should not see what he has so often, with perfect good humour, confessed, that though not guilty of the sins of commission, he is not so guiltless as to omission in points of attention.' *[133]

The ruse succeeded. The next day there was not the least evidence of any disposition to resign.[134]

If the reasons which disabled North from breaking the chain that tied him to his office are traceable to his character and upbringing, it is not so easy to understand the King's purpose in taking so much trouble to hold an unwilling man to his word. Certainly it was not based on any over-estimation of

---

* North had once confessed himself 'the worst correspondent in England.' B.M. Add. MSS., 38304, 85.

North's ministerial capacities. He was, on the
contrary, fully alive to his Premier's shortcomings.[135]
Nor, for one instant, would he have admitted that
his own personal views had anything to do with the
matter. He would never allow that his intentions
clashed with those of the bulk of his people. To
do so would be to admit that there could be a
difference between his own happiness and that of
his country. He held on to North because, in
common with the nation, he distrusted the Opposition. The noise they made at Westminster he
realized was no indication of their esteem in the
provinces.[136] But he realized, too, that if North,
having been so long in office and so personally
identified with the war went, the Ministry must go
too, and with it America, unless those who were
taken in were prepared to sign their solemn pledge
to keep the Empire intact, and that they appeared
disinclined to do. In the interest of increased effi-
ciency he was prepared to ' draw a veil ' over the
personalities which had been bandied about and to
admit ' the Wise, the Virtuous and Respectable of
all parties,' but it must be on condition that
they would commit themselves to the war. To
say, therefore, that the King would not part
with North is not altogether accurate. After four
years of war he was ready to do so in favour of any
Minister prepared to carry on a policy which still
had the sanction of the nation, but—and this was
the second and fatal proviso—the initiative must
come from North. A curt dismissal of the man who
for ten years had possessed the King's confidence,
and was so identified with the war, must (he

reasoned) have a harmful effect at home and abroad. But how could North, as we 'have seen, conscientiously resign until he could do so with honour? And how could he do so with honour unless he could hand over to a government who he felt would not betray the country and humble the King?

And so the tragi-comedy dragged on. For three months and through a hundred pages of the King's correspondence, negotiations with various members of the Opposition opened and closed, were reopened and re-closed. A little tact, a little willingness to give as well as take, and victory would have been, if not with the Opposition, at least with Shelburne, Grafton and Camden.[137] But ' the Wise, the Virtuous and the Respectable,' declined to make any reciprocal gesture. They refused to ' divide the bearskin.' By rejecting reasonable propositions carrying with them the retirement of North, Germain and possibly Sandwich, and requiring the proscription of every member connected with the administration without reward or gratuity, they plausibly justified the King's determination to have nothing to do with them as a body. Rather than be dictated to by men whom he considered to be without principles, as they were certainly without plan, he would go to any length. And where he went, went also the unhappy North, deserted (as he moaned to Robinson) by all, unable to consult any friends because, with the exception of Robinson, he no longer had any, unable to reach any decision or attend to business and suffering such torments of mind as were impossible to describe. But, as usual, once he had reached the bed-rock of depression he started to reascend and was presently ' ready to do anything that could save the king and this country.'*

Though Charles Jenkinson's nose, never more than a couple of inches from the ground, scented internal plots by the restless Bloomsbury Gang to eliminate North,[138] in the end the Ministry was somehow lashed together in time to face Parliament and carry the address by a handsome majority.† Stormont, the most learned man the historian Winckelmann had ever met, took the Seals from Suffolk ' dead to the State long before he was dead to nature,' [139] and North's steady supporter, Hillsborough, returned to office, taking Weymouth's place as Secretary of State. The Opposition had missed their chances, and deserved to miss them.

* Quoted by Mr. Herbert Butterfield in his illuminating article, *Lord North and Mr. Robinson*, 1779, Cambridge Historical Journal, 1937.
† The plotters were, of course, the ever restless Bloomsbury Gang. (Fort., iv. 472.)

Chapter VIII

DEBACLE

' Oh, for a lodge in some vast wilderness,
Some boundless contiguity of shade,
Where rumour of oppression and deceit,
Of unsuccessful or successful war,
Might never reach me more.   My ear is pain'd
My soul is sick, with ev'ry day's report
Of wrong and outrage with which earth is filled."

Cowper, *The Task.*

Until the close of the year 1779 North's principal concern had been the preservation of a majority, and the countering of Opposition attacks within the House of Commons.   Outside the Chamber his worries were more intermittent and less personal. Except in the cities of London and Bristol, and in Yorkshire and East Anglia, where local interests were either in the hands of Opposition magnates or merchants affected by the loss of American markets, the country was, whatever the Rocking-hamites might assert to the contrary, not ill-disposed towards the Ministry, or certainly not sufficiently well-disposed towards the minority.   No government could have survived the successive shocks of Saratoga, and the entries of France and Spain into the struggle, had this not been the case.   The vociferous mobs which, from time to time, choked the approaches to Parliament and hooted Lord

303

North were not more representative of British, than a resolution of New York Tories would have been of American, public opinion. With the Ministry's determination to assert the authority of the Mother Country over its ungrateful and rebellious children the nation still agreed, in principle. With the mounting expenditure that such a policy entailed there was every year less satisfaction. In this field lay North's principal cause for anxiety, as the war entered its fifth year.

' In December, 1779, a political agitation, on a scale surpassing anything which was reached until the crisis of the Reform Bill of 1832, rose like a thundercloud from the blue, and spread with startling rapidity throughout our island.' [1] To use a less elevated simile, the Opposition ceased at last to rake amongst the ashes of Saratoga and Ushant, and broke newer and unquestionably more fertile soil. A people, in times of widespread taxation unrelieved by success, is prepared to reconsider political allegiance, not because it disapproves intrinsically of a government's policy, but because its pockets are being picked without prospect of compensation. If the war was likely to become unpopular, it would not be because it was thought unjust or unconscionable, but because it was unsuccessful, unproductive, and expensive. As soon as the Opposition started to reorientate itself along these lines, so soon did it start transforming itself from a purely factious place-hunting body into one inspired by some sort of disinterestedness and conviction. Its battle-cry was the easiest of all to adopt in wartime—economy.

A Chancellor of the Exchequer who budgets for a protracted war is easy game for critics, even though, like North, he had the advantage of being able to consult Adam Smith's *The Wealth of Nations* (published in the first year of hostilities) for inspiration. At the start it had been, in accordance with the author's precepts, only the well-to-do who had suffered. Their land tax had been increased. Their cards, their dice, their male-servants, their post-chaises, their houses had one by one been taxed.[2] But four years of unsuccessful warfare, the cost of which North himself had been privately confessing could never be recouped by any miraculous victory, was a luxury no leisured class could bear exclusively, and required a degree of patience no taxpayer could be expected to possess. Certainly not the country gentlemen great and small upon whom the burden had fallen particularly heavily. It was not difficult to persuade them that some substantial alleviation could be made to their lot by the abolition of sinecures by which it pleased Opposition vanity to think the Ministry alone survived. Thus their thirst for office, and the country gentleman's anxiety to be more lightly taxed, met on common ground. This consideration should be enough to qualify any exaggerated opinion about the campaign which opened in those last months of the year. To all but a handful of idealists it was just another phase in the struggle for place. To see in the debates and resolutions and petitions which followed the dawn of Liberalism is warranted neither by what preceded nor by what followed. The host of

x

sinecures and jobs, with their ridiculous titles and
bloated emoluments, offered so obvious a mark,
that had the Opposition been whole-heartedly
sincere they could never have neglected such a
topic for over a decade. Fox, Rockingham, Savile
and Burke were unquestionably inspired by the
purest of motives, but the rank and file, whose
numbers crept up and up till they finally topped
those of the Ministry, would have found the utmost
difficulty in resisting some handsome office of profit
and idleness. Indeed, when the fortress finally
capitulated, even their leaders, Dunning, Camden
and Burke himself, made no scruple to accept for
themselves or their kin sinecures against which
they had been fulminating.*

The Economy drive, specious and question-
begging, spread rapidly across the country, and
transformed the session of 1779–1780 into one of the
most critical in North's career. For the Opposition,
in their light-hearted campaigning, had unleashed
forces which came nearer to revolutionizing the
Constitution than anything which had happened
since the death of Queen Anne. Yet it all began
sedately enough with a motion in the Lords
praying the sovereign to set a personal example of
economy and a statement in the Commons from
Burke to the effect that in the New Year he would
introduce an Establishment Bill. Now the least
hint of the axe laid to the root of the sinecure at once

* Forty years later there was no name in England which stirred the honest
Cobbett to such wrath as that of Camden. ' This great and awful sinecure
placeman . . . (he wrote of the Lord Chancellor's son). Not much less than
thirty years he held a place, a sinecure place, that yielded him about thirty
thousand pounds a year.'—(*Rural Rides*, i. 223.)

placed an eighteenth-century First Lord of the
Treasury and Chancellor of the Exchequer (for
the offices were generally held in common) in a
quandary. If, as Chancellor, he must welcome
anything that eased his commitments, as First
Lord he knew too well the value of a rich office to
silence some dangerous opponent or, more frequently, to encourage some valuable waverer. It
had been so in the days of Walpole, and was to
continue to be so long after North was in his grave.
It was a pull of opposite interests which, neither by
training nor by nature, was Lord North competent
to overcome.

Had the Opposition confined themselves to
checking waste and abolishing a few of the more
outrageous sinecures it is likely that North would
have accepted the measure in principle. But in the
Christmas holidays a more ominous note was
sounded. It came as an echo to some words uttered
a few days earlier by Charles Fox. ' It is the duty
of members of Parliament (he had declared) to
conform to the sentiments and in some degree
even to the prejudices of the people.' ³ Six hundred
freeholders of Yorkshire met, and not content with
passing their famous Petition to reduce all ' exorbitant emoluments,' appointed a Committee ' to
carry on the necessary correspondence for the
effectually promoting the object of the Petition,'
and to prepare the plan of an Association to support
such other measures as would restore the freedom of
Parliament. Put more crudely, the intention was,
or seemed to be, to take a leaf out of the books
of the American and Irish Correspondence

Committees and Associations respectively, in order to browbeat the legislature in to compliance. In other words, economy ceased to be an end and became one of the means of subjecting Parliament to external dictation. If, as Fox believed, it was the duty of members to conform to the whims of constituents, Parliament (it was objected) might presently become nothing more than a body for the registering of popular edicts.*

The Yorkshire example, so flattering to freeholders and burgesses, and extremely well publicized, was quickly followed up and down the country. It was never difficult to convene meetings or to ensure unanimity. As for a Petition, it cost very little more than the cakes and ale for the patriot who arrived on foot, hungry and thirsty. By the time Parliament reassembled a pile lay upon the table, and there were more on the way. Savile began by presenting his Yorkshire Petition, Burke produced his Bill in one of his greatest oratorial efforts, Barré moved for a Commission of Accounts, and pressed Savile for a list of all Patent Places with their salaries. As usual the full force of the attack was met by North. As usual, his tactics were reminiscent of those equally critical first days of his Ministry, although he told Eden he was no longer the man he had been.[4] Now, as in 1770, he gave way here, temporized there; but with this important difference, that when he capitulated he

---

* Sir George Trevelyan makes great play with the all but unanimous voting at the Yorkshire meeting. It was unanimous only because one of the leading peers of the county, Carlisle and nine other notables decided it was hopeless to attend. Their tenants and friends naturally followed their example. (Add. MSS., 34416, f. 489.)

did so out of conviction and not by way of policy. Thus he accepted the Yorkshire Petition, remarking that the need for economy was so self-evident that no sane man could possibly controvert such a proposition as it contained. He took the wind out of Barré's sails by gratefully adopting his idea, and himself setting up an impartial committee to supervise accounts. Savile's motion he accepted, subject to an amendment. Burke's noble effort he acknowledged with the graceful comment that, though the House contained men of very brilliant parts, none but he could have made such a speech. But the plan, notwithstanding the relief it promised to give the Exchequer, was far too revolutionary in design for one of North's training and habits to accept without reservation and long consideration. He would not even approve it in principle, although heartily agreeable that leave should be given to bring forward the five Bills it contained.

As Burke developed his ideas in a succession of motions through the months of February and March, North, consistently to his word, opposed them step by step. He pointed out the incongruity—not, however, surprising in one who at heart was a greater Tory than North was ever alleged to be— of sparing sinecure places granted for life while interfering with the Civil List which had been granted on similar terms to the sovereign.[5] He successfully fought the abolition of the third or American Secretary, and preserved that office for two more years of unhappy life. But his majorities, which Rigby unhelpfully remarked ' hardly deserved the name,'[6] failed to hold a week later when

Burke returned to the attack with a motion to abolish the Board of Trade. The debate was remarkable for an outbreak of Billingsgate between the Prime Minister and (of all people) the Speaker of the House of Commons. As the result of a red herring tossed across the discussion by a member of the Opposition, Fox had appealed to the Speaker to learn whether Parliament had an inherent right to control the Crown in any exercises which tended to support government by influence or corruption. Sir Fletcher Norton, who had been out of favour at Court ever since, three years before, he had lectured the sovereign on the virtues of economy,* thereupon rose and, after settling the point at issue, gratuitously discharged an accumulation of venom against the Ministry. He turned upon North, declared he was no friend to the noble Lord in the Blue Ribbon, and had repeated proofs that the same noble Lord was no friend of his. As evidence of this entirely irrelevant attack he instanced a promise, alleged to have been made to him when, in January, 1770, he had accepted the Speakership, under which, when the time came for him to retire (and this was obviously approaching), he should have a principal post in the legal profession. Although he was at the time mute on the point, this was clearly meant to be the Chief Justiceship of Common Pleas, which he had learnt to his mortification was being kept simmering for Wedderburn. North, for the moment, was startled by the unexpectedness of the charge, but he had no cause to fumble for an answer. Even if the Speaker's assertions were

* On occasion of a further increase in the Civil List.

correct, which he denied, he was clearly not bound
by promises of a previous Prime Minister. A long
and personal altercation followed, on which the
Parliamentary History is discreetly silent, except to
record a slashing and final speech directed against
the Speaker from the lips of Wedderburn, whose
tongue had lost none of its power of invective since
the day he had seared Benjamin Franklin. After
such an interlude, the abolition of the Trade Board,
carried against the Government by eight votes, was
almost an anti-climax. It was certainly the real,
though not the apparent, low water mark in
North's fortunes that session. A week later the
House handsomely rejected a clause in Burke's
Bill to suppress the Treasurer of the Chambers, and
after the Easter recess similar motions to abolish the
Board of Works and the office of the Great Ward-
robe. Burke thereupon withdrew his Bill in order
that ' it should be neither an eyesore to his adversaries, nor call for the tiresome and useless attendance of his friends.' [7]

While Burke's Establishment Bill, with all the
difficulties in which it must have landed any
Premier, was being progressively killed in Committee, another topic had come forward with a speed
that made Fabian tactics out of the question.
April 5 had been allocated to the consolidated
consideration of the Yorkshire and some thirty-nine
other petitions. No sooner had their titles been
read out than John Dunning, who had been
Grafton's Solicitor-General, jumped to his feet and,
dilating at length upon their highest common
factor—economy in public expenditure—moved the

startling but not very germane rider that ' The
influence of the Crown has increased, is increasing,
and ought to be abolished.' Its jingling refrain and
happy euphony has given this famous motion a
posthumous notoriety not at all apparent to its contemporaries. To them it was an exceedingly
astute and disconcerting move in the direction of
place-getting. A general election was due under
the Septennial Act in the forthcoming year, and
Members were already becoming conscious of the
existence of constituents. To tack on to the consideration of the petitions a resolution so tendentious
was obviously a master-stroke of electioneering
tactics. Either, as Sir Fletcher Norton, still smarting under Wedderburn's lash, pointed out, Members
must accept the resolution, or reject the petitions,
in which case he wished them joy in their constituencies. Coming from such an authority as the
Speaker, this argument fell with crushing weight
upon the waverers and independent members.
North, who had expected defeat from the instant
Dunning released his thunder-bolt, now regarded
it as a certainty. In those circumstances he would
probably have contented himself with registering a
silent vote against the resolution but for a bitter
and personal attack. Thomas Pitt, nephew of
the Great Commoner, cried out that the motion
required no more convincing proof than the career
of the Minister himself, who, though he had lost
America, and had wasted millions of money and
rivers of blood, still held his place, to the dishonour
and degradation of the country.[8] Twice only in
his life is North reported to have lost his temper in

Parliament, and this was the first occasion. [9]   In
view of the weeks of strain and hard work which
had preceded, the certainty of a mortifying defeat,
and then, on top of all, such a provocative attack,
this is no more surprising than that his reply was
reckoned as being below form.   Frequent inter-
ruptions, which at other times no one knew better
how to deal with effectively, now disconcerted him.
The pith of his speech consisted of the rather trite
assertion that it was not because of the influence of
the Crown that he kept his place, any more than it
was because of his own abilities, unequal as they
were to the situation; but because the people at
large distrusted the Opposition and all their works
as dangerous to the Constitution and their liberties.
Subject to a trifling amendment the Resolution of
Dunning was carried by 233 votes to 215, less than a
dozen country members voting with the Government.[10]

Rarely has so much prominence been given to so
barren a victory.   Instead of being the penulti-
mate milestone on the road to office, it proved a
very mockery of a triumph.   The sixty country
members or so who had been carried off their feet
on the night of April 5 (including such die-hard
Tories as Sir Roger Newdigate and Sir John
Rushout) felt, when they had slept off the effects,
that they had sufficiently squared their consciences
by asserting their tradition of independence, and
had thereby qualified for their constituents' continued support.   Within a week they were con-
tentedly back at heel, assisting to throw out by a
majority of twenty-nine a Bill to disenfranchise

Revenue Officers. This successful counter-attack
North was able to consolidate through the illness of
the Speaker, which entailed a ten days' adjournment. The more cooling time allowed to the
temperature reached on the night of April 5, the
more difficult would it be to generate sufficient
power to displace the Administration.* The effects
of the delay, which was due to no sinister motive,
were evidenced as soon as Parliament reassembled.
When Dunning returned to the fight by moving
that the King be requested not to prorogue Parliament till the Petitions had been redressed—a
corollary, in effect, to his Resolution—he was, to the
wrath and mortification of Fox, defeated by no
fewer than fifty-one votes. To believe, with Sir
George Trevelyan, that this turn-over was due to
' the subterranean operations of Mr. John Robinson, the Patronage Secretary to the Treasury,' is to
do an injustice to a body of men who, however
narrow their vision, were, hardly without exception,
incorruptible and indifferent to office. The country
gentlemen returned to their allegiance, not because
they were bribed, but because, all things considered, they placed more confidence in the Government than they did in the Opposition.† What
the country party felt after Easter, the country was
feeling before six weeks had elapsed.

* This adjournment had its comic aspect and illustrates the difficulty
of reaching truth in political warfare. The King believed it to be an
artifice of the Opposition to be able to attend Newmarket Races (Fort., v.
44); the Opposition regarded it as a trick on the part of the Ministry to
give them a respite.

† There was another reason. According to Wraxall full attendance
could never be obtained after the Easter recess, many members being
disinclined to return to London (*Memoirs*, ii. 557). Certainly during
North's Ministry the most critical debates were before the Easter holidays.

On June 2, the Gordon Riots burst upon an astonished and unprepared London. Nothing more outrageous and preposterous had been witnessed in the memory of man. In the midst of a war with a jealous world, with the Southern Counties liable at any moment to invasion, the capital of the Empire was subjected to the licence of an ignoble mob. The Wilkite throng, which shattered North's coach, might imagine they were making a gesture in defence of liberty. Lord George Gordon's *canaille* who poignarded North's hat could only plead that they were rioting for an intolerance that might have brought a blush to the cheeks of a Puritan. Ever since an Act, sponsored by Sir George Savile and warmly supported by North, had been passed in 1778, giving a small degree of toleration to Roman Catholics, there had been an agitation amongst militant Protestants to have its modest concessions repealed. Their brethren across the Border, having by riotous behaviour dissuaded the Government from introducing a similar measure for Scotland, a dangerous precedent had been set.* What had been done in Edinburgh might equally be done in London. Early in the New Year Lord George Gordon recently elected President of the Protestant Association, addressed a communication to the Prime Minister, and followed it up with a personal call at

* Trevelyan, rarely missing an opportunity of exhibiting North in the worst light, accuses him of conniving at riots in Edinburgh such as he set out to punish in Boston. (*Op. cit.*, ii. 290.) This unsubstantiated accusation is completely refuted by a letter which the Scottish Catholics addressed to him in alarm, beseeching him for their own sakes to forego any attempt to place them in the same position as their co-religionists in England. (See Castro, *The Gordon Riots*, 12.)

number 10 Downing Street. The next day North dispatched the following letter to Gordon:

' 5 January, (1780).

' My Lord, after having fully considered all that passed . . . at my house, I see no reason to alter the opinion I then expressed, and must beg leave to decline presenting the Petitition your Lordship left with me, or engaging to support any Bill that may be brought into Parliament for repealing the Act for the relief of Roman Catholics . . .' *

Notwithstanding this rebuff, petitions, all thoroughly inspired, were presented almost daily to the House. They were given the contemptuous reception they deserved, and that was all. When, therefore, it was learnt on the last day of May that yet another was to be presented, accompanied by some 20,000 true-blue Protestants, the Government might be excused for failing to anticipate any untoward event.

The Gordon Riots which began in consequence of this Petition on June 2, and raged, with only one day's intermission, till the 8th, fall outside the scope of this book. Parliamentary business came to a standstill. Politics ceased, or, in Walpole's phrase, became ' riotic.' Even the war was forgotten. The man who really counted was not the Prime Minister, who could jest while the mob were howling round his front door, but was incapable of riding such a tempest. It was the King, who never lost his nerve, and, when the Chief Justice of the King's Bench was quivering like an aspen leaf, was deter-

---

* A statement from the most questionable source that was possible— from the pen of Gordon himself—accuses North of subsequently *waiting upon* him and offering him money and ' a leading situation in Parliament ' in return for deserting the Association. (Castro, 23.)

mined that there should be at least one magistrate
who should do his duty. While a full Privy
Council hummed and hawed before an old opinion
of Hardwicke's on the use of troops to suppress
riots, George III cut in by asking Wedderburn
whether it was necessary to await the reading of
the Riot Act. On receiving a negative reply, he
instantly gave orders for the military to act accordingly, and in this wise brought the riots to an end.
Though North's house was one of those marked
down for destruction, and though Gordon threatened that he could, with one word, have him torn in
pieces (and North on his way to the House for the
second time in his life came near to such a fate) it
was with the effects, not the course, of the Riots
that he was principally concerned.

One night, at the height of the disturbances,
North with some guests had ascended after dinner
to the roof of 10 Downing Street. As the glare
from seven distinct conflagrations flickered on their
faces, the Premier turned to Sir John Macpherson
and asked the obvious question: ' What is your
remedy for this evil? ' Sir John replied: ' I should
try to effect a junction or open some communication
with the heads of the Opposition for the protection
of the country.' ' You talk,' retorted North, not
without reason, ' as if the thing could be done;
but it's not practicable.' [11] Eight weeks earlier, in
fact, through the intermediary of Sheridan, an
abortive meeting had actually taken place in the
Opera House between him and Fox. Certainly the
hour had not been altogether propitious. Dunning's Resolution was not ten days old, and the

Opposition still very much cock-a-hoop. In consequence Fox's manner had been ranting and menacing. Though North had expressed his wish to retire and his readiness to make concessions, the other had blustered and threatened to such an extent that no agreement could be reached.* With the memory of such a signal failure green, North might be excused for thinking a coalition still impossible. Nor was there now any need for *him* to make advances. The Gordon Riots, which disgraced Britain in the eyes of Europe, and killed a secret mission of Richard Cumberland to detach Spain from the war,[12] brought to the Premier a sense of security he had not known for years. To the average citizen it was not far-fetched to see a connexion between the County Associations and the Gordon rioters. Both aimed at intimidating Parliament. In the circumstances, it was felt safer to trust and strengthen the present Ministry than to encourage an Opposition which had toyed with Associations.

Nor was the Opposition any longer the solid phalanx it had been. The riots had broken down Party barriers, which some, at least, were not eager to re-establish. Burke and Savile, for instance, had been no less objectionable to the mob than North and Mansfield, and the special protection which the Premier had given to Burke's house had touched the warm-hearted Irishman. Rockingham, always acutely sensitive to popular excesses,

* Wraxall makes this interview take place *subsequent* to the Gordon Riots, and his authority has been uniformly followed; but a letter from Jenkinson to the King and another to Robinson given in the King's Correspondence prove it to have been not later than April 14, and probably on that date. (Fort., v. 42–45.)

was quickly warbling the cry of ' moderation ' now as during the Middlesex riots, and Conway was dreading, ' the heavy hand of the people.' [13] A few days later when North fearlessly contested a supine motion of Savile's to repeal his own Act, he even found himself in the same lobby as Fox.* The stage was more favourably set for a coalition than ever before, but this time the suppliants were those in Opposition, not those in office.

To the first approaches from a chastened Opposition North in his scepticism made no return, thereby giving some to think he had still no intention of parting with any power.[14] However, when a personal friend, Frederick Montagu, one of the Rockingham Party, took up the negotiations, he responded readily enough. The rough terms provided for North's remaining at the Treasury, the passing of the Contractors, Revenue Officers, and Burke's Establishment Bills, and some departmental changes. The King at first was agreeable —even to the inclusion of Fox in some lucrative office. It was the most promising contact yet made. But it was not promising enough. The war, as before, proved the stone of offence. On this occasion, indeed, there were words indicating that America was not to be abandoned. But they were not sufficiently categoric for the King, who, in this matter, required explicit promises under seal. Although not exceeding his legitimate powers in the choice of Ministers, George III has been sharply criticized for this insistence. Yet it is hard to find

* The Bill to repeal nevertheless passed the Commons, but, to their honour, the Lords threw it out.

any grounds for trusting a body of men who still deplored every British victory. Negotiations thus petered out, and, by the time Parliament was prorogued, all further thoughts of coalition had given place to those of a General Election.

As long as Party Government exists it is idle to expect those in office not to take every advantage to prolong their tenure. Not only had the Government regained much ground as a result of the riots, but the Opposition had become more divided than ever. Failure to make the most of such circumstances when, in any case, an Election was due within a year, would have been reprehensible in any Prime Minister. North made no such mistake. Within a few weeks of the riots the subject was officially discussed and approved by all the Cabinet save the Chancellor, whose curmudgeonly manner and want of co-operation in this as in other affairs threatened to revive all North's miseries.[15]

Dissolution came on September 1, and, Trevelyan writes, hit the Opposition like a ' thunder-clap.' If it did so, they had only themselves to blame. If their political senses were not acute enough to realize what must be in the wind, there were rumours enough, even before the end of July.[16]

Despite every favourable factor, North had been expecting no Opposition landslide. He was therefore not displeased when, after five years of exhausting warfare, the Ministry neither lost nor gained ground. But after a decade at the Treasury he knew too much about the habits of the political animal to raise Te Deums over so volatile a thing as a majority. The absence of Party discipline

made members, if anything, more susceptible than
they might otherwise have been to popular feeling
without and oratory within.   And to the wealth of
talent already crowding the Opposition benches
were now added the voices of William Pitt and
Richard Brinsley Sheridan. As it turned out,
indeed, the Parliament of 1780, elected at a higher
cost* to the Treasury than ever before, and exhibiting to the Opposition a still heartbreaking Government majority, was, within the space of eighteen
months, to place the Ministry in a minority and to
drive North at last from office.†

The first business of the new Parliament was the
election of the Speaker. No Ministry could be
expected to tolerate the continuance in the chair
of one who had shown himself so partisan as
Norton, and North hoped that he would have had
the good sense not to put himself forward.[17] On
the other hand, so far was he from desiring a ministerialist in Norton's place that he had been doing
everything in his power to induce Frederick
Montagu to take the Chair. Only when the latter
declined on the score of ill-health (to the regret of the
King as well as of North) was a Government candidate selected. Throughout the debate which followed North sat silent and refused to be drawn,

---

* The *net* cost was roughly £50,000, of which half went in assisting
eight candidates in six constituencies only. Nor was this sum greatly in excess
of the normal. (Fort., v. 465–7 and 480.)

† It may be questioned whether the Party Whip and the postcard—
usually from a vociferous minority of his constituents—has not made a
Member in the twentieth century less free than his predecessor two hundred
years before. Were not immediately post-war Parliaments, for example,
declining for so long to repeal the unpopular ' kill-joy ' clauses of D.O.R.A.,
in a sense more unrepresentative of public opinion than any Georgian
Parliament passing its Enclosure Acts or Game Laws?

Y

despite the taunts which were hurled across the floor. To have taken part, after his quarrel with the late Speaker, would have been to appear vindictive, if not improper. Nor was he in any condition to embark upon what would certainly have been another personal wrangle. The work of a strenuous recess in which he had allowed himself ' no pleasure, nor dissipation, nor vacation,' had told upon a never very robust constitution.[18] At the moment of the debate he was sickening for a very severe chill, and by the next night he was bad enough to be blooded.[19]

As North went straight home to bed, excusing himself from attending upon the King, he must have felt less dissatisfied than he had done for several years. The election of Charles Cornwall as Speaker in a House not much more than half full by a majority of sixty-nine, was a fair indication of the sort of working majority the Government might expect. The year which was closing, moreover, had been the most successful in the war. In January Rodney defeated the Spanish fleet off Cape St. Vincent. In May, Clinton had captured Charleston and its 5,000 defenders. In August Cornwallis gained the completest victory of the war at Camden. A month later Arnold, the most enterprising of the American generals, deserted to the British. This culmination of so woeful a tale of disasters produced a profound and general depression in the colonies. In fine, after five years, it seemed as if Britain was not much more than a musket shot from victory. All that her enemies could preen themselves upon was the capture of an important convoy, and the setting up by the Northern powers of the Armed Neutrality, theoretically directed against all belligerents, but in practice bearing almost exclusively upon Britain.*

From so favourable a situation, which North might now soon be enabled to quit of his own accord, and with honour, there had for some time come no pleas to be relieved. Though, on the eve of Parliament there was made the routine-like reminder that his frailties were on the increase, it was largely force of habit. Yet already, even as he lay sick, events were developing that were to make the coming year as disastrous as the passing had been glorious, and do for him what ten years of Opposition rhetoric had failed to achieve.

Papers captured aboard an American packet in September had disclosed plans of a treaty between the United States and Britain's old ally, Holland. Strictly speaking, the negotiations had been carried on by the Pensionary of Amsterdam, and therefore independently of the States General. On the other hand, relations between Britain and Holland had been deteriorating since the early months of the war. The Dutch, according to Trevelyan, those ' quiet and industrious people, whose ambition it was to live by selling their own wares,' [20] had made their West Indian island of St. Eustatius such an entrepôt for supplying Americans with every requirement that, according to Rodney, it had

---

* The fact that only one such convoy was captured in seven years of war is a noble testimony to the abilities of Sandwich, whom Radical historians, for over a century, have delighted to calumniate on the most questionable of evidence, i.e., that of his political enemies. Yet it was one of these (the Earl of Bristol) who declared, in 1779, that if any but a professional sailor was fit to preside over the Admiralty, it was Sandwich.—(Adolphus, iii. 342.)

become more detrimental to Britain than all the forces of her enemies combined.[21] In spite of being represented at the Hague by an ambassador who had been twenty-seven years in the country, England was unable to obtain any satisfaction. While invoking a treaty of 1674 under which, when one of the two countries was at war, the other should be permitted to trade with the enemy in all things save contraband, Holland had refused to respect two treaties giving England a claim on her assistance when involved in war with the Bourbon powers. If these treaties, dated respectively 1678 and 1716, are ignored, it is not difficult to make the policy pursued by Britain appear domineering and unwarranted.* To accuse North, who had to find additional money, and Sandwich additional ships, of wantonly provoking the Dutch, is to relegate them to the class of imbeciles. Failing to get satisfactory assurances from the Hague on the proposed treaty with America, the British Ministry, with the utmost reluctance, recalled Sir Joseph Yorke and declared war, because they believed an open enemy to be less menacing than a treacherous friend. Certainly they did no more than Chatham would have done in similar circumstances, and actually was prepared to do towards Spain in 1761. And yet they did wrong, not morally, but tactically. The addition of the Dutch fleet to the number of our enemies put too great a strain upon an already overtaxed navy. A watch on Texel, another on the route round the Shetlands, could only be effected by fatal weakening elsewhere.[22]

---

* This has been done by Trevelyan (*George III and Fox*, ii. pp. 58–61).

For North, at first, the consequences of the Dutch war were purely financial. ' Lord North is afraid,' he wrote in December, ' that the step we have been obliged to take with respect to Holland will greatly increase the difficulties of raising this Year's supplies.' [23] As Budget day drew nearer his fears became justified. Hitherto, if North's financial policy had not shown the touch of genius, it had called for little criticism. Perhaps no higher praise could be paid him than the fact that Burke had never yet divided against any of his Budgets.[24] While the country had had peace, national expenditure on the three principal items, Debt interest, Civil List, and the Services, in all amounting to some eight millions annually, had been met, though not without much anxious deliberation by North, through normal taxation. Once war broke out its extraordinary expenses had naturally to be met by loans. These, starting with one for two and a half millions in 1776, had so increased in amount that by the spring of 1780 North was forced to go into the City for no fewer than twelve millions. Because what affected the taxpayer in practice was the interest on the debt rather than the amount of the debt itself, North would have preferred borrowing at three per cent. and, as money stood at about four and a half per cent., giving a little additional stock by way of ' douceur.' But because he realized that to the imagination of an uninformed public the rate of interest mattered less than a mounting debt, he felt it right to humour their whims and get his money by other methods, rather than challenge prejudices and cause a panic.

Accordingly he had hitherto, in his War Budgets, assigned to every lender of £1,000 the equivalent in four per cent. stock sweetened by a terminable annuity and four lottery tickets. The effect of such bonuses was to induce people to lend, but not to increase the capital sum by more than the actual monies received. For five years this method had worked satisfactorily.* In the 1780 loan, however, North had detected a certain ominous coyness on the part of the underwriters. Now when, twelve months later, he summoned to a preliminary conference at the Treasury, in accordance with practice, the monied men who would be expected to take up the bulk of the loan, he discovered that this shyness had taken a crystalline form. The advent of another enemy, which had further depressed the funds, made the City disinclined to accept anything like the old terms. In the insecure state of the market they demanded a wider margin of safety, and something more negotiable than annuities. Their terms, in brief, were that for every £1,000 lent, the lender should receive £1,500 of three per cent. stock at fifty-five, £250 of four per cent. at sixty-eight, and four lottery tickets. North was completely aghast. This method was indeed agreeable to his own private views, but the scale was grotesque. In vain he countered with an offer to borrow at five per cent. The City would not look at it, fearing heavy depreciation. Thereupon North adjourned the conference for consideration. And well he might. By the terms proposed

---

* The 1778 Loan—'the Losing Loan,' as it was called—had been undersubscribed, but principally because the notification of the French treaty with America came in the same week.

he was being asked to fund nearly 21 millions in
order to raise another twelve. Luckily, a day
or so later, the rumour reached London that the
Emperor Joseph II was proposing mediation. Upon
this flimsy report, so sincere was now the general
yearning for peace, funds rose several points. At
the resumed meeting the City proved, in consequence, slightly more accommodating. They agreed
to accept the three and four per cent. stock at two
points higher respectively, and upon that basis
North, at his wits end now to find money, struck
an unwilling bargain. The Chancellor had done
as well as any man could have done under prevailing
conditions in the money market. Necessity, not
choice, had caused him to admit terms which he
felt at the time were unconscionable. Before
forty-eight hours had passed he knew that they were
for a certainty.

In their timidity or greed the underwriters had
compelled North to borrow on a basis below that of
prevailing confidence. No sooner then had a
whisper of the forthcoming loan started snaking its
way through Change Alley than a burst of specu-
lative buying drove up the price of a stock, which
had not yet had the sanction of Parliament, to
between nine and eleven per cent. premium.*
Translated into hard cash this meant that, out of
the twelve million pounds lent to the Government,
and over and above the unusually heavy douceurs,
some £900,000 had been lost to the country. To
those who watched the steps of the Chancellor for

* It later reacted to seven and a half per cent., at which it more or less
remained.

the least sign of a stumble, here was something that must have exceeded their wildest expectations. Even the dullest of them could argue with plausibility that the loan was a put-up job. George Byng, the truculent Member for Middlesex, was indeed, convinced of it 'from the bottom of his heart.' Fox, with complete confidence, insisted that the unwarrantable rise was simply a device to reimburse Government supporters for their recent election expenses.[25] Moreover, their inferences seemed entirely confirmed when allotment was made, and many were found to be left out in the cold. Those who received nothing, and even those who had received less than their anticipations, swelled the chorus of critics. Issue was accordingly joined on two grounds: the iniquity of the bargain; the partiality of the distribution. The first was committed to the management of Fox, the second to that of Byng.

Sir George Trevelyan states it to have been notorious that a loan on much more equitable terms could have been arranged through established and hereditary banking firms.[26] If this is true, then North stands convicted of careless, if not wilful, neglect of his country's interests. But the assertion is unsubstantiated, for the very good reason that there is no evidence in its support.* Quite apart from his assurance that the terms were the best obtainable, it is hardly possible that a Chancellor with North's years of experience would have

---

* The only grounds I can find are a few vague references to the possibility of better terms, and these from the lips of Opposition spokesmen and therefore carrying little weight when set against categorical and repeated pronouncements to the contrary from North.

omitted to take advantage of other and better
channels had he known of their existence. North
was accused of many things in his life, but no one
ever accused him of deliberate falsehood, or of
financial imbecility. If the Government were
searching for douceurs, what could there have been
more convenient than the funds of the rebel state of
Maryland lying at their disposal in London.[27]
If his refusal to touch a penny of this money is not
sufficient evidence of North's integrity, at least the
argument used by the Lord Advocate can hardly
fail to convince. If North, maintained Henry
Dundas, had wished to make a corrupt bargain,
would he not eagerly have closed with the *first* City
offer, and thereby have increased the rise in
premium? [28] But, as Wraxall, who was present
throughout these debates, justly observes, arguments, which later seemed perfectly conclusive, at
the time made no impression. If blame lies at
anyone's door for the scandalous rise in price, it is
with the City who, taking advantage of North's
known necessities, exacted terms unwarrantably
severe.

From the accusation of partiality in the distribution of scrip North cannot be said to have
emerged equally scatheless, nor in fact did he
deserve to do so. The Opposition probably felt
from the start that they were on the trail of something definitely damaging to the Ministry, and
developed an attack on more personal lines than
before. Whereas they had previously abused him
as a Minister, they now assailed North as an individual, whose baseness in concealing the real terms

could be surpassed only by the manner in which he had concluded them.[29]   North began by defending himself with his habitual good humour and affability, confidently declaring that, when the list was produced, the House would see no favour, or rather, unwarranted favour, had been shown. That distribution had not been made *pro rata*, and that discretion had been exercised, he freely admitted, but justified himself on the grounds of long-established practice.   That this discretion had been exercised as to political views, and not to the financial standing of underwriters, he vehemently denied.   At the same time he declined to produce his correspondence with the various applicants.   Such a demand was not only unprecedented but was, he argued, tantamount to saying: ' Give me the key of your bureau, let me empty all your drawers, look over your papers and read every letter I can find, and then I'll tell you whether I can prove my charge or not.' [30]

George Byng need not have worried.   When the list was produced he might have asked what need was there to burrow in Whitehall pigeon holes for something that was staring them in the face.   From the moment he started running over the names, the word Jobbery was on every lip.   As Wraxall watched North, listening to the names of clerks and underlings credited with tens of thousands of stock (in one case as much as half a million), no wonder he thought he had never seen him so overcome.[31] There is no doubt that the list surprised North as profoundly as it exalted the Opposition.   This time witticism and candour were not enough.   Nor was

it sufficient to excuse himself on the grounds that
he had given instructions to provide against such
abuses. His hands might be as white as driven
snow; Fox, in fact, conceded as much.[32] That was
not the point. What mattered was that the same
thing could not be said of his subordinates. Between the orders of an eighteenth-century Chancellor
of the Exchequer and their being carried out lay a
gap peopled by many a needy or none too scrupulous servant, from John Robinson down to the
meanest clerk. Out of the mass of applications,
many had obviously worked their way into the
Treasury ear-marked for preferential treatment.
Few officials, at a time when jobbery was thriving
in every Government department, could be expected
to resist the temptation to exercise improperly such
powers of discrimination as they possessed. North
obviously had too many things on hand to concern
himself with a list of some sixteen hundred names;
yet if a Minister is not to be held responsible for the
working of his own department, there is an end
of constitutional government. Those who were
shocked by the revelations of this debate were by
no means confined to Opposition benches. A
motion to set up a Committee of Enquiry was
defeated by forty-six votes only. North learnt a
lesson which he never forgot.

After the budget battle there fell something of
a lull on Parliamentary warfare. Even when the
fight was resumed, it was over less dangerous
terrain. Wilkes rose to make his annual motion for
the expunging of his expulsion order; Savile reproduced another version of the Yorkshire Petition;

Burke complained of Rodney's severities following his recent capture of St. Eustatius; David Hartley, one of the dullest members who ever emptied a House, produced a Bill to give Government powers (as if they did not naturally possess them) to negotiate a peace with America. Except on the St. Eustatian confiscations, everything had already been said which could have been said, and it caused little comment that North fell asleep more frequently than ever. But there was no slumber for the Premier when, on June 12, Fox came down with a fighting speech and a provocative motion to open immediate peace negotiations with America. The manœuvre was well timed. A few days earlier a despatch had been received from Cornwallis which possibly had more effect upon those members of the Ministry—and their number included North—who were prepared to revise their views on the American War than anything since the news of Saratoga. Just a year before North had expressed, for the first time, real doubts as to their likelihood, of preventing American independence by force, and now had come confirmation.* The General had reported on the one hand that he had gained an almost incredible victory at Guilford Court House; on the other that he had been compelled to fall back upon the seaboard. In brief, all high hopes set upon the campaign in the Carolinas had dwindled to Charleston and Wilmington. The long line of British victories since Bunker Hill might, for all their practical results, have been

* The remark occurs in a letter to Eden of June 14, 1780. In the British Museum the date is incorrectly given as 1778. (Add. MSS., 34415, f. 423.)

defeats. Only a man of the most impenetrable of skins or of the most flinty 'determination, could remain impervious to such a conclusion. North was no longer that man. When Fox moved what was the equivalent of a censure on the Government, the Premier, of all men, sat silent. He did not speak because he could no longer have felt sure of himself or of the policy with which he had been identified for six years. Once there had been a very good excuse for such a policy; now it was supported only by pride. And for considerations of pride the Chancellor of the Exchequer, no less than the country gentlemen, was beginning to think too high a price could be paid. If he had spoken as he felt he must have resigned immediately. In that case he must either hand over to the indomitable Germain, with the certainty of further disasters ahead, or he must compel the King to take on men who throughout the war had been exulting over every enemy victory and deploring every British success. He therefore left the task of defending the government to Germain and hoped for the best. The House, seeing a Prime Minister removing himself from the front bench, drew its own conclusions on Cabinet accord. Only 271 members bothered to vote, amongst whom all that Robinson could whip up were 172.

Abstentions now became progressively numerous until prorogation. Unless, during the recess, matters took a decided turn for the better, it was evident the next session must bring about a total change of Government. But instead of success there came a trail of disasters. In the West Indies

Tobago was lost to France, and on the mainland Pensacola to Spain. A foolhardy expedition of Cornwallis into Virginia had registered its habitual victory and when last heard of was retreating on York Town at the mouth of the Chesapeake river. At sea there had been the usual summer parading of the English Channel by a Franco-Spanish fleet. On the Dogger Bank, Admiral Hyde Parker had fought a very indecisive battle with the Dutch. Worst of all, Admiral Graves suffered a serious defeat by the French off the Chesapeake. Bleak as were these tidings, there was a foreboding of something infinitely worse. Early in November, Cornwallis was reported closely invested on the York Town Peninsula with the French fleet at his rear and Washington advancing towards his front. A cloud of depression now settled upon the capital. Men fidgeted nervously in Government offices or waited expectantly in coffee houses for news which, to some would be like the setting of Britain's sun, to others a happy release from a painful illness. On November 15, even the King was expressing concern[33]; on the 19th, North was trusting His Majesty would prepare himself 'in case of accidents.' [34] By the 25th all doubts were set at rest. Parliament was to reassemble in two days' time; the King's speech had been settled when, at midday, a courier clattered up to Germain's house in Pall Mall. He brought the news of Cornwallis's surrender at York Town. The American Rebellion had become the American Revolution.

·   ·   ·   ·   ·

The man who had joked away the failure of the

expedition to the South, who had survived the
effects of Saratoga, was for the moment prostrated.
It is reported North received the news as one
might a ball in the breast. He reeled, threw out
his arms and cried ' Oh, God! It's all over.' [35]

This incident, one of the dramatic high lights
of North's career, has been over-emphasized. His
cri de cœur was the immediate reaction to shock of
one who for months had been living on his nerves.
Once the worst was known and suspense ended, an
improvement set in. Bishop Brownlow, visiting his
brother the next day, was astonished to find him
far less dispirited than he had known him on previous occasions.[36] Nor was North's exclamation
applicable to the war as a whole. The struggle in
America, considered in terms of offensive operations,
was certainly over. But not the war in general.
Not even North. Not even his Ministry, if one man
could help it.

Since Wedderburn in the backwash of the Gordon Riots had at last been swept into the Lords,
the most combative and constructive mind on
the Government benches belonged to Henry Dundas, the Scottish Lord Advocate. Dundas was
not only convinced that the Ministry could be
saved but that, in the interests of the country, it
ought to be saved. Nor, notwithstanding the
wretched record of the past twelve months, was
he attempting to weave a rope of sand. North
himself was still personally popular—more popular, perhaps, than any man in either House, with
the exception of Fox. His principles and his
integrity were second to none. He still possessed a

large and devoted following; he could claim to have made three approaches towards American conciliation; he was known for some time past to have regarded the war as a hopeless and profitless undertaking. Upon him, either as Chancellor of the Exchequer or First Lord of the Treasury, no direct blame could lie for naval and military disasters. The really black elements in his administration were Sandwich and George Germain. If these could be purged, and the Prime Minister induced to adopt a firm but realistic attitude towards America, then there was every chance of his Ministry living to conclude a peace not entirely dishonourable; in any event, defeating the Opposition at the winning post. Supported actively by Rigby, and with the tacit approval of the majority of Government supporters, Dundas started a campaign to drive Germain, and, if possible, Sandwich, from office.

Had there been an Opposition possessing a constructive and patriotic policy, Dundas' scheme must have died at birth, and North swept into resignation on the morrow of York Town. But at a moment when, if ever, the country needed to present a resolute front to a hostile world, the Buff and Blue Junta* could think of nothing but motions to delay supplies and to put an unconditional end to the American War. Such conduct not only shocked the patriotic feelings of the country party, but was deplorably lacking in justification. Had Cornwallis' been the last British army in America, and York Town the last foothold, the behaviour of the

* So called from their wearing the habit of American officers.

Opposition could not have been more abject.
York Town might indeed have been a defeat more
crushing than Saratoga, but that was no reason,
as North pointed out, for lying down to die.[37]
With New York, Long Island, Charleston and
Georgia held, with more men under arms and more
ships in commission than at the height of the
Seven Years' War, with Canada able to threaten
New England no less effectively than when she had
belonged to France, Britain held advantages which
should prove of the utmost value in any negotiations
which North desired as much as his adversaries.[38]
Moreover, the Opposition still laboured under the
delusion that the American War was the isolated
affair it had been at the time of North's first Peace
Commission, when compliance with America's
terms would have put an end to hostilities. Even
if, notwithstanding Congress' almost lyrical protest
to the contrary,[39] it was possible to detach America
from her Bourbon allies, peace could be obtained
only by withdrawing every soldier, giving up all
conquests made since 1778, and granting an independence which a leading member of the Opposition was even then declaring it to be high treason
so much as to mention.[40]

In the face of such conduct on the part of the
Opposition, the country members, though badly
shaken by the news of York Town, responded
to the Prime Minister's appeal for support.[41]
The Government majority on a hastily revised
King's Speech was gratifying. So far from
the word ' resignation ' crossing North's lips, the
vigour of his language even astonished the King.

z

Dundas' plot seemed indeed to be prospering. A Cabinet decision to send no more troops to America ' under the present circumstances,' except those necessary to keep up establishments, had, as he must have anticipated, led to a breach between Germain on one side and North, together with the bulk of his colleagues, on the other. To the latter, such a step was the preliminary one in the direction of a peace on the best terms obtainable: a sort of Federal Union, if possible, in return for New York and Charleston; at worst, independence on such conditions as should ensure substantial benefits to British trade and compensation to American loyalists.[42] To Germain, on the other hand, anything which suggested the possibility of independence was out of the question.[43] Any insistence on that point and Dundas knew Germain must go. By publicly alluding to a Cabinet schism and descanting upon the infamy of a Minister who ' in order to preserve his place would submit to carry into execution measures that he condemned,' [44] he trusted to drive Germain into resignation.

The weakness of Dundas' plot was two-fold: it ignored the King, and it assumed North possessed qualities which he had never shown, even in quieter times. The King, while prepared to part with Germain, refused to give up Germain's policy. For him, too, a cessation of activity in America was a breathing space, after which Britain, refreshed and revising her strategy, was to fight upon her stumps rather than yield to the colonies.[45] Indeed, if the retaining of Germain had been essential to such a policy, he would have parted with his crown before his American Secretary. It was only because any further operations in America required the replacing of Clinton by Carleton, who, on account of a personal quarrel, would refuse to work under Germain, that George III saw Germain must go. Any successor, however, he insisted, must not be ' of the yielding side.' If North chose to act otherwise, then said the King, ' You must go further, you must remove ME.' [46] This was almost more than North could bear. There was, he moaned, to be ' no great objection to changing men, but a very great one to changing measures, and it will be expected from me to take upon myself *alone* to carry on that plan which appears to me in our present circumstances ruinous and impracticable.' [47]

In this misery of North, Dundas' scheme started to break down. Torn between his dread of offending one without whose support he saw himself unable to carry on, and his tried loyalty to the throne, the Prime Minister fell back on his old trick of deciding nothing, of leaving letters to answer themselves, of hoping some diplomatic or naval miracle might ease the situation. But it was not the age of miracles, and when the Christmas holidays were drawing to their close nothing had been done or decided. Then Dundas, in a last effort to reorganize the Ministry, declared that while he would be satisfied with ' one human sacrifice,' that one must be Germain. Failing this, he threatened to attend Parliament no longer. [48] With a pistol at his head, both Dundas and Jenkinson (the most acceptable choices) having shrewdly declined to succeed Germain, North in an evil moment turned to the septuagenarian, Welbore Ellis, the 'little manikin' of the Junius Letters. If Dundas' intentions had been to revitalize the Ministry by ridding it of its most damaging components, they ended by forcing the Premier to commit this fatal appointment. After weeks of anxious travail, the country beheld the delivery of the undersized, over-dressed Ellis. On the Government's supporters the effect was immediate. North, by failing to insist upon the elimination of the useless American Secretariat or at least upon the taking over of its duties by himself, had flung aside all his recent advantages. From this point, the life of the Ministry ebbed rapidly away.

When Fox, finished for the time being with Germain (kicked up into the House of Lords as Viscount Sackville), turned his attention to Sandwich, his motion of censure was defeated in a House of 400 by twenty-two votes only. With such a majority, on a subject so closely concerning one of of its principal Ministers, a Government could hardly hope to survive. With the kill now in sight, General Conway, after years of ineffective torpidity, suddenly dug in his spurs. A motion by him on February 22, to conclude the American War, was defeated by one vote only, no less a confirmed Tory than Sir William Dolben, the Member for Oxford University, voting against the Government. Excited by the closeness of the division Barré broke out into violent abuse of North, whom he vilified as the scourge of his country. For the second time in his life North lost his temper, an unmistakable sign that he was also losing his grip. When it was learnt later in the day that Conway was to propose a similar motion in five days time, North realized that even a bare majority was no longer possible. None the less, his principles would not suffer him to resign while there remained the slightest chance of forming a Government not committed to peace at any price. While even a majority of one belonged to the Government it was permissible to believe there was still such a chance. If he was to go, he would go fighting for what he considered the best interests of his country.

When on the 27th Conway made his second onslaught, North counter-attacked in something like his old and best style. The motion was not only inexpedient but, he protested, it defeated its own object, an honourable peace with America, by betraying to the rebels our determination to tie the hands of our generals and to deprive the Government of initiative or discretion. In a word, it was a party measure, emanating from men, not one of whom had the least idea how peace was to be made, except by throwing in the hand. He warned them that, if surrender was to be made, it would have to be made to France as well as to America, for with several thousand trained French troops in their midst, and French money in their pockets, the Americans were in no position to make a separate peace. But if, on the contrary, it was felt France should be reduced before America would consent to treat, then ' nothing could tend more to weaken our efforts against our inveterate European enemies than to keep our army in

America with their swords tied up by this declaration.' Finally he asserted that if the intention of the Opposition was primarily to put on record that the House suspected the Minister's sincerity and ability, the motion was the wrong one. In that case it was their duty to address the Crown, praying for his removal. ' A Minister ought not to be a Minister after he was suspected; he should be like Caesar's wife, not only free from guilt, but even from suspicion. If the House should withdraw their confidence from him it would be his duty, without waiting for an address for his removal, to wait upon his Sovereign and, deliver up to him the Seal of his office.' [49] His effort was, as he had anticipated, a vain one. North found himself in a minority of nineteen in a large House. Though, strictly speaking, Conway's motion had not been a vote of censure, but rather an instruction to the Government, it was so plainly the writing on the wall that next morning newsvendors in the streets were crying ' Good news for England! Lord North in the dumps, and peace with America!' [50] When, on March 4, Conway further moved that all who should advise the further prosecution of the American War be considered enemies to King and Country, North did not venture to divide. He merely pointed out that, Parliament having decided to give up the war, the motion was unnecessary.

Although Fox believed that the Ministry would still cling to office[51] he was being unjust to North. The moment had at last come when, having lost the confidence of the House, North would remain deaf to appeals by the sovereign to his honour, duty or

"The Fox and the Badger changing places."

affection.* To do George III justice he made
no such attempt, but started, on the contrary, to
work through Lord Chancellor Thurlow for a broad-
bottomed administration. If he was not to be delivered bound hand and foot to faction (his ceaseless
nightmare), it was now a race between Thurlow's
capacity to inveigle the less violent of the Opposition
into partnership with a headless North administration and the Opposition's ability to draft and
carry motions so censorious that North must
instantly resign, whatever the state of negotiations
pending. As for Thurlow's part, it was handi-
capped by the old intransigeance of the Closet.
The King absolutely refused to change from one
Party to another, and so give up principles which (he
declared) he valued above his crown.[52] As for the
Opposition, their purpose must be carried out
within the next three weeks. The House rose for
the Easter recess on March 25, and long experience
had proved that after this break it was impossible
to beat up the same numbers. If North could hold
out until then he would be safe for the moment, and
Thurlow given further time for maturing plans
for a loyal and moderate government. On March
5, to encourage his supporters in the belief he contemplated a prolonged tenure of power, he coolly
introduced his Budget with further heavy taxation
and a loan (this time by close tender) for thirteen
and a half millions. It was a fine piece of bravado,
but any effect it might have had was negatived by

* Nevertheless it is worth recording that John Hatsell, the experienced
Clerk of the House, was at this moment prepared to give fifty guineas to
receive one for every day North remained at the Treasury. (B.M. Add.
MSS., 34418, f. 337.)

the report (although a premature one) of the capture of St. Kitts and the apparent doom of all Britain's West Indian possessions. In a further wave of depression the Opposition pressed on their attack. A general vote of censure, moved by Lord John Cavendish, against the Ministers on the 8th was rejected by ten votes only. To Dundas this was the end of his hopes.[53] To North it proved the impossibility of holding out even to the recess.[54] Only the King remained sanguine, trusting in the success of Thurlow's intrigues. For the last time he talked his harassed Minister round. While there remained a glimmer of hope (and to him it was hardly even a glimmer) North still consented to cling to his post. He even announced publicly his decided refusal to resign until the House should express an unequivocal opinion in that respect. His followers (he probably reasoned) might rat on the question of America, but would hesitate to do so on such a particularly personal matter as the hounding of their Chief from office. Nevertheless, the Opposition decided to call his bluff. Conway and Cavendish had both been Rockingham Whigs, and their actions might justifiably be attributed to party bias. When on the 15th a resolution came before the House that they could have no further confidence in the Minister, it was sponsored by Sir John Rous, a Tory by tradition, and once a steady follower of North.

Though no one suspected it at the time, possibly not even North himself, this debate proved the last occasion of his addressing the House as First Lord of the Treasury. He spoke towards the close of a heated debate, and with unusual embarrassment. His speech, which ran on much the same lines as his previous apologies, calls for no comment. What really mattered was that, in a motion so personal to its leader, the Government were successful by nine votes only. Immediately notice of a similar motion to come up on the 20th, was tabled. By then it was felt pretty confidently those nine votes would no longer be cast for the Government.

The only possible result of the King's refusal to admit a completely new set of men must now clearly be North's personal defeat in five days time and his ejection from office. In three letters of unusual length he drove into the royal mind, as never before, the hopelessness of his situation. If he had written, or said, nothing else they would establish his claim to possess some of the attributes of statesmanship. This time it was not merely the well-worn plea of unworthiness or unfitness to carry on. Instead, the King was reminded that ' in this country the Prince on the Throne cannot with prudence oppose the deliberate resolution of the House of Commons.' William III and George II, it was pointed out, had been obliged to yield against their wishes to their Ministers,

' because they found it necessary to sacrifice their private wishes, and even their opinions, to the preservation of public order. The concessions they made were never deemed dishonourable, but were considered as marks of their wisdom and of their paternal affection for their people. Your Majesty has firmly and resolutely maintained what appeared to You essential to the welfare and dignity of this country as long as this country itself thought proper to maintain it. The Parliament have altered their sentiments, and as their sentiments, whether just or erroneous, must prevail, Your Majesty . . . can lose no honour if you yield at length . . . to the opinion and wishes of the House of Commons.' [55]

With unaccustomed freedom of expression the King was told that ' where an absolute necessity exists, wisdom will teach us to submit to it with the best grace possible.' As for his own prospects, North confined himself to a single paragraph. If he should be defeated on the 20th ' I must quit my office immediately, and shall remain in the Journals for ever stigmatized upon record by a vote of Parliament for my removal, which I believe has seldom if ever happened to a minister before.' [56]

No Minister, not even if possessed of twice the sense of loyalty of a North, could be expected to await such a fate, with perhaps impeachment to follow and even—if some extremists could have their way—the block. Weighing his duty to his King against his duty to Parliament, North could not hesitate as to his course.

It is said that one of North's letters reached the King as he was about to set out hunting at Windsor. He glanced at its contents, told the messenger he would give Lord North an answer on the morrow, and then, turning to a Lord in Waiting, exclaimed, ' Lord North has sent me in his resignation, but I shall not accept it.' [57] It was an idle gesture of defiance. When, on the following day, personal appeals failed to make any impression upon his Minister, he gave a grudging consent. ' Remember, my Lord,' he said at parting in words which compel admiration, ' it is you who desert me, not I you.'

That afternoon a crowded and excited House met to consider the renewed motion of no confidence in the Ministers. At a quarter-past four North entered. Coming straight from the Closet he wore full dress, with the Blue Ribbon of the Garter conspicuous across his breast. The success of his plan depended upon its secrecy. After twelve years North must have realized how insecure was the confidence of any man. And so he had told no one his intentions, not even Robinson, whom he had seen that morning. On reaching the Treasury Bench, he turned to address the Chair. At the same moment the Earl of Surrey, who had been selected to move the motion of censure, stood up. Both obstinately refusing to give way, uproar at once broke forth. While some shouted for North and others for Surrey, the two men themselves struggled to obtain a hearing. At length, in a lull, North managed to interject the startling announcement that any motion the Opposition might have to make was unnecessary, inasmuch as the Ministry had that day ceased to exist. After this, the ex-Prime Minister could hardly be denied a hearing. In phrases which revealed better than anything he had ever said, his charm of manner and lack of all pettiness, which in a word explain the secret of his lasting popularity, North went on to thank the House for its long and essential support. If ever a man should be grateful to the Commons of England, he was that man, whom they alone had made and fashioned and sustained. He thanked them, too, for their partiality and forbearance and added that though, now, to his sorrow, they had seen fit to withdraw their confidence, he should ever hold it the principal honour of his life that he had once, and for so many years, possessed it. They would, he felt sure, presently have another Leader of the House of greater abilities and qualifications; they were hardly likely to have one more devoted to their country, their constitution and their King. Finally, he reminded the House that though he was resigning, he was not running away. " Having for so many years held a public situation and being entrusted with the management of public affairs, I am perfectly conscious I am responsible for my conduct, and whenever my country shall call upon me to answer, it is my indispensable duty to answer for every part of that conduct.' [58]

It would have done the Opposition some honour could they have respected these sentiments uttered in an hour of defeat and abasement. Instead of agreeing with magnanimity to North's motion for adjournment they rushed into a ridiculous and ungenerous wrangle. Not content with having brought their enemy to his knees, the hot-heads and irreconcilables attempted to force on Surrey's motion, in order to have the satisfaction of disgracing the Minister. But nothing now could ruffle North. Smiling, alert, sweet-tempered, he conducted his own case without any help from his own front bench, and in the end, when the good sense of the House had prevailed, carried his motion of adjournment.

A long debate having been anticipated, coaches had not been ordered to attend until midnight. Proceedings having ended long before that hour,

Members were standing about in disconsolate groups; for it was bitterly cold and snow was falling. North, having persuaded one or two friends to get the credit of having dined with a fallen Minister on the day of his disgrace, appeared, passed through them, and out to a solitary waiting vehicle. Just as he was mounting the steps of his coach he turned to the envious Members, most of whom were his opponents, and said with a smile, ' I protest, gentlemen, this is the first time I have ever had any advantage from being in the secret.'

As he drove off into the snow a chapter of British and American history closed.

Chapter IX

THE SLEEPING PARTNER

'La vertu d'un homme ne doit pas se mesurer par ses efforts, mais par ce qu'il fait d'ordinaire.'

PASCAL.

WHILE members of a jubilant Opposition were spreading the good tidings through the withdrawing rooms of Mayfair, there sat down to dinner at number 10 Downing Street as cheerful a party as could be found in any London household that evening. The conversation was as lively, the atmosphere as serene, as if the amiable host at the end of the table had just been presented with another coveted ribbon.[1] The future might have its doubts and perplexities: a king estranged; a drop in income hardly short of calamitous; a threat of impeachment, said to be ready drawn in Burke's pocket. But for the evening of March 20, 1782, there was only that exquisite sense of relief, shared by the entire North family, which comes from the breaking of an intense strain. The realization that there were no more decisions of State to be made; no more budgets to produce; no more place-hunters to be considered; acted like a stimulant on North's ragged nerves, and restored his spirits to their true level. That night he lived up to his reputation of being the best dinner companion of his generation. During the week of intense political activity which followed his retirement, North remained, very wisely, almost invisible, clearing up (not altogether, as we shall learn, successfully) the loose ends in an office he had held for a dozen years. He offered advice to none; he was consulted by none. Even when the new administration was announced he limited his comment to a jocular observation. Those, he remarked, who had so lavishly accused him of publishing lying gazettes, began their ministerial careers by asserting, what was a palpable untruth, that His Majesty was ' *pleased* to appoint ' the Marquis of Rockingham to the Treasury, the Earl of Shelburne to the Colonial Secretaryship, and Charles James Fox to that of Foreign Affairs.[2] * As a family man, North's principal concern during those ministry-making days had naturally been for himself, whose income had been cut by £10,000; as an ex-Premier he was eager to see that those who had served him faithfully were not forgotten. A few hours before the new Ministers kissed hands, both anxieties had to a large extent been allayed. The royal master who, ten days before, had hysterically warned his Minister that resignation would mean the forfeiture of his regard ' for ever,' now blotted out those hasty words with protestations of his eternal friendship.[3] Moreover what North had been praying for, but without thinking it proper to request, the Cinque

---

* ' When I shall now see in the Gazette that H.M. has been *pleased* to appoint such a one to such a place, I substitute in my own mind the word *obliged*.' (Selwyn to Carlisle, *H.M.C.*, *Carlisle MSS.*, 621.)

Ports for life, was settled upon him, together with a salary of £4,000, being the equivalent of the pension given forty years before to Walpole on his retirement. As his present emolument from that office was £1,500, this would mean, he reminded the King with satisfaction, that the net cost to the Civil List would be only £2,500.[4] Robinson and Grey Cooper, his two Secretaries of the Treasury, received respectively a pension of £1,000 and £500; but poor Brummell, his private secretary, and father of the future Beau, for whom in all his years of office North had been unable to make any permanent provision, was left out in the cold.* A further offer to raise North to the Peerage was, however, declined, ostensibly on the grounds that ' if he can ever be of service anywhere, it will be in the House of Commons, and his wish is to be in that situation in which his weak abilities can be most usefully employed for His Majesty and the Public.'[5] While this excuse was probably made in all genuineness, a less altruistic reason for North's refusal must be taken into account. North felt safer in the Commons. Even if he knew (which is most unlikely) that the first Cabinet meeting of the new administration had just rejected a proposition of Shelburne to bring him to trial,[6] he would be well aware that in more favourable circumstances such a decision might easily be reversed, so long as the rank and file contained men prepared to force the hand of Government. From such attacks he would be in far less danger if present in the House, able to defend in

---

* Nevertheless on his death a short while before North he left £60,000. (*Gent. Magazine*, lxiv. 285.)

person his conduct and, should matters proceed to a division, to call upon a still respectable phalanx of friends for support.*

For some weeks following his resignation it was obviously North's best policy to draw as little attention to himself as possible. Though, to be on his guard, he attended the House constantly, presenting an unusual spectacle in undress. He spoke only when attacked, as in a motion condemning Robinson's pension. This was clearly intended to be a prelude to one against his own rewards and, but for Dundas' caustic reminder that it was their duty to get on with the peace rather than to pursue vindictive inquiries, North might have been stripped of place and pension. But, towards the end of May, there arrived news which further reduced the likelihood of any successful measure against the fallen Minister, and allowed North to modify his tactics without fear of consequences.

Had Rodney's somewhat exaggerated victory of the Saints occurred two months earlier, the government of North might even have been reprieved. As it was, it did something to rehabilitate the reputation of the late Ministry, it did rather more to vindicate the Earl of Sandwich, and it did very much more to embarrass the Government. In their insolence of triumph the Rockingham administration had decided to recall the Tory Rodney and to replace him with an admiral who, though a good Whig, had not been to sea for twenty years. North prudently resisted the temptation to take too much

* For such a call when danger seemed to threaten a few weeks later see a letter to the Earl of Hardwicke (B.M. Add. MSS., 35424, f. 37.)

AA

advantage of the awkward situation in which the Ministry now found themselves. When an independent Member, who had previously voted with the Government, very properly brought forward a motion censuring the displacement of the victorious Rodney, North contemptuously voted with the Ministers, remarking, with biting allusion to their own behaviour during his period of office, that he considered the need of unanimity in the fleet superior to all other considerations. For that reason, he declined to do anything to render the new Commander-in-Chief odious to the navy. At the same time, he could not help observing, he said, that had such a dismissal of an Opposition admiral taken place when he was in power, he would never have heard the end of it.[7]

Except in a debate on the late Paymaster's balances when, in a crowded House, the Government were defeated by eleven votes, North wisely did not open his mouth for the rest of the session. He had done enough to regain the respect of many a waverer. He had proved the Government to be not invincible. Whether he now slumbered in his seat or went home early to supper, nothing more that he could do was likely to hasten or retard the disruption of a Ministry, which so short a time before, had come into office with every prospect of prolonged tenure.

For while the Rodney episode had damaged the prestige of the Rockingham administration, a process of internal disintegration had been at work. The Ministry, from the first, had, in North's words, ' carried in its own bosom the seeds of its own weakness.' [8] Differences between the two groups belonging respectively to Rockingham and Shelburne had immediately broken out in questions of patronage, and once peace negotiations (to which both were pledged) had begun, in spheres of influence. The rivalry in Paris between Oswald and Grenville was simply a projection abroad of what was happening at home between their respective superiors, Shelburne and Fox. So long as Shelburne declined to regard himself as ' an ordinary Secretary of State,' [9] taking orders from Rockingham, and Fox refused to consider himself Shelburne's clerk, unanimity was out of the question. It is clear, too, that Shelburne, behind the backs of his colleagues, had set out to ingratiate himself with the King, with the result that when, in June, Rockingham took to his bed, from which he never rose, it was he and not Fox, nor any Rockinghamite, who possessed most influence in the Closet. The death of the Premier on the first day of July simply ante-dated an inevitable crisis. The King, who had never loved the Rockinghams for their extreme views on America, hastened to give the Seals of the Treasury to Shelburne. Nor was the choice unfair. Shelburne had reluctantly given way to Rockingham in March, and it was only equitable that he should fill the next vacancy. Fox, however, smarting under a series of rebuffs, refused to see it in this light. Without the least constitutional right, he bluntly told his sovereign that, unless the Seals were handed to a Rockingham Whig, or, more specifically, to the Duke of Portland, he would resign. Now, as Shelburne justly remarked, it was one thing to compel the King to accept a Party, it was quite another to dictate to him a choice of Ministers, as though he were the King of the Mahrattas, ' among whom it was the custom for a certain number of great lords to elect a Peishwa, who was the creature of an aristocracy, while the King was, in fact, nothing more than a royal pageant or puppet.' [10] George III very properly declined to be a Peishwa, and Fox accordingly departed, taking with him the cream of the Rockinghamites.

Three months of prosperity had dissolved an association that had stood ten years of adversity, and a re-seating took place within the Commons which no man could have had the temerity to prophesy in the spring of the year. Who, in the furious Parliamentary strife of February, could have predicted that before the conclusion of the session Fox would be sitting two rows above North on the same side of the House, opposing the man upon whose shoulders had fallen the mantle of ' the great and glorious statesman whose memory every gentleman should revere, the late Earl of Chatham' ? [11] But, before twelve months were to elapse, there was an even greater surprise in store.

Failure to take immediate measures against North, which would, if successful, have scattered his Party like chaff, had been a grave, if unavoidable, mistake on the part of the Ministry. Whether they thought the moment inopportune, or realized on consideration that they could hardly impeach a Minister without impeaching the majority of the

Commons who had supported his policy, they merely eclipsed temporarily, and failed to eliminate permanently, their adversary.   As long as their façade remained whole they could ignore the hundred or so votes North could command.   Once the Rockingham-Shelburne association was dissolved, then North and his squadron acquired an importance out of all proportion to their numbers.   Whatever might have been Fox's motives in breaking up the Government, whether it was genuine (and excusable) suspicion of one so universally distrusted as Shelburne, or whether it was simply selfish pursuit of power, it restored North as quotable stock on the political exchange.

Given three Parties, those of Shelburne, Fox and North, each of approximately equal strength, three possibilities must result.   Fox must patch up his quarrel with Shelburne; Shelburne must approach North; or—the most grotesque of the three—Fox must join with North, the man with whom he had, not long since, declared it unsafe to be in the same room. The first, owing to Fox's inflexible attitude, was ruled out.   This left two alternatives, between which North held the balance, and could hold it with effect, unless (Gibbon suggested) he fell asleep.[12]

For North it was not a question of how happy he could be with either.   There was no inducement to hold the scale impartially.   From Fox he had differed on every question of major importance, besides having suffered the most outrageous abuse. Shelburne, on the other hand, had been less hostile to the American War, and was even now jibbing at

unconditional acknowledgment of Independence,
strenuously advocated by Fox. Moreover, he was
too anxious to keep in with the sovereign to object
to North's re-admission on reasonable terms.
Finally, three of North's old colleagues, Dundas,
Jenkinson and Robinson, were either identified
with Shelburne, or committed to his support.
A generous offer from the Premier, and there
is little doubt that North would have accepted,
if not at once, at least before the end of the
year.

But no concrete proposition came from Shelburne. Richmond, Grafton, and young William
Pitt, whose maiden speech two years before had
drawn North's unstinted praise, all firmly refused to
admit North on any conditions. The objections
of the two dukes might safely have been ignored,
but what the twenty-three-year-old Chancellor of
the Exchequer willed was decisive. Pitt's objection
was as foolish and ungenerous as his father's veto
upon Bute. Invited into the Shelburne administration in some honourable but non-superintending
office, becoming perhaps, like Carteret thirty years
before, Lord President of the Council, North, in the
sunset of his life, would have brought strength
without danger and dignity without dullness. On
the other hand, to reject such a man, who had no
desire beyond ending his days in comfort and
peace, when there was another incensed Party
awaiting their chance of overthrowing the Government, was, vulgarly speaking, asking for trouble.
Pitt's sanctimonious attitude certainly brought him
within two years into supreme office, but he took a

chance which might very well have consigned him to obscurity.*

Meanwhile, the session having come to a rather tepid close, North gave himself his first real carefree holiday for years. Leaving the future to look after itself, he set out with his family for a tour of the North Country. On August 10, however, his happy-go-lucky plans received a rude set-back in the form of a letter from the King. Writing with the approbation of Shelburne, if not at his express request,[13] George III began by reminding North of his promise to assist cordially in retirement any Ministry having the royal approval. The Shelburne Administration had such approval. Accordingly North was requested, not merely to give it his most ' active support ' in the next session, but to call upon all the country gentlemen ' who certainly have great attention for him,' to turn up on time and do likewise. ' Many strange scenes,' the letter continued, ' have occurred in this country, but none more so than the present contest, it is no less than whether the sole discretion of my Kingdoms shall be trusted in the hands of Mr. Fox; Lord North has long known my opinion of that gentleman, which had been, if possible, more riveted by three months' experience of him in office, which has finally determined Me never to employ him again.' [14]

Having dispatched an answer which was perhaps intentionally vague, North passed on to Buxton, where he ran into Wedderburn, or rather Lough-

* George Rose, his friend, in fact thought at the time of the Coalition that Pitt was a spent force as a politician, and wished him to concentrate upon the Bar. (*Memoirs*, i. 45.)

borough, as he had now become, taking a solitary cure. The latter's restless mind had for some time been convinced that, taking every circumstance into account, the only stable form of government was one composed of the Northites and the remnants of the Rockingham Whigs. Between him and William Eden, who was on intimate terms with North, a conspiracy towards this end had already, in fact, begun. 'The first thing,' he had written, 'is to reconcile Lord North and Fox. The first, you know, is irreconcilable to no man; the second will feel his ancient resentment totally absorbed in his more recent hostility, which I think he has no other probable means of gratifying.' [15] But amidst the round of excursions, with North in the most holidayish of moods, and showing in his choice of diversions the same irresolution as in affairs of state, Loughborough had hardly been able to edge in a word of politics. North, unable to reveal the receipt of the royal and highly confidential letter, was altogether reticent. Any proposition of a coalition was lightly dismissed as premature, if not unduly flattering to the strength of his own Party. He did, however, refer to vague approaches having been made from both sides, especially to one from Fox, which he had treated with contempt, proposing an office without authority. Nevertheless, Loughborough parted from North with three strong impressions. The first was that North was still the same mountain of irresolution as ever. The second was North's surprisingly enthusiastic reception at Manchester, where his carriage, instead of being broken in pieces, had been dragged along by a mob, who clamoured for his return to office. The last was the delightful and unaffected simplicity of the North family life. From being merely a political colleague, Loughborough from this hour became a friend.

By the time Members had begun to post along the turnpikes to Westminster, the political situation had not varied by so much as an inch. North was thinner, though more cheerful than ever; but the burden of his conversation was neutrality, moderation, even abstention.[16] He would hear of no bargaining.[17]

' I wish to explain to my friends,' he wrote, ' how I stand with respect to the contending Parties. I am connected with neither, but as I cannot, consistently with my principles, engage in faction. . . . I do intend to give my voice for the necessary supplies, and to oppose whatever tends to render government unable to contend with its present difficulties. . . . With respect to unforeseen measures, being in no connexion, I am open to approve or disapprove of them as they appear to me to deserve or not to deserve approbation.' [18]

Against this design of noble detachment and high-minded neutrality, expounded later to a meeting of his friends, there were various forces at work. North himself was not (as Loughborough had privately admitted to William Eden) by nature fitted to be the leader of a Party out of office. His followers saw no profit for themselves in such a policy, and if he was unable to change his mind, they were prepared to do it for him. To assist them in their endeavours there now appeared a new figure in the background of North's life, displacing in influence that of Guilford and Dartmouth. George

Augustus North, his son and heir, and member for
the Treasury Borough of Harwich, had, in association with Eden, and Adam another staunch
Northite, for some time been closely associated
with certain Rockinghamites, notably Richard
Fitzpatrick, Fox's intimate friend, and Lord John
Townshend.

Though subterranean activities had been going
on between the two Parties, nothing appeared on
the surface when Parliament reassembled, and for
the time North had his way. He declined, on the
grounds of essential unanimity, to oppose the
Address of Thanks for one of the longest and most
flowery King's Speeches ever heard. In a speech
devoid of humour, but which to Nathaniel Wraxall
' breathed the genuine spirit of a statesman,' [19]
he supported the Ministry in their conceding
American independence, though he reserved the
liberty to criticize particulars of the terms. There
was not so much as a whisper of any agreement
with Fox, whose advocacy of unconditional independence he went out of his way to condemn. On
the other hand, when, a day or two later, it was
rumoured, on grounds which have since proved
well-founded, that there was an idea to cede
Gibraltar for some equivalent, North sided with the
Opposition's demand that the fortress should be
thrown into the scale only if peace was possible on
no other terms, and then its price should be com-
mensurate with its unparalleled importance.[20] But
when Fox proceeded to move for papers in order to
discover whether the provisional treaty with
America did or did not contain absolute recognition

of independence, North swerved once more to the side of the Government. In a powerful speech, in which he resumed his accustomed levity, he carried with him the House, applauding and rocking with laughter at his sallies and similes. Two excerpts will show the manner in which he treated the question. Speaking of the agreement, he argued that from its very terminology it must obviously depend upon contingencies, otherwise it could not be qualified as provisional, but would be like the Oath of Highgate, whereby a man swore he would never drink small beer if he could get strong, nor kiss the maid in preference to the mistress, provided always he did not prefer the maid. Passing to the contention that by its production the treaty might be cleared of any ambiguities in advance, he went on in an ironical strain to declare that if a Cabinet consisting of eleven men ' of great genius, immense wisdom and long experience ' could not fix a precise meaning to each and every article, how was it possible for the Commons to do so? He had often heard them called the Temple of Eloquence, the Temple of Debate, the Temple of the Constitution, the Temple of Liberty, the Temple of Fame, but he had never heard them likened to the Temple of Concord.[21] Notwithstanding North's clear intentions to vote with the Government, Fox chose to divide the House, and found himself in a crushing minority.*

Within three weeks from the opening of the session, North had completely reasserted himself. His wit was as keen as ever, his reputation as a

* 219 to 46.

speaker and as a politician was re-established, his debating faculties were better than they had ever been. Possessed of the power to make or unmake ministries, he had once more resumed his old ascendancy in the House. If only he could have continued to hold the equipoise between two Parties, now lending his weight to this one, now to that, as the interests of State required, he might have cancelled every bad impression and have gone far to rehabilitate his reputation. But North's ability to play such a rôle was wholly due to the sanction of his Party vote. Without its support he would be not much more than a Sawbridge or a Hartley, except that he would be more amiable than the one and less long-winded than the other. In effect North was no more a free agent in 1783 than he had been ten or even fifteen years before. Forces over which he had little control were bearing him every hour away from the middle course along which it would have pleased him to dally.

By the time Parliament reassembled after the Christmas holidays the preliminaries with France and Spain had been signed. These had been, in principle, the work of Shelburne, and therefore presented to Fox a much more promising line of attack than had the American preliminaries. Indeed, as if scenting trouble, the rats already were streaming away from the Government. Faced by the prospect of seeing his achievements ruined, Shelburne commissioned Pitt to approach his late colleague. Every condition advanced by Fox, save one, was to be conceded, and that one Shelburne, by the express command of the King, was unable to grant: he himself must remain at the head of the Treasury. Fox, with his characteristic shortsightedness, waited to hear no more, and the meeting broke up. Pitt or no Pitt, there remained now for Shelburne one course only—a coalition with North. Yet even in this extremity, Pitt still refused to yield an inch. He would welcome his supporters, but he himself would not sit at the same Cabinet table with North. His detestation of the late Premier blinded him to the absurdity of expecting a man, who had repeatedly shown his power to give or to deprive the Government of its majority, to accept terms so humiliating. Shelburne had sufficient sense not to attempt an approach on such a crude basis. Instead, he decided to play upon North's fears. Dundas was commissioned to point out, through an intermediary, that the Minister's situation was such that if he did not obtain support from North he must (since Fox would not serve under him) resign. In that event Pitt would gladly embrace Fox, and between them North and his Party would be crushed to extinction. Clearly then, North's only hope of salvation, it was argued, lay in coming to terms with Shelburne. Up to this point the case was unexceptional. When, however, it was required of North, as a preliminary proof of his friendly intentions, that he should support the Peace unconditionally, the proposition took on a very different aspect. It was not even a Gentlemen's Agreement. In return for supporting a motion, on which it was admitted the life of the Government hung, nothing was guaranteed; merely a vague promise was made

that something might be done, Pitt permitting, at
the close of the session. The leader of a Party of a
hundred or more, who had merely to lift a finger and
the Ministry would be destroyed, was to be treated
like some naughty boy, with a suggestion of a very
small sugar plum if he behaved himself. Fox
could not possibly offer worse terms, and would
almost certainly offer better. Dundas, by his menacing messages, in other words, overshot the mark, and
decided North, or more correctly, George Augustus
North.[22] When, two mornings later, he sought
to retrieve his mistake by personally calling upon
North, it was too late. North had consented to
meet Fox that very day.

The meeting between North and Fox, which was
to have such a momentous effect upon the politics
of the next fifty years, took place in the afternoon of
February 14, in the house of George North. At
first the atmosphere can hardly have been otherwise than strained. North was perfectly aware that
the step he was taking must be distasteful to many
of his Party. Fox had only the day before confessed
that the prospect of leaguing himself with North
was odious.[23] Yet, when two men of such warm
hearts and amiable natures sat down to exchange
views, it would have been more surprising had
they parted without reaching an agreement. For
the moment their entente was limited to opposing
the Address on the Peace, and driving from office
the man whom they both sincerely distrusted.
North, consistent with his earlier criticisms, undertook to attack all three agreements, the French and
Spanish Preliminaries, and the American Treaty;

Fox, precluded from assailing the last—largely his own work—was to confine himself to the others.

Three days later, when the great debate opened, Fox took his seat alongside North on the front Opposition bench. The Coalition had begun, and begun not without an element of humour. On the previous night the two principals had sat up till after four discussing arrangements for the next day. Such a lack of sleep for one of North's habits soon made itself felt irresistibly. Hardly had Lord John Cavendish started to move the amendment than North, as if half-ashamed, slunk off to the gallery, where he flopped down by the side of Nathaniel Wraxall and, notwithstanding the gravity of the debate below, in a moment was soundly sleeping. Acting under instructions Wraxall intermittently prodded his neighbour into semi-consciousness whenever some particularly violent line of attack was being pursued. After ninety minutes, feeling himself sufficiently refreshed, North returned to the floor, and astonished Wraxall by making a brilliant and vigorous speech confounding every argument hitherto advanced by the Government.*[24]

North's effort that night was something more than an inaugural address of the Coalition; it was a carefully prepared and slashing indictment of the Peace. Forceful, analytical and with complete mastery of his subject, he tore the Government's case to shreds in a speech which, as the solemnity of the debate demanded, was unrelieved by witticisms.

* Sandwich, rarely lavish in praise, has paid tribute to North's ability to master detail in the shortest time. ' Give Lord North a bundle of papers and he'll turn them over—perhaps while his hair is dressing—and he'll instantly know their contents and bearing.' Butler's *Reminiscences*, 167.

He first exhaustively examined the French and Spanish agreements, in order to refute the claim that they were based upon that principle of mutual reciprocity which our successful defence of Gibraltar and recent successes at sea had at least entitled Britain to expect.* Next he turned to the American Treaty and sarcastically remarked the only reciprocity he could see here was all on one side. We had quite gratuitously rubbed out the boundaries of Canada settled by his Quebec Act, and had given to the Americans a rich and extensive district to which, having been driven from Canada in disorder, they had not the least claim. The allowing of their fishermen to use the Newfoundland fishing grounds was matched by no reciprocal right to fish in American territorial waters. A much vaunted grant of free navigation of the Mississippi was, by the side of these concessions, a mere mockery. Disgraceful as were these terms, they were nothing to the crime of failing to protect those Loyalists, ' who, in conformity to their allegiance, their cheerful obedience to the voice of Parliament, their confidence in the proclamation of our generals, invited under every assurance of military, parliamentary, political and affectionate protection, espoused with the hazard of their lives and forfeiture of their properties, the cause of Great Britain. . . .'†

* Defending the terms Lord Stanhope writes, with unconscious humour: ' We retained our Indian Empire . . . we retained the Rock of Gibraltar.' (*Pitt*, i. 91.) Considering we had lost neither it might as well have been argued in extenuation that we had retained Ireland, which the enemy had once threatened with invasion, or the Isle of Wight to which, at one period of the war, the French are said to have laid claim.

† While Franklin may have been technically right in declaring that Congress had no power to compel the individual States to act humanely,

Instead of insisting upon justice being done, the Government had weakly consented to the Loyalists being thrown upon the mercies of the state legislatures, which, in every case save one, treated a recommendation to mercy by Congress with derision.*

North could, with grim satisfaction, point to the predicted effect of throwing away our trump cards by unconditional recognition of American independence, and by pusillanimously surrendering all we had gained in the war. ' Could not,' he pleaded, ' the surrender of Charleston, of New York, of Rhode Island and Penobscot purchase the security of these deserving people? Was Congress not sufficiently sensible of debility of internal resource to prosecute the war? Had she the temerity to have persevered in a war rather than have given up this opportunity of exercising her implacable and impolitic resentment? ' Only once did he allow himself to sink to a lighter level on a subject which he felt so keenly. During the course of his speech a dog, which had somehow strayed into the Chamber, ran out barking furiously. Waiting until the laughter had died away, he turned to the Chair, remarking: ' Sir, I was interrupted by a new speaker, but as his argument is concluded, I will resume mine.' 25

The Opposition amendment declining to express any words signifying approval, was carried by a majority of sixteen in a packed House. It had

it never seems to have occurred to the British negotiators to take him at his word and insist that representatives of each State should sign the Treaty, thereby binding their local governments.

* The honourable exception was South Carolina.

come from the pen of North himself, and was both
carefully and moderately worded so as not to offend
those of both Parties who had been startled at the
coalition of their leaders. Its success was evidenced
by defaulters numbering no more than nine from
the combined forces.

The coalition having survived its first test with
signal triumph, three days later it assumed the
offensive and proposed a vote of censure. This
time North left criticism to others and confined
himself to a defence of his new and much abused
alliance.

' There are certainly times and circumstances and
emergencies [he said] when it highly becomes all honest
men, of every Party and description, manfully to relinquish
their personal feuds and temporary animosities, and unite
their serious efforts by one generous exertion, in the
common interest. It is, then, that mutually convinced
of the integrity and honour of each other's intentions,
however much they may have differed in the carrying those
intentions into execution, [they] could fairly meet in one
cordial body for the public good. Every individual
inspired by the genuine love of his country would then
think it his duty to abate somewhat of the violence with
which his former opinion was maintained, and form a
junction at once honourable to himself and serviceable to
his country. . . . Our union is on public principles; and
to the public we shall always be ready to give in a just
account of our stewardship.' 26

The motion having been carried against the
Government by seventeen, Shelburne promptly
threw in his hand, to the disgust of the King, who
found the Jesuit of Berkeley Square (as he had once
called him) less responsive to his passionate appeals
than North had been.

From February 24 there followed a period of six weeks during which the country was without effective government. The twists and turns of the sovereign in his endeavour to escape from a Ministry which contained Fox, ' who every honest man must wish to the utmost to keep out of power,' [27] make tedious and unprofitable reading. Just as his grandfather, a quarter of a century earlier, had held out against an inevitable Pitt, so George III was resolved to avoid what he imagined to be nothing better than thraldom. It was in these crises that he showed premonitory signs of a now not distant insanity, and to that extent may be excused conduct so narrow and unreasonable. ' These are bad times, bad times indeed,' he shouted one day to Robinson, whom he overtook on the road from Windsor.[28] But they were largely of his own ordering. Had not his wild prejudices against Fox disabled him from recognizing the claims of a coalition to succeed the administration they had overturned, and from giving them his immediate confidence, he would have obtained two Ministers profoundly considerate and ingratiating. Fox, during his short term of office, besides discarding his faro cards, had shown remarkable deference and application to business. North's complaisancy to his sovereign could be taken for granted. While he was in the Cabinet (and Burke still retained his tongue) there would be no innovations, and certainly not the least disposition to take the Closet by storm. Instead, by doing everything in his power to escape them; by approaching first Pitt, then Gower, then Temple, then Pitt

again; by endeavouring to split them asunder by
appealing to North, first through his father and
then in person; by attempting to foment disputes
over distribution of offices; the King very naturally
provoked a feeling of deep distrust.   In self-defence
Fox was compelled to adopt an attitude which,
though it achieved its immediate objective, in time
did him and North fatal injury.   To ensure that, in
event of taking office, the Ministers should not find
themselves betrayed behind their backs, he was
led to insist upon the exclusion of Lord Chancellor
Thurlow, the most influential of the King's friends,
and the appointment of the Duke of Portland, a
poor thing, but a stout Rockingham Whig, to the
leadership of the Government.*

Forced to give way, the King very neatly rolled
an apple of discord into the Coalition councils by
requiring a list of their proposed arrangements
before giving his final answer.   It was, as he probably reasoned, one thing to agree upon the desir-
ability of ejecting a Ministry, it was another to
preserve harmony when discussing a division of
spoil.   North, while perfectly prepared, if necessary,
to stand aside,† made it clear he would consent
to no Coalition unless due regard was paid to his
friends.[29]   Had not Burke's Bill passed in the
previous year abolished so many offices of the utmost
value to a Premier, there would have been sufficient

---

* The King, after four weeks, had reluctantly agreed to admit the Coalition, but had required, consistent with an intention of making the ' Bottom '
as broad as possible, that the First Lord should be a peer unconnected with
any Party—a proviso which would have soon enabled him to acquire an overriding influence.

† *Carlisle H.M.C.*, p. 635. If that happened the King believed the Coalition
would not succeed (*cf.* Grafton, p. 375).

loaves and fishes for the indigent of both groups. But when the Northites, from Sandwich downwards, started emerging from their funk holes, it looked as if there would be little left for the Foxites. If the two leaders had personally been inspired by nothing higher than place-hunger, the Coalition must there and then have foundered. Indeed, North, in despair, had actually started to circularize his Party explaining the reasons for the wreck of their hopes,[30] when through the accommodating attitude of Fox, as well as through his own conciliatory disposition, a settlement was reached. The King's tactics were then met by a combined refusal to make any proposals until the Duke of Portland should be summoned and instructed to form a Government in a manner which would leave the country in no doubt that the new Ministry had the King's official countenance—they could hardly expect to receive his personal favour. While it is clear such an attitude was unprecedented, there nevertheless would have been an end to responsible government if the King, without insisting upon a dissolution, should persist in declining to give his confidence to a Party which held an overwhelming majority in the Commons.

When a second and eleventh-hour appeal to Pitt had failed, and after he had drafted a message announcing his abdication, the King surrendered. Even then, but for there being scarcely a farthing in the Treasury and Coke of Norfolk (at Fox's instigation [31]) tabling inconvenient questions and threatening inconvenient addresses, he might have held out indefinitely. From at least two sources he had been advised to give the Coalition sufficient rope to hang themselves. They should now have it. It was, then, in this grudging spirit, and not in that of a man fairly defeated, that the King held out his hand (while turning back his eyes and ears like a horse about to throw its rider) to ' the most unprincipled Coalition the Annals of this or any Nation can equal.' [32] Time and patience, Thurlow had growled, would solve his troubles, and time was, in the reign of George III, generally on the side of the Closet.

The Coalition was North's last contribution to political history. No sooner had he enabled it to be launched upon what was to prove a treacherous sea than he started to fade out of the picture. Its Cabinet of seven may have contained, besides himself, who took office as Home Secretary, two other members of his Party, Stormont (Lord President) and Carlisle (Privy Seal), but in practice proportion meant nothing. The Duke of Portland was the merest piece of tinsel. The firm, from start to finish, was Fox, the Foreign Secretary, and Fox only. Once North had provided his colleague with the working capital in the shape of 120 or so votes, he had done all that was required of him—possibly all that he really wanted to do—except to live out the remainder of his days freed from responsibility and financial concern. Certainly in circumstances which, to one who had led the House for half a generation, might have been humiliating, North showed no less complacency or unaffected good humour.[33] Fox would undoubtedly have spared his new friend any such feelings of inferiority

"The Union."

by raising him to the Lords, where it would be impossible for anyone to consider himself second fiddle to the mute-like Portland. With Burke and Sheridan by his side he had ample talent in the Commons, but very little that was likely to be of service in the Lords. The King, however, having resolved to adopt a policy of rigid non-cooperation, declined to give the new government the customary right of naming peers.* North was not chagrined. The reasons which had induced him to refuse the offer twelve months earlier still held good. A defence, not only of his previous conduct, but also of his recent association with Fox, could be undertaken with greater certainty of success where he could rally his own followers, not all of whom were by any means so well disposed as their leader to the new arrangement. If his own powers of ridicule and argument were insufficient he knew very well he could now rely upon such forensic giants as Burke, Fox and Sheridan. All he asked was that due notice should be given in order that he could be sure of attending and, if necessary, take his whipping as patiently as a child, though without complaint or bearing malice.[34]

But no longer did the fate of the nation's policy or pocket hang upon the words of North. For all he mattered he might have retired to Somerset. The only occasion on which he spoke as Secretary of State rather than as a supporter of the Government was when, faithful to his sentiments

* According to Pitt himself this right was of essential importance to any Ministry. *H.M.C. Dropmore Papers*, f. 219. The King's refusal was therefore unjust.

towards the Loyalists, he moved and carried a
motion giving officers of certain colonial corps the
privilege of half pay.[35]   Even his greatest oratorical
success was on a subject which was notoriously
non-party.   Reform had been one of the questions
on which Fox and he had agreed to differ.   When,
therefore, William Pitt, obtaining a call of the
House, introduced a motion to disenfranchise
certain corrupt constituencies, and to increase the
number of county members, the Coalitionists found
themselves voting on opposite sides.   Fox, with the
bulk of his Party, followed Pitt and the renegade
Dundas; North, with Burke in stalwart support, was
eloquent in rejecting the measure.   As Pitt, in his
opening speech, had cited the long tenure of North
as conclusive proof of a defective constitution,
the latter very properly paid him the compliment
of putting forth all his powers of wit and argument.
His reply was as good as any North had ever made.
Its pith was very much the same as that which in
the past had characterized his speeches whenever
there had been a suggestion of change or innovation.   His language was that which any so-called
Whig, in the years preceding the accession of
George III, might have employed.   His arguments
could, in effect, be summed up in a quotation from
the Italian tombstone which he had used a few
years earlier to demolish a proposal for shortening
the duration of Parliament: ' *Stave bene, voleva
meglio—sto qui.*' *[36]   Nothing but the most positive
demand could justify any tampering with so vener-
able an edifice as the British Constitution.   Of such

* ' I was well, I wished to be better—here I am.'

a demand the Petitions laid upon the table of the House were certainly no evidence. Only fourteen out of eighty-two counties had petitioned, and these contained in all no more than 20,000 names, of which Yorkshire, the forcing ground of reform, produced 9,000, and the county of Suffolk the solitary signature of its Sheriff. Pitt had suggested that the number of new knights of the shire should be one hundred; ' But I say,' cried North, parodying the speech of Regan, ' no, not fifty. What, not fifty? No, not one.' Before he could consent to such an innovation he required to see more incontestable support.[37] He carried the House with him in rejecting the measure by 293 votes to 149.

For the remainder of the session North was not much more than a mute spectator who, from his office, wrote formal letters to Lord Lieutenants and Colonial Governors in terms previously settled by Fox in Cabinet council. In the House the only awkward interruption to his slumbers on the Treasury bench occurred when Pitt introduced a measure for the reform of abuses in Government offices. As an instance of how necessary was the cleansing broom he referred to an item in the Treasury account under North, namely whipcord, for which £340 had been indented. Though he loathed the noble Lord in the Blue Ribbon from the depth of his soul he cast no personal reflexion on his integrity, and North was left to make the only possible excuse, that somebody had been guilty of lining his pockets at the State's expense.

If, in the House of Commons, North was able on the whole to preserve his reputation, in the Closet he could do nothing. His presence at Court was a continual reminder to the King of the man who, of all men, had delivered him over to Fox. Much as he detested the latter, he realized Fox owed nothing to him. Fox had not enjoyed his confidence or friendship for fifteen years; his necessities had never been relieved; he possessed no principles. To him, therefore, George III could be civil always, and at times even cordial.[38] But of North he could only think and speak in terms of treachery and ingratitude of the blackest dye.[39] From the correspondence he was compelled to keep up with his Home Secretary he excluded every superfluous word. Gone were those innumerable personal touches and affectionate trivialities which had characterized his letters for so many years. Even a message of condolence on the death of his son, Prince Octavius, remained unacknowledged.[40]

Notwithstanding the King's abhorrence of ' that *grateful* man, Lord North,' he made an opening some weeks before the close of the session through which, had he been disloyal to his colleagues, North might have wriggled back into favour. The Prince of Wales had long been, to his father's grief, fascinated by the society of Fox, and for some time had been a source of embarrassment to Ministers and of sorrow to his father. It was in attempting to keep the peace between the King and his heir that North had once pleaded with the Prince ' to conduct yourself differently. Do so,' he begged, ' on all accounts—do so for your own sake —do so for your excellent father's sake—do so for the sake of that good-natured man Lord North,

and don't oblige him again to tell the King, your
good father, so many lies as he has been obliged to
tell him this morning.' [41] It was one of the King's
major gravamina against Fox that he had connived,
if not encouraged, the Prince's irregularities.   All
through the period preceding the Coalition his
son had openly professed his personal support of the
man whom the King feared and distrusted—his
practical support had been confined to one silent
member of the Commons.   Now, in June, when the
Prince was about to come of age, Fox showed his
gratitude by magnanimously proposing an allowance of £100,000 a year.   George III, though
greatly shocked at ' so lavish an idea,' agreed on
condition that there should be no further increase on
marriage.   More mature reflexion, however, led
to the obvious conclusion that such a proviso would
merely encourage the Prince to persist in his
discreditable bachelor life.   He therefore suggested
half the amount, but supplemented by the revenues
of the Duchy of Cornwall—an allowance which, he
pointed out, would exceed by more than half what
he himself had received as Prince of Wales.[42]   This
counter-offer was totally unacceptable to Fox, who
felt that, having given his word to the Prince, his
honour was pledged.   A crisis instantly developed.

It was at this juncture that the King, expressing
the belief that North could never have been privy
to such transactions, wrote forwarding copies of
his correspondence, and giving him the chance to
exculpate himself.[43]   Now, whether the King had
had some inkling that all was not well in the Cabinet,
the fact remained that North, together with the

Chancellor of the Exchequer (Lord John Cavendish),
had criticized Fox's offer as far too generous.   Outspoken expression of dissatisfaction might have
gone far to remove the royal displeasure (which,
it will be seen, was not much more than skin deep),
and have re-admitted North into the royal confidence.   But North refused to play on Fox the trick
that others had never hesitated to attempt upon
himself.   Having given his word, however reluctantly, he was resolved, as he put it, to make *cause
commune* with his colleagues.[44]   To the King he
thereupon returned an answer as evasive as that of
the previous August.*   In his mortification George
III contemplated taking the extreme step of dismissing his Ministry.   Indeed, but for the restraining advice of Temple, who, with the King's
approval, had resigned from the Lord-Lieutenancy
of Ireland, ' my son's ministry ' would have been
immediately requested to deliver up their seals.
In the end the Prince released Fox from his pledge,
and consented to accept his father's terms.

In persuading George III that the subject of his
son's allowance was not a sufficiently popular
reason for dismissing the Ministry, Temple had
indicated that the autumn might very well see the
realization of the King's nightly prayer—the collapse of the Coalition.   It was not a very profound
prophecy coming from one so thoroughly versed in
the *politique des coulisses*.   It was, nevertheless, a
correct forecast, though it came about in a manner
which Temple could scarcely have had in mind.[45]

.   .   .   .   .

* *Supra*, p. 359

' Next Session of Parliament,' wrote Fox, some weeks later, ' will be a great crisis. I own I am sanguine about it. Nothing can go on so well as we do among ourselves; but in my particular situation it is impossible not to feel every day what an amazing advantage it would be to the country if it could ever be in such a state as to promise a permanent Administration in the opinion of Europe.' [46]

It was a hope that did Fox credit, but, unlike Temple's prophecy, it did not come to pass. For if anywhere a red light was burning ahead of the Ministry, it did so over East India House in Leadenhall Street. And Fox drove directly towards it.

North's Regulating Act of 1773 had very soon developed disconcerting cracks. At home, a smaller and more monied Court of Proprietors had shown themselves no improvement upon the old. In India the failure to give the Governor-General overriding powers had led to the notorious and undignified wrangle between Warren Hastings and Sir Philip Francis. The attempt to give Bengal a directing control over the other presidencies had broken down. Maladministration was hardly less black than before. Yet in justice to North it should be remembered that he never considered his Act more than an experiment, to be revised or modified as occasion required. Had not the American contest, and its extension to other theatres of war, followed so soon, something would certainly have been done before the expiration of the Company's charter in 1779 compelled attention. By then, with a French and Spanish war on hand, North was in no mind to devote himself to India, and he readily took the line of least resistance. The

Charter was on two successive occasions renewed on the same terms for a year. But in 1780 the disastrous incursion of Hyder Ali into the Carnatic brought about a state of things requiring something more than patchwork treatment. The Company were given the benefit of a ten years' extension to their Charter, and at the same time two committees were appointed to deal with judicial maladministration and the Carnatic War. By the time their reports, extending to some nineteen volumes, were published, North was out of office and Rockingham was in.

The labours of these committees, on which representatives of all Parties sat, revealed a state of affairs which raised India above the sordid level of faction and demanded instant attention.[47] Both Committees had agreed, in reporting, that the trouble lay in the disobedience to the orders of the Directors at home, and to the rapacity of the Company's servants abroad. Thus when Dundas, who had been Chairman of the Carnatic War Committee, proposed forty-five condemnatory resolutions and demanded the recall of Hastings, described as ' the soul of the system,' the House was in complete agreement. But a Resolution of the Commons was, after all, nothing more than an expression of opinion, and when the Directors obediently proposed to summon Hastings home, the Proprietors negatived the suggestion. A few weeks later the death of Rockingham and the subsequent ministerial disputes caused the subject to be shelved, until the Company's critical necessities once more forced the Government to take action. This time it was no wild declaration of dividends, but the crushing expenses which the late war in the East had entailed. On the eve of the formation of the Coalition Government, the Directors petitioned for relief. Bills to the value of two millions were on their way to London, and there was no money to meet them. Without the assistance of the Ministry they professed their inability to carry on. But, as Burke ominously warned them, this time assistance must go hand in hand with reformation.*

If there was one man more than another in the Coalition Cabinet qualified to deal with the East India Company, it was Lord North. Quite apart from the fact that India technically belonged to his own office, he had studied the affairs of the Company more intently than any Minister with the possible exception of Burke, who was not in the Cabinet. That, instead of him, it should have been Fox, assisted by Burke, who took up the task, is the most conclusive evidence of North's sleeping partnership. That the problem appealed especially to Fox, by reason of its intricacies and its humanity, could not have warranted such flagrant poaching, had not North plainly desired to take the easy road. His health, certainly, was no longer as good as it had been, and since that momentous day when he had handed over the Seals of the Treasury, ambition had been steadily dying within him. He was perfectly content to while away the recess dealing with the routine patronage and procedure of his department, while Fox, a stranger now to the gaming room on the first floor of

* *P.H.*, xxiii. 647.

Brooks' Club, was steadily thumbing his way through Committee reports.

Had Fox been inspired by nothing so much as the desire for retention of office, here was a clear case for the application of plaster. Instead, he chose to tackle the question rather than to patch it up. Purposely he seems to have taken the greater risk in order that, if successful, he might look to the future with the more confidence. No sooner had Parliament reassembled in November than he rose to introduce his India Bill, a child not of choice but, he maintained, of necessity. Commendable as had been his application and genuine his enthusiasm for the good name of Britain and the happiness of the native, it was at once evident that these qualities were not matched by tact and discretion.

The most revolutionary feature of Fox's India Bill was a development of North's earlier conception of a body in this country qualified to deal with charges arising out of oppression and peculation in the East. It was proposed to set up a Board of seven persons invested with full power to appoint and displace officials, and to control the entire government of the Company's Indian possessions. It was to work in London ' under the very eye of Parliament,' to whom all its Minutes should be submitted. Associated with this Board was to be another, composed of assistants drawn from the Proprietors, to manage, subject to supervision, the details of business. The Board, moreover, were to be named in the Bill, and to be irremovable for four years, after which nomination vested in the King.

The Bill instantly gave birth to wild and extravagant language, surpassing any rhodomontade hurled against North ten years before. Whereas the latter's Regulating Act had been reviled for transferring power from the Company to the Crown, Fox was accused of going a step farther, and seeking to transfer it from the Crown to his own Cabinet. He was charged with setting up one of the boldest, most unprecedented, most desperate and alarming attempts at the exercise of tyranny that had ever disgraced the annals of this or any other country; of proposing a system which would crush out the free constitution of Britain; of taking the diadem from the head of the King and placing it upon his own.[48] Confident in his big battalions, Fox treated these ravings with the contempt they deserved. The Bill passed through the Commons with triumphant majorities, and went up to the Lords, where, on the contrary, Fox was not so sanguine of success.

North had been indisposed throughout most of the debates on the Bill and took a very negligible part.* But on the morning of the first reading he had returned the draft Bill to Fox with this prescient comment. ' *Influence of the Crown and influence of Party against Crown and people* are two of the many topics which will be urged against your plan. The latter of the two objections will not be sounded so high and loudly in the House of Commons, but it may be one of the most fatal objections to your measure. It certainly ought to be obviated as

* Dr. Holland Rose, without quoting any authority, asserts somewhat invidiously that he alleged indisposition. (*Pitt and the National Revival*, p. 143.) But there is no evidence that he purposely left the labours to others.

much as possible.' [49] The risk of the Bill being regarded as a party artifice to increase and secure influence should have been as clear to Fox as it was to North. Through his habitual lack of statesmanship Fox failed to take this into account at a time when Government and patronage were practically interchangeable terms. Although his motives were, there is no doubt, of the purest, he committed a cardinal error in the choice of his Board. Had he named four from among his own ranks and the remaining three from those of the Opposition, he must have disarmed criticism that the Bill was nothing less than a gigantic job to bolster up his Ministry for the next four years at least, by constructing around it an unassailable barrier of patronage.* Instead, every member named in the Bill was found to be a professed follower of the Coalition, and one of them North's own son, George Augustus. In the Commons the recital of these names had produced no more than a few guffaws, and not a word of criticism against their competence but only against alleged tyranny of the general proposals. It was in the Lords, as North feared, that the composition of a Board possessed of such powers of appointment, was likely to become a principal object of attack. To their Lordships there was only one word to which their ears were more sensitive than British Constitution, and that word was Patronage.

Closely in touch with the House of Lords through his two personal and confidential advisers, Thurlow

---

* He had an excellent precedent in North's secret committee of 1772 on which the latter had been careful to place men of all opinions.

and Temple, George III realized that the moment was favourable for the exercise of power not warranted by the Constitution, but justified, as he believed, by circumstances. He gave Temple a card on which he had intimated that he should consider as his enemies all who voted for the Bill, and then followed it up by bringing pressure to bear on his Lords of the Bedchamber. It being impossible to keep these overtures a secret, there followed a breathless last-minute canvass of peers by Government supporters. Though some affected to be sanguine of the result, their number did not include North. On paper there might appear to be a Government majority of two to one,[50] but his experience must have told him that in a comparatively restricted House of Lords the displeasure of a Sovereign counted, in the last resource, for more than the pleasure of a Ministry. The woolly reply of Archbishop Moore that he would be ' more than friendly ' might be taken as a text for all who were not definitely pledged to the Coalition. North's fears were well grounded.

On December 17 the Bill was rejected by ninety-five votes to seventy-six, Moore and others, upon whom the Government might, in ordinary circumstances, have counted, voting in the majority. ' I own,' said North quizzically, ' I own I never quite liked this awkward phrase, *more than friendly.*'[51]

In a sense this defeat might be considered as a sort of poetic justice for North. The Minister who, in his time, had seen so many inconvenient measures poignarded by the Lords, had now himself become their victim. Perhaps over more than one Dis-

senting breakfast table next morning there were
smug references to the engineer hoist with his own
petard.

The House of Lords might have spoken; but the
House of Commons had shown in no uncertain
manner their confidence in the Ministers.   Would
the King now proceed to further unconstitutional
acts by dismissing an administration which enjoyed
so preponderating a majority?   In the councils of
Fox and North there were doubts, discussions, but
not very much alarm.   In fact it was far from being
a despondent party which, on the following evening,
dawdled over supper in North's town house.   By
eleven o'clock, when gentlemen of the eighteenth
century may be presumed to have drunk themselves
into a state of extreme good humour with each other
and the world without, Evan Nepean, North's
Under-Secretary of State, was, to his Chief's
astonishment, introduced into the company.   He
informed them, after a few moments of embarrassing
silence, that he had a message from His Majesty.
He handed it to North.   The communication was
briefly worded, and ran:

' Lord North is by this required to send me the
Seal of his Department, and to acquaint Mr. Fox
to send those of the Foreign Department.   Mr.
Frazer or Mr. Nepean will be the proper Channel
of delivering them to me this Night; I choose this
method as Audiences on such occasions must be
unpleasant.' [52]

While his guests stared at each other in consternation, North, whose admirable good-humour
and command of temper never deserted him in

such moments, turned blandly to his Under-Secretary. 'If such be the case, Nepean,' he said, 'you will have very little trouble with me. My Seals are in your custody—you have only to take them to the King.' *

George III, after all, *had* dared to strike. The Minister, who for twelve years was alleged to have been kept in power through the force of royal influence, was, by an avowed use of that same influence, displaced; while William Pitt, who had hitherto reckoned himself a Whig, came into office crouched upon the back of Prerogative.

* It is with regret that the story of North's being in bed when Nepean arrived, and telling the embarrassed secretary that if he must see him he must see Lady North too, has to be dismissed in favour of Nepean's own account as given to Sir James Bland Burges by Sir Evan Nepean himself. (See *Life and Corr.*, p. 64.)

Chapter X

TWILIGHT

' In moderation placing all my glory,
While Tories call me Whig, and Whigs a Tory.'
                                                POPE.

No event in North's life has been more hotly criticized than his coalition with Fox—in the closing
years of his life even he himself was heard to express
his remorse for what he had done.[1] His clinging to
office during the war might be excused on the
grounds of a mistaken sense of duty, of continued
Parliamentary support and of a constitutional
inability to resist royal entreaties. But in forming
the Coalition there was no extraneous pressure.
North was a free agent. No question of duty was
involved. He knew he was acting in the teeth of
the King's disapprobation. Yet he deliberately
embraced, of two parties, the one which had been
most violent in its denunciation of himself and
his King. His conduct, it is alleged, was even
more reprehensible than Fox's, because Fox, having
no principles, could sacrifice none.[2] But here was
a man who had hitherto justified his conduct by
the most high-minded of motives, ignobly jettisoning
everything he had held dear for the sake of crawling
back into office.

This formidable indictment, nevertheless, has its source in three premises, only one of which will, on examination, appear to be well-founded. They are: that North was in 1783, and always had been, a Tory; that the Coalition at the time of its inception was unpopular; that it was a failure.

.   .   .   .   .

That North was a Tory.   Even if it were assumable that North was a Tory, it does not follow that by coalescing with a Rockingham Whig he was doing anything shameful. He would not have been the first nor the last statesman to change his convictions. But if it be asked by what right North is reckoned a Tory, we are confronted by this disconcerting fact: nothing that he ever wrote or said can be construed into an admission that he belonged to the Tory camp. That he was the son of a Tory signifies nothing in one born between the years of 1730 and 1750. It will be recollected North had entered Parliament at a time when Party ties were dissolved, and his first steps had been watched and guided by men of the old Whig school, who certainly never regarded him as a Tory. When, in due course, he stood upon his own feet, he was merely one of the rising generation, whose political creed had been influenced by the Pitt-Newcastle coalition. On the one side he retained Pitt's dislike of the Old Whig family connexion, and his faith in measures above men; on the other he believed in what Newcastle had stood for before being driven into opposition: the preservation of the Constitution with its nice adjustments and the sovereign enjoying his lawful prerogatives, subject always in the last resort to the overriding authority of Parliament.

With full confidence he had in the first weeks of the Coalition defied his enemies:

' To specify a single instance in which I ever attributed to the Crown any other prerogative than is vested in it by the Constitution, or than it is acknowledged to possess by every sound Whig, and by all those authors who have written on the side of liberty. I never did, or wished to, extend this branch of the legislature one inch beyond those limits which are prescribed to it by law.' [3]

It was North's attitude towards Parliament which really determined the colour of his politics. To say that he took his orders from his sovereign as obediently as the royal coachman[4] is true only in matters where he knew the sentiments of the House corresponded with those of the Closet—and for the greater part of his twelve years in office this was the case. When the former eventually withdrew its confidence, not all the appeals, threats and injunctions from the latter were able to deflect North from his purpose.

' I was the creature of Parliament in my rise; when I fell I was its victim. I came among you without connexion. It was here I was first known; you raised me up; you pulled me down. I have been the creature of your opinion and your power, and the history of my political life is one proof which will stand against and overturn a thousand wild assertions, that there is a corrupt influence in the Crown which destroys the independence of this House.' [5]

This was not the language of Tories, of Egmont, or Thurlow, or Jenkinson. Walpole, or Pelham, or Pulteney might have said as much, but Carteret, who lived and died officially a Whig, would never have made so Whiggish a pronouncement.

Equally insubstantial is his frequently cited refusal to acknowledge the title of Prime Minister. It proves him, on the contrary, to be anything but a Tory. To the Hardwicke-Newcastle school this term stank as something sinister and un-Whiggish. As long ago as 1741 it had been the subject of a Lords' Protest that Walpole had attempted to become ' sole or even first minister, an officer unknown to the law of Great Britain and inconsistent with the Constitution.' [6] Forty years later it was one of Grafton's complaints against Shelburne that he aimed at becoming Prime Minister. [7]

The New Toryism of George III, with its loose Cabinet organization, was none of North's work. It developed in his despite, while he feebly clung to the traditions of his early years in politics. A greater man than he, a Chatham, a Pitt or a Canning, might have triumphed over such handicaps. That North failed to do so may very properly relegate him to the second class of statesmen; but it does not make him a Tory. ' Actually (writes the historian of the Tory Party) North was not a party man at all. . . . If North must be labelled, which he would have disliked, he can only be called a Conservative.'* And so also can only be called his new colleagues with the exception of Fox, and even Fox under the mellowing influence of office would almost certainly have shed his Radical tendencies. North's decision to coalesce with such men as these may have been a mistake but hardly more a

* Keith Feiling, *The Second Tory Party*, pp. 100-101.

betrayal of principles than would have been a junction with Shelburne and Pitt.

That the Coalition was unpopular. It is argued that what could shock an eighteenth-century conscience must be indefensible. But here again there is very little evidence that, at the time of its inception, the Coalition was nationally unpopular. The three Ministers who were compelled to seek re-election encountered no difficulty. In North's case this was not surprising; but Lord John Cavendish, representing the Borough of York, met not the least opposition, while Fox received from Westminster notorious for its rowdy Radicalism only a few catcalls. Too many men were still alive who could remember the coalition of Pitt and Newcastle, and even of Carteret and the Pelhams, to be shocked at any combinations of politicians. The Coalition was at the time unpopular (as well as ' infamous and unnatural ') principally in the eyes of those who by it were ejected from office. The real source of its general unpopularity came posthumously, and as a result of the third and correct premise.

That the Coalition was a failure. As with every other Coalition, success was necessary for justification. A blank record and a brief life make it easy to plaster any political association with opprobrious epithets, in this case not altogether deserved. The failure of the North and Fox Coalition came from without, not from within. Possessing some of the finest Parliamentary talents and many of the most disinterested members, it might have given the country years of wise and moderate government. As long as North and Burke lived there would have been no drastic innovations; the Crown would have been no more restricted than it was soon to become when good fortune rather than good management brought Pitt into power. But the sovereign declined to show the same accommodating spirit as his Ministers, and by the time he shook them off they had had neither the tenure nor the opportunity to carry out their intention of supplying the country with a strong and beneficial government. When, on top of its barren achievement, followed Fox's mistaken tactics, and an election campaign with the Government's unscrupulous denunciations of the India Bill as a monster of graft and iniquity, the reputation of the Coalition was blasted for ever.

However unfavourable may be the verdict upon the Coalition, the criticisms which can be applied to Fox are not applicable to North. Fox had been threatened with extinction by no one. He had been the inspiration for years of an Opposition, half of whom were in office, and ready to work with him. He had had a poor excuse for breaking away in the first place, and none at all for refusing to repair the breach and join up with his natural ally, Pitt. North, on the contrary, had been all along the passive party. He had been the wooed, not the wooer. He acceded to the advances made because they offered terms honourable to himself, not unfair to his followers, and seemed likely to give the country, what it desperately required, a strong government. In return he sacrificed nothing. The American War over, the differences between himself and Fox were reduced to questions like reform, which cut across party distinctions. And even on such matters his liberty to differ from his colleagues was expressly reserved. Had he had the opportunity of associating instead with Pitt and the Shelburnites on the same terms, and had deliberately rejected them in favour of the Foxites, there might, in view of the King's special appeal in August, have been the shadow of a reason for calling his conduct 'incredibly base and unmanly.' [8] But to applaud Pitt for rejecting North, and yet condemn North for defending himself from extinction, is to adopt an unconscionable standard of political ethics.

.　　.　　.　　.　　.

With the dismissal of the Coalition, North passed out of office for ever, and to all intents out of history. The text-book knows him no more. His death nine years later is scarcely worthy of record. His influence upon the course of politics ceased altogether. His loyal army crumbled away, demoralized by defeat, and disheartened by exclusion from the good things of life. In the estimate of the rising generation of Parliament-men he soon counted for not much more than a dozen votes. But if his political death was progressive, it was not galloping. In the pages of the *Parliamentary History* he lives on as new subjects come crowding in: Warren Hastings, the Regency Bill, the French Revolution. Ceasing to count, he ceased to offend and, save only in the cold grey heart of William Pitt, who rarely rose without reviling him in some way or another, animosities died down. He was heard with consideration and with pleasure, for his faculties remained unclouded till the last, and his wit died only with the man.

And yet, had Fox's statesmanship matched his talents, these last years of North's life might have been somewhat different. When Fox took his place beside North on the front Opposition bench on the afternoon of December 19, a mighty army in his rear, rows of empty seats before him, the game, could he have played his cards with circumspection, was his. The proper course should have been to arraign Temple for his action in the rejection of the India Bill, and to have proposed a vote of no confidence in the callow Premier. In such circumstances Pitt must have resigned, or requested a dissolution. In the first place, the Coalition would have returned stronger than before; in the second, by making full use on the hustings of the King's interference, they would very likely have done so. Instead Fox allowed his resentment to master his judgment. Determined to teach George III and Pitt a lesson for having challenged the supremacy of Parliament, Fox, always the gambler, staked his majority upon a struggle between the privilege of Parliament and the prerogative of the King; or, as Johnson chose to express it, between his own tongue and the sceptre of George III. In the mistaken idea that time must hopelessly discredit the new government and convince the country that he was its true friend, he set out to resist immediate dissolution by casting a spanner into the Parliamentary machine.

Nine months' association with Fox had, for North, converted a business association into intimate friendship, all the stronger for their agreement to differ on certain fundamentals. But on that of the supremacy of Parliament there was no differing. North could with honesty declare he would not have remained in office for five minutes had he, like Pitt, found himself in a minority of three to one. He could, with perfect consistency, protest that government lacking the confidence of the House was a violation of Parliamentary privilege, and that if prerogative should prevail over those privileges the Commons must be enslaved. He could and did reply to his critics that ' secret influence which might formerly have been problematical was now openly avowed.' [9] Endorsing every word uttered by his colleague, whom he now made a point of calling his right hon. *friend*, he thus went gallantly into a battle which was as foolish as it was brief.

For three months Fox, flushed and impetuous, directed his matchless powers against the Treasury bench on which sat Pitt, sullen and frequently silent. For three months North, confident for the future, parried and thrust to the accompaniment of anecdotes which interrupted proceedings while the House recovered its composure. For three months both leaders wasted their strength on pinprick motions, while all the time Pitt was given scope to poison the air with the most tendentious reflexions upon the late Coalition, its origin, record and objectives. Then at last, on the same day that North was elected a member of Brooks', and the Coalition had reduced its majority to one, Pitt struck. A dissolution was announced. In a well-organized Government campaign the

Coalitionists were all but annihilated. Pitt entered upon a lease of life which was to carry him into the nineteenth century. The Whig Party passed into an eclipse which lasted for two generations.

The General Election of March 1784, which drove 160 ' Fox's Martyrs ' into the wilderness, has been hailed as a spontaneous expression of public disapproval of the Coalition. ' The victory of Pitt was more a victory of the people than of the King.' [10] Judged by results this might seem the case (although Fox himself attributed his defeat to Sayer's well-known caricature showing him running off with India House).[11] Nevertheless, there lies in the Royal Archives a paper which discounts something from Lecky's pronouncement. The document is a letter dated March 22nd, and therefore two days before the dissolution. It is from the King to Drummond, the banker, and it requests an urgent loan of £24,000. Whether, as there is every reason to suspect, this sum swelled an election fund for Pitt's use, or was used for less corrupt purposes, it reopened for North a highly unpleasant subject— his own financial dealings with the King.

It will be remembered that, seven years previously, George III had given North permission to draw upon him for £20,000, for the payment of his debts. At the time of his resignation this limit had been very nearly reached, but in a statement then forwarded to the King £4,000 was shown to have been used for public or non-personal services. However, the accounts were in such confusion that settlement was not reached until some sharp words had come from the Closet. Certain claims of North the King had refused to allow, and closed the loan account tartly by forwarding a draft for the balance reckoned to be due from him. The draft came to the comparatively humiliating sum of £20 15s. 6½d. But there still remained the settlement of the Secret Service account, and here confusion and mismanagement were even more pronounced. The details which can be pieced together from such memoranda as have survived make it extremely difficult to understand the exact position. One thing, however, is clear: in 1780, £30,000 had been borrowed from the accommodating Drummond on North's note of hand. At the time of North's resignation nothing had been repaid, and interest had been allowed to accumulate. On the King's private election account North then pointed out that there stood a debit balance against the sovereign for £13,000. When this was cleared off there would remain on the general account about £22,000, which he airily suggested ' may be rub'd off, by Cheques, by the £1,000 a month, out of the Privy Purse.' [12] To the King, faced now with the prospect of drastic economies by the Rockingham Administration, here was a thunder-bolt indeed. The £13,000 he would, he replied, make himself responsible for, and as an earnest, presently sent off a draft for seven thousand on account.[13] The balance, amounting actually to £19,754 18s. 2d., he professed himself unwilling and, indeed, unable to pay. Consequently, when North passed on the £7,000 to Drummond he seems to have undertaken implicit responsibility for the £20,000 outstanding. At least, he informed the King that he was endeavouring ' to arrange his affairs in such a manner as to be able to apply the whole income of his office [*sc.* Cinque Ports] to the gradual extinction of the debt.' Meantime he requested the King to withhold the £6,000 outstanding until his own arrangements were completed, which would be in a few months time.[14] Whether it was just good-natured optimism or whether there was some subtle purpose behind his offer, it is quite certain that North, on his shrunken income, could not possibly wipe off such a debt. Nevertheless, he had trusted that Drummond would not be unduly pressing, and he trusted not in vain. When, in reply to the King's letter of March 22, the banker called on the King, the latter heard to his very great surprise that, though two years had elapsed, not a penny had been repaid, and (what was worse in his eyes) not the least effort had been made to do so.[15] In high indignation he wrote off to Robinson, who passed the communication over to North.*

In consequence of the King's letter there followed a *mauvais quart d'heure* with Drummond. North bleakly explained that, as his net income did not exceed £2,500, it was absolutely out of his power to discharge the debt.[16] Drummond, being highly useful to the Closet, could not be allowed to suffer. The King accordingly took over the debt, undertaking to repay it by instalments. At the

---

* No doubt with quiet satisfaction: early that year, on joining Pitt, Robinson had received from his old Chief a letter beginning Dear Sir, and stating ' You say you had to choose between being my friend and my enemy, and you have chosen the latter course. Your option has necessarily determined mine.' *H.M.C. Abergavenny.*

same time he made no secret of what he thought of the conduct of his once dear Minister. ' Mr. Drummond [he wrote] must see that it [the delay] was not owing to any inaccuracy in me but the most barefaced fraud on the part of Lord North.' [17]

A week later all arrangements had been made, and Robinson trusted His Majesty would personally acquaint Lord North with ' the relief and ease ' so graciously afforded. But no letter came from the incensed monarch. So far as is known he neither spoke nor wrote again to the man whom he once declared he should for ever look upon as a friend and faithful servant.[18] It was a melancholy conclusion to a friendship which had lasted through sunshine and rain for fifteen years. It is impossible not to feel that this estrangement intensified the shadows which were now lengthening around Lord North.

. . . . .

Defeat, so frequently the solvent of Coalitions, had not the slightest effect upon the association of Fox and North, proving (if proof were required) that their alliance was actuated by something higher and less interested than a craving for office. Jauntily the two friends faced the now serried ranks of the Ministry, and without concern saw in them a vista of officeless years stretching into futurity. Yet with Burke and Sheridan on their flanks they could fairly claim to possess the cream of Parliamentary talent.

In what proved to be his last Parliament North began with conscientious attendance. As before, this was not without a purpose. If his ceaseless enemy, Pitt, with an assured majority, was at last going to carry out his threats and call him to account for the disasters of the war, North, in regulation Buff and Blue, was ready, even anxious, to face an indictment. When four weeks had passed, and only a few veteran back-benchers chose to ride their favourite hobby-horse, North himself threw down a challenge. ' Let them come forward with a charge. I am ready to meet it,' he cried, ' I call for it; nay, Sir, I demand it as a right. There can be no reason for withholding it now. If I was protected before, I am not protected now.' [19]

It was more than the good speech it was generally reckoned to be; it was a dexterous speech. With so many of his former critics now on his side of the House, and his old supporters like Dundas and Jenkinson on the other, North could safely defy his opponents to bring matters once and for all time to a decision. He could hardly be arraigned by a Government, when two of its most prominent members, and one of them Pitt's own lieutenant, had been ardent advocates of himself and the war; nor could he very well be impeached without dragging in the King, who was daily rising in popular estimation. From that day onwards, no further attempt was made to revive the subject. Though the atrabilious James Martin continued to rumble on in an undertone, and Pitt still spat venom, the noble Lord in the Blue Ribbon was left alone. But before long even Pitt softened, because upon the ageing statesman was now swiftly advancing a disability that will invariably arouse pity in the hearts of the most relentless enemies. North was becoming blind.

As early as 1768 North's eyesight had been the subject of one of Brownlow's letters, but no further progress seems to have been made by the disease until some months after the fall of the Coalition, when it began to develop with rapidity. In the course of a debate on Pitt's India Bill he had jocularly remarked that he could not see whether those on the Government benches were asleep or awake.[20] But behind the walls of Bushey Park there were no more light-hearted rompings at week-ends, as the realization of inevitable blindness descended upon him. He started to lose flesh and (of all people) found sleep escaping him. The distress of one who, at home, had been more Anne North's eldest child than a Prime Minister, was painful to his family and his friends. Nor was an imprudent marriage of George Augustus with a girl of birth but no fortune calculated to raise his father's spirits. Since the couple were unable to afford a separate establishment, the effect was to provide an extra mouth for the much reduced North economy to feed.[21]

Habits of a lifetime yielded only stubbornly. Throughout the session of 1785 North made determined efforts to attend, but only on occasions when his presence was earnestly desired.[22] Even then he contributed little to debates except a misquotation while assisting to throw out Pitt's Reform Bill. In the following year it was evident that, struggle as he would, his connexion with what for thirty years had been his spiritual home was weakening. The journeys from Bushey to Westminster became more of an undertaking and less frequent. He made, instead, pathetic attempts from his own study to keep up political contacts by constituting himself a sort of corresponding Whip for his own exiguous Party.[23]   On the other hand he was, perhaps, not over-distressed that his infirmities spared him the unpleasant task of sitting through the debates arising out of the complaints against Warren Hastings whom, in the middle of the late war, he had thought it inexpedient to recall, although disapproving of his methods.

And yet it was evident that there were subjects which could still revive the dying embers and bring him up to Westminster, even though he had to be led into the Chamber and through the division lobby on the arm of his son.   In 1787 a member had proposed to repeal, at the request of the Dissenters, the Test and Corporation Acts.   North, who all his life had fought any tampering with the Established Church, would continue to do so while he retained strength to stand upon his legs.   He hoped, he said, members would realize that his opposition was due to no blind and bigoted spirit of intolerance, but to the profound conviction that, once the bulwarks of the Church were weakened, the Constitution lay exposed to danger.   The admission of persons of particular persuasions into offices of the State was something quite different from, and should not be confused with restrictions upon conscience, which, he thanked God, no longer existed.   Alluding to the hideous memory of the Gordon Riots he uttered a warning against the perils of encouraging the cry 'The Church is in danger.' [24]   His words, both from their obvious sincerity and from the disability under which the speaker was suffering, made a deep impression. For the first time the House heard a compliment fall from the lips of the Premier. The Bill was rejected, Fox dividing against his friend. North then returned to his London house well satisfied, but so exhausted that he could not sleep that night. Anne now coaxed him back to Bushey in the hope that he would find distraction amongst his peaches and vegetables; but they had lost their charm. His spirits were lower than ever: he could not amuse himself nor did he respond to the efforts of others to divert his attention. He could no longer distinguish red from white wine by sight, and if he held his hand before his face he could not see it.

Just at the moment when physical darkness was closing in upon North, there appeared one of the most graceful of the few compliments ever paid to him in his lifetime. With that forgetfulness in matters of detail which gave such a false impression of chilly aloofness, North had suffered the historian of the Roman Empire to depart from England after the fall of the Coalition without so much as a word in farewell.* If Gibbon, who had as much conceit as ability, had chosen to repay North for this neglect, he could have done so in icier compliments than any man living, save Francis. With nothing to fear, and certainly nothing to gain, he chose rather to go out of his way, in the preface to the concluding volume of the *Decline and Fall*, to immortalize his admiration of his old leader.

* For a letter from Fox semi-apologizing for North's coldness of manner, see *Egerton MSS.*, 2136, f. 232.

' Were I ambitious,' he wrote, ' of any other patron
than the public, I would inscribe this book to a statesman
who, in a long, a stormy, and, at length, an unfortunate
administration, had many political opponents, almost
without a personal enemy; who had retained, in his fall
from power, many faithful and disinterested friends;
and who, under the pressure of a severe infirmity, enjoys
the lively vigour of his mind and the felicity of his
incomparable temper.'

Meanwhile everything known to medical science,
was being tried by his fashionable physician, Dr.
Warren; a compound of ' steell and myrrh '; a course
of shower baths; a visit to Bath, the water of which,
by inducing an attack of gout, were thought to
benefit the eyesight! [25] But with the year 1788 the
last glimmer of sight vanished. At the same time
there succeeded a merciful sense of resignation.
The alternating hope and despair of averting his
fate had been crushing out his spirits. Now that
nothing more could be done, except to make the
remainder of his life easy and contented, composure
returned, his spirits revived, his health rallied.

He had in fact made a remarkable rally when,
in the autumn of the year, the King's second and
serious attack of insanity led to a series of tedious
though virulent debates. The question was, briefly,
whether the Prince of Wales stepped untrammelled
into the King's shoes as Regent, or whether it was
competent for Parliament to hedge in his office
with restrictions. Had Pitt been on friendly terms
with the Prince, no problem would have arisen.
The latter would have taken over from the King,
the former would have carried on, and North
would have remained quietly in his chair listening

to his daughters reading favourite passages from the classics. But the Prince of Wales was still the ardent Foxite he had been at the time of the Coalition, and it was as certain as anything could be in politics that, once called to the Regency, he would dismiss Pitt and summon Fox to form an administration. With the 150 Coalitionists, together with the 180 placemen who would automatically face about to any government, there was no question of lacking a majority. Pitt, thoroughly alive to this danger, and believing the King's attack of insanity to be temporary, set out to gain time. First he countered Fox's claim of right on behalf of the Prince by setting up a committee to study precedents; next he proposed certain limitations on the Regent's prerogatives. This was too much for North. Primed with precedent and argument, he dragged himself to the House, in order to fight, as he sincerely felt, the battle of the Constitution.

To the cynic North's actions were easily explainable by references to Party politics. If he was the strong Constitutionalist he had always pretended to be, should he not have come forward to support the rights of the Legislature? Such a deduction rests on a question-begging basis. Parliament was not the Constitution. Strong as was North's love of the first, it was part only of a greater love of the second. Any infringement of the prerogative as sanctioned by the Constitution he was prepared to resist as strenuously as he had done any attack upon the rights and privileges of Parliament. There was no other motive which induced him to defy the bitter weather and ice-bound streets of London in that December. For Fox and Sheridan office may have been the guiding light, and who can blame them for following it? For North office, like his sight, had become something which had passed from him for ever. Nor can considerations of Party loyalty, in one who for eighteen months had not attended Parliament, and had every excuse for continued absence, provide a convincing explanation. It is impossible to doubt the absolute sincerity of North as he stood up blind and infirm, and asserted that in Pitt's efforts to restrict the Regent's powers he saw ' a project directly violating the fundamental principles of the Constitution.' How, he asked, could a House which, by itself, had not the power to receive a petition for a turnpike road, proceed to legislate upon the Crown?

' The plain road of proceeding was short and easy. Proceed to nominate a regent and then, when the third branch was restored and the legislature was complete, they would become a parliament, perfect in all its constitutional forms and might legally pass any laws, either of limitation, restriction or of any other kind. But to attempt to proceed otherwise was to trench on the prerogatives of the Crown while they lay at their mercy.' [26]

Was it, he asked, Pitt's intention to ' parcel out the royal prerogatives like an auctioneer in lots, in order to dispose of the Regency on the easiest terms?' [27] To appoint, as Pitt intended, someone to the office of Regent and at the same time to deny him the right to make peers or to give any office save during pleasure affected the fundamentals of the Constitution.[28] In all, North made ten speeches on the Regency question, many of

them stocked with historical learning; altogether
an astonishing performance in a blind and ailing
man.   Though it is clear (as one Member pointed
out) he was barking up the wrong tree—the purpose being to make a Regent and not a King—
the disinterestedness of North's intentions were
evident in every word he uttered.   The fact that
there was hardly a grain of levity or wit may well
be taken as proof of how deeply the discussion
affected him.

While Parliament wrangled over the disposition
of his prerogative, the King slowly recovered his
sanity.   In his more lucid moments he had shown
his real feelings for North by declaring he loved him
better than any man in the world.   He even (it is
said) suggested making him Speaker.[29]   Before
Pitt's Bill with its restrictions, carried through the
Commons by force of numbers, could reach the
Lords, he was restored to health and to his senses.
The crisis was over.   Pitt had played for time, and
he had won.   The Opposition consigned their
provisional list of appointments, in disgust, to the
wastepaper basket.

With one more fling later in the session against a
renewed attempt to tamper with the Test Act,
North passed through the division lobby for the last
time.   ' He loved the constitution (said the King
many years later) not as those do who professing
to love it wish under the pretext of reform to alter
or overturn it.' [30] His last act in the Commons was
thus symbolic of his whole life.   Within three
months the Bastille had fallen, and opposition to
reform was reinforced by terror of the sansculotte.

Sometime before his last appearance in the Commons, North and his family had begun passing a considerable period of the year at the Grove House, Tunbridge Wells. It was there that he ran into his old antagonist Barré, now like himself blind, and greeted him with the words ' nobody will suspect us of insincerity if we say that we should always be overjoyed to see each other." [31] It was there, too, that the dramatist and amateur diplomatist, Richard Cumberland, became one of the large circle of friends who were always dropping in to enjoy North's wit or to bring intelligence hot from Westminster. During the American War, Cumberland had gone on a mission to Spain, and on his return had advanced certain monetary claims against the Exchequer. These had been ignored at the time, and remained ever afterwards unsatisfied. He had, therefore, no disposition to love the late Minister, and his testimony is of infinitely more value than the partial and not very accurate evidence of a daughter.*

' I do not know the person,' wrote Cumberland, ' to whose society a man of sensibility might have given himself with more pleasure and security than to that of Lord North; for his wit never wounded and his humour never ridiculed: he was not disposed to make an unmerciful use of this power, which superiority of talents endowed him with, to oppress a weaker understanding: he had great charity for dullness of apprehension, and a pert fellow could not easily put him out of patience: there was no irritability in his nature.'

Divested of that ' incidental greatness, which

* This is to be found as an appendix to Brougham, *Statesmen of George III.*

high office for a time can give, self-dignified, independent [North] rose to real greatness of his own
creating which no time can take away.' [32]

Cut off now from acquiring fresh impressions,
North was thrown back upon those which he had
gleaned from extensive reading and the course of
his own eventful life; and his memory, sharpened
by his blindness, supplied him plentifully with
anecdote and recollection. Nor was he ever in
want of an audience. Burke, Fox, Sheridan and
Loughborough continued faithful to the last; the
Prince of Wales who, when he chose, could be the
most considerate man in the country, did not fail
on his visits to Tunbridge Wells to call at Grove
House.[33]   Nor did his friends come out of charity to
a blind man, but because they enjoyed the charm
and wit of his conversation, and his apparently
inexhaustible store of reminiscences.

Except on the occasion of his 1781 Budget, the
Opposition had never attacked North as a man, but
as a Minister only. Now that the Minister was no
more, it was possible for his adversaries to feel something like affection for one who had never had an
unkind word to say, and, though he had slept during the tedious ramblings of politicians, had never
been guilty of deliberate rudeness or high-handed
behaviour.   Indeed to such an extent did he carry
his habitual courtesy that he forbade his family
ever to apply the word *bore* (then coming into
fashion) to any guest.

But in his circle of guests there were gaps, and
it was when he thought of those who should have
filled them that he visibly saddened.   Those who

had opposed him he had gladly forgiven; but what of those who had fought by his side and then, in the hour of defeat, had gone over to the enemy? What of Dundas, his stalwart lieutenant, Robinson, Jenkinson, and, last of all to rat, Eden? North would have forgiven these too. He had borne no grudge throughout his life, and was not likely to begin to do so now. But for them it was not easy to shake the hand they had deserted, and they stayed away, and—what probably pained their old chief —they prospered in their desertion.

'They can't go on without more of my friends,' he had exclaimed, on hearing that Jenkinson had at last climbed into the peerage. Though he spoke playfully, behind the remark there lay much pathos. North was an exile dying in a foreign land. The friends who tended him were many, but they were not the friends of his youth, nor even of his middle age.

In 1790 the Earl of Guilford at last died, and two things happened to North. He succeeded to the title, thereby ceasing, after thirty-five years, to represent the town of Banbury, and the spoils of three Lady Guilfords, together with the North property, fell into his lap. Besides Wroxton there passed to him Waldershare in Kent and Kirtling in Cambridge. But the fortune came too late to be enjoyed. A year or two earlier he had confessed to Cumberland his intention to have engaged some young man of learning to be a companion and reader (for the society of the young pleased him the most) but for the inadequacy of his means. Now that he could afford that young man, he had grown too habituated to the services of his three devoted daughters. Besides, his journey's end was already in sight. North spoke five times only in the stranger atmosphere of the Lords. The last occasion was six months only before his death. The subject was one he had spent the best part of his life considering, the repeal of certain taxes and the reduction of the National Debt. His final utterance, for all its pathetic ring, is therefore deserving of respect.

He had the misfortune (he said) when in office, and afterwards when out of it, to maintain upon the subject of finance, a doctrine that was very unpopular. He was now too old to change his opinion, and the point of popularity should not now bias it; he had known the effects of it formerly, and had withstood them. He had received a lesson upon that subject in a manner too plain to be misunderstood, and too severe to be forgotten; the result of the whole was, that he was taught that popularity was at an end with him, and he gave his opinion totally without feeling anything upon that point; and he confessed that in that view he regarded the Bills in question as dangerous, and he hoped that the temporary popularity which the reduction of these taxes would procure to the present, would not lead a future administration to follow their example. He wished the people of this country as much wealth, comfort, and happiness for ever as they now enjoyed. But he could not help saying, that the best way to keep them in the present happy situation would be to call on them to avail themselves of the present moment to support

their burthens when they were so well able to bear
them, that they might be able to meet the exigency
of a future war, without incurring fresh taxes that
might then be felt as burthensome. The people
of this country were now free, opulent and happy,
and they should bear their burthens now, for the
purpose of reducing the national debt, if they
wished the country to preserve and enjoy its freedom
and its happiness for ages to come.[34]

Shortly after these valedictory reflexions, symp-
toms of advanced dropsy developed. There came
a loss of appetite and a return of insomnia. Dr.
Warren no longer attempted to conceal the hopelessness of his patient's condition. North received
the news that his end was at hand with the same
composure he had shown throughout his life.
Across the Channel he saw chaos and revolution
arising, and he was glad that he would not live to
witness the anarchy and bloodshed which must
follow. He had only one care now left in the
world. As he lay awake at nights it was inevitable
that his thoughts should return to Parliament and
to the days of his Ministry; and he wondered
anxiously how he would stand in the estimation of
posterity. And yet, as he wondered, he knew he
was being weak. But there!—it was a weakness,
he confessed, he could not resist.[35] Perhaps he
felt with the prescience of a dying man that once
his own voice was still, it must go hardly with his
memory. Of those who had fought shoulder to
shoulder with him the older ones were, like himself
dying off, the younger were revolving within the
orbit of Pitt; the friends of his later years, much

as they loved the man, could scarcely be expected
to defend the memory of the Minister they had for so
long and so fiercely opposed. On the contrary,
there would be a general inclination amongst all
descriptions of politicians to turn their backs
upon those days of national eclipse associated
with his name. There would be no incentive even
to attempt to appreciate the difficulties which had
encompassed him during so many years of his
Ministry. He was likely to be dismissed with few
obsequies as the protagonist of a scene all good
Britons were eager to forget.

' He was a man,' wrote one of the greatest patriots
who ever lived, ' he was a man of admirable parts;
of general knowledge; of a versatile understanding
fitted for every sort of business; of infinite wit and
pleasantry; of a delightful temper; and with a mind
most perfectly disinterested. But it would be only
to degrade myself by a weak adulation and not to
honour the memory of a great man, to deny that he
wanted something of the vigilance and spirit of
command that the time required.'[36] This reflexion of Burke was a just and fair estimate of
North's life and character and one which, had he
lived to read it, would certainly have been cheerfully endorsed by North himself. But if so qualified a verdict could come from one, who had every
inclination to speak favourably of his deceased
friend, what might be expected from others less
compassionate?

On August 5, 1792, Frederick North ceased to
concern himself with the opinion of posterity. On
that day footmen were drawing the blinds of the

house in Lower Grosvenor Street. Eleven days later, while Hell was being let loose in Paris and Old Europe was being dragged up by the roots, the body of the third Earl of Guilford was being lowered into a grave in the quiet churchyard of Wroxton.

Within the church, hard by the chancel steps, a slab of marble commemorates the career and death of a statesman. The language is singularly free from the prolix pomposities so characteristic of eighteenth-century memorials. It briefly records (as North would have wished) his offices and his honours; but no extravagant words attempt to panegyrize his merit. It is enough that surmounting the tablet there stands Britannia looking bravely before her, a spear in one hand, a shield in the other. At her feet a lion lies couched. Viewed in the half-light of the little country church no grouping more fittingly symbolizes the life of the honest, single-minded Englishman who loved his King, his Church, and his Country. ''

BIBLIOGRAPHY

MANUSCRIPT SOURCES.

British Museum :	Auckland Papers.
	Egerton MSS.
	Hardwicke Papers.
	Liverpool Papers.
	Newcastle Papers.
	Robinson Papers.
Public Record Office:	Treasury and State Papers.
Windsor Castle:	Papers of George III.
Bodleian Library:	North MSS.
Private Collections:	Barrington MSS.
	Minto MSS.

PUBLISHED SOURCES.

ACTON, LORD, *Lectures on Modern History.*

ADAMS, R. G., *Political Ideas of American Evolution.*

ADOLPHUS' *History of England*

ALMON'S, *Biographical Anecdotes.*

ANDREWS, C. M., *Colonial Background of American Revolution.*

Annual Register

AUCKLAND, LORD, *Journal and Correspondence.*

BARRINGTON, VISCOUNT, *Political Life.*

BECKER, CARL, *Eve of the Revolution.*

BEDFORD *Correspondence*

BEER, G. L., *Commercial Policy of England.*

    ,,   ,,   *British Colonial Policy.*

BLAND-BURGESS, SIR J., *Life and Letters.*

BLUNT, R., *Mrs. Montagu (Queen of the Blues).*

BROUGHAM'S *Statesmen of George III* (1853 edition).

BUCKINGHAM, DUKE OF, *Memoirs of the Court and Cabinets of George III.*

BURGOYNE, SIR J. (Fonblanque).

BURKE, EDMUND (Prior).

    ,,   ,,   *Correspondence.*

418

BUTLER, CHARLES, *Reminiscences.*

Caldwell Papers

Cambridge Modern History, Vol. VI.

CAMPBELL'S *Lives of the Chancellors.*

CARTER, MRS. ELIZABETH, *Letters.*

CASTRO, J. de, *The Gordon Riots.*

Cavendish Debates, edited Wright.

CHANNING, E., *Barrington-Bernard Correspondence.*

CHATHAM *Correspondence.*

CHATTERTON'S *Poems.*

CHESTERFIELD'S *Letters.*

CLARK, D. M., *British Opinion and the American Revolution.*

CLIVE, LORD (Malcolm).

    ,,   ,, (Forrest).

COKE OF NORFOLK (A. M. W. Stirling).

Complete Peerage.

COOKE, *History of Party.*

CRADOCK'S *Memoirs.*

CUMBERLAND, RICHARD, *Memoirs.*

CURTIS, E. E., *British Army in the American Revolution.*

DELANEY, MRS., *Autobiography and Correspondence.*

Dodington Diary.

DOWELL, STEPHEN, *History of Taxation.*

EGERTON, H. E., *Causes of American Revolution.*

EINSTEIN, LEWIS, *Divided Loyalties.*

ELDON, LORD (Twiss).

ELLIOT, HUGH, *A Memoir.* (Countess of Minto.)

ELLIOT, SIR GILBERT, *Life and Correspondence.*

ELLIOT, G. F. S., *The Border Elliots.*

FEILING, KEITH, *The Second Tory Party.*

FISK, HARVEY, E., *English Public Finance.*

FORTESCUE, J. W., *History of the British Army*, Vol. III.

FOX, CHARLES JAMES, *Early Life* (Sir G. Trevelyan).

    ,,   ,,   ,, (Fell).

    ,,   ,,   ,, (J. L. Hammond).

    ,,   ,,   ,, (Hobhouse).

    ,,   ,,   ,, *Memorials and Correspondence* (Russell).

FRANCIS, SIR PHILIP, *Letters and Memoirs.*

FRANKLIN, BENJAMIN, *Works.*

FREDERICK THE GREAT, *Memoirs* (especially Vols. V and VI).

GEORGE III AND LORD NORTH, *Correspondence* (Donne).

George III's *Correspondence* (Fortescue).

George III and Charles James Fox (Sir G. Trevelyan).

George III (J. H. Jesse).

„   „   (J. D. G. Davies).

„   „   (C. E. Vulliamy).

Gibbon's *Correspondence*, edited Prothero.

Glenbervie, *Diaries*, edited Bickley.

Grafton's, *Autobiography*.

Granby, Marquis of (W. E. Manners).

Grego, *History of Parliamentary Elections*.

Greville, Robert Fulke, *Diaries*.

Grenville, *Correspondence*.

Halévy, E., *History of the English People*, Vol. I.

Hardwicke, Lord Chancellor (Philip Yorke).

Haydn's *Book of Dignities*.

Hertz, G. B., *British Imperialism in the Eighteenth Century*.

„   „   „   *The Old Colonial Systems*.

Historical Manuscripts Commission (referred to as H.M.C.)
    Abergavenny MSS., *Carlisle MSS.*, *Dartmouth MSS.*,
    Dropmore Papers (Vol. I), *Lothian MSS.*, *Rawdon Hastings
    MSS.*, *Rutland MSS.*, *Stopford-Sackville MSS.*

History of the Second Ten Years (1770–80), Anonymous.

Hume's *Correspondence*.

Hunt, W., *Political History* 1760–1801.

James, W. M., *The British Navy in Adversity*.

Jepson, Henry, *The Platform*.

Jesse, J. H., *George Selwyn and His Contemporaries*.

Johnson, Samuel, *Various pamphlets*.

Junius, *Letters*, edited C. W. Everett.

Keith, *Memoirs of Sir Robert*, edited by Mrs. Gillespie Smyth.

Knox, *Extra-State Papers* (1789).

Labaree, L. W., *Royal Government in America*.

Laprade, T. W., *Parliamentary Papers of John Robinson*.

Lecky, W. E. H., *History of England in the Eighteenth Century*.

Lennox, Lady Susan, *Life and Letters*.

Lewis, G. C., *Administrations of Great Britain*.

Lyttelton, *Memoir of Lord* (Phillimore).

Macaulay, *Essays*.

Macdonald, W., *Documentary Source Book of American History*.

McIlwain, C. H., *The American Revolution, A Constitutional
    Interpretation*.

MAHAN, *Influence of Sea Power on History.*
MALMESBURY *Letters.*
MAY, SIR T. E., *Constitutional History of England.*
MONTAGU, MRS. ELIZABETH, *Letters.*
MORISON, *Documents Illustrative of American Revolution.*
MUMBY, FRANK, *George III and the American Revolution.*
NAMIER, L. B., *England in the Age of the American Revolution.*
 ,, ,, ,, *The Structure of Politics at the Accession of George III.*
New Foundling Hospital for Wit.
NICHOLLS, J., *Recollections.*
NORTH (Reginald Lucas).
Parliamentary History.
PITT, WILLIAM (Lord Stanhope).
 ,, ,, (Lord Rosebery).
PITT (Chatham) (Basil Williams).
William Pitt and the National Revival (Holland Rose).
PORRITT, E. and A., *The Unreformed House of Commons.*
Quebec Act (Reginald Coupland).
ROBERTSON, SIR CHARLES GRANT, *England under the Hanoverians.*
ROCKINGHAM *Memoirs.*
ROMILLY, SIR SAMUEL, *Memoirs.*
ROSE, GEORGE, *Diaries and Correspondence.*
Sandwich Papers. (Naval Records Soc.)
SCHLESINGER, *The Colonial Merchant.*
SHELBURNE (Fitzmaurice).
SHERIDAN (Walter Sichel).
SMITH, ADAM, *Wealth of Nations.*
STANHOPE'S *History of England.*
STIRLING, MRS. A. W. M., *Annals of a Yorkshire House.*
STRYIENSKI, CASIMIR, *The Eighteenth Century.*
THOMSON, M. A., *Secretaries of State.*
Thoughts on the Present War (Anon.) 1783.
Tomlinson Papers. (Naval Records Soc.)
TURBERVILLE, A. S., *House of Lords in the Eighteenth Century.*
TREVELYAN, SIR GEORGE, *The American Revolution.*
VAN TYNE, CLAUDE H., *Causes of American War of Independence.*
 ,, ,, ,, *The War of Independence.*
WALDEGRAVE, *Memoirs.*
WALPOLE, HORACE, *Letters* (Toynbee edition).
 ,, ,, *Memoirs of George III.*

WALPOLE, HORACE, *Last Journals.*
WHITTON, COL. F. E., *American War of Independence.*
WILKES, JOHN, *The North Briton.*
Windham Papers.
WINSTANLEY, D. A. *Personal and Party Government.*
    ,,   ,,   *Lord Chatham and the Whig Opposition.*
WRAXALL'S *Memoirs.*
WRIGHT, THOMAS, *Caricature History of England.*

NOTES

CHAPTER I

[1] P. 2. Gleig, *Warren Hastings*, ii. 469.
[2] P. 4. Lucas, *Lord North*, i. 9.
[3] P. 10. *Lord Hervey's Memoirs*, ii. 435.
[4] P. 10. *Cf.* Walpole, *Last Journal*, December 1773.
[5] P. 10. *North American Review*, Vol. 176, 781.
[6] P. 12. *North American Review*, 176, 780.
[7] P. 12. *Girlhood of Queen Victoria*, ii. 290.
[8] P. 13. *North American Review*, Vol. 176, 780, and B.M. Add. MSS., 32728, 317.
[9] P. 13. *North MSS.*
[10] P. 14. B.M. Add. MSS. 32730, 241.
[11] P. 15. *North American Review*, 176, 781.
[12] P. 16. H.M.C. (11th Rep., Pt. IV, Dartmouth, 330), and B.M. Add. MSS., 32728, 163.
[13] P. 16. B.M. Add. MSS. 32729, 128.
[14] P. 17. *European Mag.*, xxx. 82; Lord Brougham, *Statesmen of George III*, i. 243.
[15] P. 18. *North MSS.*
[16] P. 18. *Complete Peerage*, H.M.C. *Hastings*, iii. 118.
[17] P. 19. *North MSS.*
[18] P. 19. *North MSS.* and Walpole *Letters*, vi. 172.
[19] P. 20. Brougham, *op. cit.*, i. 244.
[20] P. 21. *North MSS.*
[21] P. 22. *North MSS.*
[22] P. 22. *North MSS.*
[23] P. 22. *North American Review*, 176, 172.
[24] P. 23. *North MSS.*
[25] P. 23. *Ilchester*, Lord Holland, ii. 268.
[26] P. 24. *Fortescue*, iii. 479.
[27] P. 25. *North MSS.*
[28] P. 26. *North American Review*, 176, 783.

CHAPTER II

[1] P. 32. Namier, *England in Age of American Rev.*, p. 122.
[2] P. 33. *Shelburne* (Fitzmaurice), i. 68.
[3] P. 39. Namier, *Age of American Rev.*, p. 105.
[4] P. 40. Wraxall, ii.
[5] P. 41. *Cam. Mod. History*, vi. 423.
[6] P. 42. Namier, *England in Age of American Rev.*, p. 94.

[7] P. 42. *Memoirs of George III*, i. 13.
[8] P. 44. Quoted by Basil Williams, *Pitt*, ii. 204.
[9] P. 45. *Minto MSS.*
[10] P. 46. Namier, p. 177.

CHAPTER III

[1] P. 51. *Debates*, Cavendish, i. 298.
[2] P. 52. *North MSS.*
[3] P. 52. Chatterton, *Resignation, Cf.* also H.M.C. (various) viii. 163.
[4] P. 52. *Cf. Bedford Corr.*, ii. 152.
[5] P. 54. *Grenville Corr.*, ii. 86.
[6] P. 55. *Cav.*, i. 297.
[7] P. 55. *P.H.*, xvii. 1335.
[8] P. 57. *Cf. North Briton*, No. 5, and Wilkes' Introduction to *Johnson's Fall of Mortimer*.
[9] P. 57. B.M. Add. MSS., 32948, 188.
[10] P. 59. *Grenville Corr.*, ii. 151.
[11] P. 59. *Grenville Corr.*, ii. 153.
[12] P. 59. *North American Review*, 197, 783.
[13] P. 60. Walpole's *Letters*, v. 385. *P.H.*, xv. 135.
[14] P. 60. Postgate, *That Devil Wilkes*, p. 76.
[15] P. 60. Walpole's *Letters*, v. p. 396.
[16] P. 62. Namier, *Structure of Politics*, i. 103, 135.
[17] P. 62. *European Magazine*, xxx, p. 82.
[18] P. 62. *North MSS.*
[19] P. 63. *North MSS.*
[20] P. 63. *Cf.* Lord Holland's *Memoirs* in *Life and Letters of Lady Susan Lennox*, p. 24.
[21] P. 65. *Minto MSS.*
[22] P. 65. *Fort.*, i. 125–155.
[23] P. 66. Walpole, *Letters*, vii. 3.
[24] P. 67. *Fort.*, i. 295.
[25] P. 67. Chatham, *Corr.*, ii. 438.
[26] P. 68. *North American Review*, 176, 174.
[27] P. 68. *North American Review*, 176, 174.
[28] P. 70. *Cav.*, i. 581.
[29] P. 71. B.M. Add. MSS. 32977, 41.
[30] P. 71. *The New Political Creed* (*New Foundling Hospital for Wit*) iv. 68.
[31] P. 72. *Glenbervie*, i. 231.
[32] P. 73. *Grafton Autobiography*, p. 113.
[33] P. 73. *Grafton Autobiography*, p. 123.
[34] P. 74. *Grafton Autobiography*, p. 123.
[35] P. 75. *P.H.*, xvi. 91–103.
[36] P. 76. *North American Review*, 176, 187.
[37] P. 77. *Bed. Corr.*, iii. 408.
[38] P. 78. *Grafton Autobiography*, p. 127.
[39] P. 81. *European Magazine*, xxx. 83.
[40] P. 81. *Cf. Ann. Reg.*, 1767, 54.
[41] P. 81. *Grafton Autobiography*, p. 196.
[42] P. 83. Franklin, *Memoirs*, iii. 308.

[43] P. 83. *Fort.*, ii. 21.

[44] P. 83. *Grafton*, p. 201; *North MSS.* and *Newcastle Papers*, May 16, 1768.

[45] P. 83. *Postgate*, p. 151.

[46] P. 84. *Cav.*, i. 49.

[47] P. 84. *North MSS.*

[48] P. 85. *Cav.*, i. 183.

[49] P. 85. *Cav.*, i. 107–9.

[50] P. 86. *P.H.*, xvi. 545.

[51] P. 86. *Cav.*, i. 123.

[52] P. 86. *Cav.*, i. 183.

[53] P. 87. *Cav.*, i. 351, the italics are mine.

[54] P. 88. *Cav.*, i. 383.

[55] P. 89. *P.H.*, xvii. 319.

[56] P. 90. *Cav.*, i. 55.

[57] P. 91. *Cav.*, i. 56.

[58] P. 92. *Ann. Reg.*, 1769, 64.

[59] P. 94. *Cav.*, i. 298–299.

[60] P. 96. See illuminating letter from Sir George Savile to Rockingham, *Memoirs*, ii. 132-136, also Walpole, *Memoirs*, ii. 254.

[61] P. 97. *Grafton*, p. 237, and *Rockingham*, ii. 83.

[62] P. 97. *Rockingham*, ii. 142–143.

[63] P. 97. *Cf. Rockingham*, ii. 143.

[64] P. 98. *North American Review*, 176, 190.

[65] P. 99. *Minto MSS.*

[66] P. 101. *Minto MSS.*

[67] P. 101. *Fort.*, ii. 126.

[68] P. 102. King to Barrington, *Barrington MSS.* (8.5 a.m., Jany. 28, 1770).

CHAPTER IV

[1] P. 104. *The Memoirs of Sir P. Francis*, p. 362

[2] P. 105. *Cav.*, i. 435.

[3] P. 106. Elizabeth Montagu, *Letters*, iv. 80.

[4] P. 107. *False Alarm, Works*, xii. 109.

[5] P. 107. Calcraft to Chatham, *Corr.*, iii. 412.

[6] P. 107. Chatham, *Corr.*, iv. 332.

[7] P. 108. *Cav.*, i. 547.

[8] P. 108. *Cav.*, i. 439.

[9] P. 110. Hume's *Letters*, ii. 214–215.

[10] P. 110. *Fort.*, ii. 128.

[11] p. 110. Chat., *Corr.*, iii. 415.

[12] P. 110. *Taxation the worst Tyranny*, p. 8.

[13] P. 111. Namier, *Structure of Politics*, i. 86.

[14] P. 113. Burke, *Corr.*, pp. 420–9.

[15] P. 113. Peter Pindar, ii. 13.

[16] P. 114. *Keith*, ii. 120; Walpole *Letters*, ix. 270.

[17] P. 114. *Corr.*, i. 112.

[18] P. 115. *P.H.*, xvi. 1949.

[19] P. 116. *Cf.* Walpole, *Memoirs of George III*, iv. 23.

[20] P. 117. *Minto MSS.*

[21] P. 117. *Rockingham*, ii. 177.
[22] P. 117. *Minto MSS.*
[23] P. 118. *Cav.*, i. 522. *P.H.*, xvi., 876.
[24] P. 119. Eldon, *Twiss*, i. 340.
[25] P. 120. *P.H.*, xvii., 707.
[26] P. 120. *Fort.*, ii. 247.
[27] P. 120. *North MSS.*
[28] P. 120. *Cf.* Walpole, *Letters*, vii. 378.
[29] P. 120. *Rockingham*, ii. 178–182.
[30] P. 121. *North MSS.*
[31] P. 123. *North MSS.*
[32] P. 124. *Cav.*, ii. 42.
[33] P. 124. *P.H.*, xvi. 951.
[34] P. 124. *Cav.*, ii. 42–62.
[35] P. 124. Calcraft to Chatham, *Corr.*, iii. 488.
[36] P. 125. *Cav.*, ii. 52.
[37] P. 126. *Cav.*, ii. 52, and *P.H.*, xvi. 1050–1053.
[38] P. 127. *Cav.*, ii. 76–77, *P.H.*, xvi. 1123, *North MSS.*
[39] P. 127. *Cav.*, ii. 223.
[40] P. 128. *Cav.*, ii. 198.
[41] P. 128. Selwyn *Corr.*, iii. 1.
[42] P. 128. Chatham, *Corr.*, iv. 60.
[43] P. 128. *Fort*, ii. 174; Malmesbury, *Corr.*, i. 291.
[44] P. 128. *Fort.*, ii. 175, and Malcolm, *Clive*, ii. 270.
[45] P. 130. *Letters*, ii. 237.
[46] P. 130. *The Eighteenth Century*, Stryienski, p. 197.
[47] P. 130. Quoted Hunt, *Political History of England*, 1760–1801, p. 114.
[48] P. 130. *Fort.*, ii. 191.
[49] P. 131. *P.H.*, xvi. 1343, and *Cav.*, ii. 27 and 298.
[50] P. 132. See North's speech on the Timber Bill, April 1771 in *Egerton MSS.*, 240, f. 168, and *Annual Register*, 1774, p. 53.
[51] P. 132. Chatham, *Corr.*, ii. 488.
[52] P. 132. *Fort.*, ii. 171.
[53] P. 133. *Letters*, viii. 1.
[54] P. 133. *Gibbon*, i. 221.
[55] P. 134. *P.H.*, x. 806.
[56] P. 135. *Fort.*, ii. 220.
[57] P. 136. *Cav.*, ii. 378n.
[58] P. 136. *P.H.*, xvii. 151.
[59] P. 137. *Cav.*, ii. 416.
[60] P. 137. *Fort.*, ii. 233.
[61] P. 138. Walpole's *Memoirs of George III*, iv. 200.
[62] P. 139. Walpole's *Letters*, viii. 25; *Annual Register*, 1771, p. 85.
[63] P. 139. *Cav.*, ii. 479.
[64] P. 139. Calcraft to Chatham, *Corr.*, iv. 127.
[65] P. 140. *Cav.*, ii. 479–80. Chatham, *Corr.*, iv. 139.
[66] P. 141. Chatham, *Corr.*, iv. 55.
[67] P. 142. Malmesbury, *Letters*, i. 220; *Fort.*, ii. 226.
[68] P. 143. *P.H.*, xvii. 165.
[69] P. 143. *State Papers Dom.*, xxxvii. 9.

[70] P. 143. Chatham, *Corr.*, iv. 187.
[71] P. 143. Burke, *Corr.*, i. 506.
[72] P. 146. *Egerton MSS.*, 228 (April 10).
[73] P. 146. *P.H.*, xvii. 868.
[74] P. 146. *P.H.*, xx. 1251.
[75] P. 146. *P.H.*, xxiv. 204.
[76] P. 147. Holland Rose, *Pitt and the National Revival*, p. 8.
[77] P. 148. *Anecdotes of the life of Richard Watson, Bishop of Llandaff*, 138.
[78] P. 149. *Cf. Grafton*, p. 303.

CHAPTER V

[1] P. 150. *P.H.*, xvii. 232.
[2] P. 152. *Egerton MSS.*, 232, ff. 160–1.
[3] P. 153. *P.H.*, xvii, 273.
[4] P. 153. *Cf.* some interesting reflections on this in Bishop Watson's *Life*, i. 132.
[5] P. 153. *P.H.*, xvii. 228.
[6] P. 155. *Gibbon*, i. 154.
[7] P. 155. *Cf.* Walpole's *Letters*, viii. 154.
[8] P. 156. *Fort.*, ii. 325.
[9] P. 156. *Egerton MSS.*, 239, f. 24.
[10] P. 156. *Egerton MSS.*, 239, f. 196.
[11] P. 157. *Egerton MSS.*, 235, f. 227.
[12] P. 157. *Fort.*, ii. 332.
[13] P. 157. Walpole's *Letters*, viii. 154.
[14] P. 158. *Fort.*, ii. 335.
[15] P. 158. *Fort.*, ii. 335.
[16] P. 159. *P.H.*, xvii. 489–490.
[17] P. 160. *North American Review*, 177, 263.
[18] P. 160. *North MSS.*
[19] P. 161. *North MSS.*
[20] P. 161. *Sandwich Papers*, i. 21.
[21] P. 161. *North MSS.*
[22] P. 161. *North MSS.*
[23] P. 161. *Cf. Grafton*, p. 169 and *cf.* also *The Man of Feeling*, p. 216 seq.
[24] P. 162. *Quoted* Forrest, *Clive*, ii. 311.
[25] P. 164. *Cav.*, i. 261.
[26] P. 164. *Grafton*, p. 110.
[27] P. 165. *P.H.*, xxii. 108.
[28] P. 165. *Cf.* his speech, March 1773, *P.S.*, xvii. 802.
[29] P. 165. *Cf. Egerton MSS.*, 244, f. 287.
[30] P. 165. *Egerton MSS.*, 244, f. 287.
[31] P. 165. *Cav.*, i. 252.
[32] P. 166. *Cav.*, i. 225.
[33] P. 167. *Egerton MSS.*, 240, f. 246.
[34] P. 167. *Powis MSS.*, quoted *Forrest*, ii. 380.
[35] P. 168. Walpole, *Last Journal*, i. 161.
[36] P. 168. *Fort.*, iv. 276.

[37] P. 168.   *P.H.*, xvii. 233.
[38] P. 168.   *Gibbon*, i. 163.
[39] P. 168.   *Forrest*, ii. 382.
[40] P. 169.   *Egerton MSS.*, 239, f. 252, and 244, f. 280.
[41] P. 169.   *Grafton*, p. 120.
[42] P. 169.   *Egerton MSS.*, 239, f. 252.
[43] P. 169.   *Egerton MSS.*, 240, f. 254.
[44] P. 170.   *R.O. Treasury*, xxvii, f. 424.
[45] P. 171.   *Fort.*, ii. 407.
[46] P. 171.   *Egerton MSS.*, 244, ff. 280–296.
[47] P. 172.   *P.H.*, xvii. 832.
[48] P. 172.   *P.H.*, xvii. 804–806.
[49] P. 172.   *Memoirs of Sir R. M. Keith*, i. 394.
[50] P. 173.   *Caldwell Papers*, iii. 217.
[51] P. 173.   *Egerton MSS.*, 246, f. 241.
[52] P. 174.   *Egerton MSS.*, 250, f. 299.
[53] P. 174.   *P.H.*, xvii. 890.
[54] P. 175.   *Memoirs, Sir P. Francis*, i. 369.
[55] P. 175.   *P.H.*, xvii. 868.
[56] P. 175.   *P.H.*, xvii. 891.
[57] P. 175.   *P.H.*, xvii. 902.
[58] P. 176.   Burke, *Corr.*, i. 390.
[59] P. 176.   Chat., *Corr.*, iv. 278.
[60] P. 176.   *Adolphus*, i. 535.
[61] P. 176.   *P.H.*, xvii. 464.
[62] P. 177.   *P.H.*, xvii. 853.
[63] P. 178.   *Egerton MSS.*, 246, ff. 170–189.
[64] P. 178.   *Egerton MSS.*, 248, f. 193.
[65] P. 179.   *Egerton MSS.*, 248, ff. 193–4, and *Fort.*, ii. 491.
[66] P. 179.   *Egerton MSS.*, 248, ff. 340–341.
[67] P. 179.   *Keith*, i. 314.
[68] P. 180.   *Egerton MSS.*, 248, f. 198.
[69] P. 180.   *Dart. MSS.*, H.M.C., iii. 201.
[70] P. 181.   *Dart. MSS.*, H.M.C. 13, rep. app. iv. 500.
[71] P. 182.   *P.H.*, xvii. 920.
[72] P. 185.   *Egerton MSS.*, 251, ff. 152–3.

CHAPTER VI

[1] P. 186.   Lecky, ii., 241.
[2] P. 188.   Quoted Adams, R. G., *Political Ideas of the American Revolution*, p. 42.
[3] P. 189.   Johnson, *Taxation no Tyranny*.
[4] P. 192.   *Barrington MSS.*, February 17, 1772.
[5] P. 192.   Van Tyne, *Causes of the American War of Independence*, p. 345.
[6] P. 192.   Quoted Egerton, *Causes of the American Revolution*, p. 5.
[7] P. 192.   *Present State of the Nation*, 1769.
[8] P. 192.   Beer, *British Colonial Policy*, p. 210.
[9] P. 193.   *Cf.* C. N. Andrews, *The Colonial Background of the American Revolution*, pp. 126 *seq.*
[10] P. 195.   L. W. Labaree, *Royal Government in America*, p. 35.
[11] P. 195.   Van Tyne, p. 83.

[12] P. 195. Hume to Mure, *Caldwell Papers*, iii. 259.
[13] P. 195. Quoted Van Tyne, p. 1.
[14] P. 196. MS. Letter to Lord Buchan.
[15] P. 196. Quoted Lewis Einstein, *Divided Loyalties*, p. 26.
[16] P. 197. Gage to Barrington, May 5, 1772. *Barrington MSS.*
[17] P. 197. May 13, 1768, *Barrington MSS.*
[18] P. 198. General Ruske quoted Phillimore, *Life of Lyttelton*, p. 604.
[19] P. 198. Van Tyne, p. 69.
[20] P. 199. *Fort.*, iii. 59.
[21] P. 199. Mumby, *George III and the American Revolution*, p. 211.
[22] P. 200. *P.H.*, xvi. 1315.
[23] P. 202. May 7, 1766, *Barrington MSS.*
[24] P. 202. June 4, 1771, *Barrington MSS.*
[25] P. 204. *Documentary Source Book of American History*, pp. 123-131.
[26] P. 205. Carl Becker, *Eve of the Revolution*, p. 65.
[27] P. 205. Rockingham, ii. 76.
[28] P. 205. Chatham, *Corr.*, ii. 355.
[29] P. 206. *Cav.*, i. 299.
[30] P. 206. *P.H.*, xviii, 222.
[31] P. 206. *P.H.*, xix. 762.
[32] P. 206. *P.H.*, xix. 765.
[33] P. 207. *Barrington MSS.*, June 26, 1768.
[34] P. 209. *Grafton*, p. 216.
[35] P. 209. H.M.C., *Rawdon Hastings*, iii. 148.
[36] P. 210. *Basil Williams*, ii. 227 note.
[37] P. 210. *Franklin Memoirs* (1839 edn.), iii. 290.
[38] P. 210. *Lecky*, iv. 125.
[39] P. 211. *Cav.*, i. 204.
[40] P. 211. *P.H.*, xvi. 478.
[41] P. 212. *Cav.*, i. 485.
[42] P. 212. *P.H.*, xvi. 853.
[43] P. 212. *Grafton*, p. 233.
[44] P. 212. *P.H.*, xviii. 940 and 1362.
[45] P. 212. *P.H.*, xviii. 723.
[46] P. 212. Rockingham, ii. 238.
[47] P. 214. H.M.C., *Various*, vi. 96.
[48] P. 214. Quoted *Adolphus*, i. 198.
[49] P. 215. *Dartmouth MSS.*, H.M.C., xiii. Rep. App. iv. 502.
[50] P. 215. *Dartmouth MSS.*, H.M.C., Rep. part v, p. 336.
[51] P. 216. *North MSS.*
[52] P. 217. Letter from Committee of Bill of Rights to S. Carolina House of Assembly, *Ann. Reg.* 1770, p. 225.
[53] P. 218. *Mumby*, p. 311.
[54] P. 218. *Cf. P.H.*, p. 177.
[55] P. 219. *P.H.*, xix. 763.
[56] P. 220. Van Tyne, pp. 386 *seq.*
[57] P. 220. Burke, *Corr.*, i. 453.
[58] P. 221. Franklin's *Works*, iii. 312.
[59] P. 222. *Works*, iii. 334.
[60] P. 224. *Annual Register*, 1774, 63.
[61] P. 224. *P.H.*, xvii. 1159.

[62] P. 224.   Blunt, *Mrs. Montagu*, f. 139.
[63] P. 224.   *P.H.*, xvii. 1166.
[64] P. 225.   *Annual Register*, 1774, p. 64.
[65] P. 225.   *Fort.*, iii. 55, and Walpole, *Last Journal*, i. 317.
[66] P. 226.   *P.H.*, xvii, 1164, 1171 *seq.* and *Egerton MSS.*, 254, ff. 86–89.
[67] P. 227.   *P.H.*, xvii. 1275.
[68] P. 227.   *P.H.*, xvii. 1192 *seq.*
[69] P. 228.   *P.H.*, xvii, 1315.
[70] P. 228.   *Annual Register* 1774, p. 72.
[71] P. 228.   *Second Ten Years of George III*, Anon., p. 152.
[72] P. 229.   *P.H.*, xvii. 1316.
[73] P. 231.   *Cf.* North's Speech, *P.H.*, xxii. 715.
[74] P. 231.   *P.H.*, xviii. 771.
[75] P. 232.   Quoted *Docs. of Canadian Constitution*, Kennedy, p. 126.
[76] P. 233.   *P.H.*, xvii. 1123.
[77] P. 234.   *P.H.*, xvii. 1243, and *cf. P.H.*, xviii. 781.
[78] P. 234.   *P.H.*, xvii. 1320.
[79] P. 234.   *P.H.*, xvii. 1358.
[80] P. 235.   *Dartmouth MSS.*, H.M.C., 13 Rep. App. iv. 501.
[81] P. 236.   *Atlantic Monthly*, 1884, p. 660 note.
[82] P. 236.   *Fort.*, iii. 147.
[83] P. 236.   Quoted Van Tyne, p. 443.
[84] P. 236.   *P.H.*, xviii. 771.
[85] P. 237.   *Fort.*, iii. 153.
[86] P. 237.   *Fort.*, iii. 256.
[87] P. 237.   *Donne*, i. 219.
[88] P. 237.   *Fort.*, iii. 134.
[89] P. 237.   *Fort.*, iii. 152 and *Memoir of Hugh Elliot*, p. 74.
[90] P. 238.   *Fort.*, iii. 16, and Laprade W. T. *John Robinson Papers*, p. 26.
[91] P. 238.   *Dartmouth*, ii. 251.
[92] P. 238.   Walpole, *Last Journal*, i. 414.
[93] P. 238.   *Adolphus*, ii. 169, and *Donne*, i. 219.
[94] P. 239.   *Malmesbury Letters*, i. 288, and *P.H.*, xviii. 264.
[95] P. 239.   *Fort.*, iii. 177.
[96] P. 240.   *P.H.*, xviii. 322.
[97] P. 240.   *P.H.*, xviii. 233.
[98] P. 241.   *P.H.*, xviii. 321.

CHAPTER VII

[1] P. 242.   *Cf. Fort.*, iv. 135.
[2] P. 243.   Walpole Letters: *Romilly*, i. 172, and *P.H.*, xviii. 193.
[3] P. 244.   *Cf.* North to Eden, B.M. Add. MSS. 34417, f. 35.
[4] P. 244.   *Fort.*, iii. 278.
[5] P. 244.   *Fort.*, iv. 444.
[6] P. 244.   *Fort.*, iv. 146 and 153.
[7] P. 245.   *Fort.*, iv. 55.
[8] P. 245.   *Fort.*, iv. 48 and 29.
[9] P. 245.   *Fort.*, iv. 78.
[10] P. 245.   *Fort.*, iv. 501 and 135.
[11] P. 245.   *Fort.* iv. 135.

[12] P. 245. *Fort.*, iv. 55.
[13] P. 246. *Fort.*, v. 143.
[14] P. 246. *Fort.*, iv. 216.
[15] P. 246. *Fort.*, iv. 132.
[16] P. 246. *Fort.*, iv. 356.
[17] P. 246. *Fort.*, iv. 95.
[18] P. 246. *Fort.*, iv. 382.
[19] P. 246. *Fort.*, iv. 27.
[20] P. 246. *Fort.*, iv. 63.
[21] P. 246. *Fort.*, iv. 135.
[22] P. 247. *Fort.*, iv. 500 and v. 62 and 338.
[23] P. 247. *Fort.*, iv. 504 and v. 543.
[24] P. 247. *Fort.*, v. 87.
[25] P. 247. *P.H.*, xix. 208.
[26] P. 247. *North American Review*, 177, 270.
[27] P. 248. *Patshull House MSS.*, quoted Lucas, ii. 98.
[28] P. 249. *Fort.*, iii.
[29] P. 250. *Fort.*, iii. 478.
[30] P. 251. *Cf. P.H.* xii., 955.
[31] P. 251. *Egerton MSS.*, 2232 f. 11.
[32] P. 251. *Fort.*, iv. 66.
[33] P. 252. *Fort.*, iv. 61 and 217.
[34] P. 252. *Fort.*, iv. 358.
[35] P. 252. *Fort.*, iv. 503.
[36] P. 252. *Fort.*, iv. 356.
[37] P. 252. *Fort.*, iv. and v. 61.
[38] P. 252. *Fort.*, iv. 72.
[39] P. 253. *Fort.*, iv. 132.
[40] P. 253. *Cf. Grafton* 287 and *Caldwell Papers*, iii. 217.
[41] P. 253. *Cf.* Burke, *Corr.*, ii. 13.
[42] P. 254. *Fort.*, iv. 59.
[43] P. 254. *Fort.*, iv. 92.
[44] P. 254. *Fort.*, iv. 164.
[45] P. 254. *Fort.*, iv. 222.
[46] P. 254. H.M.C., *Carlisle*, 482.
[47] P. 255. *P.H.*, xviii. 994 and *Cf.* 1156.
[48] P. 256. *Cf.* North to the King, *Fort.*, iv. 216 *infra*.
[49] P. 256. Sandwich, i. 240.
[50] P. 256. Walpole, *Last Journal*, ii. 48.
[51] P. 256. *Fort.*, iv. 142.
[52] P. 257. *Fox*, ii. 38.
[53] P. 257. H.M.C. *Abergavenny*, 33.
[54] P. 258. Keith Feiling, The Second Tory Party, 126.
[55] P. 258. *Elliot, Memoir of*, p. 78.
[56] P. 259. *The Duenna*, Israel Pottinger, p. 34.
[57] P. 259. *Cf. P.H.*, xviii. p. 27 and Selwyn, 112.
[53] P. 262. *Barrington MSS.*
[59] P. 262. *Barrington MSS.*
[60] P. 262. Curtis, E. E., *Organization of the British Army in the American Revolution*, p. 66.
[61] P. 263. *North MSS.* and Walpole, *Last Journal*, ii. 76.

[62] P. 264.   *North MSS.*

[63] P. 264.   Walpole, *Last Journal*, i. 511.

[64] P. 264.   *North MSS.*

[65] P. 265.   North to Barrington, August 24, 1775. *Barrington MSS.*

[66] P. 266.   Walpole, *Last Journal*, i. 569, and *Dartmouth*, iii. 229.

[67] P. 267.   Van Tyne, ii. 259.

[68] P. 268.   Add. MSS., 344, 414, f. 310, and H.M.C. (*Stop.-Sackville*), 82.

[69] P. 268.   *Tyranny the worst taxation*, p. 25.

[70] P. 269.   *P.H.*, xviii. 781, and H.M.C. *Sackville* ii. 25.

[71] P. 269.   Sackville, ii. 83.

[72] P. 270.   *Fort.*, iii. 290.

[73] P. 270.   On the whole question see *Fort., History of British Army*, iii. 185–6, and *Adolphus*, ii. 367.

[74] P. 272.   *Sackville*, H.M.C., ii. 67.

[75] P. 272.   Wesley, *Corr.*, vi. 160.

[76] P. 273.   H.M.C. Various, ii. 139.

[77] P. 273.   *Cf.* Elliot, p. 149.

[78] P. 273.   Donne, ii. 90.

[79] P. 273.   Add. MSS., 34414, f. 304.

[80] P. 274.   H.M.C. Various, vi. 139.

[81] P. 274.   *Fort.*, iii. 504.

[82] P. 275.   Add. MSS., 29, 475, f. 13.

[83] P. 275.   *Fort.*, iv. 77.

[84] P. 275.   *Cf. P.H.* xx. 336.

[85] P. 276.   *L.J.*, ii. 112.

[86] P. 277.   *Fort.*, iv. 27.

[87] P. 278.   Add. MSS., 34414, f. 399

[88] P. 278.   H.M.C. Various, vi. 146.

[89] P. 278.   Add. MSS., 34415, f. 237.

[90] P. 279.   *P.H.*, xix. 765.

[91] P. 279.   *Annals of a Yorkshire House*, ii. 26

[92] P. 280.   *Fort.*, iv. 38.

[93] P. 280.   *Fort.*, iv. 60.

[94] P. 280.   *Life and Letters*, Earl of Minto, i. 74.

[95] P. 282.   *Fort.*, iv. 67.

[96] P. 283.   *Fort.*, iv. 102.

[97] P. 283.   *Fort.*, iv. 144–6.

[98] P. 283.   *Fort.*, iv. 167.

[99] P. 284.   *Cf.* Minto, i. 76.

[100] P. 284.   Add. MSS. 29, 475, 15.

[101] P. 285.   Gibbon, i. 338.

[102] P. 286.   *Fort.*, iv. 115.

[103] P. 286.   B.M. Add. MSS. 37833, f. 227, also *Egerton MSS.* 2429 and *Fort.*, v. 201.

[104] P. 286.   *Fort.*, v. 162.

[105] P. 287.   *P.H.*, xxi. 909 and 920, also *cf.* Wilkes' speech, xxi. 892 and Walpole's *Letters*, xi. 72.

[106] P. 288.   *Political Life of Lord Barrington*, 165.

[107] P. 289.   *Fort.*, iv. 216.

[108] P. 290.   Add. MSS. 37, 834, 39.

[109] P. 290.   *Fort.*, v. 223.
[110] P. 290.   *Adolphus*, iii. 23.
[111] P. 290.   *P.H.*, xix. 1223.
[112] P. 290.   *Fort.*, iv. 264.
[113] P. 291.   *Fort.*, v. 281–6.
[114] P. 291.   *Fort.*, iv. 275.
[115] P. 292.   Add. MSS. 38306, 120, and *Fort.*, iv. 292.
[116] P. 292.   *Cf. P.H.*, xx. 197–8 and 946.
[117] P. 293.   *P.H.*, xx. 335.
[118] P. 294.   Butler, *Reminiscences*, i. 166.
[119] P. 295.   *Dart.*, ii. 474.
[120] P. 295.   *Fort.*, iv. 356.
[121] P. 295.   *Fort.*, iv. 356.
[122] P. 295.   *Fort.*, iv. 361 and 377.
[123] P. 296.   *P.H.*, xx. 937.
[124] P. 297.   *P.H.*, xx. 949–50.
[125] P. 298.   B.M. Add. MSS., 34416, 456.
[126] P. 298.   *Fort.*, iv. 410.
[127] P. 298.   *Fort.*, iv. 435.
[128] P. 298.   *Fort.*, iv. 461.
[129] P. 298.   *Fort.*, iv. 444, *Mem. of Fox.* i. 212 and 245.
[130] P. 298.   Trev., ii. 253.
[131] P. 299.   *Egerton MSS.*, 2232 f. 17.
[132] P. 299.   *Fort.*, iv. 397.
[133] P. 299.   Add. MSS. 37835, 30–6.
[134] P. 299.   Malms., *Letters*, i. 442.
[135] P. 300.   *Cf.* King's Letter to Robinson, B.M. Add. MSS. 37834, f. 88.
[136] P. 300.   B.M. Add. MSS., 37835, f. 44.
[137] P. 301.   *Cf. Fort.*, v. 2–5.
[138] P. 302.   *Fort.*, iv. 472.
[139] P. 302.   *P.H.*, xxi. 55.

CHAPTER VIII

[1] P. 304.   Trevelyan, ii. 226.
[2] P. 305.   See *Wealth of Nations*, iii. Book V.
[3] P. 307.   *P.H.*, xx. 1379 (italics mine).
[4] P. 308.   B.M. Add. MSS. 34417, f. 41.
[5] P. 309.   *P.H.*, xxi. 174.
[6] P. 309.   *P.H.*, xxi. 189.
[7] P. 311.   *P.H.*, xxi. 621.
[8] P. 312.   *P.H.*, xxi. 361.
[9] P. 313.   H.M.C., *Rutland*, iii. 26.
[10] P. 313.   Watson, *Remns.*, i. 123.
[11] P. 317.   Wraxall, i. 346.
[12] P. 318.   Cumberland *Mem.* ii. 37.
[13] P. 319.   Keith, ii. 108.
[14] P. 319.   *Fort.*, v, 87.
[15] P. 320.   B.M. Add. MSS. 34417, f. 102 and *Abergav.* H.M.C., 33
[16] P. 320.   *Cf.* Walpole's *Letters*, xi. 254.
[17] P. 321.   *North MSS.*
[18] P. 322.   H.M.C. *Abergav.* 33.

[19] P. 322.   Add. MSS. 37835 f. 186.
[20] P. 323.   Trev., ii. 58.
[21] P. 324.   Sandwich, iv.
[22] P. 324.   See Sandwich, iv.
[23] P. 325.   *Fort.*, v. 163.
[24] P. 325.   *P.H.*, xxi. 1349.
[25] P. 328.   *P.H.*, xxi. 1338.
[26] P. 328.   Fox, ii. 358.
[27] P. 329.   *P.H.*, xxi. 1332.
[28] P. 329.   *P.H.*, xxii. 22.
[29] P. 330.   Wrax., ii. 273.
[30] P. 330.   *P.H.*, xxi. 1355.
[31] P. 330.   Wrax., ii. 371.
[32] P. 331.   *P.H.*, xxii. 31.
[33] P. 334.   Sand., iv.
[34] P. 334.   H.M.C. *Aberg.*, p. 46.
[35] P. 335.   Wrax., ii. 435.
[36] P. 335.   *North MSS.*
[37] P. 337.   *P.H.*, xxii. 716.
[38] P. 337.   *Cf.* H.M.C., *Aberg.*, 46.
[39] P. 337.   See *Ann. Reg.*, 1782, p. 303.
[40] P. 337.   *Ann. Reg.*, 1782, p. 146.
[41] P. 337.   B.M. Add. MSS. 34418, 213.
[42] P. 338.   See *Fort.*, v. 335-7, and *P.H.*, xxiii. 454
[43] P. 338.   *Cf. P.H.*, xxii. 829.
[44] P. 338.   Wrax., ii. 449.
[45] P. 338.   *Cf.* Germain's Memo., H.M.C., *Stopford-Sackville* 216-20.
[46] P. 339.   H.M.C., Various, vi. 276.
[47] P. 339.   H.M.C., *Abergavenny*, 46.
[48] P. 339.   *Fort.*, v. 359
[49] P. 342.   *P.H.*, xxii. 1077.
[50] P. 342.   Romilly, i. 152.
[51] P. 342.   Fox, *Mem.* ii. 279.
[52] P. 343.   *Egerton MSS.*, 2232, 51.
[53] P. 344.   H.M.C., *Aberg.*, 51.
[54] P. 344.   *Cf. Fort.*, v. 381.
[55] P. 346.   *Fort.*, v. 395.
[56] P. 346.   *Fort.*, v. 398.
[57] P. 346.   Wrax., ii. 595.
[58] P. 348.   *P.H.*, xxii. 216-8.

CHAPTER IX

[1] P. 350.   Fox, *Mem.* i. 277.
[2] P. 351.   Romilly, i. 277.
[3] P. 351.   *Fort.*, v. 397, 421.
[4] P. 352.   *Fort.*, v. 409.
[5] P. 352.   *Fort.*, v. 407.
[6] P. 352.   Shelburne, ii. 104.
[7] P. 354.   *P.H.*, xxiii. 81.

[8] P. 355.   *P.H.*, xxiv. 255.
[9] P. 355.   *Fort.*, v. 502.
[10] P. 356.   *P.H.*, xxiii. 192.
[11] P. 356.   *P.H.*, xxii. 691.
[12] P. 357.   *Corr.*, ii. 24.
[13] P. 359.   Rose, i. 27.
[14] P. 359.   *Fort.*, vi. 97.
[15] P. 360.   Auck. *Corr.*, i. 9.
[16] P. 361.   Gibbon, ii. 14–5.
[17] P. 361.   Fox, ii. 32.
[18] P. 361.   *Egerton MSS.*, 2136, f. 213.
[19] P. 362.   Wrax., ii. 224.
[20] P. 362.   Wrax., iii. 235.
[21] P. 363.   *P.H.*, xxiii. 317.
[22] P. 366.   Fox, ii. 31 *seq.*
[23] P. 366.   Grafton, 355.
[24] P. 367.   Wrax., iii. 264.
[25] P. 369.   *P.H.*, xxiii. 443–454.
[26] P. 370.   *P.H.*, xxiii. 557–8.
[27] P. 371.   *Fort.*, vi. 97.
[28] P. 371.   Add. MSS. 37837, f. 203.
[29] P. 372.   Fox, Drinkwater, 237.
[30] P. 373.   Walpole, *Last Journal*, ii. 605.
[31] P. 373.   *Coke of Norfolk*, Stirling i. 214.
[32] P. 374.   *Fort.*, vi. 329.
[33] P. 374.   Wrax., iii. 390.
[34] P. 375.   *P.H.*, xxiii. 781.
[35] P. 376.   *P.H.*, xxiii. 1051.
[36] P. 376.   *P.H.*, xxi. 601.
[37] P. 377.   *P.H.*, xxiii. 847–53.
[38] P. 378.   Fox, ii. 199.
[39] P. 378.   Buckingham *Memoirs*, i. 301.
[40] P. 378.   *Fort.*, vi. 374.
[41] P. 379.   Eldon, Twiss., i. 152.
[42] P. 379.   *Fort.*, vi. 400.
[43] P. 379.   *Fort.*, vi. 402.
[44] P. 380.   Fox, ii. 117.
[45] P. 380.   Buckingham, *Memoirs*, i. 301.
[46] P. 381.   Fox, ii. 208.
[47] P. 382.   *Cf.* Fox's speech, *P.H.*, xxiii. 1189.
[48] P. 385.   *P.H.*, xxiii. 1279 and xxiv. 135.
[49] P. 386.   Fox, ii. 218.
[50] P. 387.   Gilbert Elliot, *Life and Letters.* i. 89
[51] P. 387.   Fox, ii. 25.
[52] P. 388.   *Fort.*, vi. 476.

CHAPTER X

[1] P. 390.   Glenbervie, i. 180.
[2] P. 390.   *Cf.* Lecky, v. 215.
[3] P. 392.   *P.H.*, xxiii. 559.

[4] P. 392. Drinkwater, p. 63.
[5] P. 392. *P.H.*, xxiii. 852.
[6] P. 393. Lecky, v. 283 note.
[7] P. 393. Grafton, p. 361.
[8] P. 396. Pitt, p. 129.
[9] P. 398. *P.H.*, xxiv. 291.
[10] P. 399. Lecky, v. 287.
[11] P. 399. Eldon, i. 162.
[12] P. 400. *Fort.*, v. 462.
[13] P. 400. *Fort.*, v. 474.
[14] P. 401. *Fort.*, vi. 27 and Windsor Archives.
[15] P. 401. Windsor Archives.
[16] P. 401. Windsor Archives.
[17] P. 402. Windsor Archives.
[18] P. 402. *Fort.*, v. 421.
[19] P. 403. *P.H.*, xxiv. 992.
[20] P. 404. *P.H.*, xxiv. 1202.
[21] P. 404. *North MSS.*
[22] P. 404. B.M. Add. MSS., 34, 120, 25.
[23] P. 405. *Cf. Egerton MSS.* 2136, 273, and 2137, 3
[24] P. 405. *P.H.*, xxvi. 818–23.
[25] P. 407. *North MSS.*
[26] P. 409. *P.H.*, xxvii. 750–1.
[27] P. 409. *P.H.*, xxvii. 834.
[28] P. 409. *P.H.*, xxvii. 952.
[29] P. 410. *Diaries of Robert Fulke Greville*, 159, 166.
[30] P. 410. Glenbervie, i. 234.
[31] P. 411. Walpole, *Letters*, xiv. 39.
[32] P. 412. Cumberland's *Memoirs*, ii. 173, 349.
[33] P. 412. *North MSS.*
[34] P. 415. *P.H.*, xxix. 1006.
[35] P. 415. Glenbervie, i. 61.
[36] P. 416. Burke, *Letter to a Noble Lord.*

INDEX

A

Adam, William, 362
Adams, John, on Boston Tea Party 219; 220; 236
Adams, Samuel, 216, 219, 230
Alfred, King, George III's beau ideal 40
Ali, Hyder, 382
Augusta of Saxe-Gotha, Princess of Wales, influence on son 41; 57, 64; death, 150
Anne, Queen, 29, 35
Anson, Lord, 127 n.
Arnold, Benedict, desertion to the British 322

B

Barré, Col. Isaac, 79, 106, 123, 136, 166, 241, 255, 308; violent attack on North 340; 411
Barrington, Viscount, 69 n., 70, 76, 101, 244 n., 259, 261; letters from North 262, 264, 288
Beckford, William, 106, 116, 117, 143
Bedford, 4th Duke, 46
Bessborough, Earl, 26
Bolingbroke, Viscount, 42
Boston Tea Party, 219; second incident 226
Bradshaw, Thomas, 179
Brandywine, Battle of, 273
Brooklyn, Battle of, 267, 270
Brummell, William, 352
Buccarelli, Don Francisco, 121, 126, 130
Burgoyne, Sir John, 169, 170, 176, 178, 179, 260, 271, 273, 274, 287
Burke, Edmund, 65; description of

Chatham Ministry 72; 79; corrected in false quantity 85; 94, 97, 106, 113, 115, 123, 135, 143, 145, 153, 161, 162, 166, 170, 175, 290, 306, 308, 309, 311, 318, 325, 332, 350, 371, 375, 376, 383, 394, 402, 412, appreciation of North 416
Bute, 3rd Earl, 22 n., 33; influence exaggerated 39; relations with Pitt 43-47; 50; offers place to North 51, 52; resignation 53; 57
Byng, George, 328, 330

C

Calcraft, John, 132
Camden, Charles Pratt, 1st Earl, 58, 69 n., 99, 100, 106, 209, 213, 301, 306
Camden, Battle of, 322
Carlisle, 5th Earl, 278, 308 n., 374
Carteret, Viscount, 6, 358, 392, 394
Cavendish, Lord John, 344, 367, 380, 394
Charles II, 31, 38
Chatham, William Pitt, 1st Earl, 6, 19, 21; alleged jealousy of North 22; his offer of office 23; 24, 26, 35; refusal to co-operate with Bute 43-47; resignation 50; 57, 64, 65, 69 n.; forms ministry 67; offer to North 68; Earl of Chatham 69, 71; the Chatham Creed 71; illness 72; resignation 74; 89 n.; on Middlesex election 96-99; opinion on North 107; 114, 117,

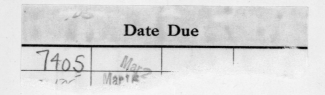